Taming the Dragon

In the early 21st century, environmental risks such as climate change, bio-diversity loss, resource scarcity, large-scale migrations, and conflicts over critical resources have become our lived reality in a world where nearly 8 billion people struggle to thrive. These crises have proven impossible to address without fundamental transformations of our economic institutions—exactly as predicted in this groundbreaking work. First published in 1994, *Taming the Dragon* offers a careful investigation of the processes that have led to global environmental change. It is based on a new and original analysis of economic mechanisms as the result of complex processes of cultural evolution. This analysis enables the author to develop both a short-term strategy and a long-term perspective for managing the global environmental crisis. Demonstrating how and why world economic and environmental policies are dangerously out of sync with each other, Jaeger arrives at an understanding of human reality that stresses the importance of interpersonal relations both in private life and within the world economic system itself.

Taming the Dragon

Transforming Economic Institutions in the Face of
Global Change

Carlo C. Jaeger

Routledge
Taylor & Francis Group

First published in 1994
by Gordon and Breach Science Publishers

This edition first published in 2025 by Routledge
4 Park Square, Milton Park, Abingdon, Oxon, OX14 4RN

and by Routledge
605 Third Avenue, New York, NY 10158

Routledge is an imprint of the Taylor & Francis Group, an informa business

© 1994 by OPA (Amsterdam) B.V.

Publisher's Note
The publisher has gone to great lengths to ensure the quality of this reprint but points out that some imperfections in the original copies may be apparent.

Disclaimer
The publisher has made every effort to trace copyright holders and welcomes correspondence from those they have been unable to contact.

A Library of Congress record exists under LCCN: 00297973

ISBN: 978-1-041-14699-5 (hbk)
ISBN: 978-1-003-67572-3 (ebk)
ISBN: 978-1-041-14702-2 (pbk)

Book DOI 10.4324/9781003675723

TAMING THE DRAGON

TRANSFORMING ECONOMIC INSTITUTIONS IN THE FACE OF GLOBAL CHANGE

CARLO C. JAEGER

*Swiss Federal Institute
for Environmental Science
and Technology
Zurich, Switzerland*

Gordon and Breach

Switzerland • Australia • Belgium • France • Germany • Great Britain
India • Japan • Malaysia • Netherlands • Russia • Singapore • USA

Gordon and Breach Science Publishers S.A.
Y-Parc
Chemin de la Sallaz
1400 Yverdon, Switzerland

British Library Cataloguing in Publication Data

Jaeger, Carlo
    Taming the Dragon: Transforming Economic
    Institutions in the Face of Global
    Change. – (International Studies in
    Global Change, ISSN 1055–7180;Vol. 5)
    I. Title II. Series
    330.9

    ISBN 2–88124–638–9   (hardcover)
    ISBN 2–88124–637–0   (softcover)

Contents

Introduction to the Series   vii

Preface   ix

1   **Introduction**   1
   1.1   Environmental Crisis and Conflicting Interests   1
   1.2   The Development of Human Ecology   8
   1.3   Plan of the Book   13

2   **The Accountable Animal**   19
   2.1   The Emergence of Persons   21
   2.2   Culture and Social Structure   28
   2.3   Biographies and Personal Identity   44
   2.4   Common Madness and the Reality of Evil   54

3   **The Evolution of Human Ecological Systems**   73
   3.1   Conceptualizing the Environment   75
   3.2   Kinship and Gender   86
   3.3   Public Happiness   98
   3.4   Vocational Cooperation   115

4   **The New Enlightenment**   131
   4.1   Cultural Regeneration   133
   4.2   The Legacy of Mechanistic Thinking   147
   4.3   Tracing an Older Tradition   159
   4.4   Ecosystems and Moral Orders   176

5   **Transforming the Economy**   187
   5.1   A Fresh Look at Eco–Eco Problems   188
   5.2   The Juggernaut of Quantitative Growth   199
   5.3   Mechanisms of Qualitative Growth   212

5.4   A Steady–State Economy? 232

6   Managing the Environmental Crisis   247
6.1   Global Change and Sustainable Development 251
6.2   Innovation Processes and Regional Milieus 257
6.3   The Energy Challenge 262
6.4   Human Agency and Cultural Regeneration 270

Bibliography   277

Subject Index   295

Name Index   307

Introduction to the Series

This series brings together under one banner works by scholars of many disciplines. All of these researchers have distinguished themselves in their specialties. But here they have ventured beyond the frontiers of traditional disciplines and have developed new, innovative approaches to the study of social systems and social change.

Why? What has prompted this foray into uncharted territory? What is the reason for broadening theoretical perspectives and developing new methodologies? The impetus comes from the world we seek to understand. Scholars have traditionally made "boundary" assumptions that limited their scope of inquiry to the concerns of a discipline. Such limitations facilitate concentration, though they have always been artificial. The interpenetration of social, economic and environmental phenomena, and the precipitous pace of change in the late twentieth century make it clear that such convenient intellectual boundaries are not only unrealistic, they are untenable.

How complex waves of change sweep through the contemporary world, altering the natural environment, technology, the economy and social systems; the interaction of these forces, their impact on nations, communities, families and individuals; and the response to them by individuals and collectivities—this is the focus of the research to be presented in this series. The scholars writing in the series are themselves engaged in social change—the restructuring of our way of thinking about the world.

Carlo Jaeger's *Taming the Dragon* is an important book by one of the finest minds working in human ecology. Jaeger uses a scholarship of impressive breadth and depth to reconceptualize the links between ecology and economics. His insight is clearly demonstrated when he offers innovative suggestions on how to design institutions to manage environmental change. *Taming the Dragon* will stimulate much deeper thinking about human–environment interactions and environmental policy. It is a major contribution to the new human ecology we need to understand global change. We are very pleased to have it as part of our series.

Tom R. Burns
Thomas Dietz

Preface

The following study of human ecology includes, almost inevitably, a mixture of errors and insights. While I alone must assume full responsibility for the errors, I owe many of the insights to several people who provided me with help over a number of years; some of these people I would like to mention here. Ruedi Lüscher and Alois Rust showed me how to make use of philosophical arguments for the present task. Adrian Linder, by operating as a theological consultant, challenged my self–critical skills. With Thomas Schmid and Peter Niggli I shared the transformation of traditional forms of political awareness in the face of ecological problems. Charles Sabel was a surprising teacher of the art of carrying on a debate as a process of sociological inquiry. Eberhard Ulich sharpened my perception of the psychological aspects of the labor process. Bertram Schefold showed me the necessity of studying today's mathematical economics without ignoring the humanities; years ago, Joan Robinson encouraged me to advance in this effort further than she herself had felt able to go. Gisela Jaeger–Weise shared with me the passion for thinking as well as the compassion for suffering people and maltreated beings.

The help of anonymous reviewers consulted by the Swiss Federal Institute of Technology and by Gordon and Breach Science Publishers was invaluable. Vilem Mudroch, Meinrad Rohner, Ingrid Shockey, Arnd Weber, and especially Matthias Wächter improved the manuscript by patient and detailed criticism. During the 1980s the Human Ecology Group at the Swiss Federal Institute of Technology formed a node in a truly interdisciplinary network, which inspired me again and again. The Department of Environmental Sciences, in which this group was formed, offered the opportunity for participating in the adventure of transforming the tradition of science by exposing it to today's environmental problems.

Other insights are due to the literature I have consulted. This requires some comments on the use of scientific literature in interdisciplinary research. Most readers will probably have a professional competence in some of the fields discussed in the present book, while being quite unfamiliar with others. Such a situation is a presupposition of, not a hindrance to, interdisciplinary cooperation. I will argue that the theme of this book requires interdisciplinary cooperation in a very strong sense. Accordingly, I have used the work of sociologists, economists, philosophers, psychologists, geographers, and others.

The bibliographical references serve mainly two purposes. On the one hand they place my arguments in the context of various research traditions and indicate the sources of specific results and conjectures. This should be of help mainly to the specialists in the fields concerned. On the other hand the references should help readers unfamiliar with a specific field to get an orientation which will enable them to further pursue the subject if they wish to do so. This approach necessarily leads to a highly selective list and I must excuse myself for often limiting my quotations to only one or two examples out of a much larger set of equally valuable publications on some given topic. I hope that thanks to this procedure the book will prove to be useful both within the frameworks of specialized research activities and within the context of more general debates.

Night before last I had a singular dream. I seemed to be sitting on a doorstep (in no particular city perhaps) ruminating, and the time of night appeared to be about twelve or one o'clock. The weather was balmy and delicious. There was no human sound in the air, not even a footstep. There was no sound of any kind to emphasize the dead stillness, except the occasional hollow barking of a dog in the distance and the fainter answer of a further dog. Presently up the street I heard a bony clack–clacking, and guessed it was the castanets of a serenading party. In a minute more a tall skeleton, hooded, and half clad in a tattered and moldy shroud, whose shreds were flapping about the ribby latticework of its person, swung by me with a stately stride and disappeared in the gray gloom of the starlight.

Mark Twain, A Curious Dream. Containing a Moral

Chapter 1

Introduction

1.1 Environmental Crisis and Conflicting Interests

Until now nature has been patient with us. We are polluting the atmosphere and the oceans, devastating the soil all over the earth, decimating the various species of the biosphere—and nature is still providing us with the means of life without which we would not be able to exist.

Meanwhile, however, we have become aware that we are playing a dangerous game. For generations, insight into particular natural processes has enabled us to make increasing use of them for our purposes. But now we are beginning to understand that it is exactly by this capacity that we are menacing the interplay of the natural processes on which our very existence depends. The fear is spreading that before long nature could lose its patience with human beings.

One of the problems that inspires such fear is the danger of climatic change induced by the burning of fossil fuels and other human activities. Human beings behave immoderately in activities critical to the environment—from the volume of global traffic to the clearing of tropical rain forests. But nature remains patient, for the time being. The strain on the atmosphere by greenhouse gases has been increasing for generations, but real climatic change as a consequence of the activities in question has not yet been observed. Climatic models elaborated by scientists, however, convey a glimpse of what can be expected, if human immoderation should meet a less patient nature.[1] What exactly the tolerance limits of our biophysical environment will be with respect to the above mentioned and other phenomena lies beyond our knowledge. There is no longer any doubt, though, that human beings at the end of the 20th century are stressing those tolerance limits dangerously.[2]

Fortunately, in this situation an increasing number of voices are heard pleading for humankind to change its course in order to develop a moderate way of dealing with the environment.[3] If nature remains patient, this could lead to the now vague idea of *sustainable development* gradually taking shape in the coming decades.[4] Should nature be less indulgent, however, human moderation would produce less striking progress, but would at least enable initial steps towards sustainable development. Continuing the present immoderation, on the other hand, would lead to the kind of global environmental catastrophes that many people consider inevitable. This constellation of possible futures for humankind and its environment can be illustrated in terms of game theory by considering two partners each of whom has two strategies at his or her disposal.[5]

---

[1] Houghton, Jenkins and Ephraums [134].
[2] D.H. Meadows, D.L. Meadows and Randers [187].
[3] Gore [102], Schmidheiny [245].
[4] The World Commission on Environment and Development [275].
[5] This is, of course, metaphoric language, which should help us to raise fruitful scientific questions. They include the question of whether human beings are part

	patient nature	impatient nature
moderate human behavior	sustainable development	steps towards sustainable development
immoderate human behavior	actual state of affairs	global environmental catastrophes

Figure 1.1: Possible "strategies" of humankind and nature

The conceivable results may then be represented as in figure 1.1.[6] Given this situation, many scientists concerned about environmental problems try to avoid an unreasonable strategy by pointing out the more or less inevitably related *ecological risks*. In order to lend more impact to their warnings, some of them have been moved to evoke images of the end of the world in a nearly prophetic manner.[7] In the past, most prophecies of doom contained a moral. Presently, scientific research on the disastrous environmental effects of humankind's current way of life is often perceived along similar lines by the general public; the moral seems to be that there is something wrong with our way of life and that we ought to search for new ways to live in better accordance with nature.

However, science has a long–standing tradition of deliberately trying to avoid "ought"–statements by separating them from "is"–statements. This makes scientific prophecies of doom particularly difficult to handle. In—not necessarily conscious—reaction to this difficulty, the prophecies are often treated as plain forecasts, and consequently further research is called for in order to improve the accuracy of the predictions.

In the present work, I will pursue another strategy. I will consider it to be a well–established fact that humankind is currently disrupting its biophysical environment in many morally unacceptable ways. This fact has both an ecological and a moral dimension. The ecological dimension can be described in considerable detail, thanks to our present knowledge of phenomena like the ongoing mass extinction of biological species, the greenhouse effect or the production of toxic waste. The moral dimension can be spelled out in many ways ranging from philosophical

---

of nature or not, as well as the question concerning the right measure in dealing with the environment.

[6] Following Costanza [52, p. 4].

[7] Some scientists were reinforcing a belief in the prophetic gift of science by gladly accepting funds from political authorities inspired by that belief.

reasoning to artistic representation.[8] I deem both the ecological and
the moral tasks worthy of effort, but I also think that enough evidence
is already available to take the above mentioned fact as a starting point
for another kind of inquiry focused on the simple question: *"How can
the only species which has begun playing havoc with the biosphere learn
to take care of it?"*

However easy to ask, this question is not at all easy to answer. In
order to approach a sensible answer the initial question has to be split
into a series of single problems, the investigation of which resembles
the solving of a puzzle: the puzzle of human ecology.

According to a dictionary definition, puzzles are problems designed
to test a person's knowledge, ingenuity, and the like. Here, however, we
seem to be facing one of those puzzles, which (like some riddles in fairy
tales) are a matter of life and death. But even if today's environmental
crisis is alarmingly real—problem solving can be a joyful activity, and
we cannot afford to lose this joy when dealing with a problem whose
urgency requires creative abilities to the highest degree. Therefore,
even if the fate of humankind should be at stake, the reader is kindly
asked to always remember that this book offers him a puzzle: a test for
a person's skill, patience, and temper.

In order to answer our initial question it is necessary to consider environmental problems in the context of *cultural evolution.* The current
environmental crisis involves a combination of very different processes.
Some of them are reversible, some are not; some have a time horizon of
decades, others of centuries and even millennia. Anybody wishing to
study the combination of these processes will find a serious challenge
for his or her skill, patience, and temper; and this is the first reason
why I use the metaphor of a puzzle here.

The second reason is the fact that any serious attempt to solve our
problem needs to handle pieces of knowledge originating from very different disciplines. By integrating these pieces in appropriate ways it
will be possible to develop a reasonably complete picture of the role of
humankind in environmental disruption. However, once major features
of this role have been at least roughly understood, it will also become
possible to depict a possible state of affairs in which humankind would
have resolved the environmental crisis by developing a sustainable life
style. Such a state cannot be attained earlier than in several generations' time; but it is a central thesis of this book that strategies aimed

---

[8] Meyer–Abich [189] and Hösle [132] provide examples of a philosophical treatment.

	responsible "South"	reckless "South"
responsible "North"	sustainable development	loss of wealth in the "North"—maximal growth in the "South"
reckless "North"	maximal growth in the "North"—conflicts and catastrophes in the "South"	present state of affairs

Figure 1.2: Combinations of strategies in the "North"–"South"–conflict

towards achieving this goal can be implemented in a sensible way under present conditions.

Admittedly, simply pointing out the ecological risks connected to the unreasonable strategy of immoderation can never be sufficient to abolish that strategy. Humankind is not a single agent with clearly defined interests, but a contradictory structure. If one just introduces the rough distinction between "North" and "South" or between industrialized and developing countries, one points at enormous *conflicting interests*. In view of such conflicting interests each side can figure out its chances to gain advantages at the cost of the other side, even with the overall environmental situation deteriorating.

Such a constellation is illustrated in figure 1.2. The present state of affairs may well be described as a combination of ecologically reckless strategies of both North and South. In contrast to this situation, a perspective of sustainable development implies that both sides turn to a strategy which can be labeled as "responsibility for the whole planet". This perspective may well be considered advantageous by both sides, compared with the present state of affairs. Nevertheless, it will be hard to realize this goal if the temptation continues for both sides to reap, by their own recklessness, the fruits of the other side's responsible strategy.

The North may expect maximal economic growth in a situation where the South is forced to observe regulations of ecological moderation while the North continues its present wasting of resources. The South, on the other hand, may hope for maximal growth if it succeeds in increasing its exploitation of resources while the North tries to curb its immoderation. The North has to fear economic and ecological damage if the South does not support its strategy of responsibility; in the reverse case, the South has to be prepared for heavy social conflicts and ecological catastrophes as a consequence of global environmental strains.

This kind of situation can be described in terms of game theory as a *prisoner's dilemma*. Accordingly, it is compared to the situation of two prisoners expecting their sentence. They may reduce the expected sentence if neither of them discloses their common secret; each, however, may completely avoid punishment if he betrays the other—as long as that one does not forestall him. This metaphor contributes to an understanding of the global environmental crisis in so far as it illustrates how hopeless our situation is as long as the agents concerned recklessly pursue their special interests. Admittedly, in reality there are not simply two agents in symmetric respective positions. The position of the "North" is obviously much more comfortable than that of the "South", and both terms refer to a variety of different agents. The "North" comprises the USA, Japan, the Western European countries, as well as countries situated in the geographical South, like Australia. The "South" includes the OPEC–states as well as India and Costa Rica. Besides those national agents, however, an immense number of other organizations are relevant for the dynamics of the ecological crisis, above all the business firms comprising today's global economy.

Finally, the ecological crisis cannot be understood without considering the billions of individual people living today. If a single person pollutes the environment in order to make his or her life comfortable or simply bearable, she or he gains an actually perceivable advantage, while his or her contribution to global pollution is infinitely small—no matter whether the rest of humankind behaves moderately or immoderately. If, on the contrary, an individual person dispenses with a similar advantage, she or he really feels that sacrifice whereas the corresponding ecological relief is infinitely small.

Yet it is just this aspect of taking into account not only institutional agents but also individual persons which allows us to conceive at least hypothetical ways out of the planetary prisoner's dilemma. It is quite a remarkable fact that, in spite of the constellation described above, an increasing number of individuals has not only begun to worry about the current environmental crisis, but is also trying actively to contribute to a solution.[9] This development makes us assume that, in view of the global environmental crisis, a human individual's situation is not sufficiently described by the simple notion of a socially isolated agent occupied with maximizing his or her individual benefits. A more realis-

---

[9] See Dunlap and Mertig [64] for a case study focussing on the U.S.

tic description is required to identify possible ways out of the planetary prisoner's dilemma. With that purpose in mind, this study tries to consider the importance of social relations for the constitution of personal identity[10] and to discuss *the role that human individuals and social institutions play in the global environmental crisis.*

This will lead to a discussion of strategies for approaching solutions to this crisis. A quick solution of today's environmental problems, however, should not be expected. Taking into account the time–span required for a stabilization of the world population at a sustainable level, it must be admitted that any process for solving the environmental problems of the present will stretch for several generations. We will arrive at a similar time horizon if we take seriously the technological and institutional changes required for the transition from today's lifestyle to a sustainable one. It thus seems reasonable to think about a process involving three or four generations. Clearly the changes which will take place during such a time–span will reach much deeper than the introduction of some new laws and the invention of some new technologies.

Furthermore, there can be no single institution, let alone a single human being, steering this process. Political authorities, business firms, trade unions, scientific institutions, churches, private households, etc., will all have their say. A myriad of institutions and of individuals will bear responsibility for the final outcome. Therefore, I will not look for a single comprehensive strategy leading to the goal of a sustainable lifestyle. The present study should instead provide indications concerning different strategies, which could be implemented by different agents in a mutually consistent way. Solving the puzzle of human ecology is an exercise in pluralism; it requires the willingness to engage in a process of conversation and joint action, thus avoiding the two great enemies of the human mind: pure order and thorough chaos.

---

[10] A similar approach with respect to the prisoner's dilemma is to be found in Sen's [252] remarkable essay. The interesting attempts to find ways out of a prisoner's dilemma by repeating the "game" until the agents have found an optimal state of affairs (Axelrod [8]) can well be combined with such an approach. Taken on their own, however, they will not be sufficient for a discussion of the global environmental crisis, as a long sequence of iterations, for instance with respect to the depletion of the ozone layer, would not be a sensible procedure. As to the real negotiation processes concerning protection of the ozone layer, cf. Benedick [18].

1.2   The Development of Human Ecology

When talking about *human ecology* in this study, I wish to emphasize
that I am concerned with the ecology of a particular biological species,
namely humankind. Moreover, there is an interdisciplinary research
tradition bearing the name of human ecology, and our task would be
greatly simplified if the puzzle of human ecology could be solved with
the means presently available within this research tradition. Until now,
however, this tradition has not been able to fulfill such high expectations. Nevertheless, it does form an essential part of the scholarly
context on which this work relies, and to which I hope this work can
contribute. Therefore it seems appropriate to give a short outline of
how the research tradition of human ecology has unfolded so far.

This research tradition originated after World War I within the
framework of the so–called Chicago School of Sociology. In their studies
of the modern metropolis, researchers of this school examined waves of
immigrants in analogy to the succession patterns discovered by plant
ecologists. The analogy led to fruitful research of spatial mobility in
metropolitan regions, and as a result social processes of segregation and
displacement were carefully documented.

While biological processes as such did not figure prominently in
these studies, much research was focussed on spatial processes involving
human beings. In the 1920's R.E. Park, one of the founding fathers
of human ecology, wrote a programmatic paper entitled "The Urban
Community as a Spatial Pattern and a Moral Order".[11] He starts with
the analogy between plant communities and human societies and then
presents findings on the spatial patterns of modern cities. "Every large
city tends to have its Greenwich Village just as it has its Wall Street"
(p. 23). From the discussion of such phenomena he goes on to "a
further speculation", and writes (p. 27): "Reduce all social relations to
relations of space and it would be possible to apply to human relations
the fundamental logic of the physical sciences".

He then explains that such a possibility will never be fully realized
because of the importance of less tangible phenomena like communication, consensus and self–consciousness. "Ultimately the society in
which we live invariably turns out to be a moral order in which the
individual's position, as well as his conception of himself—which is the
core of his personality—is determined by the attitudes of other individuals and by the standards which the group upholds. In such a society

---

[11] In the following I quote from Park [207]. See also Park [208].

the individual becomes a person" (p. 30). While he therefore fully acknowledges the existence of moral orders, which are quite different from spatial patterns, he emphasizes the paramount importance of spatial patterns for any empirical study of moral orders and ends up by claiming that: "it is only as social and physical facts can be reduced to, or correlated with, spatial facts that they can be measured at all" (p. 31). This tension between the importance of a spatial context for humans as physical beings and the importance of a moral context which once and again plays an essential role in human life is no doubt characteristic of the origins of human ecology.

The Chicago School is sometimes criticized for ignoring the differences between biological and social realities by applying biological concepts to social reality. The flaw of this criticism is that it takes the use of biological analogies at face value. In their studies of urban communities, researchers like Park quite explicitly tried to combine processes which may be described in biological terms with the specific human reality of moral orders. One may well say that their study of the latter was inadequate, but that is another matter. Far from having ignored the differences between human beings and other organisms, the pioneers of human ecology searched for ways to study the reality of persons existing in a context of moral orders without forgetting the physical and biological conditions of such existence. Even if their search was only partially successful, it was no doubt a fascinating intellectual adventure worthy of being continued in improved ways.

In order to pinpoint a crucial weakness of the Chicago School it is important to understand that what the pioneers of human ecology took from biology was not an understanding of specifically biological processes, but rather some vague and powerful ideas about the spatial interaction of individual entities. These ideas have less to do with biology than with the atomism of classical mechanics. They relate to a world constituted by individual entities in such a way that all social phenomena could "be reduced to the elementary movements of individuals, just as physical phenomena, chemical action, and the qualities of matter, heat, sound, and electricity are reduced to the elementary movements of molecules and atoms".[12] This is the world–view of mechanistic thinking. Its scientific ideal is Newtonian mechanics, understood as an axiomatic theory reducing a rich variety of phenomena to a single kind of entity.[13] The Chicago School, however, never developed a

---

[12] Park [207, p. 27].
[13] Mechanistic thinking will be a main theme of chapter 4.

coherent theory of its field of study, neither in mechanistic nor in any other terms.[14]

Clearly, the program of human ecology at that time hoped to develop a kind of social science which would share the amazing trustworthiness of the natural sciences. The use of analogies from biology seemed to provide a promising start for this purpose, and the search for general principles seemed to be the obvious way of proceeding. It is interesting to see how the same hope in a rather different shape captured the whole profession of geography after World War II in the form of the so–called quantitative revolution in geography. Now the emphasis was no longer on biology and the environment but rather on quantitative methods and spatial analysis. In this spirit the quantitative revolution tried to meet what were perceived as the standards of hard science.

An important result of this effort was the impressive series of studies belonging to the research program of urban ecology.[15] This program was related in several ways to the tradition of human ecology, for instance by the fact that some of these studies originated in Chicago. Deeper relations lay in the focus on cities as objects of study, and, above all, in the attempt to study social relations by analyzing spatial data.

This time new instruments were used, for example, the mathematics of factor analysis implemented on electronic computers. Huge quantities of data on the spatial distribution of various variables from population density to tax revenues were boiled down to a few crucial dimensions of differentiation.[16] In modern cities, the most important of these dimensions seems to be the socio–economic status of various inhabitants, while a second major role is played by different household or family types to which the inhabitants belong. Finally, in the U.S. cities, the ethnic composition of the population has been detected as an in-

---

[14] The emphasis on spatial patterns, which is characteristic of the origins of human ecology, was reinforced by Barrows [15], who in a renowned presidential address to the Association of American Geographers proposed to develop geography straightforwardly as human ecology. In line with mechanistic thinking, he proposed a search for general principles which would underlie the co–existence of people on a given territory. The geographers of the time were rather sceptical with regard to such principles and the proposal did not receive much of an echo. For a more recent discussion of the relation between geography and human ecology, see Steiner and Wisner [264].

[15] Urban ecology, in this context, does not mean the study of ecosystems in urban situations, which has attracted increasing interest in recent years. It rather denotes an approach which studies spatial patterns occurring in urban systems. That approach is documented in Berry and Kasarda [25].

[16] See Timms [278, p. 54ff] for an overview.

dependent dimension. In cities with smaller ethnic differentiation—as in some Western European cases—a similar role is played by mobility characteristics of the population.[17] The discovery of this threefold differentiation of contemporary cities is a major research achievement that will help us in the present study.[18] Whatever flaws one may find in the overall approach of both human ecology in general and urban ecology in particular, such a discovery is proof of the fruitfulness of these approaches.

Another remarkable aspect of the research on urban ecology was the fact that geography and sociology were combined. In the context of sociology, the tradition of human ecology was revived in theoretical terms, too. A major contribution was Hawley's prolonged attempt to overcome the theoretical weakness of the Chicago School.[19] He retained the ideal of axiomatic theory, but instead of trying to explain social phenomena in terms of the spatial movements of individuals, he sought a strictly social theory, which would be quite independent of assertions about individuals. A major feature of his approach is the extension of the idea of ecological equilibrium from ecosystems to social systems embedded in larger environments. Hawley's work has vigorously influenced urban ecology.[20] Without meaning to deny its merits for urban ecology, I will, however, argue in chapter 2 that the idea of a purely social theory is highly problematic, and its difficulties may be exacerbated in the context of human ecology, where the relations between human beings and their biophysical environment are a main focus of interest.

A human ecological approach will have to study individual and social realities in terms of their mutual interdependence. Basic ideas of modern individualism, which have deeply influenced modern science, will have to be relativized while keeping in mind the importance of individual freedom of action. This is by no means an easy task; it requires a philosophical discussion of the high–handed way of dealing with nature that modern natural sciences have made possible.[21]

---

[17] Friedrichs [91, p. 187].

[18] See section 6.2.

[19] Hawley [121, 122, 123].

[20] Sometimes it is necessary to distinguish between urban and social ecology, since a specific line of research in social ecology, unlike in urban ecology, is mainly concerned with the interactions between organizations and their socio–economic environment (Emery and Trist [71], Micklin and Choldin [191], Hannan and Freeman [115]). This work helped effectively to inspire the research of urban ecology.

[21] Picht [218].

Another discipline of considerable relevance for the research tradition of human ecology is cultural anthropology.[22] In the framework of the Chicago School and of urban ecology, the environment under study is mainly the built environment, often conceptualized in theoretical considerations as pure space. Cultural anthropology, however, has always been strongly concerned with the relation between human cultures and their biophysical environment. An important contribution, on which I will draw in chapter 2, was made by Bateson, who tried to develop an interdisciplinary theory of human communication, which would shed light on the processes leading human beings to destroy their environment.[23] His line of argument originated in anthropological field–work performed decades ago. Its further development, however, was strongly influenced by recent debates about global environmental problems.

More generally, these debates inspired what may be called the new human ecology. Since the 1970's, the tradition of human ecology has been renewed on the basis of shared environmental concern.[24] In this context, the concept of the environment has been firmly rooted not only in social processes and spatial relations, but also in biophysical realities. On this basis, interdisciplinary cooperation in human ecology has been enlarged so as to include biologists, physicians, psychologists, philosophers, architects, and so on. Environmental concern seems to be an excellent basis for interdisciplinary cooperation in very different contexts, ranging from education to environmental policy. However, at least until now, the new human ecology has not been very fertile in terms of scientific research. An important reason for this unfortunate situation could be the legacy of unresolved theoretical issues which the new human ecology has inherited from its predecessors.

An innovative attempt to tackle this legacy was made by Catton and Dunlap.[25] They claim that the development of humankind since the end of the Middle Ages has been increasingly shaped by what they call "the dominant western world view". This world view sees human beings as masters of their destiny and treats all other beings as possible means for the attainment of human goals, or, in the author's words, as objects of human domination. According to Catton and Dunlap, traditional social theories—including the human ecological theory elab-

---

[22] The *locus classicus* for the relation between human ecology and cultural anthropology is Steward [265]. An excellent overview is provided by Bargatzky [13].
[23] Bateson [16].
[24] Borden [30], Boyden [37] and Young [299, 300] .
[25] Catton and Dunlap [47, 48] .

orated by Hawley—are academic expressions of this very world view. They then formulate the hypothesis that since the 1960's a "new ecological paradigm" has been emerging in the context of contemporary societies. The new paradigm sees human beings as embedded in the comprehensive web of nature, which they are currently disrupting, but which they need in order to survive in the long run.

This approach has yielded significant research results, especially in the empirical study of environmental attitudes, where the development of an "ecological paradigm" has been tracked with the help of survey methods.[26] However, criticizing traditional social theories does not necessarily lead to a superior alternative. Established social theories offer important possibilities for the design and coordination of meaningful social research. How can the "new ecological paradigm" be used for this purpose? This question is still unsettled among the specialists whom it concerns most directly, i.e. among environmental sociologists.[27] A major problem lies in the fact that the vague ideas conveyed by the so–called ecological paradigm largely neglect the necessity of a rigorous analysis of interactions between political and economic processes.[28]

My sketch of the research tradition of human ecology shows that this tradition provides a stimulating scholarly context for an inquiry into the puzzle of human ecology. I will, however, rely more on the questions which have been formulated in this context than on the answers which have been proposed so far.

1.3 Plan of the Book

Given this background, I will gradually develop a tentative answer to the puzzle of human ecology, which I have defined above with the following question:

1) How can the only species which has begun playing havoc with the biosphere learn to take care of it?

I will structure this question into five different problems, which indicate the main themes of chapters 2 through 6. They are:

2) Can the way in which humankind is disrupting its own habitat be understood as the result of some collective madness?

---

[26] Cotgrove [53], Dunlap and van Liere [65], Milbrath [192].

[27] Dunlap and Catton [63] and Buttel [45] provide careful overviews of environmental sociology.

[28] This necessity is illustrated in a sociological context by Schnaiberg [246], in an economic context by Perrings [215].

3) Is such a state of madness reinforced by characteristics of contemporary society, especially of the modern world economy?
4) Does the experience of the Enlightenment provide a model for improving contemporary economic institutions?
5) How can a sustainable world economy be envisaged?
6) What kind of strategies aiming at that goal can be implemented under present conditions?

In chapter 2, I will argue that human agency cannot be understood independently from the speech acts with which persons account for their conduct. (In chapter 5, this will lead me to consider the rules of economic accountancy as a special case of social accountability.) This approach to human agency implies that social and psychological realities are the results of a process of co–evolution, in which neither of the two can be said to be more fundamental than the other. I will stress that at least some interpersonal relations of accountability are indispensable for the development of personal identity. From the point of view of the person whose identity we are studying, these are internal relations with other persons. Impairment of such internal relations may damage personal identity, possibly to the point of madness. Several theorists have claimed that forms of madness involving hampered personal identity can afflict not only single individuals, but also whole populations. I will introduce the concept of common madness in order to describe such situations, which seem quite relevant to the current environmental crisis.

A main advantage of this approach lies in the possibility of identifying structural causes of global environmental problems without presenting them as the necessary consequences of some Satanic system. This is a widespread tendency, which often condemns domination as the systemic cause of evil. In my inquiry into the puzzle of human ecology, I am not going to ignore the fact that persons can do evil, nor will I ignore the reality of power. I will try, however, to resist the temptation to explain away the problem of evil by referring it to a system of unaccountable behavior, and will instead hold persons to be morally responsible agents. Common madness is not a system, but rather an indication of the state of disarray of human ecological systems, which are formed by humankind together with its biophysical environment.

In chapter 3, I will describe the cultural evolution of human ecological systems. No "laws of motion" for human society will be stated, no simple story of progress or decline will be told, but today's ecological problems will be related to several forms of social change, whose time scales vary from a few decades to several thousand years. The point of my argument about cultural evolution is the identification of three layers of socio–cultural reality, which determine the formation of personal identities in the contemporary world: The oldest layer is an archaic one based on relations of gender and kinship, which are reproduced in the realm of private life. Later, a political layer was added, which for several thousand years has shaped societies according to power structures developed in public life. But the polarity of private and public life is misleading in the contemporary world, because, in the meantime, a third realm has emerged. This is the social reality of vocational life, which is linked to the use of money in a world–wide system of markets. There can be little doubt that this reality is transforming the biosphere to an astonishing and sometimes frightening extent.

In chapter 4, I will discuss the experience of the Enlightenment as an especially significant process of cultural evolution. I will argue that the Enlightenment stands in a long tradition of emancipatory experiences, but that it is flawed by a tendency towards mechanistic thinking, which I consider to be a crucial component of the so–called dominant western world view. As I will argue, mechanistic thinking is, to some extent, actually giving way to a "new ecological paradigm", which I will address as an evolutionary cosmology. This development can be very helpful for an inquiry into the puzzle of human ecology. It would, however, be a dangerous illusion to believe that conjuring up the "new ecological paradigm" would be a way of solving our puzzle. An evolutionary cosmology may be in the making, but it is at best in its beginnings. And if my analysis is correct, the further development of such a cosmology will depend to a considerable degree on transformations of scientific research traditions.

The most elaborate and also the most influential research tradition in the human sciences is the one of economics. I will review its contributions and limitations with regard to the puzzle of human ecology in chapter 5. The main message conveyed by the famous metaphor of the invisible hand is a warning addressed to politicians. This metaphor is often interpreted by saying that there is no better way of promoting social welfare than by allowing everybody to pursue his or her self-interest. According to this interpretation, moral arguments may have a role to play in the political definition of basic rules of economic actions, but not within economic life as such. An important conclusion of this line of argument states that if politicians want to preserve the environment, they should not try to achieve this goal by forcing economic agents into a specific course of action. Instead, they should provide suitable incentives and let the appropriate course of action develop through market processes. I will support this conclusion, but not the premise. I will argue that the metaphor of the invisible hand should not be interpreted in terms of moral philosophy, but in terms of an analysis of markets as information systems. Such an analysis can better explain why markets have their remarkable adaptive capacity, which political authorities would be well advised to not to interfere with.

Within the framework of this analysis, one can conceive an economy in a "steady state", where further growth would no longer be considered desirable, and where rates of interest as well as rates of profit would fluctuate around zero. The systematic tendency of today's economy to generate increasing environmental risks would come to an end under such conditions. However, the "steady state" is at best a long run perspective, which can help to design appropriate strategies given our present condition. But a transition to such a state will remain completely unrealistic as long as earning money is seen not only as an important aspect of economic activities, but as their main objective. I will introduce the concept of an external goal to describe forms of human agency where the goal is considered to be independent of the means. And I will argue that the research tradition of economics presupposes a concept of labor which implies external means–ends relations.

In chapter 6, I will discuss some processes which in the course of three or four generations could lead to sustainable ways of life of humankind on earth. Here I will restrict myself to characterizing such ways of life by the following features. Money still plays a major role in human lives, but no longer as an external goal of action. Rates of interest and profit fluctuate around zero, and while technological change continues, economic growth has come to an end in a situation where a decent standard of living has been attained by the so–called developing countries as well. Rent yielding natural resources have an infinite price, and rents have displaced taxes as the main source of revenue of public authorities. Critical environmental variables are controlled by tradeable emission permits, which business firms acquire in public auctions. The greatest part of stocks and shares is owned by pension funds run by vocational organizations. These organizations include people sharing a common vocational tradition, be they wage earners or not. Vocational traditions play an essential role in the structuring of the human skills on which the world economy relies. As a consequence, economic activities are not experienced primarily as instrumental for the acquisition of consumption goods but as opportunities for self–fulfilment.

The world economy has become a mosaic of regions, each of which enjoys a considerable degree of economic and political autonomy. Kinship networks are an essential component of regional social structures, religious traditions may be vital for regional cultures. The state offers public education, which is supplemented by educational activities of vocational organizations. As a rule, scientific institutions have been separated from the state, in analogy to the earlier separation between the state and the church. Scientists are still consulted in the process of political decisions, but so are, for example, artists and other people. Esthetic criteria play a major role in decisions affecting landscapes, and talking about love is no longer focused on sexual relations. Sexual motives and gender differences still play a crucial role in human life, but co–presence of men and women is the rule in private life as well as in political and in economic contexts. The world population has been stabilized somewhere well below ten billion people. World politics takes shape within the framework of a society of democratic nations, which have police forces, but no armies. If some nation tries to undermine this state of affairs, it is restrained by coalitions of other nations, not by any central authority. People can still do evil, and if enough of them decide to do so, large scale environmental destruction, as well as a history of wars, tyrannies, etc., can begin once more.

But, stranger, when I first read it this morning, I said to myself, I never, never believed it before, notwithstanding my friends kept me under watch so strict, but now I believe I am crazy; and with that I fetched a howl that you might have heard two miles, and started out to kill somebody—because, you know, I knew it would come to that sooner or later, and so I might as well begin. I read one of them paragraphs over again, so as to be certain, and then I burned my house and started.

Mark Twain, How I Edited an Agricultural Paper.

Chapter 2
The Accountable Animal

In this chapter, I will argue that the emergence of interpersonal relations of accountability marks the transition from biological to cultural evolution. The difference between human beings and other animals depends, to a considerable extent, on the complexity of the human brain. This brain shares many dispositions inherited from older species. However, biological evolution has led to increased flexibility in animal behavior. One can imagine that the older parts of the brain store fixed behavioral programs, which are inhibited or triggered by more recently developed parts of the brain. In human beings, this flexibility has reached a point where the more sophisticated dispositions of the brain can be activated in a coherent manner only if the individual organism is embedded in a network of social relations.

Given this background, the first two sections will describe in general terms persons and the social reality in which persons are embedded. Persons are regarded as agents combining biological motives, habits, and reasons in the design and pursuit of projects. As a result of biological evolution, biological motives are related to the biophysical environment in which humankind was formed. As a result of cultural evolution, habits are related to social networks including persons and human artifacts. Moreover, as a further result of cultural evolution, reasons are related to webs of social rules, which make up human culture. I will introduce the concept of a normative field to describe the combination of culture and social structure.

In the third section, I will discuss some aspects of human biographies, especially the fact that personal identity is shaped by relations with other persons. I will call such relations internal ones. I will then argue that the identity of a person can be described in terms of selected projects, abilities, beliefs, and relations. Finally, I will attempt to show that at least some cases of damaged personal identity can be explained by the total or partial absence of internal relations with other persons.

In the last section, I will develop the concept of common madness, without which one can hardly understand how humankind comes to disrupt its own habitat with such frightening resolution. For this purpose, two related difficulties must be dealt with. On the one hand, identifying some state of affairs as a situation of common madness should not be an arbitrary choice; on the other hand, it should be made explicit whether or not the critical connotations of such a concept are warranted in the context of a scientific inquiry. I will handle these difficulties by arguing that scientific inquiry, like other human practices, presupposes an ability to identify nonsensical beliefs. Given this background, the situation of common madness relevant to the environmental crisis will then be described as a combination of two clusters of such beliefs.

The first cluster suggests that personal identity can be defined and developed without referring to interpersonal accountability relations. By doing so, such relations are considered to be merely external relations. The second cluster suggests that human activity can be described and organized by treating the relations between means and ends as external relations, too. I will argue that an important cause of common madness are normative fields requiring people to act according to such beliefs. Such fields can be described by means of the sociological concept of anomie.

One way of disregarding the importance of interpersonal accountability relations for the constitution of personal identity originates in the extreme individualism of modern times. Another variant of common madness, which in historical terms seems to be much older, tries to reduce the constitution of personal identity to membership in some social group. Common madness is not a static entity, it has developed in different variations in the course of cultural evolution. Describing this development will be one of the tasks of the following chapter.

2.1 The Emergence of Persons

In this section, I will take a first look at the equally common and amazing reality of human persons. Persons have emerged from the natural history of the biosphere, including the natural history of plant and animal societies. Meanwhile, persons are a major factor shaping the future of the biosphere. They are able to design and pursue projects, and they do so with astonishing and sometimes appalling efficacy. In their activities, persons are influenced by biological motives, whose roots are not directly accessible to consciousness. Furthermore, human activity is also shaped to a large extent by habits; those form the realm of practical consciousness. Finally, human action is influenced by reasons, i.e., beliefs by which the action in question can be accounted for in conversations. Such beliefs form the realm of discursive consciousness. Discursive consciousness cannot arise in isolation. It is only in the context of social networks and accounting conversations that human organisms become persons.

Persons are able to influence the biophysical environment from which they once originated, and in this sense they can be described as emergent causes.[1] One is often inclined to say that newer entities consist of older ones because one can try to explain the formation of the former in terms of causal interactions of the latter. This is quite often misleading. Nobody would say that slices cut from a loaf of bread consist of the original bread. Everybody knows that there is no way of transforming the slices back into the loaf. Where the newer entities may reasonably be said to consist of the older ones, as with dough made out of flour, there still may be no way of reversing the process. In the world we live in, from time to time new entities emerge which simply cannot be reduced to already existing entities. Rather, they can be characterized by new causal powers able to act back on pre–existing entities. This happens both in the situations encountered in the kitchen and in those studied in astrophysics.

---

[1] The idea of emergent causality is used in a wide range of literature including Popper [222], Bhaskar [28] and Sperry [260].

It seems that a long time ago a spatio–temporal reality involving sets of elementary particles and physical fields started to unfold with a big bang.[2] After some time, new entities like atoms or galaxies were formed. In the course of time, molecules, comets and many more beings appeared. Later, under very specifc environmental conditions, microscopically small living beings emerged on planet Earth. In a long process of biological evolution, they developed into an immense variety of plants and animals.

Biological evolution quite often led to the emergence of organisms with new properties, which were, so to speak, neutral in a given environment.[3] Such properties may then enable a new species to expand into habitats which were forbiddingly hostile to its ancestors. The evolution of the human brain can be discussed in such a way. It was not just an accommodation to a given environment, but an *evolutionary breakthrough*, which not only proved feasible in the given environment, but which also opened up an amazing array of new possibilities, leading to a species whose history cannot be understood merely in biological terms.

Our ancestors shared with other animals a brain with two anatomically differentiated parts. It seems that with respect to some forms of communication (like the songs of certain birds) one of the two hemispheres plays a crucial role. In human beings, this differentiation has become very pronounced. Usually the left hemisphere is specialized in sustaining the linguistic abilities so peculiar to humankind.[4] The complexity of the human brain is a necessary condition for the ability to engage in conversations.

Perhaps some day we will be able to describe the human brain in very detailed ways; this, however, would still not provide us with a sufficient condition for the explanation of linguistic skills. To get the whole picture, one must consider—together with the evolution of the human brain—also the natural history of social relations. The flight of a bee may depend on the dance of another bee, the gesture of a chimpanzee on the grimace of another chimpanzee. Clearly, chimpanzees are involved in intense social relations such as the one between mother and child. Long ago, out of the network of such couplings human conversations emerged. And with the emergence of ordinary day to day talk social relations developed a new quality.

---

[2] This idea has a mythical quality linked to the biblical History of Creation.

[3] Gould [103, p. 332].

[4] Sperry [260], Gazzaniga [93, p. 199ff].

The initial topics of conversation of our ancestors could have revolved around all kinds of things, actual, possible or imaginary. No doubt they talked about animals, plants, rivers, clouds, the rain, the sun, and so on. Obviously, they also started talking about themselves. At some point they learned to use words like "I" and "thou".[5] Thereby they deeply transformed the network of social relations, which they previously shared with other animals. They enabled each other to become persons.

I have started with the concept of emergent causality and related it to the evolution of the human brain. By considering the transformation of social relations among animals into conversations among human beings I have started describing a process of co–evolution leading to the dual existence of persons and of conversations, of a psychological and of a sociological reality. I shall take very seriously the idea that these two realities cannot be understood in isolation from each other any better than the phenomena of magnetism and electricity could adequately be understood separately.

Persons are able to effect changes in the material world. They can walk around, gather flowers, plant a tree, light a fire, etc. What they do may depend on what another person says. A hunter walking in the mountains may change his direction because a peasant tells him that he has seen an ibex on the top of a certain precipice. The word "because" is used in a straightforward sense here: Talk can cause action. One should carefully distinguish causality from empirical regularity. A cause is linked to its effect by a relation of necessity, not of predictability.[6] Under the given circumstances, the effect would not have happened without the cause. The given circumstances, however, are rarely known in detail and their repetition is even more rare. If a specific action occurred as the consequence of some speech act this surely does not imply that the same talk will regularly produce the same action as its consequence.

We have to take the causal power of speech quite seriously. By talking to the peasant the hunter is led to a certain belief about the location of an ibex. This belief constitutes the reason for his subsequent action. It can be offered as an explanation of that action and it will usually be accepted as such. I will treat reasons as kinds of causes

---

[5] The crucial role of this pair of words has been emphasized by Buber [40].

[6] A feather in the air may rise or fall, but it is inevitably attracted by the earth. An act may or may not conform to the actor's moral beliefs, but these beliefs inevitably tend to shape what the actor does.

which are peculiar to humankind.[7] A reason, according to this view, is a *tendency* of a person. The tendency may be latent, as the power of hydrogen to burn into water in the absence of oxygen. The tendency will be exercised under suitable conditions. In the case of reasons, the crucial condition for an actualization of the tendency is the combination of reasons with what may be called natural will.[8] By this I mean the fact that human beings act spontaneously: being active is part of their nature. Human activities contribute to the satisfaction of needs and wants, but basically human activity is not driven by some exterior necessity. One might even say that activity is for human beings what blowing is for the wind.[9]

Natural will and clusters of reasons become linked when human beings make *projects*.[10] A project is something a person tries to do. This presupposes a world which is quite different from the one imagined by mechanistic thinking.[11] For projects to be possible, the future must offer degrees of freedom. The future is not a predetermined trajectory of a given system, it is not even an array of neatly defined possibilities. The future has to be understood as a mix of necessities, possibilities and true surprises. By surprise, I mean here not the realization of

---

[7] Bhaskar [27, p. 121f].

[8] St. Augustine was the first to describe in philosophical terms the reality of the human will, which had largely been ignored by Greek philosophy. To him, it seemed quite obvious that talking about the human soul would not make much sense without explicit consideration of religious matters. Today this attitude may seem somewhat awkward. What is generally considered necessary for a serious discussion of human will are not the traditions of religion, but of psychology and philosophy. I will follow this approach, but will try to avoid the *hybris* of thinking that religion has nothing important to say on these matters.

[9] There are important cultural traditions emphasizing capabilities of contemplation (in ancient Greece) or of *dolce far niente* (in a country full of works of art). Such traditions will be relevant for our discussion of labor and common madness. For the moment, let us draw a distinction between the broad concept of human activity, which focusses on the fact that human beings tend to cause a wide variety of effects, and a narrower concept, referring to attempts to control these effects. These traditions can then be discussed as facilitating the powers of human creativity by stopping such attempts to control its effects.

[10] In a moment, I will discuss the idea that beside reasons projects also involve habits and motives.

[11] I will consider mechanistic thinking in greater detail in chapter 4. Shotter [254] discusses the contrast between mechanistic thinking and a sensible description of human agency. He relies heavily on the notion of intentionality. I prefer to avoid this notion for two reasons. First, what I need to say concerning human agency can be said without it. Second, it is linked to a great amount of philosophical confusion, which I will not try to clarify here. An important aspect of this confusion is the tendency to neglect the difference between speech acts and other forms of human action.

a given possibility, but the appearance of new possibilities. Without surprises human action could be reduced to the choice between given alternatives. Projects often have a creative component which cannot be described in such terms, though. "When I have to choose between two clear cut alternatives I always take the third one" says a Jewish joke of considerable practical relevance.

Clearly, projects may fail. They may be impossible to realize or the agent may commit errors in the attempt to carry them out. Moreover, the realization of a project always involves an interplay between the causality displayed by some human agent and other causes beyond his or her control. This interplay will by necessity lead to unexpected effects. These may change some of the reasons involved in the project—a person may change his or her mind and modify the projects in response to such effects, as well as to other causes.

Reasons, natural will and projects are treated here as emergent properties of human beings. Could it be that someday one would be able to reduce them to physical properties of human brains? This possibility could not be realized in the sense implied by the science of physics. Physics is an experimental science and experiments are projects depending on the will of human agents with an open set of shared beliefs. No doubt brain research will produce fascinating and maybe frightening results of great relevance for the study of human agency. If it should cast serious doubt on the very concept of human agency, however, this would lead to an end of the practice of scientific experiments, not to new experimental results. Now this is conceivable and one may speculate about the kind of culture which would evolve under such conditions. It could not be a culture holding beliefs sustained by experimental science. Rather it would be a culture which considers our beliefs on neurology, biochemistry, and the like, as superstitions. Such speculation may be healthy gymnastics for the mind; it strengthens rather than weakens basic notions of human agency.

The conversation between the hunter and the peasant clearly is not necessary for the hunter's project of searching for an ibex in a mountain region, but a surrounding field of actual and possible conversations is required for something to count as a reason. A reason is something I can mention in conversations when I am engaged in accounting for my conduct. The fact that accounting occurs in conversations is related to the importance of beliefs in accounting for human actions. ("Why did you go up to the mountain?"—"I believed that the ibex was there.")

A belief is something which may be true or false. Whether these two cases structure a universe of discourse in the way proposed by classical

logic is open to debate.[12] It is hard, though, to deny that the possibility
of being true or false is unique to linguistic entities like statements and
propositions.

I do not want to decide whether all reasons are beliefs[13] or whether
some reasons are not beliefs at all. The fact that reasons are used
in *accounting conversations* leads me to link the notion of reasons to
the concept of discursive consciousness.[14] A human agent, or, for that
matter, a person, is characterized among other things by his or her
discursive consciousness. This is, so to speak, the stock of reasons
available for the account of one's conduct in conversations.

Now it is clear that reasons are not the only causes of human conduct. Take the example of habits.[15] A habit may become a reason
if the person involved is able to talk about it and if in the relevant
conversations such talk is accepted as a form of accounting. A man
may explain his walking on top of the holy mountain with his habit of
meeting an angel there, but clearly a habit may also cause conduct independently of any discursive practice. A football player may have some
minor habit in the way he kicks a football of which he is as unaware as
his fellow players; nevertheless a trained observer may explain a goal
of that player with that habit. This leads to the familiar distinction
between "knowing that" and "knowing how". Human conduct requires
both, but it would be impossible if it did not continuously allow for the
latter without the former. Children learn walking and talking, but they
do not learn to walk by learning to talk about it. I use the notion of
"practical consciousness" in order to describe this dimension of human
action.[16]

It is important to note that practical consciousness is strongly related both to routine action and to improvisation. It is a rather strange
myth that improvisation and routine should be mutually exclusive. The
tradition of Jazz music provides an excellent example of the fact that

---

[12] I consider two–valued formal logic as a formal language which stylizes some important features of natural languages. There are other similarly important features
of natural languages, however, which are not represented in such a logic. I would
oppose any attempt to install formal logic, whether Boolean or not, as an ideal for
human conversations. Actual conversations can and sometimes must be criticized,
but such criticism needs a broader ground than the one offered by formal logic.
In particular, it needs some notion of material, not formal error. Clearly, such
notions are presupposed in any scientific practice—including the one of logicians.

[13] As Bhaskar [27] supposes.

[14] This concept has been introduced by Giddens [99].

[15] See Bourdieu [32, 33] for some far–reaching discussions linked to problems of habit
formation.

[16] Again following Giddens [99].

routine is a necessary condition for improvisation. Moreover, the notion of practical consciousness is helpful in discarding the misconception of human activity as a sequence of discrete projects. As persons we make decisions from time to time, but our life is continuous (and even decisions may ripen in a continuous process). Discrete projects are not the building blocks of human life, they are the product of social practices which structure the continuous conduct of human life.

Beside reasons and habits, projects also involve biologically rooted motives.[17] Human agents are embodied beings. This implies that like other organisms they need specific conditions and opportunities for existence: air to breathe, a certain range of temperature, food, time and a place to sleep, etc. They also share a wide range of dispositions. On the one hand, there are, so to speak, ready made dispositions for certain reactions (for example, fear) and behavior (for example, exploring a situation). On the other hand, there are second order dispositions for the learning of certain abilities (walking, talking, sexual behavior, etc.). Biological evolution has produced increasing flexibility in these matters.

An instructive example is provided by the case of territoriality.[18] The territorial behavior of chimpanzees is more flexible than that of "older" monkeys, and mammals generally show more flexibility than reptiles. Cases of brain damage show that older, more rigid dispositions are still grounded in the parts of the brain which an organism has inherited from older species. In these cases, newer parts of the brain have the ability to inhibit or to trigger such tendencies depending on the circumstances. It seems reasonable to assume that in human beings such a process has led to a situation where the operation of bio-

---

[17] My use of terms like "cause", "reasons", "will", "project", "habit", and "motives" differs from other usages which can be found in the literature. Until the present, however, no satisfactory use of these terms has been established, so there is no compelling reason for introducing a supplementary terminology. Nor do I wish to use the terms to arbitrarily re–label well–known phenomena. Rather, I use them to identify certain poorly understood processes which are characteristic of human agents. While sometimes all causes of action are called motives, I use the word motives only for biologically predetermined causes of action. We may be consciously aware of such motives, for example, when we are hungry. To say "I am hungry" clearly involves discursive consciousness, but it presupposes the operation of biological processes of which we are not aware and of which we can probably never be fully aware. In this sense, such motives emerge from the unconscious realm. If for some reason the unconscious fails to be well integrated into a person, the causal influence of motives on actions may become very problematic.
[18] Dürrenberger [68].

logical motives is shaped both by the acquisition of habits and by the conversations in which persons account for their actions.

In the course of their individual development, humans develop motives such as hunger or a delight in exploring new situations. What distinguishes persons from other organisms, however, is that such motives always operate in conjunction with reasons and habits. Accordingly, I characterize human agents by the triad of *discursive consciousness, practical consciousness* and the *unconscious.*[19] Neurophysiological findings plausibly suggest that dreams play a crucial role in the integration of the older parts of the human brain with parts which are more directly responsible for conversations.[20] Dreams could be essential for the integration of the biologically rooted dispositions of a person into projects formed in practical and discursive consciousness. Along such lines, the psychology of the unconscious could be integrated into a more comprehensive understanding of persons.

Clearly, the psychology of the unconscious is of major interest in cases where, for some reason, the connection between practical and discursive consciousness with the unconscious fails. The latter can then be transformed so as to include mutilated motives which result from its failed integration into practical and discursive consciousness. Moreover, under certain circumstances the unconscious can break through in its "brute" form, such as with the consequence of brain damage. Furthermore, there are situations when more recent parts of the brain are temporarily suspended, as in some cases of danger. There are much more complex cases of a defective integration of the unconscious with practical and discursive consciousness, related to problems of mental illness, which will be important for the discussion of common madness.

2.2 Culture and Social Structure

So far, I have offered a sketch of persons as integrating motives, habits and reasons in spontaneous activity. I have also introduced the notion of a project combining reasons with natural will as well as motives and habits. I have treated motives, habits and reasons as three specific kinds of causes. This fits well with neuro–biological brain research, provided, however, that the latter does not fall into the reductionist trap.

---

[19] This triad is discussed by Giddens [99].
[20] Winson [295].

The concept of emergent causality should help to avoid neurological reductionism.

However, one should reject not only neurological, but also psychological reductionism. Brain researchers seem heavily influenced by the latter even if they reject the former. They may disagree on whether psychological reality can be satisfactorily explained in biochemical terms, but they usually take it for granted that social reality is to be explained in psychological terms. This is quite understandable at least as far as psychological reductionism leaves emergent mental causes as more or less co–extensive with brain processes: If mental states are "within" isolated individuals, no doubt brain research somehow leads very "close" to such states. The use of the computer metaphor in cognitive sciences has greatly enhanced such views. Yet this application has been criticized with strong arguments. I will discuss some of those arguments in order to emphasize the links between personal and social reality.

For this purpose, I will proceed in three steps. First, I will distinguish between social rules and algorithmic instructions. The latter describe possible operations, which may or may not be executed. The former indicate standards of accountability, which are invoked, criticized, modified, explained, and so on, within the context of accounting conversations. Social rules establish interpersonal relations of accountability, which enable human beings to become persons. In the second step, I will discuss how social rules enable persons to refer to something in their utterances and, on that basis, to construe representations. This discussion will help us later to reflect on problems of truth, error, and madness. In the third step, I will consider two basic dimensions of social reality: culture and social structure. Human beings are animals suspended in webs of social rules; these webs, which make human life meaningful, constitute human culture. They are reproduced and transformed in accounting conversations. These conversations take place in the context of networks of persons and human artifacts; these networks constitute social structures. Cultures and social structures form units, which I call normative fields. Persons and normative fields are the result of a process of co–evolution, and neither of them is reducible to the other.

Suppose, to take Wittgenstein's example, that everybody has a small box whose contents we call a "bug".[21] Nobody can look into a box which is not his or her own. Still, people may use the word "bug" in

---

[21] Wittgenstein [298].

conversations: This may be part of what Wittgenstein calls a language game. Now one might say that everybody learns what a bug is by looking into their own little box. The bug is a metaphor for mental states conceptualized through psychological reductionism. If we consider joy as an example we would say that individuals know what joy is by generalizing the results of introspection to other individuals. We can contrast this account with the fact that babies show specific reactions to a joyful face before they show specific reactions to a red thing.[22] It seems that babies are able to perceive joy before they are able to perceive colors and that they perceive faces before they perceive things.

Let us consider the real case first and deal with the bugs later. Joy is perceived as a property of the face; this seems to be a case of direct perception.[23] The face is not perceived as a thing with certain physical characteristics from which an inner state of the person involved is somehow inferred. A human being encounters a joyful person. There are no sense data here, what is given is the encounter. The recognition of colors, shapes and similar characteristics of things requires more elaborate perceptive skills than those involved in the recognition of the mother's smile. Asking how the baby's eyes are involved in this encounter leads us toward an approach to perception processes which emphasizes the relations between organisms and their natural environment, and is thus ecologically oriented.

Sensory organs are a result of evolutionary processes during which organisms have developed in specific environments. That is why the human eye, for example, is suited to the wavelengths of natural daylight. The environment of a baby involves, in the first place, its mother. The baby's system of visual perception can readily pick up its mother's smile. To pick up a smile does not mean to construct an inner representation of it. It means being able to respond to it in certain specific ways. Representations become relevant only much later.

The baby's facial muscles are capable of smiling, and, at some point, the baby learns to smile. The ability to perceive a smile as well as the ability to display a smile are not the goals of the learning process, rather they are its starting point. What the baby learns is how to use these abilities in a social context; it learns rules of smiling. This may appear as a progressive restriction of an originally unconstrained ability, but it is, in fact, something very different. The social rules which the baby learns to follow enable it to do things which it could not do before. A

[22] Shotter [254, p. 57ff].
[23] Michaels and Carello [190].

very important example is the ability to greet other people. A smile may be a way of greeting somebody, but to use it in such a way requires compliance with some relevant rules.

The point is that the mother's joy is not something in her head which is displayed on her face like a computer output is displayed on a video screen. The joy is on her face where the baby perceives it; in the course of its later life the baby will learn to perceive joy—as well as other emotions, for example, fright—in a greater context. Eventually, the child will also learn to display joy not only on its own face, but also in all kinds of behavior and in various arrangements. Joy may be present in a painting as well as in a way of breathing. No doubt a skillful person may perceive another's joy in very inconspicuous details. A person also will learn both to display joy in a wide variety of ways and to hide his or her joy in some cases. In this process, a psychological reality is formed, a reality which is usually quite inaccessible to anybody except the person involved. This, however, is not the starting point of personal development and it necessarily allows for exceptions.

Suppose everybody has learned what a butterfly is in a world full of butterflies. Everybody is then given the instruction to catch a butterfly and to put it into a little box. Only under exceptional circumstances (say at one's birthday) are people allowed to have a look into other people's boxes. Clearly, people may talk to each other about their personal butterflies in meaningful ways. We may invent a fairy tale where the boxes grow into personal gardens and the butterflies there live as happily as the ones fluttering through nature outside.

What the metaphor should emphasize is that it takes *social rules* to form a psychological reality.[24] By contrast, cognitive science and mathematical linguistics have led to the conceptualization of rules as something operating within a computer or a brain. A rule, in this sense, is a programming statement like:

$$\text{If} \quad (x = \text{target}) \quad \text{do stop, else do} \quad (x := x - 1) \qquad (2.1)$$

I call such "rules" algorithmic instructions. They specify the behavior of a system which can operate in solipsistic fashion. If there were

---

[24] Wittgenstein sometimes seems to be arguing against anything like an "inner" reality of persons. I do not want to discuss here either Wittgenstein's texts or his intentions in detail and simply wish to state that I consider the existence of such a reality to be perfectly warranted as long as it is not understood as providing the atomistic building blocks of social life. As a consequence, I consider it meaningful to ask what Wittgenstein wanted to say when he wrote his notes and what these notes mean. It is, however, dangerously misleading to confuse the meanings of the texts with the intentions of the author.

only one computer in the world it could obviously be said to follow an algorithmic instruction like formula 2.1. Algorithmic instructions do not require being cited in conversations to account for the actions to which they refer.

In contrast, persons are related to each other by social rules.[25] These are invoked in the conversations where people account for their actions. To follow a rule implies linguistic skills, especially the ability to invoke the rule in conversation. Therefore I make a distinction between habit formation and the learning of rules. Somebody may have the habit of getting up early in the morning, though as a guest in a monastery she may not know that the monks get up early in the morning as a rule. Even if she does what the rule requires, we would not say that she was following it. Sometimes habits may be described by algorithmic instructions and in some cases biological motives may be specified by such instructions as well. The difference between motives and habits would then show in the different rigidity of the instructions involved. Using the metaphor of a computer program, we might say that motives are programmed genetically, whereas habits are programmed by repetition. The repetition of some course of action may be produced by any set of circumstances. An important case is obviously the imitation of an example.

A person can also be given verbal instructions to do something again and again. In such cases, it is often difficult to distinguish habit formation from rule learning. Nevertheless, it is possible to design training programs—in the context of sport, industrial production and so forth— where verbal instruction is used to form a habit without thereby establishing a rule. The very ability to talk to each other, though, already involves numerous social rules. Human language presupposes both motives and habits, which in some cases may be described in terms of algorithmic instructions (for example, in the realm of phonetics). Yet learning to use a language also involves learning to follow social rules. There are habits of greeting people which are formed by repetition, but children are also told explicitly how and when to greet somebody. Chil-

---

[25] It was one of Wittgenstein's concerns to show that the algorithmic instructions used by mathematicians presuppose the social rules which mathematicians share with so–called ordinary people. Mathematical linguistics inspired a variety of efforts to show the opposite: Social rules are derived from algorithmic instructions which are genetically programmed into human brains. The whole issue is intimately related to the fascinating and largely unsettled question of the foundation of mathematics. Without discussing these latter questions in much detail, Baker and Hacker [12] have nevertheless argued quite convincingly why social rules cannot be meaningfully reduced to algorithmic instructions.

dren are also taught rules for using words. A language is constituted and stabilized among other things by a multitude of rules formulated with the help of the language in question.

Rules have a very important temporal relevance. A rule typically indicates a series open for continuation. To teach a rule we may give some examples and explain their point; as the pupil develops we comment on his or her actions both by criticism and approval. Once the pupil is able to account for his or her own actions we may take it that she or he has learned the rule (although she or he will still make mistakes from time to time). Rules, as it were, link the past to an undetermined future. They enable and constrain human beings to shape a common future by enabling and constraining their *relations of accountability.*

Clearly there are sanctions for cases where a rule is broken, but the importance of sanctions is often misperceived. To follow the rules of a language enables a human organism to be a person talking to other persons. This is not just the reward for correct behavior. The inability to communicate which has to be faced by somebody who does not follow such rules is much more dramatic than simply a sanction for deviant behavior. On the other hand, there are cases where a rule can be broken without harm, and there are cases where rules are not so much broken as they are transformed. In–between we find cases where somebody breaks a rule and thus is excluded partially, though not completely, from a given community. The problem which then arises is how such a person can be reclaimed by the community in question. This is where sanctions in a specific sense become important: They offer ways of re–entering. The simplest example is the requirement that after certain cases of misbehavior an apology is expected. In this sense, the connection between sanctions and social rules is much more subtle regarding the relationship of responsibility between persons than in cases of similar connections in animal societies.

"Certainly animals display regular behavioral patterns, including regular *reactions* to regular behavior. Moreover, certain kinds of deviation from regular behavioral patterns typically meet with distinctive aggressive reactions (for example, in cases of failing to conform to the pecking order). Such behavioral interplay appears to be a rule–like phenomenon. What grounds might we have for refusing to take the additional step of attributing genuine normative behavior to non–language–using creatures? It is that, in the absence of a capacity to formulate a rule or recognize a rule–formulation, a creature lacks other capacities distinctive of rule–following; it cannot *justify* its behavior by reference to a rule, cannot *consult* a rule in guiding its behavior in doubtful cases, cannot *correct* its behavior by *referring* to the rule and cannot *criticize* its own or others' behavior by alluding to the rule".[26]

It is constitutive for persons that they are related to other persons by relations of responsibility. Such relations imply that persons are causes because responsibility implies accounting for one's impact on the world. Moreover, these relations require the possibility that persons could have acted otherwise than they actually did: the concept of responsibility would be pointless if the actions under consideration could not be modified by practices of accounting. Finally, relations of responsibility presuppose social rules, because accounting conversations refer behavior to rules.

There is a widespread tendency to distinguish human action and animal behavior not in terms of rules, but in terms of meaning. This is a misleading contrast. The point of the foregoing argument lies in taking seriously Wittgenstein's contention that in order to study the meaning of a sentence it is often appropriate to describe its usage. To describe the usage of a sentence, it is not sufficient (and sometimes not even necessary) to identify the purposes for which it may be used. Nor would it suffice to produce statistics on the linguistic contexts in which the sentence appears, or to ask "native speakers" about expressions which can be substituted for the sentence in question without altering the meaning. All this may be useful, but the crucial task is to identify the rules which are involved in the usage of a linguistic expression. To understand the sentence "How do you do?" means being able to follow the social rules specifying how that sentence is to be used. To follow a rule implies an ability to account for what one is doing by invoking that rule while talking about one's actions. The meaning of an action is determined by the rules invoked in conversations accounting for the action. What does it mean to plant a tree? It depends on the rules to which people refer when they talk about planting it.

The situation is confused by a habit of thought running more or less as follows. A name refers to an individual—be it a person, a dog, a country, etc. The name is a sign for the individual and using the name evokes a mental representation (a "mental image") of the individual named. To study the meaning of a name means studying the correspondence between the name and the mental representation which it

---

[26] Baker and Hacker [12, p. 254–255].

evokes.[27] A similar correspondence must exist for other linguistic expressions as well—"red" refers to the property of "redness" and evokes a mental image of a specific color, and so on for verbs, sentences, and exclamations. Finally, this generalization is extended beyond the linguistic realm in order to include symbols, actions, and the like.

This whole argument starts with a misleading description of reference. How do we use a name? Certainly the practice of addressing somebody plays a major role here. To address somebody is a practice involving a whole family of social rules. Such rules specify, for example, whether I may call somebody by her or his first name, or how I should react when somebody calls me by name while I am engaged in a conversation. More generally, to be able to refer to something in one's utterances means to act in accordance with certain rules. It is the description of those rules which helps us understand the meaning of acts of reference; conversely, acts of reference cannot explain the meaning of rules.

The line of argument which I am criticizing starts by confusing acts of reference with the relation between a representation and a state of affairs represented. It then introduces mental representations and tries to explain meaning as a representational relationship between a signifier and a signified. Next, truth is depicted as some isomorphism between the former and the latter.[28]

If somebody refers to a tree by telling me "Look at that tree!" the meaning of that sentence is not a tree or the concept of a tree or the concept of looking at a tree. The meaning of the sentence is that I should look at the tree. Human beings learn to understand such sentences by learning to organize the movements of their eyes and bodies according to certain social rules. These rules do not prescribe trajectories of movement, rather they connect our bodily movements with accounting conversations.

From this perspective, acts of reference do not necessarily involve *representations*. If two persons in a conversation both refer to the same tree they do not need to "have the same mental representation of a tree". To understand each other is not a matter of sharing representations. Rather, human beings construct representations with the help of acts of reference. Once a child has learned to refer to trees and to

---

[27] This concept has become influential mainly by structural linguistics inspired by Saussure [242].

[28] The labyrinth is complete when intentionality is linked to meaning by claiming that the meaning of my words is grounded in the intention I have when I utter them.

play with words, she or he may take a stick of wood and say "that's a tree!". We check whether the child knows what she or he is saying by continuing to monitor its further behavior. To handle a representation again involves social rules.

Finally, there are rules for talking about errors, truth and the like. If a child says that mountains are small, we may teach her that she is mistaken and inform her about the effect of distance. If she remembers correctly some past event we may emphasize the truth of her account. The rules concerning matters of truth are not primarily rules about the relationship between a representation and something represented. If a child says "that's a snake" to a stick of wood and uses the stick as a representation of a snake, we may join him in his play. If he says "that's a stick of wood" to a snake and tries to catch it, we may severely criticize him and teach him some truths about snakes.[29]

What about a misleading map, which, for example, prevents tourists from finding the seaside resort they wish to visit? Do we not encounter here the paradigmatic case of a concept of truth formulated in terms of a match between a representation and the state of affairs it represents? This powerful metaphor was elaborated in terms of the formal language of mathematical logic in Wittgenstein's *Tractatus*.[30] Later Wittgenstein showed how natural language enables us to describe the rather narrow limits of this metaphor. These limits are revealed in the instructions for using the map. Without such instructions, it would not make sense to say that a map is misleading. Rules related to truth and errors do not apply to a map as such, but only to a map in the context of more or less specific instructions for its use. A map may be an excellent guide for locating a certain building and nevertheless be useless for an assessment of the area within that building.

A similar argument applies to concepts of mental maps, mental images, and the like. Clearly, one can imagine a dolphin and even a unicorn while looking at the clouds wandering through the sky. Getting acquainted with a certain state of affairs usually involves enhancing one's ability to imagine that situation. It is not limited to that enhancement, however, but rather the development of imaginative abilities goes hand in hand with the growth of all kinds of practical and discursive

---

[29] Even being aware of the fact that we have just saved a child's life from a poisonous snake need not prevent us from realizing that reality cannot be described independently of language games, and that different language games can imply very different descriptions. This is a major theme of the "internal realism" advanced by Putnam [226].

[30] Wittgenstein [297].

abilities. Learning to play the piano will probably result in some improvement in the ability to imagine playing the piano, but it usually also results, for example, in the ability to hit a key without having to look at it, or in the ability to link one's practice with statements like "let's play the blues". Moreover, a person acquainted with some situation does not use only one mental image of that situation, rather she or he is able to generate a wide variety of changing mental representations of the situation in question. Talking about a piano does not mean referring to a mental representation of a piano, although it may involve a whole family of such representations.

So far, I have argued that there are social rules enabling individuals to perform acts of reference and constraining the ways in which they might try to do so. Moreover, there are social rules enabling and constraining persons to treat some beliefs as true or false (human life would be a dull affair if such identification was always easy). A third family of rules concerns representations, with the important distinction between what may be called material and mental representation.

Using the concepts of mind and matter is quite dangerous here, but it is harmless when compared with the use of the polarity of public and private which also frequently occurs in the same context. There is a difference between Michelangelo's *David* and somebody dreaming of king David last night. We may try to grasp the difference by noting that the statue is made of stone and by supposing that dreams are made of "the same stuff" as we are. Alternatively we may note that the statue is set up in a public place while dreams are usually considered as part of our private lives. But a king may tell his people about the dream of David he had during the night before his coronation and there may even be a public ritual requiring him to do so. Conversely, somebody may sculpt a little statue of a person he loves and use the statue in a purely private context. I therefore prefer to distinguish social from psychological representations, and to link both to social rules as in the example of bugs and butterflies previously discussed.[31]

---

[31] I should perhaps emphasize that the foregoing discussion owes much to Wittgenstein without being in line with mainstream Wittgensteinians. Wittgenstein's philosophy is permeated by moral indignation against the kind of talk common in the philosophical circles of his time. I do not want to assess how far this indignation would disappear if Wittgenstein was to assist in more recent debates in ordinary language philosophy, but I wish to emphasize that one of the reasons why I use the concept of social rules as elaborated by Wittgenstein lies in the fact that the critical power of this concept is by no means limited to elitist philosophical circles. An important suggestion of the social and historical range of

Human reality is twofold, as it has a personal and a social component. These cannot be separated, since they cannot exist independently
of one another, but they can and must be distinguished in the sense
that they causally interact with each other. This interaction cannot be
understood in terms of the classical analogy equating the relation between a society and its members with the relation between an organism
and its organs. Social reality is not composed of persons. Instead, a
more elaborate concept is needed. Such a concept can be developed by
distinguishing between two different kinds of entities, which are both
composed of actions: on the one hand, personal biographies which include the series of all actions performed by a specific individual; on the
other hand, social structures which include the actions performed in a
specific cultural framework.[32]

Social structures are best introduced by examples: families, nations,
firms, the line at the bus stop, the community of mathematicians, children playing together in a neighborhood, etc. Social structures involve
persons performing mutually interlocked activities and they involve the
human artifacts which are reproduced in these activities. A person is
an embodied being, and from birth to death every person describes
a trajectory in the overall space he or she shares with other physical
bodies, be they human beings or pebbles. Social structures share with
persons the fact that they are spatio–temporal entities.[33] A simple

---

critical analysis of language games was given by the Austrian writer Karl Kraus,
whose satirical work was deeply appreciated by Wittgenstein. I should add that
Wittgenstein himself was somewhat one–eyed in his polemical efforts because he
lacked a criticism of Humean concepts of causality (recently, such a criticism has
been developed in Bhaskar [28], and Harré [118]). These remarks are not meant
as a contribution to philosophical debates. Rather, they should emphasize that
although the argument developed here uses concepts first introduced in Wittgenstein's "Philosophical Investigations", it is not necessarily susceptible to a series
of criticisms which may be quite appropriate with regard to some philosophers
strongly influenced by Wittgenstein.

[32] This approach was first introduced by Parsons and Shils [211]. It has been further
elaborated by Luhmann [169], who drops the assumption that there are atomistic
actions. This involves two steps. First, a shift in emphasis from action to communication, whereby action is constituted by processes of ascription which define
certain events as effects of certain systems. Second, communication itself is seen
as a complex event generated by the very systems which exist in light of this
communication. Luhmann's arguments are stimulating and have been important
for my argument in many respects. Nevertheless, they lack a realist approach to
human agency and thereby create a tangle of conceptual problems which may be
avoided by following the lines of argument proposed in Giddens [99] concerning
the relation between personal and social reality.

[33] Other notions which may be used to refer to social structures as spatio–temporal
entities are Wittgenstein's concept of a life form or the concept of a social form

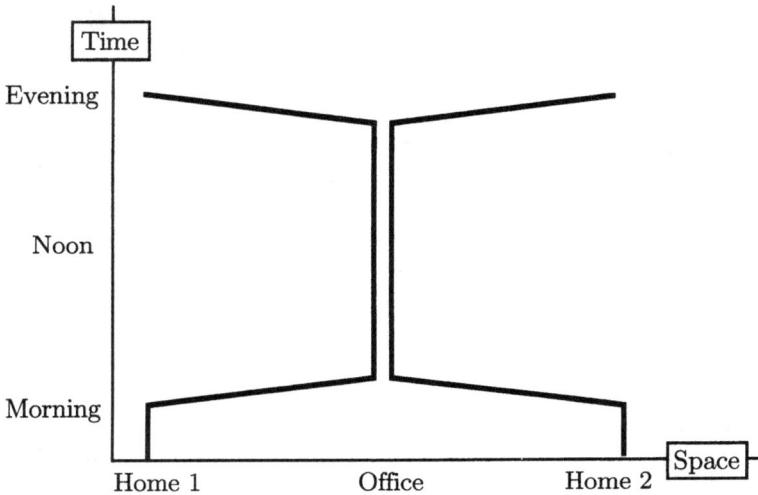

Figure 2.1: A working day.

example is provided by the representation of a working day involving two people in figure 2.1: The early morning is spent at home, followed by commuting to the office, where the two persons remain during the day; in the evening, commuting the other way takes place, and, after spending the night at home, the same pattern can be repeated. Persons live on the surface of the earth, and therefore, for many purposes, the spatial dimensions of social structures can be represented by a two-dimensional map, onto which a time–axis can be imposed vertically. Time may be clock–time but it may also be a series of culturally relevant phases like the ones defined by the weekly rhythm introduced by the Jewish religion. Space may be Euclidean space but it may also be a patchwork of culturally relevant territories as, for example, workrooms and homes or the territories of different nations. The trajectories of people and of artifacts like buses or bus stations can be combined in the same framework.

The notation of time–geography[34] is quite useful for the study of social structures. The original idea of time–geography was to study the phenomenon that as people try to realize projects they face spatio-

---

proposed by one of the pioneers of modern sociology, the German sociologist Simmel.

[34] Introduced by Hägerstrand [112].

temporal constraints. These constraints may be partly defined by given technologies of transport and communication, and partly by social rules regulating the crossing of various territorial boundaries. An important kind of constraint stems from the fact that many projects can be realized only if specific persons and things meet at some place. Such meetings are called bundles, while places where people must remain stationary in order to work on some project are called stations. It can be shown that in everyday life people are engaged in remarkably stable networks constituted by different bundles involving other people.[35] Often, such networks are patterned in small groups involving perhaps a dozen people. Although such a group may never meet as a whole, it is nevertheless integrated by a strong network of face to face contacts. Different groups are interconnected by selected members with relatively frequent external contacts.

The approach of time–geography has been criticized in different respects.[36] In the present context, two points seem especially important. First, often one is interested not simply in the trajectories of people and things, but in the activities with which people are engaged. An elegant possibility to enrich the notation of time–geography consists of considering colored trajectories. Suppose we are interested in a set of conversations. We may then assign the color green to the trajectory of a person at any place where the person in question talks to another person. In such a way, we can consider not only the bodily movements of persons, but also the changing character of their activities. If a social structure is understood as a set of interconnected activities, it may be represented as the set of all segments of trajectories marked by certain colors.

Second, social reality does not simply constrain individual projects. Instead, social reality is simultaneously constraining and enabling: Without it there would be no human agents at all. In time–geography, this fact is not taken seriously enough. It is misleading to introduce social reality simply as a set of constraints limiting the possibilities of individual projects. Instead, we better remember the basic sociological insight that rules are an essential part of social reality. In considering any social structure, one can always ask which rules are necessary for its reproduction. We can, for example, consider the totality of speech acts performed in Italian as a social structure. The grammatical rules of the Italian language then form a cultural reality linked to that structure.

---

[35] Influential studies on such networks are presented by Törnqvist [280]. Wellman and Berkowitz [292] offer a synthesis of newer research on personal networks.
[36] Giddens [99, p. 166ff, p. 172f].

For most purposes, the time–geographical description of social structures is quite insufficient without the description of the set of rules, i.e., a cultural reality, associated with that structure.

It is a peculiar characteristic of *culture* that it does not exist independently of its effects.[37] A set of social rules exists only in so far as it influences some set of human actions. Obviously, one can consider rules which might come into existence, as in the case of a parliament deliberating a proposal for a new law. Furthermore, it is often very important to ask whether some conceivable cultural pattern is possible under the given circumstances, and what consequences its realization might have.[38] While a magnetic field exists independently of the question of whether any metallic objects are in fact influenced by it or not, culture exists only if it plays a role in the practices of human agents. This might seem to lead to a vicious circle where an effect creates its own cause. The circle, however, is avoided by the explicit consideration of time together with the distinction between discursive and practical consciousness. Culture is reproduced in accounting conversations while it influences social structure, which, in turn, influences culture via accounting conversations.

Conversations are subsets of social structures; they involve only speech acts while social structures involve all kinds of practices, verbal and non verbal.[39] In these practices, persons reproduce social struc-

---

[37] Bhaskar [26, p. 79ff].

[38] This leads to questions about the cultural evolution of rules, which I will discuss in chapter 3.

[39] There is an important parallel in Wittgenstein's late philosophy: language games are embedded in life forms. As is well known, Wittgenstein first claimed that every sentence has a precise meaning, which can be elucidated by logical analysis. The economist Sraffa, a friend of Wittgenstein's, shook this conviction by challenging him to produce a logical analysis of a gesture common in southern Italy. To convey the flavor of this gesture, one may recall an anecdote told by the Sicilian novelist Lampedusa in his novel "Il Gattopardo". Garibaldi with his thousand brave followers tried to liberate Sicily. There he met a day–laborer lying under an olive–tree. The hero told the sluggard about the great historical task to be performed. As an answer, the taciturn native slowly moved the back of his hand from his throat along his chin toward the foreign speaker. Wittgenstein might have replied to Sraffas objection by stating that this gesture has a precise verbal equivalent (namely the italian expression "me ne frego") and then claiming that this verbal expression of indifference has a propositional content whose truth conditions can be analyzed following the lines proposed in Wittgenstein's *Tractatus*. This would have been in tune with much semantical work of the present day, but instead Wittgenstein was silenced. Later he noted that he felt like a tree with all its branches cut (Malcolm [176, p. 57]). Only many years later did Wittgenstein

tures, and in their speech acts they reproduce cultures by accounting for their conduct in terms of social rules.

Culture is not a sub–system of society which would exist beside sub–systems like politics or the economy. Instead, culture and social structure are the two basic dimensions of all social reality.[40] However, my approach to the relationship between rules and representations implies that culture should not be considered simply as a set of symbols or as a code. A culture includes symbols and codes, but basically it is a moral order, consisting of a dynamic network of rules. Symbols and codes are nodes and patterns in such a network. Moreover, I am deliberately talking about rules, not about values. Obviously, it would be interesting to discuss how far the existence of rules entails the existence of values, but here this question can be left open. According to my analysis, the existence of social rules does not presuppose a realm of values. In chapter 3, however, I will discuss how, in the process of cultural evolution, certain generalized goals of action, which could be described as central values of contemporary human culture, have emerged.

How does the unity of a culture come about? On the one hand, a social rule always presupposes other social rules: A rule is reproduced in conversations and it takes more than one rule to unfold a conversation. Therefore, rules are mutually interlocked to a greater or lesser degree. On the other hand, there is a direct link between cultures and social structures. The rules of chess are uniquely related to the games of chess actually played in the world. However, if we consider these games as forming a social structure, then we must include not only the moves made by the players, but also other related activities such as the production of chessboards, etc. More importantly, we must include the comments which the players make about their games and also the forum by which a wider public observes and comments about such games—for example, when somebody learns to play, or when some rule is historically modified. The interface between a social structure and

feel able to cope with Sraffa's gesture by describing the interplay of language games and life forms which takes place in such situations. In the subsequent philosophical literature most attention was directed to language games and very little to life forms. On the other hand sociological literature, which is often concerned with life forms, usually does not pay much attention to language games.

[40] Haller, Hoffmann–Nowottny and Zapf [114]. Giddens [99] denotes a similar duality with the notions of social system and social structure. Unfortunately, this terminology is a bit confusing, because it re–labels social structures as social systems, while using the notion of structure to refer to culture. This seems to be an unnecessary tribute to the analysis of culture proposed by French structuralism.

the corresponding culture is formed by the conversations taking place in the structure.

The unity of a social structure is mainly due to the fact that the activities belonging to it are spatio–temporally linked by recursive causal chains. People meet to play chess and play chess to meet, tournaments are organized, newspapers publish chess columns, newcomers are taught the rules of the game, chess pieces are used and reproduced, and at any moment in time each one of these activities depends directly or indirectly on a great number of earlier activities. In this process, the social structure is reproduced and its unity sustained until the structure either splits up into separate structures, merges into a greater unit, or simply ceases to exist.

The boundaries both of social structures and of the corresponding cultures are not always precisely marked. In most cases, it is quite easy to find actions about which it is impossible to say whether they belong to some structure or not; the same holds for rules with regard to culture. As James Joyce showed in writing *Finnegan's Wake*, the boundaries of the English language may be even fuzzier than the coast of Britain. The existence of borderline cases, however, is perfectly compatible with the existence of uniquely identifiable cultures and social structures.[41] I denote the unity of a social structure with the corresponding culture as a normative field.[42] Alternatively, it may be described as a social system.

The identification of normative fields or social systems is quite often a very difficult task. Was there a European normative field in the Middle Ages? Is there one presently? Is there a modern social system? Is there a capitalist system? Are they identical? What about neighborhoods, people meeting in the streets, etc.? Anyhow, it is important to emphasize the fact that normative fields constitute boundaries both of time and space, such as school bells, garden fences, customs barriers,

[41] Contrary to a widespread fashion in contemporary general systems talk (shared by Luhmann [169]) I do not identify a normative field on the basis of a border drawn (either by the observer, or by the system itself) between the field and its environment. To identify the normative field of a prehistoric population one may start by examining some of its remains and notice, for example, certain similarities among pieces of pottery found by archaeologists. Traces of wooden houses and the like may be added, and on the basis of such evidence the normative field in question may be tentatively described. The question of its borders is only one of many interesting questions to be studied. The practice of definition in the literal sense of drawing a border is a useful metaphor for the practice of identification precisely because the latter is much more difficult to describe than the former.

[42] Following Heintz [128, p. 280]. This notion can be related to the work of Lewin [163], who introduced field concepts into psychology.

foundation protocols, and so on. The identification of a normative field is not based on an external observer's more or less arbitrary drawing of a defining line through the continuum of social processes. An observer could instead try to deduce the existence of a normative field out of a variety of interlinked social phenomena, among whom there are more or less exactly defined boundaries and border areas.

Social reality is made up of pairs of social structures and cultures; some of them we know to a certain degree, while about others we have only vague ideas. Moreover, normative fields are by no means mutually exclusive, rather they overlap in all possible ways. However, one can distinguish broad categories of normative fields. For example, there are systems like multinational corporations which emerged at some historical point in time and are therefore obviously not universal to humankind. On the other hand, there are normative fields of kinship, which apparently seem to have existed since the origins of humankind and which may therefore be called universal. Quite understandably, this category of normative fields plays a major role in the development of human personality. This is my next theme, a theme which requires a careful integration of sociological and psychological arguments.

2.3   Biographies and Personal Identity

Social reality enables human organisms to become persons, who in turn reproduce social reality by their actions. Persons are individuals in a very strong sense of the word: every person has a unique biography, in which that person's identity can develop. It is only in the context of a personal biography that motives, habits and reasons can be woven into a more or less coherent whole. This occurs in such a way that the little word "I" denotes a being conscious of itself, which, with this consciousness, is able to shape its existence and assume responsibility for itself. I will approach the theme of biographies by considering some classical themes of psychoanalysis. Freud tried to use the analysis of dreams in order to understand the dynamics of biographies, and, in this analysis, he placed great emphasis on sexual motives. While empirical evidence contradicts many of his more specific claims, there is also evidence supporting the hypothesis that dreams are essential for the integration of biological motives, habits, and reasons, as well as for the maintenance of continuity in personal biographies. I will argue that the uniqueness of a person is not a matter of stable character traits, but of a combination of several factors. These include long lasting projects, important abilities, crucial beliefs, and accountability relations with other persons. I will label interpersonal relations which shape one's personal identity as internal relations. This will introduce the theme of madness, because the development of personal identity can be severely impaired by poorly developed internal relations.

When scientific psychology was born at the end of the 19th century, the conviction that the experimental method would somehow lead psychological research toward reliable truths was shared by an extremely wide array of researchers. This expectation does not seem to have been fulfilled, and one may wonder whether Wittgenstein was not right in his suspicion that the experimental method in psychology is inadequate in coping with the conceptual confusions which make our psychological knowledge so unreliable.[43]

It is a remarkable feature of psychoanalysis that although Freud hoped to link psychology with medicine by basing it on neuro–biological facts (and thereby conferring on the psychiatrist the authority of the surgeon), he did not primarily try to achieve this goal by experimental research. To those who see this methodological choice as an abandonment of scientific principles, it may be replied that the science of astronomy also has to study the stars without being able to push them around in the laboratory. Clearly, astronomy has strong links with laboratory experiments, and psychoanalysis could probably gain quite a lot from stronger links with laboratory research in psychology. The crucial point though is that it is rather difficult to conceive meaningful experiments with *biographies*. Clearly, a main obstacle lies in moral barriers, and this is not an accidental difficulty. Among the conditions under which biographies unfold are the specific moral orders with which they have to cope, and it is a basic property of moral orders that they cannot be manipulated at will.[44]

In discussions of psychoanalysis, the emphasis is usually placed on the concept of the unconscious, and on the importance of sexuality inherent in this concept, rather than on the study of biographies. Nevertheless, a fresh look at the matter may be useful here. Consider, for example, the idea of the Oedipus conflict, which in psychoanalytic theory is seen as establishing the complex known by the same name.

---

[43] Wittgenstein [298, p. 232].

[44] Biographies don't unfold in a social vacuum. Normative fields enable and constrain human beings to enter specific biographical transitions in the course of time. This is the focus of the sociological literature concerning the life–course. See Buchmann [41] for an instructive example of this approach.

First of all, the Oedipus conflict marks a cluster of events determining a passage within a biography. In the years before this passage, the child will have given considerable attention to sexual matters in play and talk, after which a phase of latency begins where sexuality seems to have much less importance. Later, sexuality re-emerges as a theme of considerable biographical relevance, in particular with respect to the coordination of biographies involved in marriage.

Given this background, one can try to describe links between features of adult biographies and experiences made in childhood. The concept of the unconscious is used to understand the hidden character of the bridges connecting childhood experiences with adult life, and dreams are used to look at those bridges—much in the way that astronomers use telescopes to get a closer look at the stars.[45]

It is important to understand that such a general approach can be elaborated in very different special theories of biographical passages. A good case in point is the description of the Oedipus complex in feminist terms given by Shulamith Firestone.[46] She starts with the plausible assumption that the child first experiences a strong emotional bond with her or his mother while a similar bond with the father is formed only later. This is combined with the pessimistic, if not unrealistic, assumption of deep conflicts between mother and father. The child, therefore, experiences a painful need to choose between its parents. Although the bond with the mother is stronger in the beginning, the child perceives the father to have access to a much wider world. The boy usually seeks a similar access by shifting emphasis from his bond with the mother to some kind of identification with the father. For the girl, such an identification is more troublesome and after some attempts at establishing a strong bond with the father, the girl either identifies with the mother or reaches a more ambiguous position. In both cases, sexuality is tied to basic choices about one's own biography before the period of latency.

Now clearly with such approaches to psychology there is considerable danger of getting lost in a game of arbitrarily combining anecdotal evidence. It is well worth recalling the story of the computer scientists who finally achieved the challenging goal of building a machine which

---

[45] A similar argument holds for the kind of dream analysis developed by Jung [151]. In Jung's approach, sexual relations lose their paramount importance and instead symbolic figures—similar in certain respects to the gods of the great Homeric tales—are used as points of reference for the discussion of personal biographies.

[46] Firestone [77]. A recent argument with similar implications for the Oedipus conflict is developed by J. Benjamin [19].

by any available test seemed to be able to think. Excited, but still puzzled, one of them decided to ask "it" directly. "Can you think?", he slowly typed on the keyboard. After a moment, which seemed to him one of hesitation, the machine produced on its video–screen the answer: "Well, this reminds me of a story ...". Anecdotal evidence and story telling surely present great opportunities for talking nonsense; but they do so precisely because they are one of the most important ways in which human thinking actually develops. Shakespeare's phrase that we are such stuff as dreams are made on may well indicate the reason why psychoanalytic theory with all its oddities cannot be simply discarded in any serious attempt to reach a scientific understanding of human reality.

Newer neurological findings provide some support for the hypothesis that dreams play an important role in establishing continuities in the conduct of human lives by relating current experiences to older emotional and cognitive patterns acquired during earlier periods of life.[47] Under such circumstances, dream telling may very well have an important part to play in therapeutic processes concerned with the reorganization of a person's conduct of life.

On the other hand, the attempts of different analysts, or even of the same analyst on different occasions, to interpret dream reports so as to uncover their latent meaning often lead to widely diverging results. It seems more reasonable to assume that dreams have no "true meaning" at all, but are rather part of the processes by which human beings learn to cope with the experiences and problems they face in their lives by drawing upon earlier experiences and innate dispositions.[48] Thereby, they mobilize and rearrange feelings, memories, and the like in ways which may produce hints for future courses of action. This does not at all contradict the view that at least some dreams document unconscious links between different segments of personal biographies, especially between early childhood and later stages.

In the dynamics of those links, sexual motives may well play a major role. This role, however, is not easily expressed in words. It is often very difficult to find appropriate words for talking about sexual experience. Besides, it is not always easy to find words for telling a love story, in

---

[47] Lehmann and Koukkou [161]. In this context it is interesting to notice that the duration of dream phases per night is much larger in children than in adults.

[48] Winson [295]. This line of argument could contribute to an explanation of the fact that although the evidence for a therapeutical efficiency of psychoanalysis is rather weak there may be good reasons to take psychoanalytical theory quite seriously.

spite of and perhaps because of impressive literary examples. After all, the artistic way of telling such stories follows a long tradition claiming that love is a mystical reality which words cannot depict.[49] But cannot sexual relations, at least in some cases, be characterized by a painful inability to talk to each other due to the damages of a historically given language?[50]

Language is not simply one of the instruments which human beings use for their attempts to realize projects. Of course, talking can be part of the attempt to realize a project. This, however, does not provide a complete basis for understanding human talk. What is the project leading to the utterance "Good bye"? Obviously this depends on the context in which the utterance takes place. Although a person may be engaged in all kinds of more or less well defined projects which are somehow relevant to such an utterance, the main explanation for it may simply be some personal habit shaped in the course of time by social rules. The distinction to keep in mind in such cases is the one between the meaning of an expression and the projects involved in a specific utterance of that expression. This is essential, because otherwise one would relapse into some kind of methodological individualism where atomistic agents constitute meanings by planning individual projects.

Human beings are *animals suspended in webs of rules*, which they themselves have spun.[51] One has to keep in mind, however, that persons do not produce those webs individually. Rather, each person is confronted with pre–existing webs of rules, which are reproduced and transformed in the context of accounting conversations. Individual projects are then formulated within those webs, and the attempts to realize such projects are the subject of further accounting conversations. As I have already noted, the social rules which constitute those webs are distinct from algorithmic instructions by the very important property of leaving the future largely undefined. Without this property, personal projects would be unwarranted and even impossible.

However, in a world characterized by surprise, situations may arise which cannot be handled with the existing social rules. New rules will then emerge or the community in question will cease to exist. Moreover, new or modified rules may emerge without any external pressure, just as an unintended consequence of some combination of personal

---

[49] de Rougemont [234].
[50] In literary terms, such a situation is described by Stefan [262].
[51] Modifying a metaphor introduced by Geertz [94, p. 5].

projects. The transformation of social rules may even be an explicit part of personal projects. This does not contradict the statement that the whole web of rules could not be produced by an individual project. First, even the most radical plan to create new social rules—for example in revolutionary attempts in the fields of politics, arts, gender relations—would be impossible without pre–existing rules. Second, a new rule may be proposed by a single person, but it becomes a social rule only if it is adopted by other persons as well, if interpersonal relations of accountability are established in which the new rule is invoked in accounting conversations.

For the sake of convenience, let us label as "fundamentalist anarchism" the project to abolish not only the rules enforced by the power of the state, as in classical anarchism, but all social rules whatsoever. Such a project is quite similar to the idea of letting a person live without oxygen. What is possible, and in fact does take place all the time, are transformations of social rules. Such transformations are necessarily gradual in the sense that discontinuity in some rules is always accompanied by continuity in others; and they are necessarily social in the sense that such transformations are always the product of the joint action of several persons. Transformations of social rules will always be the consequence of projects in so far as human organisms would not be persons without such projects. Whether some transformation of social rules is explicitly envisaged by such projects, or whether it just happens as an unintended consequence of human action, depends on the circumstances.

The notion of a project should not be misconstrued simply as a mental representation defining some goal which has to be reached in order to satisfy individual needs. Situations which may be described in this fashion represent but one of several categories of projects. Quite often projects involve not so much an attempt to realize an imagined state of affairs as an attempt to do what is prescribed by certain rules. Suppose somebody comes into a village in a foreign country. She or he may very well have the intention of doing what the people there expect a stranger to do, without actually knowing what these expectations are. In developing a project, she or he may imagine past situations, which are somehow relevant to the present one, but his or her project cannot strictly define a final state of affairs. Rather, such a project involves the willingness of a person to place his or her trust in a largely unknown web of social rules.

When one adds to the importance of projects for human life the fact
that human beings are extremely capable of acquiring new abilities, as
well as the further fact that they tend to retain acquired abilities, one
comes to a good position to discuss some aspects of *personal identity.*[52]
To talk about personal identity means placing psychological reality in
a social context. Consider the case of self–reference. As I have already
noted, reference is a way of conduct governed by social rules; it is a
social practice.[53] Language, too, is largely governed by social rules.
Natural languages offer possibilities for self–reference: I can talk about
myself.[54] To study such possibilities in the first place involves not so
much a discussion of psychological matters, as a careful study of whole
families of social rules.

Taking the possibility of self–reference for granted, we can ask what
it is we are referring to in cases of self–reference.[55] If we had to give a
clear cut answer to the charming question: "What is a self?", we could
start by saying: "A person". What then is a person? It is a living
organism engaged in relations of responsibility with other beings of its
own kind. Here we could add a description of human agency along the
lines proposed in earlier sections of this chapter, but the persons so
described would all be alike. They would lack personal identity—and
thereby would not be persons at all. How then do we identify not just
people in general but distinct persons?

As persons are embodied beings, we can clearly identify them by the
same means by which we identify other living organisms or solid bodies.
Basically, such identification is linked to location in space at a given
time. If we ask for the description of a person, however, we will surely

---

[52] An overview of newer debates on personal identity is provided by Shotter and
Gergen [255].

[53] I am talking here about the case where persons refer to something, for example,
a sunrise. The relationship between the person and the being referred to must be
distinguished from the relationship between this being and a word which can be
used for the purposes of reference (for example, the word "sunrise"). I call the
latter relationship denotation. Many words do not denote at all (in the foregoing
sentence, for example, "many" and "not"). To say that a word denotes something
implies that the word in question is used in successful practices of reference.

[54] With the terminology introduced in the preceding footnote one can distinguish
between self–reference and self–denotation. Gödel's theorem in mathematics is a
special case of self–denotation: A word contained in a sentence which is stated in
a formal language denotes that very sentence. The activity of the person using
those formulae does not appear in the realm of discourse associated with that
formal language.

[55] For a careful discussion of this question see Harré [119]. Compare also Heckhausen [127, p. 492ff].

be rather dissatisfied if we only get a description of that person's body. We will also expect some hints about what may be understood as that person's psychological being. However, we should not assume that such a personal being can be expressed as a set of psychological properties which are more or less stable through a person's biography.

Clearly, we would not accept as a description of a person's identity the statement that somebody was sad last Monday morning. The statement that somebody is a joyful person, however, would be much more acceptable. Such a statement indicates certain abilities of the person in question—she or he can smile and laugh, they may let you forget your sorrows, they may be able to sing in specific ways, and so on. Now persons differ in their abilities and in their ways to develop their abilities by learning, and possibly they use these abilities to distinguish themselves from other people. In any case, an acceptable description of a person will indicate some abilities of that person. Usually the abilities in question may reasonably be assumed to last for a considerable portion of a human biography (as I have noted, it is a natural property of human beings that they acquire abilities much easier than they lose them).

Included among a person's projects may be attempts at shaping one's biography. Such projects will enter a careful description of that person. For example, the project of becoming the president of the United States or the project of being a perfect mother may each shape a person in deep and lasting ways. One does not need to share Sartre's radical attempt to define persons only in terms of such projects in order to accept his emphasis on the irreducible role of projects in creating personal identity.[56]

Both abilities and projects involve matters of knowledge and belief. Although such matters today often are affiliated with the so–called cognitive domain, one should not be misled into separating them from emotional issues. Learning to know a landscape involves going through a variety of feelings and emotions. It is very strange indeed to suppose that persons can acquire knowledge without being emotionally transformed as well.[57] This is especially true with regard to knowledge about persons: To learn to know another person more than superficially always is an intense emotional experience.

---

[56] See Sartre [241] for a striking example.

[57] Studying the practical consequences of this idea is of great importance in our historical context, where the growth of knowledge is separated by institutional barriers from most aspects of the emotional growth of persons.

When talking about personal identity, we are not only concerned with properties, but also with relations. To be a certain person means to stand in certain relations to other beings, especially to other persons. A friendship may be as important for somebody's personal identity as an ability or a project. Clearly, the importance of social relations for personal identity is not limited to the immediate present: A past friendship can be essential for somebody's personal identity his or her whole life long. There is a strange tendency to frame investigations of personal identity by asking what remains of a person if we ignore their relations—of ownership, dependency, authorship, authority, solidarity, etc., to other beings. This implies the assumption that all relationships with which a person is engaged are external relations. However, if persons exist by virtue of relations of accountability—as I am arguing—this assumption is easily seen to be absurd. *Internal relations* to other people are a necessary condition for the unfolding of personal identity.

Philosophically speaking, an internal relation is one which has to be valid in order for a certain identification to be possible.[58] For example, a number is even if and only if it is divisible by two. A person is a mother if and only if another person is her child. Persons are individuals linked by internal relations. A strictly atomistic world view implies that there are only external relations. On the other hand, an extreme holism is given by the thesis that all relations are internal ones. In some sense, one may say that whether a relation is internal or external depends on our way of defining the things that may be related internally or externally, but possible definitions are not completely arbitrary. For example, it is impossible to describe numbers without referring to relations. Here I will argue that a person can only develop a consciousness of himself or herself by being related to other persons.

A reasonable description of a person involves relations, beliefs, abilities and projects. Obviously, there will be elements in all these dimensions which can be neglected in the description of the person's identity, just as there will be elements which may be considered to be essential. One can then attempt to identify elements which form a stable core, which would enable us to speak of personal identity as running through a whole biography. As Wittgenstein has remarked in a famous argument, however, the strength of a thread does not depend

---

[58] The distinction between internal and external relations has been elaborated by Whitehead [293] among others. For the present task, a general discussion of relations is not necessary as my argument will involve only three specific kinds of relations: Relations between persons, relations between means and ends, and the relation between those two relations.

on the existence of one fibre running through the whole thread but on a multitude of interlaced fibres. In a sense, this metaphor justifies an argument against the search for a unique personal identity and supports the notion of a multitude of "souls" which would make up a person.[59]

Still, there is a drastic difference between a person formed by a rich variety of experiences and a human being at the mercy of frequent alterations from one "near–person" to another, as described in the literature dealing with multiple personality. This is the problem of personal coherence, which is sometimes framed in terms of mental illness. Talking about illness here is a medical metaphor referring to a reality which cannot be reduced to organic damage, although it may be affected by such damage. I want to insist, however, that problems of madness are real and that they are related to questions of personal identity.[60] Personal identity can be damaged and it is important to understand how such damage comes about and how it can be reversed. Clearly, this requires considerable understanding of how personal identity develops in less dramatic cases, too.

In a crucial sense, personal development begins with a mother's love for her child.[61] The child first develops in an intimate symbiosis with its mother; in the course of time, other adults, among which the father usually plays a significant role, build up similar relations of symbiosis with the child. Sooner or later the child enters into very different kinds of social relations in the context of peer groups. It seems plausible that peer groups are important for learning to follow rules, because in such groups following specific instructions is less important than in the symbiosis with adults, while accounting conversations are very common. Be that as it may, when entering the world of peer groups the child is already acquainted with gender relations from her or his symbiotic experiences. The social differences between the sexes offer the child the fundamental experience that persons are not all alike and that there are complementary relationships between different persons. Later on, when the child becomes an adult member of human society, say a woman, her biography will be profoundly shaped by the way she handles her position in kinship structures and gender relations.

---

[59] This notion is defended by Lévi–Strauss in Benoist [21].

[60] See Coulter [54] for a careful discussion of some of the relevant epistemological questions. Following Bateson [16], I will argue that a concept of madness is essential for an adequate discussion of ecological problems.

[61] Shotter [254, p. 107ff].

An acceptable theory of human affairs must allow scientific discourse about love to acquire greater significance than is presently the case. An important step in that direction is to realize that love is not a mental state. To say "I love you" usually implies a bundle of commitments regarding situations which may arise in the future. If we consider a commitment as a project for which I make myself responsible to other persons, then love may be regarded as a source of certain commitments—and the example of a mother taking care of her child is a case in point. Extending the metaphor, one may say that this source is located not within a person, but within an internal relation between persons. Thus, it perhaps becomes easier to accept that love is not accessible to a direct scientific study. For in scientific terms, love is a cause which may be identifiable only through its effects. If one of those effects would be a willingness to talk more carefully about the cause, this might even be of some help to scientific progress.

2.4   Common Madness and the Reality of Evil

I will begin this section with a discussion of three attempts to develop a view of mental illness which applies not only to relatively rare individual cases, but also to whole populations. They refer to the emergence of civilization, to the practice of war, and to the rise of Nazism. I will argue that at least the last two instances warrant a concept of common madness, which in modified form can also be applied to current processes of environmental destruction. I will consider common madness as a case of impaired personal identities. After having discussed some strengths and shortcomings of psychoanalytic approaches to common madness, I will reflect upon the approach by Bateson, which explicitly relates results of research about schizophrenia to the present environmental crisis. Bateson analyzed the phenomena of madness in analogy to mathematical paradoxes. I will argue that the analogy can be very useful, if it is freed of misleading connotations by setting it in the context of accounting conversations.

Common madness can then be studied as the outcome of clusters of nonsensical beliefs. A combination of two such clusters deserves special attention. The first cluster suggests a notion of personal identity without internal relations between persons, while the second one suggests a notion of human activity without internal relations between means and ends. I will argue that important causes of common madness are normative fields lacking internal coherence. In the sociological tradition, such a lack of coherence is referred to as anomie. Finally, I will suggest that an explanation for large–scale environmental disruption by humankind is to be found in situations of anomie and common madness—together with the plain fact that human beings are capable of doing evil if they wish to do so.

It is one of Freud's lasting achievements that he led the human sciences to take seriously the themes of love and sex, as well as to consider their possible connections with madness. He did so by his attempt to develop an effective therapeutic procedure for individual cases of neurosis. Here, however, I am interested less in the therapeutic use of psychoanalysis than in its use for the study of the relations between humankind and the biosphere.[62] Such a study should not ignore the fact that the Freudian analysis of mental illness has been generalized to a view of *mental illness afflicting whole populations.* Three different arguments are important here. One is Freud's speculation about some prehistoric event which gave rise to the kind of personality structure formed by the Oedipus conflict. The second argument is Freud's attempt to understand the reality of war as the dreadful expression of an uncontrolled death–drive. Third, there are the attempts of the Frankfurt School to combine psychoanalytic arguments with Marxist analysis in order to understand the emergence of Nazism.[63]

Basically, Freud's speculations on the emergence of civilization in prehistoric times run as follows.[64] The repressed sexual and other desires of adult persons indicate that the natural state of human beings is one of barbarism. In its origins, humankind evolved in small hordes of people without any comprehensive social order. Typically, each horde consisted of an aggressive male with several females and their children. The father feared his sons and chased them away before they became adults.

At some point, a group of sons murdered their father. After the murder, they were able to stabilize their alliance by repressing their sexual desire for the horde's females. This repression was facilitated by a sense of guilt, which led to a new emphasis on obedience toward the father. A social order based on the incest taboo was formed, and it was reproduced by children exposed to the Oedipus conflict. The experience

---

[62] It could well be that the basic approach of psychoanalysis to biographies is sound in scientific terms, while its application in therapy still leaves considerable room for improvement.

[63] In particular Horkheimer [131], Adorno et al. [2].

[64] Freud [86].

of that conflict made the children internalize the incest taboo, and hence reproduce the social order, including the Oedipus conflict, into which they plunged the following generation.

In this conflict, children develop a superego by experiencing the contradiction between their incestuous desires and the authority of the father, which enforces the incest taboo. Civilization is based on repression, therefore we are rarely completely happy with it; but without it we would fall back into a state of destructive chaos.

There is a remarkable similarity between this line of argument and Thomas Hobbes' theory of the state. His starting point is expressed by the phrase "*homo homini lupus*". In his view, the central authority of the state is necessary to guarantee a peaceful social order. This philosophy of the state grew out of an atomistic ontology, which tried to explain social institutions in terms of individuals.[65]

In order to judge the above speculations, it is useful to take notice of a few facts about the emergence of civilization (established mostly after Freud formulated his speculations).[66] Before states were formed, there were cases of ritual head–hunting, but no generalized wars. Stable patterns of kinship involving incest–taboos, as well as more general rules of endogamy and exogamy, are much older than the major civilizations of the past. The dominant position of the father was not originally part of those patterns, but arose roughly at the same time as states were formed. Long before this happened, our ancestors had learned to organize themselves by speech and by rule–oriented behavior involving speech.

War can hardly be attributed to some natural state of humankind, as it was "invented" long after stable ways of organizing human lives in a shared cultural context evolved and stood the test of time during a long period. This point should not be confused with the question of whether aggressive behavior as such is biologically rooted in human beings.[67] Wolves surely have a biologically determined tendency to display aggressive behavior under certain circumstances, yet there are no wars among wolves. Hobbes referred to a situation of civil war, which ended by the monopolization of power by the central state. Hobbes is actually describing a historical experience, but the inception of this experience cannot be traced to a natural state of affairs, nor can war be understood as a regression to a natural state of generalized destruction.

---

[65] The same ontology is to be found in the political philosophy of Locke [165].
[66] I will come back to these topics in chapter 3.
[67] Groebel and Hinde [108].

These findings are relevant for Freud's concept of the death drive, which he developed in the historical context of World War I.[68] The temptation of psychological reductionism here would imply an explanation of the reality of war with the internal dynamics of the biographies of the individuals involved. It may well be that a war is favored by certain biographical properties frequent among the populations involved,[69] but it is impossible to explain the occurrence of wars in terms of individual biographies. If, for example, biographies in the German Reich of the 1930s showed something like a propensity toward war, then this fact requires a social explanation.[70] Moreover, the occurrence of wars is clearly a major factor structuring human biographies.

In the following chapter, I will further pursue the point that biographies are irreducibly socially shaped. Here I want to consider a specific, if crucial aspect emphasized by feminist critiques. To analyze the social determinants of individual biographies has always been a major concern of Marxist theory, but in that theory sexual relations play at best a secondary role. It was no doubt a lasting achievement of psychoanalysis to consider sexual relations in the context of modern society as a field of experience of paramount importance. Marx tended to ignore private life, Freud emphasized its relevance. Freud, however, tended to analyze social phenomena in terms of a psychological reductionism. The feminist critique of the patriarchal system shares the emphasis of sexual relations and of private life (including the realm of housework to which Freud did not devote much attention). Yet it refuses the reductionist approach: Private life itself is described as a social reality. This implies that the distinction between public and private is by no means identical to the one between the social and the personal. Freud claimed that the events of public life are in fact dominated by processes taking place in the private realm, and that social reality is shaped by personal reality. That the two claims are not identical is shown by the fact that feminist critique denies the second claim but not the first one.

If Freud's attempt to reduce social processes to the dynamics of personal biographies is unsatisfactory, this does not imply that the opposite position of considering personal biographies as mere expressions of social realities is any more valid. This kind of sociological reductionism can be found quite often in Marxist approaches, to which psychoanalysis represents a major challenge. Freud may have exaggerated his theoretical emphasis of sexual relations, but there can be no doubt

---

[68] Freud [87].

[69] See Theweleit [276] for an argument along such lines with respect to Nazism.

[70] Drucker [61] tried hard to offer one.

that in modern societies conflicts between the sexes are much more frequent and important than would be suggested by the marginal role which they play in Marxist theory. Under these conditions, attempts to avoid the temptations both of psychological as well as of sociological reductionism deserve our interest.

A series of such attempts has been undertaken in the empirical studies of the Frankfurt School. An influential argument from this tradition concerns the emergence of Nazism in Germany. It sees the so–called authoritarian personality as the link between family structures and Nazi politics. According to this view, the dominance of the father in many German families at the beginning of the 20th century tended to produce personality structures with a weak ego unable to cope with a rigid and very demanding superego. This psychological authoritarianism then coincided with the need of the ruling class in Germany to defend its power in a situation of economic crisis. The result was the development of growing authoritarianism by political elites, who nevertheless were accepted by a large part of the population. Ultimately, this development led to the atrocities of the concentration camps and of World War II.

The Frankfurt School used Marxism to understand the political economy of fascism, while psychoanalysis supplemented the understanding of its private dimension. A first hint at difficulties with this approach is given by the fact that the economic crisis of the early thirties in America did not lead to increased political authoritarianism, but rather to Roosevelt's New Deal. How can this be understood in a framework of personality structures? One could try to distinguish different family patterns, including an authoritarian type, represented mainly in Germany, and a liberal type, represented in Anglo–Saxon countries.[71] Obviously such an argument can help explain the different responses to the Great Depression. Nevertheless, it is hard to deny that diverging political traditions played an important and autonomous role which is systematically overlooked in Marxist approaches.

The Marxist part of the argument was further shaken by the reality of Stalinism and the failure of all attempts toward a socialist revolution in industrialized countries. On the other hand, the psychoanalytical part of the argument was in fact explaining personality traits in terms of family structures and in doing so did not get very far in avoiding sociological reductionism. The Frankfurt School undertook a conscious effort to allot space to personal agents in social theory. It

---

[71] Such a distinction is proposed by Todd [279].

tried to do so by combining psychoanalysis and Marxism, but in fact this resulted in an explicit consideration of private life without much personal autonomy.[72]

This is not to deny that experiences like World War I and Nazism make it highly plausible that madness can afflict whole human populations, and that in order to understand such situations economic, political and private dimensions have to be combined. No doubt the Frankfurt School has made a lasting contribution to the analysis of such problems, but it has also shown that a combination of psychoanalysis and Marxism is insufficient for this purpose.[73] I think that a better approach can be found by considering the basic human experience of making an error.

The ability to hold true beliefs is one of the most remarkable properties of persons. Truth becomes accessible only in the process of living together with other persons. Children gradually acquire the ability to hold true beliefs by being exposed to certain normative fields. These fields take into account the possibility of errors: A child learns what truth is, among other ways, by learning how to correct errors. These are factual errors which can be handled within the usual framework of relations of accountability between persons. To err is human and no doubt everybody holds erroneous beliefs from time to time. This may be quite innocuous but in critical situations it may obviously do great harm.

Beliefs may be wrong, as in the case of a belief that some painting is an original by Rembrandt while it is in fact the work of a pupil of Rembrandt. Besides being simply wrong, beliefs can also be nonsensical

---

[72] In a sense, it is exactly this absence of true personal being which the pioneers of the Frankfurt School presented as the main discovery of their social theory. Horkheimer and Adorno [130] developed a sophisticated philosophical argument to discuss the lack of personal autonomy in modern society. This leads to a remarkable paradox. Marx formulated his theory with the explicit goal of showing how true human agency emerges in the struggle against capitalism; Freud developed psychoanalysis as a framework for therapeutic processes, which under the conditions which Marx described as capitalism should enable the patients to become autonomous persons. The combination of the two approaches in the analysis of Nazism led to the description not only of Nazism, but of modern society in general, as a social reality which does not allow personal autonomy at all. There may be some truth in such a conclusion, but it contradicts a good deal of common sense as well as the basic premises of the two theories combined.

[73] Habermas [110] has renewed the Frankfurt School by substituting Piaget for Freud and, in certain respects, Parsons for Marx. This has enabled him to discuss arguments from very different sources, including Wittgenstein, Max Weber, and many others. I will consider some aspects of his approach in chapter 6.

as in the case of the belief that the antipodes are people who spend their life hanging upside down from the other side of the earth. Somebody who holds such a belief did not really grasp the concept of an antipode. Again, nonsensical beliefs are quite frequent and usually inoffensive. Nonsensical errors are not harmful as isolated errors, but rather by the compound effect of several nonsensical errors. Human agents may entangle themselves in whole *clusters of nonsensical beliefs* to such a degree that their status as persons becomes questionable: This is the case of madness. I do not want to discuss here the problem of how, in given social systems, cases of madness are identified and how different institutions and people try to handle such situations.[74] It must be emphasized, however, that cases of madness differ widely both in kind and in degree. The role that cerebral biochemical processes play in the formation of large clusters of nonsensical beliefs will not be assessed here.[75] What is important is to treat a belief as the psychological property of a person, and not as a biochemical property of an organism, though quite obviously psychological properties may be influenced by biochemical, social, and many other factors.

In order to proceed, we need a minimal understanding of how, beside biochemical disturbances, social factors can influence personal madness. For the latter point, the work on the so–called double–bind hypothesis formulated by Bateson requires consideration. Bateson's original idea was that the paradoxes of set theory provide a paradigmatic case for the study of madness. Set theory was developed in the 19th century with the belief that a set is the totality of all entities sharing some arbitrary property. A wide array of mathematical disciplines could be reformulated with this approach by treating numbers, functions, geometrical figures, etc., as different kinds of sets. As is well known, this approach led to difficulty in the case of the set $\mathcal{P}$ which includes all sets which are not their own members. If $\mathcal{P}$ were its own member, it would have to share the set–defining property of not being its own member. If, on the other hand, $\mathcal{P}$ were not its own member, it would fulfill its own membership condition, and therefore would in fact be its own member. Both formulations lead to an intrinsic contradiction.

This paradox indicates that at least some of the original set–theoretical beliefs were nonsensical. Obviously, holding these specific nonsensical beliefs was completely harmless for the overwhelming majority of people: they could ignore the paradox, or, if they got to know

---

[74] See Foucault [83] for an example of such a discussion.
[75] Coulter [54] discusses some related issues.

it at all, laugh at it and forget about it while going on living their lives. Even a mathematician could have handled it that way; there are many other subjects in mathematics where she or he could have done useful work. For somebody like Bertrand Russell, who was determined to concentrate his work on the foundations of mathematics, things were not so easy. After all, the paradox showed that those foundations were by no means as solid as the ideal of mathematical rigor seemed to require. If mathematical proofs were built on sand, how could one trust mathematics any more? Moreover, if even mathematical arguments, those paradigms of reliable thought, were not sound, how could one rely on any other way of arguing?

This kind of generalized doubt can actually paralyze a person to the point where the problem is no longer an isolated nonsensical belief, but threatens the person in question with more or less pronounced forms of madness. Russell found his way out of this maze together with A.N. Whitehead by distinguishing between types of sets, a solution which is known as the theory of types in mathematics. A set of material objects, say the set of all the books on my desk, may be said to be of type 1. A set of such sets may be said to be of type 2. An acceptable set never has the same type as its members. The set $\mathcal{P}_n$ may then be defined as the set of all sets of type $n - 1$ which are not their own members. The set $\mathcal{P}_n$ then is simply the set of all sets of type $n-1$ and the paradox disappears. This line of argument is obviously similar to the distinction between an object language and its meta–language. The latter distinction engenders an infinite hierarchy of languages, while the former introduces an infinite hierarchy of types. In this framework, paradoxes are then seen as the result of a confusion between different levels of language.

Bateson claimed that similar situations can arise in the context of family life and called them *double–bind situations*. A mother talking to her child is said to use a verbal object–language. If she supplements her talk with gestures, facial expressions, and the like, she is said to use a non–verbal meta–language as well. A double–bind then means, for example, that the mother tells the child that she likes it while indicating the opposite with her gestures. Broadly speaking, the double–bind hypothesis states that this kind of situation lies at the heart of cases of schizophrenia.[76] Research on this hypothesis seems to suggest that

---

[76] To avoid confusion, I hasten to emphasize that this does not rule out combinations with different kinds of biochemical processes. On the one hand, the ability of children to handle double–bind situations can depend on genetic factors; on the other hand, the mental effort required from the child can exhaust some chemical

the appearance of madness in families characterized by double–bind situations tends to reinforce this condition.[77]

The double–bind hypothesis is relevant here because it has been linked by Bateson to the issues of today's environmental crisis.[78] He suggested that, together with the emergence of so–called higher forms of civilization, some kind of social change occurred by which something like a generalized double–bind situation became inscribed into human culture. From this perspective, earlier social systems were able to sustain a more reasonable relationship with their environment than so–called higher civilizations precisely because the latter are afflicted with some kind of common madness. How far the so–called higher civilizations are in fact marked by a double–bind structure is not precisely elaborated by Bateson. The spirit in which he tries to grasp the problem of common madness can perhaps be illustrated by the following image.

Today's global society knows the distinction between workday and Sunday. On working days, we account for our actions in an object language, while on Sundays, in a meta–language. In the object language, we talk about labor, about purposefully dealing with material things, about holding one's ground in a merciless competition. The meta–language of today's Sunday—the leisure world—, on the other hand, talks about purposeless desires, about luck, and once and again about love; thus, it renews in secularized form the religious theme of redemption by the divine power of love.

The messages transmitted in those two languages are not compatible with each other, and are rarely put in relation to each other. This inconsistency provides the cultural grounding for a work of destruction which is done on working days and palliated on Sundays. In other words, that situation seems to be a double–bind based on a highly ambiguous relation between immanence and transcendence. This image offers a way to proceed from the idea of individual schizophrenia caused by a double–bind situation to a concept of common madness.

The notion of common madness is intuitively warranted by phenomena like war, slavery, and global environmental disruption, but it raises an important objection.[79] Possibly, the concept of common madness

---

substances which are vital for the proper functioning of the brain. Our discussion of social conditions of madness is not committed to the contention that there are no biochemical conditions of madness.

[77] Stierlin [266, p. 50ff].

[78] Bateson [16].

[79] I will discuss the case of slavery in chapter 3.

expresses nothing except some arbitrary value judgement. The analogy with biological processes can be of some help in clarifying this problem. We may feel strong aversion to diseases while liking healthy organisms. Identifying a disease is nevertheless an important and perfectly sensible scientific practice. In a similar sense, scientists can try to identify instances of common madness without being confused by the fact that people may or may not detest war and like peace.

Care must be taken, however, not to be trapped by the biological analogy which I have just introduced. I have insisted on the fact that persons are emergent entities which transcend the realm of biological evolution. Therefore, the analogy between madness and disease can be used only by maintaining the distinction between the personal and the biological. It must be possible to roughly sketch the identification of madness as a phenomenon lying beyond the scope of biology. This is exactly what I did by linking the phenomenon of madness to the possibility of nonsensical beliefs.

Then a remarkable consequence arises. Biologists may dislike the disease of cancer, but in scientific terms they do not criticize cancer any more than a geologist criticizes an earthquake. On the other hand, to discover that some cluster of beliefs is largely nonsensical means ipso facto to criticize it.[80] This critique does not condemn a state of affairs in the name of some subjective value; rather, the critique arises on the grounds of what Wittgenstein might have called a shared life form, namely the practice of correcting not only factual errors, but also errors rooted in nonsensical beliefs.[81] This life form is not restricted to any scientific community, but rather it is shared by every mother who helps a baby to become a person. Clearly, most persons talk nonsense from time to time, and sometimes—such as when playing with nonsense in the context of a joke—persons are even required to do so. Being a person implies the ability to identify and correct both factual errors and errors involving nonsense.

In order to discuss the topic of common madness more specifically, I must go back to the theory of types once again. If there is such a thing as common madness involved in the current conversation of humankind, then scientific rationality should not be considered immune

---

[80] Remember that in talking about madness I am not concerned with isolated beliefs.

[81] I am concerned with erroneous beliefs here. Obviously, other forms of errors become relevant if one considers various kinds of actions, including the action of expressing a belief. For example, there may be rules of politeness which make it inappropriate to express some true belief under given circumstances.

to it.[82] Taking the paradoxes of set theory as a paradigm case for the study of madness may be an important step for this reason, too. Then it must be acknowledged that Bateson's insistence on the theory of types looks a bit out of fashion today. Today mathematicians usually avoid the well known paradoxes with different strategies.[83]

I will argue that the basic idea behind the double–bind hypothesis can actually be strengthened by dropping its reliance on the theory of types and other versions of set theory as well, and by turning instead to Wittgenstein's interrelated notions of language games and life forms.[84] Wittgenstein devoted a great deal of his effort to finding a better answer to the paradoxes of set theory than the one offered by the theory of types. This led him to major innovations in the philosophy of mathematics.[85] Far from separating the debate on the foundations of mathematics from issues of madness, Wittgenstein emphasized the strong links between the two. Bateson hoped that the theory of types, which had so strongly inspired his thoughts on madness, could actually be used as a tool in the study of this subject. Wittgenstein, however, seems to suggest that the debate on the foundations of mathematics is an example of the same problem which is found in the conversations of many inmates of psychiatric institutions: How can we handle beliefs which are not factual errors, but rather instances of nonsense?

To take an example, the belief that the axioms of set theory are similar to the bedrock on which the skyscrapers of Manhattan are erected could be quite nonsensical. Maybe such axioms are more comparable to a new roof on top of a house that has been built over a long period of time. Maybe the metaphor of a house is simply misleading if one wants to understand the reliability of mathematics. There is no need to discuss these issues further once the relationship between the notion of

---

[82] Quite the opposite, as many would argue with Feyerabend [76].

[83] Such strategies are discussed by Quine [227].

[84] Wittgenstein's practice of philosophy may be understood as an attempt to find a cure for instances of common madness. Some related arguments can be found in Kreilcamp–Cudmore [158].

[85] The tremendous impact of Plato's philosophy on Western culture is due to a considerable extent to the fascination exercised by the Platonic account of mathematics. If—as authors like Shanker [253] or Baker and Hacker [12] suggest— Wittgenstein's philosophy does not offer a further footnote to the Platonic account of mathematics, but actually marks the beginning of a more adequate account, it will surely take a long time to work out its consequences. Finding a cure for common madness could then turn out to be the process which Plato misleadingly identified as a one–way shift from sensory experience to the contemplation of ideas. Still, Plato's metaphor of leaving the cave in which humankind is trapped is one of the most suggestive metaphors for the problem of common madness.

madness and the paradoxes of set theory has been reassessed. Madness should not be explained in terms of the theory of types, but in terms of the notion of nonsensical beliefs. This notion can then be applied to the discussion of the foundations of mathematics, as well as to any other human conversation.

When talking about nonsensical beliefs, care must be taken to consider the fact that an expression which is nonsensical in English may be perfectly meaningful in German. The distinction between sense and nonsense is possible only within the context of some normative field. It is therefore possible that what seems to be nonsense to one person is quite meaningful to another, but only if they orientate on two different normative fields. To say that a belief is nonsensical is relevant only in the context of the normative field where the belief is expressed. If, on the other hand, this context is taken into account, the identification of nonsensical beliefs is not purely a matter of opinion. Once we know that a group of children is playing football according to some set of rules, we can assess a specific move as a case of foul play. In the same way, we can identify isolated nonsensical beliefs as well as cases of madness once we know the normative fields involved.

Therefore, there seem to be two different ways out of situations of madness. On the one hand, a person may learn to correct a cluster of nonsensical beliefs in such a way that his or her ability to act in a given social context is improved. On the other hand, the social context in which the person in question is involved may change in such a way that beliefs which were once considered nonsensical become perfectly meaningful. It is as if in a given language community somebody started to utter meaningless expressions and the community was then to develop new rules whereby those expressions became part of the language. This possibility helps to understand the widespread suspicion that there is an intimate link between cases of genius and madness. Madness may in fact prefigure social forms which will later emerge. Such prefiguration, however, may also happen without involving cases of madness, and madness may happen without involving such prefiguration.

The forms of therapy which have been developed on the basis of the double–bind hypothesis actually tend to modify the social system in which a case of madness arose (usually a family) in such a way that nonsensical beliefs become quite intelligible.[86] This seems especially

---

[86] See Fischer [78] for a more detailed discussion with explicit reference to Freud's psychoanalysis. In such discussions, there is the danger of confusing the process by which a nonsensical expression becomes meaningful with an alleged discovery of a hidden meaning. There are interesting parallels here with the fate of math-

appropriate when the social system in whose context a case of madness arose is seen as a cause of this process. The double–bind hypothesis indicates a causal link between certain kinds of social situations and forms of personal madness. Under such circumstances, the nonsensical beliefs involved in this madness may lead to a therapeutic process involving not simply an individual patient but also the whole family. The original situation may be transformed in such a way that the nonsensical beliefs developed by a person struck by madness may later become meaningful as a form of protest against that situation. This can imply far–reaching changes in the family concerned. If such changes do not take place, the person concerned may participate in the development of other social systems which allow him or her distance from the original family life. I do not want to discuss here the specific problems associated with the cases of madness usually labelled as schizophrenia. What I want to emphasize is the broader possibility that an important cause of madness can exist in certain features of social systems.[87]

Such a feature was identified by the double–bind hypothesis as the recurrence of paradoxical communication in the social system of a family. Paradoxical communication was originally described by metaphors taken from the theory of types. This description can be improved by noting that in so–called double–bind situations it becomes impossible to establish or maintain relationships of responsibility. For example, a child may find itself in a situation where for an important set of her actions she can conceive no account—be it a justification, an excuse, or anything else—that seems understandable to its mother. This means that the child sees no chance of reaching agreement or even disagreement, but only the possibility of ongoing misunderstanding. In other words, the relationship of accountability between mother and child is severely impaired. If there are no other persons which can offer alternative relationships of responsibility, the child is forced into irresponsible action, not in the sense of doing something which is clearly wrong, but in the sense of losing the opportunity to embed its actions in accounting conversations.

Such an impairment of accounting relationships is often caused by the simultaneous relevance of two conflicting rules. This is the basic feature

---

ematical conjectures (Shanker [253]). A closer analysis of these problems would focus on the relationship between empirical sentences and grammatical sentences, on which both Fischer and Shanker draw in accordance with Wittgenstein.

[87] Again, I want to emphasize that this does not at all exclude the relevance of other—biochemical, psychological, etc.,—causes.

of double–bind situations, whether they are described in terms of the theory of types or not. In sociological terms, such situations can be studied with the concept of *anomie*.[88] In the present context, I will label as anomic a normative field which makes it impossible for some persons involved in the field to act according to the field's social rules. A main form of anomie is provided by the existence of contradictory rules. It must be noted that the notion of a contradiction between rules makes little sense outside of the specific situations where those rules are applied.[89] Anomie is not a property of culture alone, but of a normative field including culture and social structure.

In the present context, I want to discuss issues of individual madness only to the extent to which they are indispensable for the study of the self–destructive tendencies which seem to characterize humankind in the 20th century. For the moment, I will rely on the rather abstract insight that clusters of nonsensical beliefs can impair relations of responsibility, which are a necessary condition for the development of persons. This leads us to the possibility that certain normative fields tend to produce cases of personal madness. While this possibility may be of considerable relevance to the problems of schizophrenia and of family therapy, here I am interested in more mundane forms of insanity, which I have labelled as common madness and which may express themselves in phenomena like war, slavery, and environmental disruption.

Common madness implies the existence of a cluster of nonsensical beliefs which, so to speak, infect the cultural heritage of humankind. What then are these beliefs? If my hypothesis should indicate an actual state of affairs, then this question might turn out to be rather tricky for the simple reason that I must suppose that I am, to some extent, sharing those beliefs. In principle, this is not an insurmountable difficulty. A nicotine addict may easily describe his addiction as including a whole set of beliefs which he is able to criticize in a way that has some plausibility, even for other addicts. Still, his self–criticism may be quite confused on details. This does not mean that it is unwarranted, but

---

[88] For a careful discussion of this key sociological concept, see Orrù [203].

[89] This means that when one talks of a problem caused by some contradiction between different rules, one is in a sense always concerned with a deficiency of the corresponding normative field. A supplementary rule could eliminate the situation of anomie. The well–known example of the arithmetical rule which states that division by zero is not allowed is a perfect example of such an elimination of anomie. Often, additional rules increase the complexity of the normative field in question. They can also simplify it, mainly by increasing its coherence, but also by making whole clusters of older rules obsolete.

rather that it is incomplete. Its completion may actually require the addict to get rid of his addiction. While this can be easily said in principle, it may require great patience and a great deal of luck in practice. With the hypothesis of common madness, one should be prepared to encounter a similar situation.

Consider the notion of a human *soul*. I have discussed in the preceding sections how the identity of a person, its soul if you like, is constituted by intertwined threads, including abilities, relations, projects and beliefs. Now let us consider instead a spatial metaphor which suggests that a person's soul is something like a core deep inside the person in question, protected by a boundary which separates that person from the rest of the world. What happens if a person comes to believe that their identity is constituted by such a boundary? What happens if normative fields sustain beliefs of this kind in virtually every person who has grown up in the context of these fields?

These questions offer a useful approach to the phenomenon of common madness. In human life, there are all kinds of boundaries. There are the contours of objects, like a mountain or a stone; there is the skin of animals and people; there are watersheds and rivers. Then there are the boundaries which are relevant for territorial behavior, often rooted in physical boundaries like the edge of a forest or the wall of a house. Finally, there are boundaries in metaphorical space, as when we speak about limits which separate permitted from forbidden actions. Clearly, persons are able to cope with boundaries, to avoid crossing them or to cross them in an appropriate manner, to abolish, draw or re–draw some of them, and so forth.

However, if I try to define myself in terms of boundaries which separate me from other beings, then I will be attempting, among other things, to sustain a personal identity which is independent from my interpersonal relations. A cluster of nonsensical beliefs will lead me to treat all interpersonal relations as being external to my personal identity, and to ignore the fact that without at least some interpersonal relations which are internal to the persons involved, there would be no persons at all.[90] The beliefs in question are nonsensical in the same way as solipsistic ideas, which I criticized in section 2.2 with Wittgenstein's metaphor of the bug in a box.

---

[90] A nice metaphor in this context is provided by the notion of an aura, as proposed by W. Benjamin [20] (see also Stoessel [267]). Using this metaphor, one can contrast the attempt to define things and persons in terms of boundaries with a representation of these entities as embedded in an aura formed by a dense network of relationships.

Using this strange but widespread view, human agency is detached from relationships of accountability. The human subject is depicted as acting upon its environment in splendid isolation. A person may talk to other people about what she or he does, but their actions occur prior to such talk. It is as if a baby started acting like a human being and later only incidentally started to comment on its actions verbally. Treating interpersonal relationships of accountability as if they were external to personal identity may well mean misconstruing human agency—by starting from the case of an isolated individual acting on some object in their environment. The relationship between human agents and their environment is then detached from the social reality which enables and constrains those agents to sustain relationships of responsibility with each other.

The nonsensical belief that interpersonal relations are external to the persons involved makes it very difficult to grasp the internal relations which exist between many means and ends of human activity. Instead, nonsense leads to nonsense, namely to the idea that solipsistic agents employ means of action which are only externally related to the goals pursued. Take the classical example of music. In order to play the flute, I perform certain movements with my tongue. Playing the flute is the end, while a means to this end are the tongue movements. That there is a difference between means and ends is shown by the fact that to some degree tongue movements can be described in physical terms which do not refer to music at all. There are always cases, however, where there is no better way to describe the movement of the tongue than by saying that it punctuates a melody with a brilliant staccato. These are cases where means and ends are internally related. Symmetrical cases can be found starting from the ends. It is, for example, impossible to explain the practice of playing the flute without referring, among other things, to the fact that it is performed by means of the human breath.

The above argument does not imply that it is impossible to build a robot which would produce the sounds of a flute sonata by pressing the appropriate keys of a flute and generating the appropriate airstreams. It would, however, be at best highly metaphorical talk to say that the robot employed these means to the end of playing the flute. It might make sense to say that some engineers use such a robot with the goal of reproducing the sounds of a flute sonata. Means–end relations make sense in the context of accounting conversations. Therefore, a robot which would really play the flute by itself would need the ability to coordinate itself with other musicians in the context of such conversations, just as engineers who really try to build such robots coordinate themselves.

The cluster of beliefs which try to represent the human soul as existing independently of interpersonal relations cannot grasp the internal means–end relations which are established in accounting conversations. Instead, one can try a solipsistic representation of human agency. From this perspective, an isolated individual could choose the means which seem appropriate to the pursuit of its predefined ends. Means and ends are then treated only as being externally related. If such beliefs are widely held, human agency is deeply modified in the sense which may be expressed by saying that agency degenerates into *labor*.[91] If human agency often degenerates into labor, then such beliefs will be reinforced by this experience. I therefore venture to characterize common madness by a cluster of shared beliefs which try to organize personal identity in terms of boundaries and which misconstrue human agency as labor.

Common madness may be sustained by normative fields sharing a twofold property. On the one hand, there are rules which require human agents to define their personal identity in the literal sense of the term "definition": Personal identity has to be organized and described in terms of boundaries. On the other hand, these demands are complemented by rules which require that human actions are conceived following the paradigm case of labor. However, such rules can be effective only if the relations of accountability between various human agents are rather weak. (Otherwise neither interpersonal relations nor means–end relations could be treated as exclusively external relations.) As I have discussed in section 2.2, though, the establishment of relations of accountability lies at the very root of social rules. If accountability relations are weak, then social rules are wanting in the first place. In this sense, normative fields sustaining common madness are a case of anomie.[92]

Until now, I have developed the notion of common madness in a rather abstract way. It is time to become more specific and to attempt to reconstruct how this notion can be used with respect to the cur-

---

[91] This critical concept of labor owes much to Tronti [283] and to Dahrendorf [55]. It is closely related to the psychological distinction between intrinsic and extrinsic motivation (Heckhausen [127, p. 455ff]).

[92] Anomie is not simply a question of how many rules exist. A family, for example, may entail a normative field with plenty of very detailed rules which regulate all kinds of events from breakfast to holidays, but still may lack a few simple rules which would enable and constrain the parents to gradually involve their children in conversations where the parents' actions are discussed.

rent environmental crisis. This will be the focus of the next chapter. Here I must end with a warning. The environmental disruption which humankind is presently causing raises some very serious moral issues. Any explanation of this disruption in terms of social realities is open to abuse by eliminating questions of personal responsibility from the debate of environmental problems. Similar abuse is possible when a person's actions are explained by describing that person as mentally ill. The notion of common madness offers both possibilities of abuse at once. However, it is a fact of life that human agents can choose to do something which they know to be wrong. Freedom includes the possibility to do evil. Whenever this possibility is realized, there is no use hiding this sad fact behind more or less accurate analyses of social and psychological phenomena. This has to be kept in mind during the following analysis of the role of common madness in the evolution of human societies.

At first it used to vex me because, with all my watching, I was never smart enough to be around when the water was running uphill; but now I do not mind it. I have experimented and experimented until now I know it never does run uphill, except in the dark. I know it does in the dark, because the pool never goes dry, which it would, of course, if the water didn't come back in the night. It is best to prove things by actual experiment; then you *know*; whereas if you depend on guessing and supposing and conjecturing, you will never get educated.

Mark Twain, Eve's Diary.

Chapter 3

The Evolution of Human Ecological Systems

In this chapter, I will try to analyze some of the main steps of the process of environmental disruption in which humankind has been engaged for a long time. To prepare the ground, I will begin in section 3.1 by developing the notion of a human ecological system. I will introduce two concepts for the study of the interaction between humankind and the biosphere: technomass and the entropy margin. The first concept refers to flows of material, the second to flows of energy. However, such physical characterizations are by no means sufficient for an analysis of environmental disruption by humankind. For the purpose of such an analysis, I will discuss the cultural evolution of human ecological systems. I will distinguish three phases characterized by irreversible discontinuities of cultural macro–evolution—in contrast to the more continuous and often reversible processes of cultural micro–evolution.

The first discontinuity corresponds with the so–called neolithic revolution, which marks the end of archaic human ecological systems. These systems, which will be the main theme of section 3.2, were characterized by their very limited impact on the biophysical environment, and as a rule they were also characterized by rather careful ways of interacting with this environment. An important aspect of this situation was the fact that archaic systems put great emphasis on rules of kinship and reciprocity, both of which were not restricted to human beings.

In section 3.3 I will discuss the emergence of dual human ecological systems. These systems are characterized by a polarity between a public and a private realm. The private realm is the result of a transformation of older archaic systems, while the public realm represents a new emergent reality. In the public arena, a certain end of action plays a crucial role: the goal of gaining power. Power is a generalized end of action in the public sphere. This is not to say that power is the only goal of public action, but it means that public action can hardly be understood if the role of relations of power is neglected. Sex plays a similar role as a generalized end of action in the private realm.

With the first step of cultural macro–evolution, a process of cultural degeneration took place. As a result, dual systems were afflicted to a considerable extent by common madness. In this process, both sex and power became external goals of action, thereby contributing to the degeneration of human agency into labor. This degeneration led to increasing environmental disruption in dual systems. As the technological and organizational capabilities of dual systems largely exceeded those of archaic ones, their environmental impact became much more pronounced.

However, environmental disruption at a truly global scale set in only after dual systems were replaced by a more comprehensive triadic system, which took shape in Europe during the period lasting from the Renaissance through the Reformation and until the Enlightenment. This is the second step of cultural macro–evolution, which will be discussed in section 3.4. It resulted in the emergence of vocational systems, which added a third layer to the previous realities of private and public life. This layer of social reality formed the world economy, in which money is the generalized end of action. Again, this seems to be an external goal for many kinds of human activity, in particular in the context of wage labor. Moreover, an overwhelming tendency to minimize wage costs per unit of product resulted from anomic traits of the world economy. This tendency was encouraged by the discovery that the use of human energies can be enormously amplified by suitable technologies, especially by burning fossil fuels.

Meanwhile, environmental disruption has reached the point at which the search for a sustainable lifestyle has become one of the most urgent tasks of humankind. How can the process of cultural degeneration which began at the time of the first discontinuation of cultural macro–evolution be reversed into a process of cultural regeneration? This chapter is meant as a preparation to the approach of this question.

3.1 Conceptualizing the Environment

The emergence of humankind in the course of biological evolution took place in a given natural environment. Air is an essential part of this environment; we breathe it. Water is just as essential, although the rhythms of drinking allow for larger breaks than those of breathing. Our legs and feet are related to the ground, which naturally supports human beings. Our eyes are able to perceive the light of the sun.

The attempts of the ancient philosophers to understand the whole world in terms of a few basic elements like earth, air, water and fire owe their far–reaching fascination, at least in part, to the fact that they hint at basic interfaces between human organisms and what may be called the world at large. Such an anthropomorphic access to the world was misleading as long as it was linked to the claim that somehow the beings of our world were made out of these "interfaces", which were then termed elements. Meanwhile, we do know that water consists of hydrogen and oxygen, not the other way around. Still, we could never have reached an understanding of hydrogen without first having encountered water again and again.

I do not want to settle venerable ontological questions about the elementary categories of being. What I am looking for is a conceptual framework which could help to describe and study the biophysical environment in which personal beings and social relations are embedded. Three complementary traps must be avoided here.

The first one is the attempt to start with an explicit ontology framed in terms of the philosophical tradition. Beautiful questions invite speculation: What is the relationship between event and object, between subject and object, between subject and predicate, between predicate and relationship? Human ecology has much to gain from and maybe something to offer in an enduring dialogue with philosophy, but there is no point in trying to find a solid base for an inquiry into the present environmental crisis by settling such philosophical questions in a definitive manner.

The second trap is to regard the theories of the natural sciences as being the above mentioned conceptual framework. Obviously, the natural sciences study the environment of human beings and are therefore indispensable to any serious study of human ecological systems. The natural sciences mainly try to grasp natural phenomena which are either drastically larger or smaller than the common environment of human beings. Here, I am interested in criteria of relevance directly linked to human life: In this context, water is more elementary than hydrogen, air more elementary than oxygen. I am not looking simply for a theoretical basis provided by the natural sciences, but for a frame which could help to use the results of these sciences in a meaningful way for the study of human ecological systems.

The third trap is to be satisfied by the different descriptions of the environment offered by the large variety of human cultures. With this approach, both philosophy and the natural sciences become nothing more than frameworks presented by certain specific cultures. Even if these frameworks were adopted in a more or less uniform fashion all over the globe, they would still have to be considered in some sense equivalent to the mythologies and concepts of any other culture.[1] Anthropological reports about the way different cultures represent and describe the environment of human beings are of paramount importance for anybody trying to study human ecological systems; the same holds for psychological findings about perceptions and descriptions at the level of the individual. In any case, the question arises whether a framework can be found which would help to use such findings without falling into the trap of naive relativism. We must be able to take the Homeric tales of Poseidon, god of the seas, seriously, while knowing that the tides are caused by the attraction of the moon.

For this purpose, the distinction between air, water, earth, and fire[2] as four elementary realities of the directly perceptible human environment is quite helpful. To this distinction one may add broad categories of entities which are essential to the environment of humankind. Human beings encounter plants and animals long before they discover hydrocarbons and photosynthesis. The human world is populated by

---

[1] Why not consider the different ways in which different individuals look at their environment? Why not go further and emphasize that even one individual describes the same environment in very different ways over the course of time?

[2] Where the sun can be considered as the paradigmatic example of a huge fire.

plants and animals as well as by things and stuff. They are all involved in a myriad of processes including events like birth and death, as well as the growth of a forest, the formation of a mountain, or the blowing of the wind.

The environmental framework introduced so far is still incomplete for one paradoxical, though very important, reason. From month to month the moon grows and wanes; there is hardly any human culture which ignores this fact. Even when the moon is invisible it still forms a part of the world in which we live. Hidden beings are a fact of life. Human beings are usually well aware of the fact that there are many hidden beings which may be very important for their life, even when very little is known about them. From time to time, previously hidden beings are discovered, but the realm of hidden beings is not abolished by people becoming familiar with some of them. Radio waves and elementary particles belong to this realm, but there is no need to exclude the possibility that there could be more hidden beings than just those identified by modern science.

The ground on which we walk, the air which we breathe, the water which we drink, the sun which gives us light, the plants and animals which give us food, the things and stuff which we meet, and the hidden beings of which we may be aware, constitute the human environment. Social reality is closely meshed with this environment. Thus, for instance, the social structure of a family usually is linked to a segment of the built environment, which characteristically includes a specific array of things. Persons interlinked by cultural rules and social structures, together with their specific environment, form a *human ecological system.*

Where exactly the boundaries of such a system lie is an empirical question. To answer it, one must take into account that the boundaries of human ecological systems are defined through the interplay of just these systems. It is, for instance, by no means left to a scientist's arbitrariness to define where the border of a country lies, not even if this border is partly diffuse and perhaps a matter of dispute. Human ecological systems cannot be defined simply by means of the boundaries that separate their specific environment from the environment in a broader sense. We seldom describe a family in terms of the apartment in which they live. If, however, we want to investigate a specific family, we may ask about the size of their apartment.

The family may also share with other people pieces of common ground which they use regularly. The specific environments of different human ecological systems are not necessarily mutually exclusive. On the other hand, the specific environment of a single human ecological system may be disconnected in time and space: A family living in town may be linked to some country club where they go during weekends, or the family may move to a foreign country. The specific environment of a nation is often defined by a coherent territory with rather stable boundaries. Nevertheless, nations, too, may include spatially separated territories, and their boundaries can vary strongly over time. Again there may be shared environments of great importance—the oceans, for example. It would be a mistake to identify the specific environment of a nation only by its territory.

The case of occupational systems is especially instructive. Consider the example of miners. Obviously, it would be absurd to study such an occupation without studying a very specific environment. This environment includes specific portions of the ground and of the air. It also includes certain stuff (for example, coal) and things (for example, certain machines).[3] The specific environment of miners is scattered over the whole planet and may be subject to drastic changes depending, for example, on the depletion of old mines and on technological change both in mining itself and in activities which rely on the products of mining.

If instead of miners we consider lawyers, obviously the specific environment will become very different. Books will be essential here, light will play a very different role, the culturally defined territories of courts will require careful analysis. Passing from occupations to organizations again introduces new problems for research. The distinction of single–plant and multi–plant firms will become important, and a distinctive case of the latter, the multinational firm, will deserve special study.

Describing the boundaries of specific environments often goes hand in hand with identifying the boundaries of normative fields. There is no way of identifying national territories without explicitly considering the social reality of nations. The same is true of all kinds of specific environments.[4] It would also be a mistake to attempt to describe the

---

[3] It is worth emphasizing that one of the first uses of the concept of a socio–technical system was developed in the context of mining (Trist [282, p. 7ff]). This concept was used to criticize engineers who designed technical systems without taking social reality into account—a criticism which is still highly relevant both with regard to stubborn Tayloristic approaches to organization, as well as with regard to the analysis of environmental risks (Perrow [217]). The criticism is relevant to social analysis, too, where such analysis tends to neglect the specific environment.

[4] This statement implies that there is no simple determination of social reality by ecological constraints.

social reality of a nation as if its specific environment was somehow accidental. The recursive reproduction of the nation's normative field is interlocked with the reproduction of its specific environment, both by biophysical processes which are independent of human will and by human actions themselves.

To emphasize the link between socio-cultural realities and specific environments, one may make the somewhat provocative statement that contemporary social theory can hardly be improved as an independent theory. To achieve further improvement, it is necessary to overcome two theoretical separations. One is the separation between personal and social being. As I have discussed in chapter 2, this is a distinction between two different realities which are interdependent to such a degree that no general theory considering only one of them can be satisfactory.[5] Special theories of psychological or sociological problems obviously can still be perfectly meaningful in the context of a more comprehensive view of human reality. Furthermore, the theoretical need to study personal and social life as interdependent realities does not at all mean that the vocational differentiation between psychologists and sociologists is of no practical value. However, the human sciences will suffer unless both disciplines develop the modesty to acknowledge that they cannot formulate a satisfying general theory in isolation from one another.

Even if one accepts the fact that the distinction between personal and social reality should not be misunderstood as a fundamental theoretical separation, a second problem remains. It is often identified—somewhat pathetically—as the separation between "nature" and "culture". Clearly, distinguishing between the two realms denoted by these concepts is indispensable if we are to avoid the pitfalls of social Darwinism and similar doctrines on the one hand, and the snares of full blown idealism on the other. The creativity of human beings is unmatched by the causal powers of stones and trees, but at the same time human beings are unable to create stones and trees. The "nature–culture" distinction is, in fact, important enough to require the development of human sciences which cannot in any meaningful sense be reduced to the sciences concerned with physical and biological reality. In the development of the human sciences, on the other hand, this distinction has led to an unfortunate separation, treating human reality as a realm

---

[5] As I will discuss in chapter 4, special and general theories can be analyzed as different kinds of research traditions.

which can be perfectly understood without dealing with the biophysical environment in which human existence actually unfolds.[6]

Meanwhile, this separation is severely handicapping the understanding of both psychological and social reality. This is especially relevant with regard to spatial relations. Space is not just a physical dimension in which human beings may operate, but rather an essential condition for the constitution both of human persons and of human societies.[7] As I have discussed in chapter 2, the notion of space, or better, of space–time can help us to formulate a reasonable concept of social structure. The abstract dimensions of space and time can be fleshed out using the framework for the study of human environments introduced above. Along these lines, it is possible to distinguish "nature" and "culture" while acknowledging their interplay in human ecological systems.

In such systems, a specific social reality is linked to a specific environment. However, it is important to note that this link is necessarily an indirect one: Stones do not follow social rules and social rules do not touch stones. The link is provided by persons who follow rules when touching stones. To introduce a genuine ecological dimension into social theory necessarily requires a major psychological contribution. As the research tradition of ecological psychology has shown, the understanding of sensory perception and organic movement can be greatly improved by considering the kind of environment in which such perception and movement have evolved.[8] Thereby, the spatio–temporal properties of such an environment are combined with the rich variety of other properties which are characteristic of the beings existing in this environment.[9]

However, while the environment of a frog is the pond, the environment of human beings is, in a very important sense, simply the whole world. When sketching a framework for the description of the human environment I have purposely refrained from isolating a portion of the world in the same way by which the pond may be isolated when we want to study the frog. In particular, the category of hidden beings

---

[6] My argument implies that in a sense the human sciences should be developed as a branch of the natural sciences. Not by pursuing the old dream of reducing human reality to physics, but by studying the emergence of molecules as well as the emergence of nations as steps of one and the same natural history.

[7] This idea has been developed by geographers like Thrift [277].

[8] I am referring to the work of Gibson [98] and his followers.

[9] Another psychological concept which seems relevant here is the notion of a "life–space" in Lewin [163]. Again, it represents an attempt to take seriously the problem that the study of human beings is greatly hindered by the widespread practice of considering humans in isolation from their environment.

allows all kinds of unperceived and even unperceivable beings to be part of the environment under consideration.[10] The framework has been so designed that it allows for the access of human beings to the whole universe, and I would like to introduce the term *"multiverse"* to denote this all encompassing environment. In fact, some such concept is required in order to grasp the relationship of human beings and their environment, in contrast to the relation of organisms and environment in biology.

Still, the examples of families, nations, occupations, and so on, show that social structures are linked to specific parts of the world in which we live. I will therefore distinguish between the multiverse, to which all human ecological systems are related, and the specific environment included in a human ecological system. I talk of a multiverse in order to account for the fact that the world at large may be perceived and represented in many different ways. There is some truth to the expression that there are "ways of world–making"[11] and one may be tempted to say that every human ecological system is a world of its own. One must also acknowledge, however, the fact that human beings are able to talk to each other about their common world and that they are able to situate themselves in this world. The concept of the multiverse is an attempt to handle the tension between the specificity of different worlds and the common world we all share. However, the multiverse is not an "environment" in the sense of something surrounding some specific being: if a person talks about "the world" or if a human ecological system presents some representation of it, both necessarily include themselves in this world.

The relationship between humankind and its environment is a main focus of economic theory. Traditionally, economics has been concerned mainly with the relationships between people and those items of the biophysical environment which have a finite positive price. The multiverse, however, also includes goods which may be free or not tradeable at all but which are nevertheless presupposed by any economic activity. We therefore need some broad concepts to discuss both economic and non–economic relationships between humankind and its environment, concepts which are not restricted to the realm of economics. One such concept refers to material entities whose existence and/or position must

---

[10] As an example, consider the case of magnetic fields, for which we do not have sensory capacity.
[11] Goodman [101].

be explained as an effect of human action. I will call the ensemble of all these entities at any given moment in time *technomass*.[12]

Food and beverage are the most trivial examples of technomass; excrements and garbage are inevitably related to them. The human body itself will be included because the reproduction of humankind is the result of human action. Clothes and houses are other familiar examples, together with all kinds of tools, weapons and instruments. By choosing a suitable list of categories, these entities can be represented as a vector. Such a list will be grounded in categories of material things which have been developed in the course of cultural evolution. This includes both categories of natural kinds like "goats" or "carbon dioxide", as well as categories of culturally constituted objects like "flutes" or "typewriters". The nth element of the vector then indicates the total weight which the nth category contributes to overall technomass.

At any historical moment in time some finite list of technomass may be more or less appropriate, but there is no need to limit oneself to actually existing entities. Rather, it is often useful to consider some set of possible components of technomass. For this purpose, I will consider a vector with infinitely many components. Only a finite subset of these will have a positive value, indicating that the component in question actually contributes to technomass in the situation considered. All the other components will have zero values, indicating that they represent mere possibilities, which may or may not be realized at some later moment in human history.

Obviously, human beings use existing technomass to gather food, build houses, produce tools, etc. These activities involve changes in technomass, whose compound effect can be described as a mapping of the technomass vector at time t (the input vector) into the technomass vector at time $t+1$ (the output vector). As I am concerned here with a process taking place on a planetary scale, the annual cycle of the earth around the sun is a convenient time unit. A technomass vector is then understood as consisting of average values for a given year.

In the dynamics of technomass I distinguish several processes. First, there is the production of new technomass. A simple example is the cutting of branches in order to weave baskets. I denote material entities which newly enter technomass in the year under consideration as raw

---

[12] This concept owes much to the mass–balance approach in environmental economics (for a remarkable work in this tradition see Perrings [215]). The concept is obviously related to Boyden's [37, p. 192ff] notion of techno–metabolism, as well as to the concept of a metabolism of the anthroposphere (Baccini and Brunner [10]).

materials. Using this terminology, the branches of a tree (or the oil under the sea) are only potential raw materials. The branches only become actual raw materials when they are cut (as the oil becomes a raw material when it is extracted from the ground). Next, there is the transformation of technomass, as for instance, by the actual weaving of branches into baskets. This also includes simple wear and tear, such as with the use of baskets.

Finally, there is the elimination of technomass as when the traces of a camp of hunters and gatherers slowly disappear in the process of renewal in a tropical forest. I denote material entities which leave technomass in the year under consideration as disappearing technomass. Disappearing technomass then designates the opposite of raw materials. It should not be confused with waste and garbage. If a tribe leaves a camp in the forest, huts and other traces may remain as identifiable technomass for many years. During this time, the waste materials are a component of technomass, but such debris may actually disappear when it is reintegrated into the biochemical cycles of the forest. This means that the fact that a specific carbon molecule in a plant was incorporated into the arrow of an Indian years ago will be an irrelevant explanation of the plant's present existence and position.

The possibility that technomass may actually disappear depends on specific features of the biosphere. Consider a simple hydrological cycle. Clouds are formed over the sea and blown toward mountains. There the rain falls on the ground, where the water is collected in a river, which brings it back to the sea. Part of this water may be used by human beings to drive a mill, after which the water is led back to the river. Suppose that the water outside the river–bed has, at any given moment, a total weight of ten metric tons. If this is the average value over a given year, then these ten tons will be included in the year's technomass. They are both raw material and disappearing technomass with respect to the period of time considered. If, on the other hand, the water of the river is collected in a storage lake, raw material and disappearing technomass will be two distinct volumes of water, both of which are only fractions of the technomass stored in the lake. In any case, the existence of hydrological cycles is one factor which leads to the disappearance of technomass. Another factor is given by the various chemical cycles which take place in the biosphere. On a global scale, an especially important one is the carbon cycle, which concerns the human use of plants, animals, and fossil fuels.

The disappearance of technomass is not limited strictly to periodical processes. The biosphere involves many circulation processes which show recurrent patterns without being strictly periodical. Human beings can extract materials from such processes and return them without altering the overall characteristics of these processes. Clearly, a main feature of present–day environmental problems is the fact that human beings can actually alter these overall characteristics as well. As an illustration, let me recall the possibility that Manhattan could be flooded by the ocean as a consequence of the greenhouse effect which is due to the burning of fossil fuels.

The biosphere is a closed system only with regard to physical matter. With regard to energy, things are different. As is well known, the existence of the biosphere depends on a more or less constant throughput of solar energy of about $1.73 \cdot 10^{14}$ kilowatts. The accumulation of technomass involves a wide array of energy flows which are modified by human action. For a long time such flows were simply irrelevant on a global scale in comparison with the continuous stream of solar energy. Meanwhile, the total energy flows taking place within the framework of the world economy amount to the order of magnitude of $7 \cdot 10^9$ kilowatts. This is a fraction of about 10^{-5}. I call it the Prometheus fraction.

In order to understand the ecological relevance of this fraction, one must consider the global entropy flow through the biosphere. The flow of solar energy entering the biosphere carries with it an entropy flow. The two flows are linked by a straightforward formula which states that the entropy flow is equal to the energy flow divided by the temperature at which the solar energy is absorbed by the biosphere. The same formula holds for thermal radiation through which the biosphere releases energy back into outer space. Now it is important that the earth always has one side illuminated by the sun while the other side lies in the shadow. If the earth always had the same face turned toward the sun, solar energy would be absorbed at the temperatures prevailing on the day side and this energy would then be released at the same temperatures. As the two energy flows would have the same size, the entropy flow leaving the earth would be of the same size as the flow of incoming entropy. Because of the daily rotation of the earth, however, a considerable part of the energy flow which leaves the biosphere is released at night temperatures, which are lower than those prevailing during daytime.

The same amount of energy, therefore, carries a greater entropy flow with it when it leaves the globe than it did when entering it. I call this difference the *entropy margin*. One consequence of this margin is that the biosphere can persist in a state far from thermodynamic equilibrium. Without it, hydrological and biochemical cycles would break down and so would the evolution of life. All these processes involve the production of entropy, and if this entropy could not leave the biosphere, the physical and chemical processes taking place on earth would run toward a thermodynamic equilibrium, where they would be reduced to the random movement of molecules. What characterizes the biosphere in thermodynamic terms is not equilibrium but rather a series of stable disequilibria, which rely on the entropy margin. Therefore, from the point of view of the biosphere, the basic form of pollution may be the production of too much entropy, the critical amount being determined by the entropy margin.[13]

Given the complexity of the biosphere and the non–linear character of the processes sustained by the entropy margin, it would be nonsensical to attempt to specify the maximum level of the Prometheus fraction sustainable in the biosphere. At the end of the 20th century, there are serious reasons for thinking that humankind is crossing thresholds set by the entropy margin. It is very difficult to identify these thresholds precisely and still more difficult to foresee them before they are crossed. Research into such thresholds is obviously important, but it is even more important to understand that in many cases they are actually unforeseeable.

A physical system displays foreseeable behavior under the condition that the quantitative effects of a change in an input variable converge toward zero if the input change itself converges toward zero. One of the main results of research in the field of non–linear thermodynamics is the appreciation of the fact that the behavior of systems far from thermodynamic equilibrium is often not foreseeable. However, such systems can form dissipative structures displaying foreseeable patterns. Human ecological systems rely on such patterns, for instance on recurrent weather situations, oceanic currents, and biochemical cycles. However, if the entropy flows involved in dissipative structures are modified beyond some critical range, chaotic behavior with unpredictable results must be expected.[14] This is the situation which human ecological systems are facing at the end of the 20th century. In order to identify possible ways of coping with this situation, we must consider how human ecological systems have evolved, starting with their very beginnings.

---

[13] Stressing the importance of entropy flows for today's environmental problems was a main concern of Georgescu–Roegen [95]. However, he referred mainly to the tendency toward thermodynamical equilibrium and less to the cyclical processes which characterize dissipative structures far from thermodynamic equilibrium.

[14] See Schieve and Allen [244] for an analysis of such situations.

3.2   Kinship and Gender

Human beings have always existed with at least a few supplementary pounds of technomass per head beside their body weight. Food and beverage, clothes, various tools, maybe a hut were the main items before the development of stable settlements. In some cases, one would have to add the traces of fire with which human beings cleared a piece of forest, or maybe a brooklet whose course was corrected by human action. In the context of tribal societies, technomass per head would hardly ever have surpassed twice the weight of a human body. Given that ten thousand years ago the world population of human beings comprised less than 10 million people, one arrives at a sensible order of magnitude if one assumes that total technomass amounted to maybe 1 million metric tons of matter.

It seems rather obvious that in those remote times technomass showed nearly no change from year to year, neither in composition nor in size. Over longer periods, considerable oscillations no doubt did take place; they were centered around a growth trend which lay in line with the demographic growth of humankind. From time to time new technologies emerged, be it as an adaptation to changing environmental conditions, or perhaps as a result of spontaneous creativity. In any case, the technomass vector slowly increased, not only with regard to the total mass involved but also with regard to its number of components.

Technomass is continuously reproduced by human action. This process is intimately linked to the existence of interlocked systems of routine action, which remain more or less stable over specific spatial realms and temporal periods. Human beings have habits of eating, sleeping, dressing, playing, etc. These habits are organized in human ecological systems, which are indispensable for the physical reproduction of adult persons, as well as for the development of newborn infants into adult persons. Clearly, such habits are related to biological motives, but the amazing variety of life forms which has been documented by cultural anthropologists shows that there is no simple correlation between habits and biologically rooted motives. With the formation of human organisms, biological evolution has come to a point where biological motives do not define behavior, but indicate broad ranges of problems, which may be solved in widely differing ways.

During the long period in which humankind found its food by gathering plants and hunting animals, the human ecological systems which organized basic habits of human life involved quite limited numbers of people. I call the systems formed in this period *archaic systems*. The smallest of them obviously involved two people, as in the paradigmatic case of the mother–child symbiosis. Larger systems involved groups of perhaps a dozen people, who camped together in different places. The largest systems involved maybe several hundred or at best a few thousand people, who could share a common language, kinship relations, a broad territory, etc. Such systems occasionally split up, and, thanks to slow demographic growth and migratory movements, they eventually spread over nearly the whole terrestrial surface.

Amazing as the variety of such systems may be, they share at least one common trait, namely the paramount importance of *kinship relations*. Whether this came about by chance or by necessity may be difficult to decide, but in any case one has to accept this fact, which shaped the whole subsequent history of humankind. Kinship relations are rooted in biological differences. There are, on the one hand, differences of age, especially the gap between adults and children. During its life, a human being will usually cross some or all such differences. On the other hand, there is the difference of sex, which cannot be crossed in the course of a usual individual biography. This difference determines motives of fundamental biological importance, namely sexual ones. In the process of their ongoing reproduction, human ecological systems continuously shape motives into habits. Archaic human ecological systems focus on kinship relations and hence on sexual habits, they thus attribute a special importance to sexual motives.

The development of a person requires the formation of habits out of motives, of practical consciousness out of unconscious being. The importance of gender in this process implies that it is impossible to become a person in general. The biologically rooted relations between men and women are not external to persons; persons are constituted as being male or female.

In archaic systems kinship relations form rather stable networks which interrelate several persons by various rules. In this framework, persons are able to handle not only relations between men and women, but also between mothers and children, between siblings, between children and fathers, and they know how to handle concatenations of such relations, for example with a brother–in–law. Beside actual relations, potential relations play a crucial role in archaic systems (as they do in all human ecological systems). There are habits and rules concerning the meeting of strangers and concerning the distinction between potential mates and other people; in particular there are rules of avoiding incestuous situations.

In archaic systems, kinship relations play a paramount role in the overall organization of day to day activities. Long before the first stable houses were built, the origins of family households were set in the daily habits of our ancestors. The organization of activities like gathering plants, hunting animals, sharing food, etc., was linked to gender differences and kinship relations, and the same held true for activities like singing and playing, finding a place to sleep, giving a farewell to the dead, and taking care of newly born children. Clearly, isolated family households would hardly have been sustainable systems in the long run Even if incestuous relations did not involve serious genetic drawbacks, they would have undermined the pattern of kinship relations on which the system was based. Archaic systems did not form isolated "households", but larger networks, whose size allowed for rules of endogamy and exogamy: if a person was to have children, they would have found their mate outside an inner circle of relatives, but inside an outer circle defining the larger system to which the person belonged.

Storage technologies were irrelevant for the human ecological systems of those times, and human life was carried on mainly as a direct process of give and take with nature at large. This general feature of archaic life forms fits in well with the emphasis on kinship relations. In the context of such relations, norms of *reciprocity* are nearly omnipresent. A multitude of rules exist which indicate how a person can and must respond to what she or he gets from other persons. This includes not only the case where person Y gets a gift from Z and responds with a gift to Z, but also the case where the gift from Z to Y leads to a gift from Y to X, etc. By analogy, such rules were often extended to the relationship between persons and the natural environment.

There is some evidence for archaic societies slaughtering whole herds of mammoths and maybe even contributing to the extinction of mammoths and other large mammals.[15] These animals had no natural enemies which could endanger their survival as a species as long as all predatory animals were of substantially inferior size. In this situation, large mammals could reproduce with rather low fertility rates. The new kind of intelligence which was characteristic of *homo sapiens* provided this animal with a hunting advantage, which may have led to the extinction of the larger animals. The same kind of intelligence enables human beings to take care of their environment, as is evidenced by many practices of hunting, gathering, and later of gardening. In

---

[15] Budyko [42, p. 310ff].

the case of large mammals, human awareness of the impact of *homo sapiens* on the environment was probably lacking.

With this possible exception, the *environmental impact* of archaic societies was quite limited, and may well be compared to that of other mammals. In particular, the human contribution to total entropy production in the biosphere, the Prometheus fraction, was insignificant. The main source of energy for human beings was their own organic metabolism, as was the case with other animals. The ability to make a fire was no doubt extremely important for human beings, but from the point of view of the biosphere the impact of human fires was negligible. In those times, human ecological systems were embedded in a vast biophysical environment which was quite independent of their development.

In general, archaic systems emerged under conditions of remarkable spatial opportunities. Human beings lived in practically unbounded areas. Moreover, the biological motives of territorial behavior in the evolution of primates and then of *homo sapiens* had become so flexible that they allowed for a wide array of possibilities in the spatial arrangement and development of human ecological systems.[16] Together with the amazing ability of human beings to explore new environments and to adapt in creative ways to new conditions, human ecological systems were allowed to multiply without much difficulty.

A very important consequence was the fact that as long as the spatial range of single systems was rather narrowly limited, many conflicts could be resolved simply by spatial separation. As long as conversations were not written down, such spatial limits were imposed by the difficulties of stabilizing normative fields over large spatio–temporal distances. This was compounded by the ecological imperatives of a lifestyle where food was not stored and transport was based almost exclusively on walking.[17] The practical result of this situation was a network of human ecological systems in the form of small groups and later of tribes with very weak connections between larger units. Within such units, on the other hand, smaller human ecological systems were nested and connected in many and often very intense ways.

Like all human ecological systems, the archaic ones included a cultural and a structural dimension, which were linked by accounting conversations. In archaic cultures rules governing gender relations and

---

[16] See Dürrenberger [68] for the development of human territoriality in the course of cultural evolution.

[17] Spatio–temporal aspects of archaic human ecological systems are a main theme of Carlstein [46].

kinship structures played a crucial role. The development of archaic normative fields was no doubt influenced by biological and practical circumstances, but basically, it must be understood as a creative process of considerable autonomy.[18] In this process, rules concerning kinship were quite often developed not only for relations between persons, but also for relations between persons and other beings, and even for autonomous relations between non–human beings. The result bears surprising similarity to a basic implication of the modern theory of biological evolution: human beings are linked with all living beings by kinship relations. It seems that the archaic normative fields of long ago took this fact more seriously than do most normative fields of our days.

It is sometimes said that archaic societies in fact considered all beings as living and even as persons. A great deal of anthropological evidence seems to point in such a direction, but forgetting some rather simple facts may make such discussions absurd. Even the most animistic hunter of prehistoric times distinguished between living and dead animals.[19] If his hunt involved plenty of rituals, it also involved the ability to hit a target. Talking to animals, living or dead, did not at all imply that catching a fish was the same in moral terms as killing a human person. There are traces of ritual head–hunting in prehistoric time, but while hunting animals and gathering plants was part of the daily routines of all human societies, it seems that murdering human beings was limited to few such societies and even then to rather exceptional circumstances.[20]

---

[18] An important example of such autonomy with regard to biological motives is suggested by rules concerning homosexual relations. It is by no means clear how far homosexuality is grounded in biological motives. But the great intercultural variety in rules concerning homosexuality can hardly be explained by a corresponding variety in biological properties of the people involved. The fact that homosexuality appears explicitly in different normative fields illustrates how biological motives define a problem area, while the solutions are elaborated by human agents involved in the interplay of cultures and social structures.

[19] This point is stressed by Wittgenstein [296, p. 4].

[20] Müller [197, p. 80f]. A somewhat similar argument holds with regard to the more widespread practice of infanticide, with the important difference that a newborn baby is at the very beginning of the process of becoming a person. This should not be misunderstood as a justification of abortion, infanticide and other forms of killing human organisms which could be said to show no explicit personal being. It is rather an explanation of the fact that normative fields permitting infanticide were no more permissive with regard to the murdering of adults and even of older children than fields where infanticide, too, is treated as a case of murder.

Discussions about animism, however, do point to another very important fact. Archaic normative fields evolved in most and perhaps even in all cases in such a way as to imply rules of conduct appropriate for actual or possible meetings with sacred beings or with traces of them. Such rules were not separable from the rest of the normative field, because such meetings were not separated from the meetings between people or between people and animals, things, and events. Archaic normative fields may therefore be said to have evolved with a spiritual horizon. This component was often directly related to kinship rules by defining kinship relationships among sacred beings as well as between such beings and human persons. Finally, the spiritual dimension of archaic normative fields was linked to the development of rules of reciprocity which play a major role in most, if not all normative fields.[21] Obtaining a gift may involve meeting a powerful spirit (in modern terms, one might call it a spirit of love), and this in turn calls for the next gift.

I have claimed in chapter 2 that personal identity involves abilities, relations, beliefs, and projects, which characterize a specific person. In the context of archaic normative fields, this is especially relevant for the ability to handle kinship and gender relations, an ability which also involves beliefs and projects referring to such relations. To handle these social relations requires an integration of motives and habits, and here sexual motives play a crucial role. Moreover, it requires the ability to account for one's way of conduct in matters of kinship and gender in all kinds of conversations. This, in turn, involves a very important belief, namely the belief that one is a person, an accountable human agent.[22] This belief may be held in very different variants, ranging from nearly total fatalism to nearly total solipsism; but accounting practices require that some beliefs be held which lie between these extremes.

The importance of kinship and gender relations implies that archaic human ecological systems cannot be understood without considering their intergenerational reproduction from the very outset. One important aspect of this reproduction are the various institutions of heredity. In archaic systems, the main heritage was cultural; parents had little or no possibility of transferring social positions and individual property rights to their children, but obviously parents and other close relatives played a major role in the personal development of children. The concept of socialization is often used to describe the processes in

---

[21] Gouldner [104, p. 190ff].
[22] Harré [119] studies the implications of this belief.

which beliefs, projects, and abilities, and thereby personal identities, are developed in the context of social relations. This is sometimes misunderstood as a process in which persons would be, so to speak, moulded out of a generic human material by society. But if it is true that persons cannot unfold without normative fields, then it must not be forgotten that such fields cannot endure without persons actively reproducing them.[23] Socialization processes cannot be added to archaic human ecological systems after these systems have been described, as they are a central topic of an adequate description of such systems.

In technical jargon one could say that the process of socialization does not relate society as an independent variable to persons as dependent variables, but that it is a recursive process dynamically interlinking persons and society. Socialization implies not only the transformation of babies under the influence of adult persons and the human ecological systems of which they are a part, but it implies as well the transformation of these persons and systems under the influence of babies.[24] Socialization itself would rapidly disappear from the surface of the earth if it did not produce autonomous beings. Autonomy by this definition does not mean unconstrained possibilities, but rather a flow of human agency taking place in a context which is simultaneously enabling and constraining. In this respect, a person's social environment is not different from the physical one: just as gravity enables human beings to walk while constraining their movements, reciprocity may constrain the actions of human beings while it enables them to love.

Archaic normative fields originally evolved together with human language. Language games would not work without both webs of cultural rules and structures of habitual practices.[25] Cultures and social structures cannot exist in isolation from each other; the link between them is established and maintained by the accounting practices of human conversations. The question of when *homo sapiens* started to talk leaves room for wide speculation. Human artifacts which can confidently be considered as traces of talking beings are not older than some tens of thousands of years, while the palaeontological evidence seems to indicate that the organic ability to learn to talk already existed about a million years ago.[26] Fixing a date for the emergence of archaic systems is all the more questionable as that process no doubt

---

[23] "Actively" means here: such reproduction requires human action, although the social reproduction may be among its unintended consequences.

[24] This point is emphasized by Giddens [100, p. 120ff].

[25] As Wittgenstein [298] insisted.

[26] Müller [197, p. 128f].

took a rather long time to run its course. Be that as it may, one can hardly deny that for the longest part of humankind's existence social reality has consisted of archaic normative fields.

During this period of time a tremendous amount of variation and change took place. Obviously, one may say that the few tribes still surviving in places like the Latin American rainforests are static in comparison with the highly industrialized nations of the present.[27] This judgement, however, is relative, it should not make one forget that archaic normative fields are, like all social reality, permanently subject to gradual change. This is simply due to the fact that social reality exists only in virtue of its continuous reproduction by human agents. Because they are agents, humans are always capable of changing a course of action. They may do so in response to problems they encounter. This should, however, not be misunderstood as just a passive reaction to external pressures. As a matter of fact, human agents are creative beings, who, however, originate new ways of conduct not ex nihilo, but on the basis of older ways. Clearly, many such attempts are more or less short lived; it takes especially favorable conditions for a new way of conduct to become stabilized to such a degree that it results in the modification of some normative field.

During the long period of time in which social reality consisted of archaic normative fields, a type of social change took place which I will call *cultural micro-evolution*. I use evolutionary terminology in order to stress the interplay of variation and selection going on in such social change. If the notion of cultural evolution should be persistently confused with biological evolution and with the idea of progress, perhaps a new terminology will eventually have to be introduced. Progress implies that the result of change is, in an important sense, better than the older state of affairs. There is, however, not the slightest reason

---

[27] The difference concerns the pace of certain changes. No doubt in many respects the pace of change in so-called modern societies has accelerated enormously during the last few generations: great spatial mobility, the massive introduction of human artifacts in everyday life, far reaching changes in social rules, etc., are important examples. Yet it should not be forgotten that such innovations are combined with astonishing stability in other realms: The City of London has maintained its financial role for two centuries, the Catholic Church maintained its religious one for two millennia, etc. The very perception of accelerating social change is due to the contrast with stable social realities, where change is not accelerating and is maybe even slowing down. Besides, the awareness of social change is related to different forms of "historicity". Normative fields may enable and constrain persons to very different forms of awareness and this no doubt also holds for the awareness of temporal relations in general and social change in particular.

to think that this is the case with cultural micro–evolution.[28] The paintings on the walls of prehistoric caves are often as perfect as anything human persons have ever produced subsequently, and so are the masks of many Indian tribes. Cultural micro–evolution has produced an amazing variety of human ecological systems, but no progress from imperfect to more perfect stages of social development. One therefore also must drop the idea of a unilinear development as it is implied in the notion of progress. A later stage is not superior to an earlier one and there is no single later stage associated by necessity with an earlier one.

The analogy between biological and cultural evolution may be productive because the tradition of cultural rules can be compared with the transmission of biological genes in interesting ways.[29] Like genes, rules only show in complex combinations, which I denoted as cultures. Cultures shape social actions and institutions to a considerable extent, and rules shape single aspects of those actions and institutions. The similarity of rules and genes should not be overstressed, though. What is important is the fact that cultural rules are necessary for the development of the human ability to act and that such rules are transformed in processes based on an interplay of variation and selection. The selection of rules depends on their compatibility with the respective biophysical environment, but at least as important is their compatibility with other rules, and also with the projects of a large number of persons.

About ten thousand years ago archaic human ecological systems underwent a process of change which cannot be described as simply another instance of cultural micro–evolution. One of its main features, which will be discussed in the next section, was the emergence of a specifically political realm of human existence and, along with it, the development of a polarity between private and public life. Another important change was a marked shift of kinship structures toward *patriarchy*. Patriarchy is not a "system", it is a cluster of gender–related

---

[28] One might drop the idea of social progress simply by claiming that it implies value judgments, which are out of place in scientific discourse. This is not my point here. Concepts of organismic growth as well as concepts of organismic healing may well be linked to value judgments. Nevertheless, they have a basis *"in re"* which makes them not only acceptable but even indispensable for many scientific inquiries. What I am denying here is that the notion of social progress has a basis in processes of cultural micro–evolution. Later on, I will consider other cases of social change where the idea of progress is actually more relevant: cultural macro–evolution, and cultural degeneration and regeneration.

[29] An efficient plea for this comparison is made by Burns and Dietz [44]. See also Sanderson [240]; Boyd and Richerson [36]; Jensen and Harré [149].

properties of a large class of human ecological systems. All human ecological systems, including those of archaic times, differentiate between
men and women, and, indeed, the very emphasis on kinship assigns
paramount importance to gender relations. With the development of
the polarity between a private and a public realm, a peculiar kind of
differentiation between the sexes became common in human life. By
and large, political life became the privilege of men.

It would, however, be a serious mistake to limit the analysis of patriarchy to the reality of gender–based discrimination. Rather, one must
consider processes of degeneration of accountability relations as well.
In chapter 2, I have suggested that human agency may degenerate into
labor and that this process comes along with a degeneration of relations of accountability. In the realm of private life a great variety of
activities has degenerated to "house labor". The exclusion of women
from public life went along with a withdrawal of men from housework.
In public life relations of responsibility between men and women can
hardly be established if situations of co–presence arise only under exceptional circumstances. In private life an analogous difficulty arises,
because situations of co–presence are quite restricted by the absence of
men from housework.

Still, co–presence of men and women occurs regularly in private life.
Clearly, in these situations people account for their actions on a day
to day basis. What then does it mean to speak of a degeneration of
accounting relations in such situations? Seen from the perspective of
social reality, this process can be described as a detachment of language games from life forms. Wittgenstein tried to describe such a
detachment in the realm of the language games of philosophers.[30] This
description was inseparable from a criticism of the contempt for ordinary people, a contempt so deeply rooted in academic institutions. To
insist, as Wittgenstein did, that academics working in philosophy de-
partments are not superior to saleswomen in department stores, does
not entail that the latter are immune to nonsense. In the context of
common madness investigations of the degeneration of language games
both of so–called ordinary people as well as of the cultural elite are

---

[30] Wittgenstein [298].

required.[31] Some remarks concerning this subject shall conclude the present section.

In contemporary culture, a remarkable link between ordinary people and the cultural elite exists with regard to the theme of sexual encounters. There is a widespread expectation that in such encounters the borders which are supposed to define the self should fade away so that talking about "I" and "you" will become meaningless.[32] This is a mystical notion, which has important roots in religious traditions of the Orient. Poetic metaphors linking this notion to the love between man and woman have been elaborated by the troubadours, who at the end of the Middle Ages renewed the tradition of western literature.[33] There can be little doubt that between the times of Petrarca and the days of Hollywood movies a deep correspondence concerning these themes has been established between ordinary language and the language of important cultural elites.

Moreover, once persons are identified in terms of boundaries, it may seem quite natural to do the same with all kinds of other beings. Such a way of talking is sometimes associated with a linguistic form which has gained great prominence in philosophical thinking. I am referring to the view that a subject linked to a predicate represents the gen-

---

[31] As was already mentioned in chapter 2, Wittgenstein appreciated the writings of the Austrian author Karl Kraus, who claimed that the horrors of World War I would not have been possible without the degeneration of ordinary language fostered by irresponsible journalism. Furthermore, did not Dostoevsky, whose novels Wittgenstein read over and over again, show that the really important issues in human life as well as the most terrible conceptual errors could be discussed among ordinary people at least as well as among philosophers? Common madness was to be found among the villagers of Tsarist Russia as well as among the fellows of a Cambridge college.

[32] Buber [40, p. 85ff] has offered a careful criticism of this view. He distinguished between I–Thou relations and I–It relations and claimed that human life degenerates when the latter are detached from the former. This is quite similar to the distinction between communicative and strategic action which Habermas [110] has proposed as an elaboration of his older distinction between interaction and labor (Habermas [111]). Another distinction of the same kind is proposed by Harré [120] when he speaks of the expressive and the practical order in social reality. The same theme is varied in yet another way by Varela [285] with the distinction between autonomy and control. These authors see the problem as one of balancing two basic modes of human agency. Foucault [84] gives a more radical account when he suggests that the scientific study of humans expresses a historical situation where human agency is defined as labor. He then suggests that the possibility of scientific inquiries into human reality is fading away anyway, and does not pursue any further the question of how human agency could be transformed from labor back into a wider context of human endeavor.

[33] de Rougemont [234].

eral structure of elementary sentences, and that this structure corresponds to the identification of human and non–human beings in terms of boundaries. "Paul sings" would be an example of such a structure. In a famous study, Whorf has claimed that the way nouns and verbs are combined into sentences in Indo–European languages is only one of several linguistic possibilities, and that the Hopi speak a language which implies a radically different world–view.[34] A main feature of this view was supposed to be an emphasis on processes expressed by a systematic reliance on verbal forms and on a different use of temporal modalities.

Whorf was advocating cultural relativism on linguistic grounds, but such relativism fails to notice the dramatic tension between contemporary Western culture and the Hopi tradition. In fact, the Hopi tribe has developed a prophecy which stands in striking contrast to such relativism.[35] This prophecy condemns the American way of life much as Israelite prophecies once condemned the imperial cultures of their time. This is not a matter of syntactical structure, but a critique of life forms. Such a view fits well with the notion of common madness. The question is not whether we say "Paul sings" or whether we develop simple syntactical forms somehow akin to "Singing unfolds in Paul's becoming". The question is rather whether we use words to enable each other to be human agents unfolding our lives in relations of responsibility, or whether we talk as if human agency was defined in terms of isolated beings, who can escape from their isolation only when language is eliminated—as it seems to be the case in some mystical traditions.

In the terminology introduced in chapter 2, one can say that accounting relations fail when discursive consciousness is cut off from practical consciousness and from unconscious motives.[36] Such a split is especially relevant with regard to sexual encounters. Unconscious motives and non–verbal abilities are of paramount importance in those aspects of life which human beings share with other animals, and sexual behavior no doubt belongs to this category. I have already mentioned that gender differentiation plays a pivotal role in the development of personal identity. In chapter 2, I have suggested that common madness can be described as a situation where personal identity is believed

---

[34] Whorf [294].

[35] Waters [288] has documented the Hopi world–view.

[36] If certain normative fields induce a split between discursive consciousness and the unconscious, one should expect that this will affect the way in which different parts of the brain are integrated.

to rely on boundaries separating one person from another, as well as from the rest of the world. In patriarchal systems gender differences are used to define personal identities essentially in terms of boundaries and not in terms of relations. Under these conditions it is quite plausible that sexual relations can entail an unending series of rather dramatic identity crises.

3.3   Public Happiness

As I discussed in the last section, about ten thousand years ago a major process of social change occurred which cannot be described in terms of cultural micro–evolution alone. A good approach to that process is offered by the evolution of human territoriality.[37] The first animals to display innate abilities of complex territorial behavior were the reptiles. In the course of biological evolution, these abilities became both more differentiated and less fixed. Animal territoriality links places to animals both individually and collectively, and territoriality also defines critical distances for flight, aggression etc. Territoriality does not simply trace boundaries between animals, but rather constrains and enables them to carry out specific forms of interaction. With the emergence of archaic human ecological systems, territoriality was further elaborated by processes of cultural micro–evolution: Households, tribes, and other systems displayed rich varieties of territorial habits and linked them to rules concerning the organization and meaning of space. A very important common trait of archaic systems was their territorial mobility: people stayed in a given place for only a limited amount of time.[38]

With the domestication of plants and animals, stationary systems became feasible. Sedentariness was no isolated innovation. The spatial density of people could be greatly increased with the development of gardening and agriculture and with the corresponding improvements in the practices of food storage. The development of metal–working, pottery, and woven textiles all contributed to this change. The maximum size of human ecological systems in terms of the number of people could greatly increase. It also expanded in territorial terms. Human practices relating to inanimate beings underwent dramatic changes with the introduction of the usage of metals and with other inventions. At least equally impressive was the change in practices relating to living beings,

---

[37] See Malmberg [177], Sack [238], Dürrenberger [68].
[38] Groh [109].

practices which accompanied the shift from hunting and gathering to gardening and agriculture. Somewhat later, practices of human communication were deeply transformed by the invention of writing. After this step, human conversations would never again be the same. With the practice of writing, conversations acquired an additional dimension, which allowed them to span much greater portions of time and space than had been the case previously.

The other remarkable transformation of human territoriality taking place within the same process was the differentiation between *private and public life*. It is quite obvious that in the context of ancient cities a household's sleeping room was private territory while the site where town meetings were held was a public one. This simple polarity had been absent from the territorial distinctions of archaic settlements. In the course of cultural evolution, biologically grounded dispositions of territorial behavior were shaped in such a way as to refer to this polarity. The integration of these two types of territories is a basic characteristic of classical urban life; and as is well known, political systems in ancient Greece were realized on the scale of individual cities.[39] A related differentiation occurred in a less obvious manner with regard to another form of territorial behavior, namely the demarcation of interaction distances.[40] Private conversations usually unfold between persons who are more or less within an arm's length of each other. This means that they can focus their eyes on each other's faces and perceive spoken words together with mimic expressions. This interaction distance clearly limits the number of persons who can easily participate in private conversations to less than a dozen people. Public debate, on the other hand, is typically carried on at considerably greater distances between speakers and hearers. Eyes are focused more on the whole body than just on the face, mimic expressions are magnified by greater gestures, and voices are more forceful than in private talk. Under such conditions, several dozen and even hundreds of people can easily meet in public conversations.

With the emergence of public conversations *dual human ecological systems* became possible—systems which beside private households also included public works like ports and roads, as well as legal codes such as the Roman law. Dual systems integrate private systems spread over some common territory. Political units are formed, be they as small as a *polis* in ancient Greece, or as large as a Chinese empire. I call

---

[39] Similar situations emerged at the end of the Middle Ages in Europe once again.
[40] Hall [113]; Dürrenberger [68].

these units nations, thus generalizing the modern concept of a nation to cover a large class of human ecological systems. A nation in that sense means an identifiable population with an exclusive claim to an identifiable territory. The population obviously varies over time, in part due to phenomena like migration. The territory usually varies over time, too, but the link between population and territory remains stable. This marks the difference between mobile and sedentary systems.

The focus on kinship and gender enabled archaic systems to reproduce through succeeding generations. On this basis, political systems could develop. It is their emergence that makes possible the inclusion of the development of agriculture, writing, metallurgy, etc., in a coherent process of social transformation. Political systems did not simply displace archaic ones. Clearly, archaic systems were deeply modified by the emergence of the new kind of social reality. Nevertheless, they survived in the form of private life. The development of a domain of public debate and of political institutions, which was distinguished from the private realm, was the first step of *cultural macro–evolution*.[41] It is a remarkable fact that this step occurred independently in different places at different times: in the Middle East, in Central America, in South–East Asia, and possibly in Africa as well.

The processes of cultural micro–evolution, which I considered in the context of archaic systems, are usually reversible. Similarly reversible processes of cultural micro–evolution take place in the context of political systems. The rise and fall of empires provides many examples to be reflected upon.[42] The emergence of political systems as such, however, was not a case of cultural micro–evolution: It did not simply transform the existing kinds of normative fields, but rather, it so to speak added a new layer of social reality to the existing one. While cultural micro–evolution can often be analyzed as an evolutionary process taking place at the level of individual rules, cultural macro–evolution involves very large clusters of rules. Actually, the first step of cultural macro–evolution brought a whole new category of rules into being. While in the case of micro–evolution irreversibility seems to be the exception, with macro–evolution it seems to be the rule. Nations are built and may dissolve again, but political reality does not get annihilated, and original archaic societies are not restored. Political transformations take place, new nations emerge and in some form or

---

[41] The second step will be discussed in the following section.

[42] Obviously, "micro" does not refer to spatial dimensions when we discuss cultural evolution.

another public life goes on, and along with it the subtle interplay of public and private realities.

Why does cultural macro–evolution occur at all? This seems to be an open question. As normative fields are continuously reproduced by human agents, it is quite obvious that cultural micro–evolution takes place and that it does so in a basically unregulated way, more or less like a random walk. It is not clear, however, why and how cultural macro–evolution takes place.[43] Considering more specifically the transition from archaic systems to dual ones, various speculations are possible. One may regard such a transition as an endogenous social transformation triggered by physical or biological events. Could climatic change have played the role of such a trigger? The fact that the transition occurred at different times in different places would make it difficult to sustain such a view in a general manner, but at least in some cases there may be some truth to such an idea. Demographic change may be considered a biological trigger.[44] Combining population growth and migration, humankind slowly expanded over a long period of time, but because of the limited size of possible human habitats on earth, population density sooner or later had to increase. Both increased density and larger social networks may have played an important part in the historical transition to political systems.

Single persons as well as larger populations are characterized, however, by a creative potential, and cultural macro–evolution can hardly be understood without taking this fact seriously. On the other hand, there are some striking similarities between the various independent cases of transition to political systems. This strongly suggests that to some extent human creativity was realizing predetermined possibilities. Adding a further stratum of social reality on top of the archaic systems could be realized by human creativity under suitable conditions. Trying to specify these conditions still provides a major challenge to research.

In section 3.2, I have noted that archaic normative fields were originally permeated by spirituality. The differentiation of philosophy and religion can be studied as part of the overall differentiation between public and private life. This does not at all imply that philosophy and religion are incompatible: Socrates, Plato, Aristotle, and others would have considered this idea as completely absurd; but public conversations

---

[43] Flannery [80] discusses some possible explanations.
[44] The argument by Boserup [31] could be interpreted in such a way.

emphasize ways of arguing which are cultivated more in philosophical than in religious traditions.

The Ancient Greeks experienced the fact that political life was possible, and after eons of life in archaic systems, this was quite astonishing. One could very well wonder how the world must be made in order to allow for such an experience. This curiosity lies at the heart of philosophy. When Aristotle described humankind as animals who engage in conversations and reason with each other (*zoon logon echon*) he stated a basic fact about humans. His description of humans as political animals (*zoon politikon*) raises a more subtle issue. Humankind existed for a long time without the kind of political practices and institutions whose emergence made Aristotle think about politics. Political institutions are by no means a basic feature of human life; but in the world of human beings political institutions are possible. The world and humankind are such that freedom is possible in a twofold sense: Not only are persons able to act, in the sense of causing events which they could also have avoided, they also have the ability to deliberate about rules of conduct and to shape them by common agreement. Without this latter ability the political institutions of democracy would never have evolved.

I am not going to discuss these problems at length here, as this would lead too far into philosophical arguments. I simply want to stress the intimate relations between such arguments and the emergence of politics. It seems plausible to suggest that the democratic traits of the Greek *polis* were essential to the success of Greek philosophy. Today, taking care of philosophical traditions may be a crucial task for any political culture emphasizing democratic institutions.

The emergence of political systems has not stopped the reproduction of archaic systems, it merely transformed them into private ones. The reproduction of private systems probably could not cease without the simultaneous disappearance of persons altogether. Political systems presuppose the existence of persons, they therefore require the persistence of systems of kinship, families, households, etc., in which persons develop in the first place. For political systems, intergenerational reproduction is much less crucial than for archaic ones. Public life goes on thanks to the continuous replacement of departed people by other persons, who were previously formed in the realm of private life. However, both kinds of systems need to be reproduced on a day to day basis by human agents.

Political practices are concerned to a substantial degree with the creation and maintenance of public works which can contribute to the territorial integration of large communities. The same goal is also supported by the formulation and the use of written social rules. In archaic and private systems, the importance of writing is limited by the fact that children learn to talk before they learn to write.[45] Political normative fields, on the other hand, in most cases heavily rely on written rules and offer explicit rules for making, applying, and modifying further rules—as in the case of law–making by constitutionally defined parliaments. To a large extent, political conversations and practices concern the creation of new social rules.

Two very important points should be noted here. First, the distinction between private and public is by no means analogous to the one between personal and social. Private life involves persons as well as social structures, conversations, and cultures just like any other realm of human existence. Second, as I have already remarked, there is a historical continuity between archaic systems and the private component of more recent human ecological systems. In so far as children first get acquainted with private systems and only later learn to act in political ones, there is some truth to the claim that tribal societies are in a sense closer to the world of children than to the world of adults of more recent societies.

Political systems can, so to speak, delegate to private systems the processes of primary socialization, which enable children to become persons. Nevertheless, intergenerational reproduction of political systems deserves careful attention. Persons become able to assume political responsibility and therefore to act in political systems only through processes of secondary socialization. The institution of the school, where children learn to read and write and to share what may be called a nation's common sense, plays an important role here. In archaic as well as in private systems, gender differences are essential for socialization. In political systems, differences and relations between nations play a similar role. Obviously, for the member of an archaic tribe, the relation between his or her group and other human collectives was of vital importance as well, but this relation was framed largely in terms

---

[45] The use of rules in private systems differs in several respects from their use in political systems. In particular, rules referring to the symbiotic relations between small children and their close relatives cannot be discussed and shaped by everybody concerned. Children learn to argue about social rules mainly in their peer groups, which they join when they are no longer that dependent on a symbiosis with adults.

of kinship rules. Two important examples are the rules of endogamy, which restrict possible marriage to the group, and the rules relating to "totemism", which establish metaphorical kinship relations between human societies and non–human beings.

Personal identity in archaic systems is rooted in a person's feminity or masculinity, in its being the child of its mother, and in its being inserted into a complex network of both literal and metaphorical kinship relations. This implies that personal development is strongly rooted in the unconscious realm of biological motives. In the context of nations, however, personal identity has both a private and a political dimension. The development of the latter requires the prior formation of the former, especially because teaching children to take part in conversations is a basic achievement of private systems. Political systems then allow for a second level of personal identity, which is less strongly linked to biological motives. Unlike gender, nations are products of cultural evolution from the outset. Still, as the example of territoriality shows, biological motives do play their part in the formation of *political identity* as well.

The foregoing argument should make it sufficiently clear why I consider it misleading to associate the distinction "public—private" with the distinction "social—personal". I also think it misleading to link the notion of politics too narrowly with the regulation of social conflicts. Clearly, social conflicts exist and it may be useful to have a specific concept to designate such processes, be they peaceful or disruptive. If the notion of politics is used for this purpose, it would clearly refer to all human ecological systems and could not be used to describe the difference between archaic and dual systems. Somehow, one has to distinguish between private and public conflicts.

Solving a conflict is a special case of problem solving. Finding a solution to a public problem, say in the realm of schooling, does not necessarily consist of solving some public conflict. The same holds for relations between nations. The basic difficulty in the case of international relations concerns the fact that different nations can coordinate themselves by forming a society of nations, but hardly by forming a superordinate nation.[46] Obviously nations may fuse into a new and larger nation, but then, by definition, they lose their status as politically independent entities. Problems of nation building are of paramount importance in human history, and the experience of contemporary Europe shows that they are by no means limited to "young nations". Beside

---

[46] I will come back to this problem in section 6.4.

the processes transforming relations between different nations into relations within a newly formed larger nation, there still remain truly international problems. The idea of a nation large enough to be free, for all practical purposes, of external problems has a long history, as the examples of the Chinese, Roman, and other empires show. In the end, the idea seems to be self–defeating: Humankind can form a society of nations, but if it tries to form a unique global nation the result will probably be no nation at all. The ability to handle differences between nations seems to be a basic requirement both for the formation of political identity in the realm of personal reality and for the building of nations in the realm of social reality. To abolish the difference between nations would mean abolishing the difference between private and public life and thereby abolishing the specific socio–personal reality of politics. This presupposes a reversibility of cultural macro–evolution which, to say the least, seems highly improbable.

A main feature of the first step of cultural macro–evolution was the emergence of *political power*. Clearly, one can use the word "power" so that it simply refers to the possibility of causal influence. One can then say that fire has the power to transform wood into ashes and that an actor has the power to make his public laugh. Using the word in this way signifies that power is a trivial ingredient of social relations, as well as of chemical or biological ones. There is another language game where we use the word "power" to refer to hierarchical relations between human beings (and sometimes other living beings as well). The two language games are linked, but this is no reason to confuse them.[47] I will not attempt to clarify the immense variety of problems which have been discussed in the vast literature on social power.[48] Instead, I want to stress the importance of a specific notion of political power. It

---

[47] Moreover, a major confusion can arise with another language game, where the word power is used to refer to physical energy. H.T. Odum [202], for example, suggests that physical energy is actually the scientifically identifiable core of the vague philosophical notion of causality. A similar fascination with the concept of energy can be found in the notion of psychological energy proposed by Freud, and also in several hints in the work of Marx, where he suggests that labor basically consists of physical energy spent by human beings. However, the concept of energy refers to a general feature of all physical processes. Therefore, if we describe a cause of any physical process we can always ask what energy flows are associated with this process. Energy is an aspect of physical causality, but understanding a physical cause takes more than stating that somehow energy is involved in its operation.

[48] See Mann [178] for a historical approach, and Barnes [14] for a theoretical approach to the notion of power.

may well be that much talk about social power involves unwarranted generalizations of a more specific notion of power, which is appropriate for the description of political reality.

How, then, can political power be described? I will start by considering the relation of command and obedience. This is clearly not by itself a specifically political relation, for it also appears in an essential realm of private life, namely in the relationship between parents and children, as has been emphasized by various attempts to match the analysis of the family with an analysis of the state. I do not wish to discuss these attempts in any detail here. Rather, I would like to stress that language games of command and obedience are widespread in human life. When we talk about a command, we refer to a speech act which is embedded in a normative field; obedience, in turn, refers to certain acts embedded in the same field. We are thus concerned with a specific relation of responsibility. The rules of commanding and obeying imply that a command is justified not simply by claiming that it indicates the proper thing to do under the given circumstances, but also by claiming that under the given circumstances to give a command was the proper thing to do. The normative fields which define situations of command and obedience also define punishments and rewards, which are used to handle proper and improper reactions to a command.

Whether one wants to say that situations of command and obedience involve relations of power may be considered mainly a matter of definition. I prefer to reserve the term power for political contexts in order to emphasize the fact that in political systems situations of command and obedience are organized in very specific ways.[49] With the cultural evolution of political systems, certain people were assigned the role of representing a political body and of coordinating the actions of its members by appropriate commands.[50] This situation I will designate by the notion of political power. Moreover, political territories are often internally structured, as in the case of different provinces belonging to the same nation. This leads to power hierarchies familiar from public authorities.

This meaning of power clearly applies to emperors and kings as well as to democratic governments. In democratic settings, every citizen holds political power in so far as voting procedures are used to determine the community's will. This is sometimes expressed by say-

---

[49] As we will see below, this corresponds to the usage of the term power in the literature on generalized media of interchange.

[50] It is interesting to compare the problem of political representation with the arguments concerning rules and representations in chapter 2.

ing that we, the people, are actually the state. In order to understand the use of such expressions, it may be helpful to consider other examples of representation. For example, when explaining the game of chess, one may say about a small piece of wood: this is the king. Such a statement inserts an entity into a context of rules. A nation involves both people who died long ago and people yet unborn, it involves a territory, which may change over time, and it also involves complex patterns of institutions and social rules. This whole human ecological system can be represented by the citizens, who, at a given moment in time, are entitled to vote. Statements establishing such a representation insert the citizens into a context of democratic rules. Such is the idea of the social contract invoked in many of the greatest works of political philosophy.

Political power becomes especially important when the coordination of large numbers of people is established, involving more people than can meet in an assembly. Archaic systems involved quite small numbers of people and knew only loose forms of coordination between each other. Political systems, on the other hand, developed the ability to coordinate large numbers of people on national territories. If some persons are said to hold political power, then these persons are related to a normative field which entitles them to give commands as representatives of some community as a whole. The emergence of political power then allows political entities to be considered legal entities, which are akin to natural persons. A nation can be held accountable for its actions, because there are natural persons representing it.

This holds true both with regard to the relation between a nation and its members and with regard to the relations among various nations. Political power as such does not enable one nation to give commands to another, but it enables nations to deal with each other and to reach agreements on all kinds of issues, including the agreement to disagree. The notion of power proposed here is quite close to the one used by the so–called realist school in international diplomacy, which considers the existence of a plurality of nations to be a major fact of political life, and asks how these nations can learn to behave as members of a society of nations.[51]

To ask such a question already implies that any description of political power would be dangerously incomplete without relating it explicitly to the practice of war and other forms of common madness. In chapter 2, I

---

[51] McKinlay and Little [185].

have suggested that with the advent of common madness human agency degenerated into labor. Since then, a long and contradictory history of attempts to escape from labor has developed. In its simplest form, this means that people simply try to refuse labor, but once labor has become the usual form of human agency such a refusal means that the reproduction of human life as such is jeopardized.[52] Few people are willing to push this risk very far. Therefore, situations that force people to go on laboring are sooner or later re–established as an unintended consequence of the simple refusal of labor. Some people, however, may attempt to escape labor by delegating it to other people. This attempt has deeply marked the history of humankind since the emergence of political reality.

Such attempts have good chances of success, because they usually provide for a mechanism which counters the tendency to refuse labor as such. The delegation of labor from one group of people to another does not simply grant the first group an unwarranted privilege. The privileged group may be seen to be making an essential contribution to the reproduction of human life, because it keeps the destructive potential of a generalized refusal of labor at bay. If, however, the degeneration of human agency into labor is due to a lack of relations of responsibility, then the delegation of labor to other people reproduces this problem. This is obviously the case for those who are expected to actually carry out the labor. The ones, though, who are supposed to be free from labor, will hardly have a chance of establishing relations of mutual responsibility with the laboring people. By this very lack of relations of responsibility, the privileged group will in fact again find itself entangled in labor.

I have already discussed a major example of such a situation in the case of patriarchy. With the differentiation between private and public life, political identity became a constituent of personal identity. Until recently, the conditions of patriarchy nevertheless made it all but impossible for most women to unfold their personal identity in the public realm. Instead, a woman often acquired what may be called a secondary identity by marrying a man with whom she could share his political identity. Obviously, in the course of history this discrimination has not always been equally strict, and many different ways of coping with such a situation have been developed. It is still a major fact of history that this discrimination has persisted from the emergence of political systems until today. The exclusion of women from

---

[52] The notion of refusal of labor was introduced by Tronti [283].

political life produced all kinds of situations where powerful men meet powerless women. The difficulties of maintaining the accountability relations necessary for the development of personal identity in the private sphere are worsened by the far–reaching exclusion of women from public life.

With regard to housework, in virtually all political societies an unequal division of labor can be observed, with women carrying the heavier burden while the authority of men is often expected to guarantee the stability of everyday life. In the realm of public life, from which women were usually excluded, human agency periodically degenerated into one of the most terrible forms of labor, the labor of war.[53] Moreover, war was instrumental in the development of various ways of assigning labor to specific groups of people, like slaves and serfs. This leads to complex interactions between war, political power, and the organization of labor. In the Roman empire, for example, the discipline of the slaves faltered from time to time, and an important aspect of military expansion was the possibility of acquiring new slaves, who, at least for a while, would perform their labor without much resistance.[54] There is no doubt that the practice of war is a major example of a breakdown of relations of responsibility between persons.

This breakdown is closely linked to the misconception that identity is defined by boundaries. The identity of a nation does not depend on boundaries, but on a large cluster of family resemblances involving historical events as well as social rules and landscapes.[55] But how often has the crossing of some territorial border been intended and perceived as a threat to some nation's identity? Afterall, the very idea that entities may be defined by their borders is based to a considerable extent on using national borders as a metaphor for the formation of identity. This metaphor is all the more important since with the emergence of political systems membership in such systems becomes an essential dimension of the process in which personal identity is formed.

In chapter 2 I have discussed how the degeneration of human agency into labor combines a neglect of internal relations between persons with a neglect of internal relations between means and ends. This is of the greatest importance in the present context, because power is a *generalized end of action*. Power is a goal of a presidential campaign

---

[53] The notion of the labor of war goes back to the Homeric epic of the Trojan war.
[54] Though veiled by the author's Marxist orthodoxy, the discussion of the Roman empire in Anderson [4] offers interesting material in this respect.
[55] Remember that by the term nation I also designate entities like the Polis of Ancient Greece or the Pharaoh's empire.

and it is a goal of foreign policy. In the operation of public authorities, attempts to gain, exert, and secure power play an essential role, and the same is true, for example, in the shaping of public opinion by mass media. In the sociological literature, this state of affairs is discussed under the label of generalized media of interchange.[56] This label was introduced in order to analyze the similarities between the role which money plays in economic systems and the role which power plays in political systems. The emphasis on processes of exchange is due to the origins of the concept in a sociological analysis of economic systems.[57] In order to avoid a bias toward economic phenomena, I prefer to stress the character of money and power as goals, which are shared by agents in economic and political contexts.

Such shared goals facilitate the coordination of the multitude of individual projects arising in human ecological systems. In political contexts, the pursuit of power by individual agents can lead these agents to represent a political communitiy in such a way as to contribute to the public happiness of the community. This kind of happiness distinguishes dual human ecological systems from archaic ones.

Consider the case where being powerful is seen as something so desirable that it justifies a very wide range of attempts to become ever more powerful. Under such conditions, hierarchies of political power become quite separated from relations of accountability, and political action degenerates into labor, in extreme cases into the labor of war. As is well known, such situations characterize a great part of the political history of humankind.

The work of Machiavelli surely represents one of the most impressive attempts to describe this kind of situation. What makes his work so disturbing is the fact that he leaves little hope for the possibility to counter the impact of power by opposing it with other, allegedly higher ends. Take the example of peace. This may be seen as a highly desirable possible state of affairs, but Machiavelli was no doubt right when he claimed that in the name of peace all kinds of outrageous actions from lies to murder have been committed time and again.

The existence of generalized ends of action is directly linked to the phenomenon of social interests. With regard to the puzzle of human ecology, interests are often invoked in order to explain why some simple solution does not work. Examples of such arguments are the following:

---

[56] Parsons [210]; Luhmann [170]; Loubser et al. [166]; Habermas [110].

[57] Parsons and Smelsers [212]. Parsons [209, p. 43ff] describes the origins of the concept.

If economic growth stopped, ecological problems would be solved, but enterprises and trade unions have an interest in economic growth. If ecological external effects were internalized into market mechanisms, everything would be fine, but, unfortunately, politicians, oligopolists and other social forces have an interest in restricting market mechanisms. If production was not controlled by profit seeking, everything would be fine, but entrepreneurs, managers, and politicians have an interest in maintaining capitalism. If patriarchy were abolished, everything would be well, but men have an interest in maintaining their privileges. Despite their mutual contradictions, statements like these convey important partial truths. These truths, however, are dangerously deformed by a simplistic view of conflicting interests, a view which has much in common with the mechanistic picture of the collisions taking place in a game of billiards.[58]

As I already mentioned in chapter 1, there can be little doubt that mastering the environmental crisis of our times will involve major conflicts of interest. Contemporary culture, however, is deeply shaped by a mechanistic vision of human society according to which partial interests are not amenable to any kind of rational argument. This vision is found in many proposed ready–made solutions to the environmental crisis. A viable solution will hardly be developed unless the study of this crisis includes the ways in which conflicting interests are generated and transformed, and the possible role of accounting conversations in these processes. Such a study requires consciously overcoming important limits of mechanistic thinking. This is not a matter of easy polemic, but of patient inquiry.

In archaic societies human beings knew how to kill each other and from time to time they did commit such acts, whether in isolated cases of murder or in various forms of ritual killing. The social practice of war, however, started with the emergence of politically structured societies, in which the pursuit of power became dissociated from accountability relations. Power became an external goal of human action and such action thus degenerated into labor. This was a crucial component in the development of common madness, a form of cultural evolution which can be described neither in terms of micro–evolution nor of macro–evolution. I describe it as *cultural degeneration*. It can be analyzed as a transformation of cultural rules, too, but not as the emergence and diffusion of new rules or new categories of rules, but rather as a loss of consistency in existing webs of rules. With an ecological metaphor,

---

[58] See the next chapter for a discussion of mechanistic thinking.

this may be described as an erosion of cultural resources, which results in large scale anomic situations.

All politically structured societies that existed for a long time developed institutions like slavery or serfdom—institutions which had been unknown to earlier societies. This fact has inspired a long tradition of thought which sees the existence of domination as the congenital defect of human civilization. The thought is expressed most clearly in the anarchist tradition, but it is to be found in some form or another in most works of social critique. More often than not, Marxist theory, too, is interpreted along these lines. Also, the split of the labor movement in the 19th century into Marxist and anarchist branches had its theoretical rationale in different approaches to the problem of political power. Anarchists saw political power as an unwarranted institutional form, which lay at the root of all social problems, while Marx tried to explain power on the basis of the historical conditions of its formation, by discussing the state as a form of the social organization of labor.

The available evidence seems to indicate that there had been phenomena of war previous to slavery but not the other way around. This contradicts the anarchist view of domination as the cause of all social evils, while supporting the Marxist approach to the extent that domination might be explained by other social factors. Marxist theory, though, depicts domination as the inevitable, if transitory, price of progress. This implies the unproven claim that cultural degeneration was a condition of cultural macro–evolution, that public happiness could not have unfolded without common madness.[59]

Another weakness of Marxist theory deserves attention here, because it reappears in much contemporary theorizing.[60] I am referring to the neglect of the processes of cultural degeneration which took place in the transition from archaic systems to private life. If power can be studied as the generalized end of action relevant in the public domain, then the relevance of sexual motives in private life deserves a careful study in the same terms. Sex is a generalized end of action, and just like power, it can become an external goal. Under conditions of patriarchy, it may be even more difficult to establish accountability relations with regard to sex than with regard to power. Moreover, the biographies

---

[59] Marx tried to justify this claim with the argument that domination was necessary to extract a social surplus under conditions of scarcity. But the available evidence seems to indicate that archaic systems knew less scarcity than the subsequent systems (Sahlins [239]).

[60] Including the renewal of the Frankfurt School by Habermas [110].

of powerful persons offer plenty of evidence for the links between these two generalized ends of action.

Until now, I have considered cultural degeneration in the context of social reality, but when human agency degenerated into labor, the relationship between humankind and the biosphere, too, became marked by irresponsibility. The ability of the Roman Empire to destroy large parts of the Mediterranean forests was not due to the construction of some terribly efficient device for cutting trees, but rather to the ability to coordinate large masses of people while neglecting relations of accountability. The normative fields of earlier societies enabled *homo sapiens* to live in very different environments without hindering the reproduction of these environments. The newer societies characterized by political institutions developed courses of action with far reaching ecological impacts, and in several cases actually destroyed important parts of their environment, as in the case of Mediterranean forests. This was all the more dangerous as the technological means of dual systems largely exceeded those of archaic ones. With the emergence of dual systems a long record of *ecological destruction* began.

In archaic human ecological systems, the growth of total technomass was due mainly to population growth on a planetary scale. This was still an important factor in the period from the emergence of the so–called higher civilizations to the emergence of the world economy at the end of the European Middle Ages. During this period, world population augmented from an order of magnitude of 10 million to about 400 million people. Technomass per head also increased considerably due to several interrelated processes. First of all, technomass increased thanks to a long list of durable items. A very important example is the domestication of plants and animals. Also, the development of pottery and weaving as well as of metal–working made possible a large number of durable items, including stored stocks of food and the like.

Beside the effect of durable items, we have to consider the importance of reproduction processes. This includes the biological reproduction of technomass as in the case of agriculture. Moreover, technological reproduction occurs when certain items of technomass are used to reproduce other items; the emergence of urban life engendered complex networks of such reproduction of technomass. Still, one should remember that at the end of the Middle Ages only a small minority of humankind lived in an urban setting. As a very rough guess, one may assume that at that time technomass per head was of the order of magnitude of a dozen times a human body weight. If one takes this sum to be about half a metric ton, one gets an order of magnitude of 200 million metric tons for total technomass.

With the emergence of so–called higher civilization, archaic rules of reciprocity were undermined by the development of military conquest, patriarchy, and slavery. The practice of taking without giving became a major feature of human civilization. This holds true quite literally for the accumulation of technomass, which was based on the extraction of growing amounts of raw materials from the natural environment. The products gained from these materials were, to a large extent, incorporated in a more or less permanent way into the total technomass.

The accumulation of technomass implies a process of taking without giving in a very trivial sense. The total physical mass of raw materials exceeds the corresponding mass of disappearing technomass. The relations of reciprocity, which dual systems inherited from archaic ones, were not formulated in terms of physical mass, though. Physical accumulation of technomass is not morally incompatible with relations of reciprocity. Compatibility, however, requires networks of rules which treat raw materials as gifts of nature, whose acceptance by humans implies an obligation to donate corresponding gifts back to nature. Under such conditions, the re–insertion of technomass into natural cycles could not be a casual matter of the disposal of waste products. Rather, the accumulation of technomass would be designed so as to yield non–polluting waste products, which could easily re–enter the circulation processes of the biosphere. Humans would also strive to express their gratitude to nature by the way they shape persistent technomass. The beauty or ugliness of cultural landscapes tells a lot about the gratitude or ingratitude of humans; aesthetic issues are intimately related to norms of reciprocity.[61]

No doubt many instances of give and take can be found in the process of the accumulation of technomass, even after the emergence of political systems. By and large, however, the accumulation of technomass was based on the practice of taking without giving, a process which became common in political life. In this process, a careless attitude toward the environment became quite normal. This carelessness is directly linked to the weakness of accountability relations. The accumulation of technomass was mainly a result of human activity in the degenerated form of labor. This had disruptive social implications in the form of slavery, patriarchy and war. It also had ecologically disruptive consequences, as in the case of the large scale deforestation

---

[61] Such rules of reciprocity are often embedded in rules of religious activity.

carried out in order to build the navy of the Roman Empire. However, the ecological implications of labor became really dramatic only after the accumulation of technomass was organized in the framework of the world economy, which is presently transforming the surface of the earth.

3.4 Vocational Cooperation

In the contemporary world, beside private and political systems, a third kind of human ecological system plays a major role. People spend substantial parts of their lives in workplaces, which are neither private nor public territories. For reasons that should become clear in the present section, I will call them vocational territories and denote the corresponding human ecological systems as vocational systems. Workshops, plants, and firms are examples of such systems. Workplaces are usually places of cooperation, where several people are engaged in common tasks. However, cooperation within firms also requires other forms of cooperation crossing the firms' boundaries. Software firms use hardware and hardware firms use software; hardware firms use plastics supplied by chemical firms, which in turn use software to control plastics production, and so on. In fact, a worldwide vocational system has emerged: the world economy. This huge network of cooperation has linked the myriad of conversations carried on by human beings into what is sometimes called the conversation of humankind. It crosses national boundaries and, indeed, has enabled and constrained different nations to undertake steps—although often very small ones—toward a worldwide society of nations.

Considering the world economy as a vocational system should help to avoid two misconceptions. The first one falsely perceives the economy as the realm of material production. This is rather strange in view of the fact that in the contemporary world economy the major part of occupations belong to the so–called service activities. Even in manufacturing firms often only a minority of the employees is actually involved in producing things. Typical economic activities today consist of the rearrangement and elaboration of texts, numbers, figures, and the like, and in talking to people both in face to face settings and by means of telecommunication technologies. Material things are, of course, produced in this process, but this doesn't distinguish human conversations carried out in the context of vocational systems from human conversations carried out in archaic systems. Material things are as essential for vocational systems as they are for private and public ones, no more, no less.

The idea of the economy as a system of material production is linked to the second misconception of the economy as the system that produces the goods needed for human life. The production of food, clothes, dwellings, and the like is then seen as the paradigmatic economic task. Most things produced in the contemporary world economy are, in fact, not necessary for human life. The simple fact that humankind existed for millennia without compact disks, movies, satellites, computer programs, etc., clearly proves this point. Maybe human life was enriched by the introduction of these items, but that is a very different matter. It would be absurd to claim that archaic tribes were less happy than we are because they did not have cars and television sets. Only when acquainted with these things may one develop a preference for a life with them as compared with a life without them.

Vocational systems respond as much to each other's demands and ideas as to the needs and wishes of private households. This can be illustrated by two analogies. The first one refers to a fairyland where software firms sell programs to hardware firms, from which they buy computers. It is often assumed that "in the last instance" the net output of an economy must be passed over to private or public households. Suppose that the investment plans of the two groups of firms were directed at expanding production at a mutually compatible rate. Then they would both buy and sell a correspondingly growing amount of products. As long as none of them lost confidence with regard to the future, they could happily continue without having to concern themselves with final consumption by private households. The latter may be interested in buying home computers and software to play chess with, and the firms would perhaps be happy to serve them. With expanding capacity, the firms may even try to persuade private households to buy ever–growing amounts of hardware and software. In some respects, this is the world in which we live.

The above mentioned analogy concerns the role of net investment as final demand. A second analogy concerns the proper dynamics of vocational creativity. It can be illustrated by a group of painters with a strong interest in each other's work. Clearly, they may look at each other's paintings, and their technique and style of painting may evolve in a process of cultural micro–evolution.[62] Moreover, they may be in-

---

[62] A similar situation arises in scientific communities, as Kuhn [159] and many others have stressed. What is often called a scientific paradigm is quite similar in some respects to artistic styles.

terested in literature, architecture, even engineering, and have friends who are active in these fields. (This kind of situation played a crucial role in the Renaissance, when vocational systems actually emerged.) Under such conditions, vocational systems can display great creativity and be of interest both to a wider public and to private households. Nevertheless, this situation could hardly be understood simply as the production of material goods needed and consumed by private households. Obviously, it would also be quite misleading to imagine that the vocational systems under consideration were closed. Artistic innovation is often triggered by changes in technologies, tastes, etc., which originate in other social contexts. Far from wanting to develop a generalized "l'art pour l'art" ideology, I would like to stress that vocational systems react to each other at least as much as they do to political and private systems.

Since Weber wrote his famous study on the Protestant ethic,[63] it has become a commonplace sociological argument to claim that the cultural emphasis on vocational life is a product of the Reformation. In fact, the very notion of "vocation" used here could not be understood without the efforts by Luther, Calvin, and others to re–define the relationship between human beings and God. Also, the importance of the Renaissance for the emergence of vocational systems can hardly be overestimated. This holds true even in the context of theological ideas. The old biblical theme of a similarity between God and human beings was developed with regard to creativity: there was a strong tendency to assume that the more creative a human being was, the closer she or he was to God. This was a crucial step in the emergence of vocational normative fields.

The Renaissance also contributed to the emergence of vocational normative fields by stabilizing a wide array of interrelated occupations. Painting, architecture, literature, as well as different forms of craftsmanship already existed in the political systems of Ancient Rome and Greece. Now a systematic cooperation of such specialized activities was established. This implied the formation of specific traditions for different occupations. I consider occupational traditions here as human ecological systems, which include sets of human practices evolving in space and time. An occupation involves a set of such practices, a set which deeply shapes the biographies of the persons who reproduce it. Moreover, occupations stand in vital relations of complementarity to

---

[63] Weber [289].

each other: they cannot exist in isolation, but only in the context of a strongly differentiated vocational system.

One may wonder whether the differentiation of occupations can somehow be related to natural kinds along the lines of the correspondence between ore and miners or wood and joiners. There is, however, little to be said in favor of such an approach. Occupations emerge, change, and disappear in the course of cultural micro–evolution, and their definition is probably best studied as the result of human creativity. Clearly, occupations are related to the environment in which we live, but their dynamics depend chiefly on their internal relations with each other. This dynamic then helps in organizing the relations between human beings and the environment.

Gender is rooted in a fundamental biological property of human organisms. This is not the case with nationality, but the link between nations and territories could make it appear quite natural that human beings are born into nations. Be that as it may, nationality is a matter of choice only under exceptional circumstances. Occupations are a different matter. There are constraints on the choice of occupations, but one does, nevertheless, have a choice. Vocational systems, however, do not simply coordinate jobs, but rather integrate biographies. This was very clear in the guilds, which the Renaissance took over from the late Middle Ages. Vocational systems are based on a kind of practical consciousness which cannot be changed easily during a single human life. They enable and constrain the ability of persons to change jobs, but they also constrain and enable their ability to stick to occupations. Persons may change their occupations, but this is a difficult and risky step requiring specific social and psychological processes of personal transformation.

With the emergence of vocational systems, the old polarity between private and public life was enlarged into a triad. The result was the emergence of a *triadic human ecological system*, in which humankind is presently living. This triad has found an expression in territorial terms, too: Private and public territories were redefined so as to leave space for vocational territories as well. This process deeply changed the face of cities and eventually led to the blurring of the distinction between city and countryside. In fact, while the emergence of vocational systems may have been more visible in urban contexts, it also took place in the countryside. The abolition of serfdom allowed serfs to become citizens and it also allowed them to become farmers. The widespread rural revolts at the end of the Middle Ages were nourished, among other reasons, by the desire of the peasants to re–define farm work as the performance of a vocational activity on a par with the work of the artisans in the cities.

It is interesting to note that, with the emergence of vocational systems, human territoriality was re–shaped also with regard to interaction distances. I have already mentioned that private contacts usually take place within smaller distances than public ones and that this is related to the number of people typically involved. Vocational contacts take place within intermediate distances of a few meters.[64] The intermediate distance of vocational contacts is related to an intermediate number of participants. Private life is, so to speak, focused on dyads and public life on assemblies; in vocational life human groups are of paramount importance.

Vocational systems form a remarkable connection between the macro–level of the conversation of humankind and the micro–level of accounting conversations in ordinary life. I have just noted that vocational conversations typically involve more people than the dyads which are characteristic of private life, but less people than public assemblies. The basic frame of vocational conversations are human groups.[65] These groups, however, form meshes of interpersonal networks of astonishing size, meshes which easily cross national boundaries. Nations occupy connected areas, while vocational systems are scattered dotwise across the whole globe.

Vocational systems display the ability to span huge spatial distances unmatched by private and political systems. Historically, the development of printing technology was essential in this regard. The invention of written alphabets deeply altered the nature of human conversations by stretching their spatio–temporal range with the support of written texts. Printing had a similar effect by increasing dramatically the number of people who could simultaneously be involved in certain conversations. This effect was compounded by improvements in transportation technology, especially ship–building and navigation. As a result, human territoriality came to the point where humankind could be said to inhabit the whole earth.

The triadic human ecological system has begun to spread over the whole globe with amazing speed. This is the second step of cultural

---

[64] Hall [113] has described how this intermediate distance has a specific meaning in Western culture while, for example, in the Arabic world this is not the case. It would be interesting to investigate whether and how Arabic interaction distances are modified with the growing importance of vocational life.

[65] This may be a major reason for the persistent importance of small firms in economic life (Granovetter [106]).

macro–evolution. The first step could run its course independently in
different places, because dual systems expanded relatively slowly. The
second step happened only once, in Europe, and we may never find
out whether this could have happened independently elsewhere. All
contemporary vocational systems can be traced back, to a considerable
degree, to the end of the European Middle Ages.[66]

The accounting conversations constraining and enabling vocational activities involve a specific normative field, which is distinct from the
normative fields of private and public life. I call it the field of vocational ethics.[67] Among its historical sources, I have already mentioned
the Renaissance with its emphasis on human creativity. As Max Weber pointed out, another source is the Reformation, but the field of
vocational ethics is by no means identical to the features of the Reformation studied by Weber. In particular, I do not wish to claim that
vocational ethics were a by–product of Calvinist notions of predeter-
mination. Nor do I want to insist here on the elaboration of ascetic
methods of self–improvement by Protestant sects. Even Weber's great
theme of rationality is not directly linked to the phenomenon of vocational ethics, although a prospering vocational ethics may help to
clarify some important problems of rationality.

The Reformation exercised a lasting impact on vocational normative fields. Among other things, this included the emphasis on mundane
activities. This emphasis renewed old features of biblical religious traditions, but it did so in a different context. For the Reformation, charity
could and should be expressed in vocational activities. A new sense
of human dignity was linked to this idea: artisans, farmers, doctors,
merchants, artists, etc., were answering, in all their different tasks, to
a divine call. Being engaged in a vocational occupation became a very
important characteristic of human beings.

Private and political normative fields shape personal identities
through processes of socialization, which reproduce and transform these
fields. The same holds true for the field of vocational ethics. The formation of *vocational identity* has found remarkable expression in the
tradition of the so–called German Idealism. Goethe's novel, *Wilhelm
Meister*, carefully describes how the experience of love in the private

---

[66] More precisely, today's vocational systems are the result of substantial interaction
between the second step of cultural macro–evolution and endogenous processes
of cultural micro–evolution in other world regions.

[67] Jaeger, Bieri and Dürrenberger [145].

life is related to the venture of learning to situate oneself in the contexts of public and also of vocational life.[68]

Vocational ethics emphasize creativity and cooperation in the context of lifelong commitments to specific occupations. It is not the case that there is one normative field concerned with the peculiarities of single occupations and another one related to creative cooperation. Rather, the rules that specify various vocational occupations constitute this cooperation. Vocational ethics add, so to speak, a third layer to personal identities already shaped by private and public processes of socialization. Once people learned to account for their way of conduct in vocational systems, they became able to engage in far–reaching cooperation, and literally able to transform the globe.

Now all of this may sound utterly idealistic to many readers, but the opposition of idealism and materialism is a source of nearly infinite confusion. Consider the case of science. What we are accustomed to describe as science is a vocational system. Activities like studying the stars with telescopes, experimenting with chemicals, making an expedition to the Galàpagos Islands all have become part of a highly complex network of occupational activities. There is no way of explaining these activities without considering the conversations going on within scientific communities, as well as across their borders. Such conversations take place at scientific conferences, in the teaching environment, in day to day research settings and on other occasions. They are heavily dependent on written texts, which are continuously being produced by scientific communities with the help of vocational systems involving publishing businesses, libraries, telecommunications, and so forth.

These conversations reproduce and transform vocational cultures especially with regard to all kinds of rules about how to do research, to teach, to publish, etc., in specific fields. These cultures organize the body of knowledge which science contributes to society at large.[69] There, scientific results are used in all kinds of techniques, which are

---

[68] The elaboration of humanist themes in the context of German Idealism has substantially contributed to the German system of higher education. It also formed an important background for Weber's work, and, together with this work, contributed to the German system of vocational education.

[69] There are rules about what to believe, and science develops such rules. This is not to say that truth is just a matter of convention. Rules may be criticized, among other reasons, because they presuppose factual errors. It is obviously a major feature of science that it tries to eliminate such faulty rules, but I am not going to discuss the relationship between rules and truth here. For the purposes of the present task, it is enough to say that science involves vocational normative fields, which organize a wide array of beliefs held by scientists and by people who

developed in the context of other vocational systems. Industrialization was a major example of this process. Vocational cultures that are reproduced in human conversations contribute to major material effects like the existence of a worldwide telephone network. The causal chain involved, however, is not a simple link. Magnetic fields influence iron, not plastic; cultures influence human agents, not things. Human agents by definition are able to influence other bodies, be they living or not, and they always have some autonomy in doing so. A material effect of a vocational culture is, therefore, always an indirect effect, which only arises in combination with the autonomous causes contributed by human agents.

The relationship between science and society can be understood, to a considerable degree, by studying it in the context of vocational systems. There is no need for the notion of a general scientific method here, and there is no reason to suppose that science is more rational than other human activities. In fact, it is doubtful whether a notion of rationality is really useful if rationality is supposed to be something fundamentally different from the interplay of accounting conversations and the human ability to give up erroneous beliefs. This interplay is not peculiar to science; it is to be found in religion and philosophy as well as in so–called everyday life.

No doubt science has some specific traits of great importance to cultural macro–evolution. With the emergence of political systems, philosophy was differentiated from religion. In a similar way, science was differentiated from both philosophy and religion with the emergence of vocational systems. This means, among other things, that science shares the internal differentiation provided by the forms of complementarity and cooperation which are characteristic of vocational systems. The affinity, however, between science and other vocational systems is blurred by the close links between science and the state. While a long series of negative experiences has led to the separation of religion and the state, the relationship between the state and science has been maintained, until now, as a close symbiosis.[70] Public authorities justify many of their decisions with scientific expertise and scientific institutions are financed to a large extent by public authorities. In particular, the state runs an educational system geared to scientific institutions. Still, the respective autonomy of politics and science is protected by strong social norms associated with the doctrine of a value–free science

---

trust them, and that these normative fields place considerable emphasis on the avoidance of erroneous beliefs.

[70] Feyerabend [76] offers a thorough criticism of this situation.

as opposed to value–bound politics. Whether this attempt to handle the relations between truth and power is a satisfactory state of affairs is another matter.

For the moment, I want to focus less on power than on *money*. In section 3.3, I have described power and sex as generalized ends of action in the contexts of, respectively, public and private life. Now it is time to stress that money plays a similar role in vocational life. The identification of the two steps of cultural macro–evolution entails the distinction between three kinds of normative fields: private, public, and vocational.[71] Sex, power and money are the generalized ends of action corresponding to each of these three contexts.[72]

Unfortunately, in the second step of cultural macro–evolution cultural degeneration has extended into the newly emerging realm of vocational life. The external relation between means and ends, which was a main feature of cultural degeneration both in private and public life, has become a main feature of vocational life as well. The possibility of treating money, power and sex as an interconnected cluster of external goals of action has, in fact, fascinated both popular and artistic imagination for a long time.

Moreover, money operates as an external goal also for paid activities which are not vocationally structured. This leads to considerable difficulty in wage determination. Consider an ensemble of firms where human activity is not organized within the framework of vocational life, but, for instance, within the framework of entirely unqualified activities. In line with standard textbooks on economics (and also with most Marxist analyses), one is then led to consider human labor as a generic category of inputs into the diverse production processes.

With this view, the input of labor is measured with the help of time units, much as in the case of electricity. But an input of electric energy is not specified simply by talking about "two hundred hours of electricity". Rather, we talk about kilowatt–hours or similar units, which combine two components. On the one hand, there is the time unit, which I call the extensive component, because it is used to measure the temporal extension of a process of energy transformation. On the

---

[71] They correspond to the three kinds of action systems discussed by Touraine [281], and to the three kinds of structural principles introduced by Giddens [99, p. 180ff], as well as to the two steps of social differentiation identified in Parsons and Shils [211, p. 28f].

[72] This helps understanding why the concept of a generalized medium of exchange becomes unbearably fuzzy when it is generalized (for example, by Luhmann [171]) to include a wide array of items like truth, love, trust, influence, etc.

other hand, there is the unit of electric power, which is used to measure the intensity of this process. In the case of labor, this would require a specific unit, which could be used to measure the intensity of labor in a given period of time. Nobody has tried harder to find ways of measuring labor than F.W.Taylor, and I will call this imaginary unit of labor intensity the "Taylor".[73] One then could speak of Taylor–hours and treat human labor in the same way as electricity.

In fact, there is no such unit. Actually, Taylor was looking for a surrogate for vocational activities. In vocational systems, the occupation of a farmer or a steel–worker is socially defined so that it makes sense to talk of twenty man–hours of farmer's work. There is no metric measure of intensity here. Instead, there is a social category of time, namely the time of a farmer's vocational activity. This social category then defines certain rhythms of activity, as well as a whole set of living and inanimate things, which are consumed, used, produced and reproduced by the processes in question. It also defines possible patterns of cooperation with other farmers, as well as with different occupations. Technically speaking, production functions involving human beings can be meaningfully formulated only if social categories of human activities exist—categories which actually define the relations described by these functions. In the realm of economic life, these categories are vocational occupations.

In the absence of such occupations, firms cannot rely on well established production functions. In practice, this means that labor productivity is nothing one can rely on, but rather is the outcome of a basically unforeseeable struggle. This struggle stakes firms trying to invest in profitable projects against people who are expected to perform activities for the sake of the external goal of earning money. This means that no normative fields organize their respective activities in a meaningful way. As a result, wages must be seen as the outcome of partially unpredictable bargaining processes—a view which fits much better with empirical data than economic equilibrium models.[74] Wage labor, then, is best conceptualized as an anomic activity in the sense discussed by Durkheim. His basic intuition as to a remedy, which would be based on a strengthening of vocational ethics in the activities involved, seems to deserve much more attention than it has received up until now.[75]

---

[73] Taylor [274].
[74] Akerlof and Yellen [3].
[75] Durkheim's argument is developed in the preface to the second edition of his famous work on the division of labor [66].

In the foreseeable future, Durkheim's approach to the problems of wage labor may be more useful than the one of Karl Marx, and all the more so if it is combined with a careful study of the theories of Max Weber. Still, there is much to be learned from Marxist attempts to explain social and especially political processes in relation to economic reality. What must be rejected is the Marxist tendency to explain the economy in terms of material production. After all, Marxist theory has always insisted that even material production cannot be understood without considering social relations. What is difficult to grasp is the fact that economic phenomena are constituted by specific kinds of social relations, namely vocational ones. This clearly implies that the Marxist emphasis on economic reality becomes rather misleading in contexts where the second step of cultural macro–evolution has taken place only partially or not at all.

Perhaps this is a major reason for the categorical mistakes involved in Marxist treatments of feudalism. Marx did identify the first as well as the second step of cultural macro–evolution and he also hinted at parallels between them. The systems which lie, so to speak, between these two steps are differentiated by processes of cultural micro–evolution. An example is provided by the difference between the Roman Empire in antiquity and the Carolingian Empire in the Middle Ages, as well as between the classical Chinese Empire and the reign of the pharaohs in Egypt. Marxist theory became entangled in considerable conceptual difficulties by treating slavery, feudalism, and the so–called Asian mode of production as if they indicated additional steps of cultural macro–evolution.

If Marxism introduced too many of these steps, then mainstream sociology committed the opposite error of conflating the emergence of political systems and the emergence of vocational ones into a single notion of modernization. The differentiation of political systems and later of vocational systems have been described within this tradition, but they have not been clearly distinguished. Instead, a simple dichotomy between traditional and modern societies has been proposed. An adequate understanding, however, of the difference between archaic and dual systems becomes impossible under these conditions. One could therefore restrict the notion of modernization to the second step of cultural macro–evolution and introduce another term to denote the first step. In this sense, one could, for example, distinguish between a process of civilization leading from archaic systems to dual ones and a process of modernization leading from dual systems to the triadic one. Both steps must be distinguished from the process of cultural degeneration, which began together with the first step and continued within the context of the second.

A realistic view of cultural macro–evolution and cultural degeneration is especially relevant with regard to the misery which is the fate of billions of people living in the so–called developing countries. After nearly all former colonies have become sovereign nations in terms of international law, more or less stable elites have become established in most of these nations. Struggles among such elites often take the form of coups d'état, and in some cases civil wars challenge the very existence of some ruling elite. In many respects these elites are very different from the bourgeoisie, which played a crucial role in the emergence of the world economy.[76] In the context of cultural evolution, an especially important difference lies in the fact that contemporary elites in developing countries define their social position mainly in political contexts and, as a rule, do not nurture the development of vocational identity. The conditions of life for the vast majority of the population in these countries surely do not favor such a development either.

So, in these countries the development of vocational identity is still quite exceptional. The monetary institutions, however, which once evolved in Europe together with vocational identities, have now been introduced into developing countries in order to organize forms of labor which lack the cultural context of vocational ethics. The search for profits is carried on in situations which would be incompatible even with minimal forms of vocational responsibility. In a sense, today's developing countries share only one half of the social setting which brought the world economy into being, namely monetary institutions. The other half is wanting, as long as in the context of business enterprises personal identity is not linked to vocational ethics. Unfortunately, even multinational firms, in whose countries of origin such a link usually exists, rarely seem to share it in the developing countries where they operate. One may even wonder whether sometimes the vocational responsibility involved in the corporate culture of such firms is not actually weakened by their involvement in contexts where such responsibility pays much less than it does in industrialized countries.

Meanwhile, the mass media and, to a lesser extent, the increased possibility of global mobility have made elements of vocational ethics available in many developing countries. Therefore, one should take quite seriously the possibility that firms will more or less spontaneously

---

[76] The difference is stressed by Elsenhans [69].

acquire the character of vocational organizations in the so–called informal economies, where they are not too strongly intertwined with the established political elites. This, hopefully, could contribute to a transformation of such elites in a direction where vocational responsibility becomes a vital feature of their own social life.

While these issues are of tremendous importance in the context of the present conditions in developing countries, they are much less dramatic from the point of view of firms operating in highly industrialized countries. The development of the social framework of the world economy since the days of Columbus has shown that this framework does hold, as long as a substantial part of the firms operating in it display the character of vocational organizations. The existence of firms in which labor is performed without any reference to vocational ethics becomes a tragic problem in countries where this is the normal case— not in those countries where the economy is run mainly by vocational organizations.

This situation raises a moral issue which is similar to the one once emphasized by Marx in the context of the rising labor movement. A state of affairs which is unacceptable by the moral standards of the persons involved is reproduced by these very persons, because they are enmeshed in specific normative fields. In the case of the struggle between the 19th century bourgeoisie and the emerging working class, the victims of such structures have seized the historic occasion for transforming their situation. The result may be unsatisfactory in many respects, but it surely has yielded an impressive surge in the standard of living over several generations. Yet, most victims of misery in the developing countries will die before they may even begin to hope for such a possibility.

The example of Japan, Taiwan, and some other Asian countries demonstrates that economic success outside of Europe is not limited to English speaking nations. Now the time factor requires serious consideration. Imagine that the misery of developing countries could be overcome through industrialization processes similar to those of Europe and America, processes which have been imitated so successfully by Japan and some other countries. There cannot be the slightest doubt that for the next decades this still implies further famines, epidemics, and wars. What makes this perspective really hopeless is the fact that it would entail an accumulation of technomass heavily impairing the biosphere's entropy margin. Today, a similar amount of crucial natural resources is consumed in the Los Angeles area as is on the whole Indian subcontinent. The *environmental disruption* implied by a situa-

tion in which the lifestyle of Los Angeles spreads over the whole world
is beyond imagination.

Still, such disruption seems the logical outcome of the accumulation of technomass within the context of the world economy. Since the
Middle Ages, world population growth has accelerated to a staggering
pace, and this is directly related to the planetary expansion of technomass. In the last 500 years, world population has augmented by a
factor of about fifteen. In the countries which underwent industrialization technomass per head has augmented much faster. This is due to
the shift from energy spent by human agents to energy controlled by
such agents.[77]

Later came the waves of industrialization and urbanization leading
to the situation in which now nearly every solid thing in a person's
surroundings is a human artifact. The oceans, the atmosphere, and
the earth's crust must accommodate a rapidly increasing amount of
technomass. This process would have been impossible if the accumulation of technomass had been constrained by the amount of energy
flowing through the human body. As the search for possibilities to
limit and even reduce wage costs became a major tendency of modern
society, however, this constraint was progressively removed. Energy
flows involved in natural processes amenable to human control were
increasingly substituted for the energy flows involved in human labor.
The total energy flowing through a human being is limited mainly by
the amount of food which is burned by the human organism, yielding an energy flow of about 100 watts. This limit, however, became
completely irrelevant as soon as human agents developed the ability to
control energy flows like those of a steam–engine or a power plant. The
world economy has been quite literally fueled by the burning of fossil
fuels.

The rising amount of energy transformations taking place under
human control induced rising entropy production. As defined in section 3.1, this means that with the rise of the Prometheus fraction human activities started to bite into the biosphere's entropy margin. By
burning fossil fuels, humankind began to produce sizeable amounts of

---

[77] A peculiar example of energy controlled by human agents is the inconspicuous
work of earth–worms, to which Darwin once devoted a careful study. The development of agriculture in Europe led not only to large scale deforestation, but also to
the formation of a layer of topsoil, which was not simply a natural resource, but,
in fact, the effect of human agriculture. Careful ploughing, fertilizing, and crop
rotation created a milieu in which earth–worms could multiply and increasingly
contribute to the formation of topsoil.

extra entropy, which no longer leave the biosphere. What precise effects this extra entropy will have can hardly be predicted. Presently, it gets locked to a considerable extent into carbon dioxide, which is no longer recycled by photosynthesis and has started contributing to the greenhouse effect. Clearly, very different processes would occur if nuclear energy could substitute for energy gained from fossil fuels. But again, a huge amount of extra entropy would be produced, which in some form or another (for example, incorporated in nuclear wastes) could again threaten the stable disequilibria of the biosphere, in which the existence of humankind is embedded. This could be true in yet other forms if solar energy was utilized to such an extent as to allow for further accumulation of technomass.

Under these conditions, one must take very seriously the proposition that the probability of future environmental hazards increases with every year in which ongoing accumulation of technomass leads to extra entropy production. As an example, consider the part of biomass which is also a part of technomass. Until now, this has been a minor fraction of total biomass, mainly because of the fact that until now the vegetation of the oceans has been nearly untouched by humankind. On land, too, considerable biomass which does not enter technomass remains, the most majestic instance being the tropical rainforests. Meanwhile, these forests are being transformed into technomass, and there can be no doubt that the corresponding destruction of biological diversity is linked to a tremendous increase in entropy. The entropy content of biomass does not necessarily increase when plants and animals are incorporated into technomass. The development of agriculture after the Middle Ages, for example, does not seem to have involved major increases in entropy production. Today, however, the accumulation of technomass is actually linked to such increases.

Technically, it is no doubt conceivable that the world economy could work with a stabilized or even a reduced Prometheus fraction. But can such a state be attained without a long succession of catastrophic breakdowns? Can the cultural and structural characteristics of today's world economy accommodate this transformation in a gradual process? There are no clear cut answers to these questions. There is, however, a rather urgent need for a variety of efforts to develop new institutional arrangements which could help humankind to enjoy its common home instead of destroying it in acts of common madness.

While I waited and looked on I presently recognized in this watchmaker an old acquaintance—a steamboat engineer of other days, and not a good engineer, either.

Mark Twain, My Watch.

Chapter 4

The New Enlightenment

Human beings as accountable animals are a product of biological evolution, but they also are engaged in a process of cultural evolution.[1] Within this process I have distinguished three very different sub-processes: micro–evolution, macro–evolution, and degeneration. The current environmental crisis is the outcome of a long process of cultural degeneration, which has stabilized a state of anomie and common madness by reducing human agency to labor. Overcoming this crisis would require a comprehensive process of cultural regeneration, which would end this state of common madness by transforming labor back into human agency.

In section 4.1 I will describe some processes of cultural regeneration which have taken place in the past. A crucial criterion for cultural regeneration is the reduction of nonsensical beliefs, especially regarding external relations between means and ends as well as between different persons. In the past, developments in this direction often have been focused on the misuse of political power as an external goal of action. These developments of cultural regeneration led to the establishment of democratic institutions in many nations. A major contribution in this sense was made by the Enlightenment. With regard to the global environmental crisis which humankind is facing, the Enlightenment deserves special attention because it saw science as a driving force of

---

[1] More precisely, I might speak of socio–cultural evolution. I use the expression "cultural evolution" for brevity, not to restrict attention to culture as distinct from social structure.

social progress. Today, recognition of the environmental crisis is due to a large extent to scientific work, and overcoming this crisis will no doubt be impossible without major contributions by the scientific community.

However, awareness of global environmental problems is often associated with a critique of the world view which resulted from the Enlightenment. A major characteristic of this world view consists of mechanistic thinking. Quite often even descriptions of environmental problems are framed in mechanistic terms. This is the theme of section 4.2, where I compare three simple models: the first one refers to biological ecology, the second to human ecology, and the third to Newtonian mechanics. Major features of mechanistic thinking are its atomistic approach, its reliance on measurement, and its emphasis on predictability. The comparison between the three models leads me to distinguish between classical mechanics, which I regard as an integrative research tradition well suited for the study of important physical systems, and mechanistic thinking, which I consider to be a problematic generalization of classical mechanics beyond its proper realm.

In order to understand how this unwarranted generalization came about, in section 4.3 I discuss the tradition which was displaced by mechanistic thinking. This was not a tradition of scientific research, but a more comprehensive tradition of inquiry, which began with the Old Testament. The emergence of Christianity marks the most dramatic transition in the development of this tradition. A less intense, but still important transition corresponds with the development of a morphological cosmology, which was based on the encounter between Christianity and Greek philosophy. The research tradition of classical mechanics might have been integrated into this comprehensive tradition of inquiry if the latter had experienced further renewal. Such renewal was actually attempted by various Protestant movements, but no new synthesis was obtained. In this situation, mechanistic thinking developed as a surrogate for a comprehensive tradition of inquiry.

Lately, the development of relativity theory and quantum mechanics, and recent work on non–linear dynamics, have undermined the plausibility of mechanistic thinking. Furthermore, the discovery of biological evolution and the identification of a possible origin of the universe in the so–called big bang theory have contributed to a new view of the world in which we live. A displacement of mechanistic thinking by an evolutionary cosmology seems possible. A new Enlightenment could assign a new role to science as one of the caretakers of the global environment.[2] The study of human ecological systems can and should take advantage of this possibility. However, we better avoid the illusion that using evolutionary metaphors, perhaps enriched by the terminology of general systems theory, is sufficient for an understanding of human ecological systems.

In order to advance toward such an understanding, it may be useful to compare purely biophysical ecosystems with human ecological systems. This is the topic of section 4.4. There I begin by discussing some rather intricate relations between ecosystem development and biological evolution. This discussion supports the view that there is no clear cut limit at which environmental disruption by human beings leads to total catastrophe. To say that humankind is destroying its own environment means making a moral, not simply a biophysical assertion. Moral orders—i.e., webs of cultural rules—are a crucial component of human ecological systems, and they deserve careful study no less than the biophysical components. Overcoming mechanistic thinking in a new Enlightenment, then, would involve an integrated study of major interactions between moral orders and environmental processes. This will be especially relevant with regard to economic phenomena, which will be the focus of chapter 5.

4.1 Cultural Regeneration

In chapter 3, I argued that one form of common madness, which developed with the first step of cultural macro–evolution, treats political power as a purely external goal of action. As I will discuss in this section, at least two major attempts at cultural regeneration tried to reverse this situation more than two millennia ago: the religious tradition formed with the Jewish exodus from the land of the pharaos and the philosophical tradition which emerged in the city–states of ancient Greece. Core elements of both traditions were blended in the experience of early Christianity. By the end of the Middle Ages, however, undemocratic pursuit of power as an external goal of action faced little criticism from the catholic church. Such criticism, however, was renewed in the name of science and human reason by the thinkers of the Enlightenment.

None of the mentioned processes of cultural regeneration was focused on overcoming the forms of common madness to be found in

---

[2] I owe this idea to Schneider [247].

the economic system, which emerged with the second step of cultural macro–evolution. Such a focus, however, was established by the labor movement. Meanwhile, the guiding ideas of the labor movement have lost much of their plausibility. These ideas never really emphasized the possibility of transforming labor back into human activity, although in the past decades the experience of the labor movement was characterized, among other things, by a widespread refusal of labor with large scale economic impacts.[3] Overcoming the environmental crisis may well require a comprehensive transformation of labor into human agency in the fields of private, political and vocational life. Major social movements of the 20th century, especially the feminist, peace, and environmental movements, can be seen as parts of a search process which might lead to such an outcome.

In order to describe the roots of this search process, it is useful to distinguish three types of religious traditions, each of which can be related to the notion of cultural degeneration.[4] The first type leads people to actively support cultural degeneration, the second one leads them to endure cultural degeneration by retreating into a realm of individual religious experience, and the third one leads them to search for cultural regeneration by joint action. Coarse as the distinction may be, it points to important differences. The religious tradition of the Aztecs, with its mass sacrifices of human beings, seems to be not very far from the first type; the Buddhist tradition, especially in its Chinese version, shares important traits with the second one. The paradigmatic case of the third type is provided by the biblical tradition.[5]

In the *Judaism* of the Old Testament, the abuse of political power as an external goal of human action was questioned time and again. The emancipation from slavery, the limitation of land ownership to usufructuary rights, the introduction of a law which was not at the disposal of kings, all became important goals of the chosen people, whether they realized those goals or not. In particular, the distinction between the different roles of kings and judges initiated a crucial step of cultural regeneration in the political realm: the introduction of a pluralistic system of power.

Such systems were to be realized more fully only much later, in the context of the Enlightenment, with the idea of a separation of powers

---

[3] This refusal will be discused below.
[4] The distinction has been introduced by Morishima [196, p. 194] in his attempt to discuss the cultural presuppositions of Japan's economic achievements.
[5] As stressed by authors like Taubes [273] and Walzer [287].

and the design of elaborate constitutional systems of checks and balances. Before we turn to later developments, however, we must ask who, according to Judaism, were the primary agents of cultural regeneration. Human beings were not assigned the most prominent role: salvation was expected as the work of God, realized through the Messiah. However, according to this tradition, God had chosen the people of Israel as his ally. As far as human beings are concerned, the members of the chosen people are the main agents of cultural regeneration.

Independently of the biblical tradition, a search for cultural regeneration was undertaken in *Ancient Greece*. Again, abuses of political power as an external goal of human action were questioned and led to the development of laws which even the most powerful person had to obey. The tradition of democratic institutions, which unfolded in Athens and later in the Roman Republic, is one of the most impressive instances of cultural regeneration in the history of humankind. This tradition cultivated ideals of rational debate, which have not lost their fascination still to this day, as is documented for example in recent instances of critical theory.[6]

Who were the agents of cultural regeneration according to the Greek tradition? In the modern versions of democratically oriented political philosophy, reversing cultural degeneration is seen as the task of human beings—using their natural faculties of reasoning, but unassisted by divine help. Such was not the view of the Ancient Greeks, nor, for that matter, of the citizens of the Roman Republic. Without talking about a comprehensive alliance between the gods and the Greek communities, the Greek tradition still emphasized the futility of all human action aiming at democracy and justice without seeking the support of the gods. The line which the Greeks drew between themselves and the barbarians had much in common with the distinction which the Jews made between themselves and the infidel.

However, both the Jewish and the Greek traditions were only partially successful in their attempts to reverse the process of cultural degeneration. They were able to develop political institutions which made viable an understanding of political power as an internal goal of political action, embedded in interpersonal relationships of responsibility. They did not achieve a similar integration of sexual motives into private accountability relations. Notwithstanding remarkable exceptions such as the poetry of Sappho, patriarchy remained largely unchallenged in both traditions. Practices of slavery were by no means absent from

---

[6] Habermas [110].

the Jewish tradition, and they were even essential for the lifestyle of Ancient Greek cities. The democratic institutions of Classical Greece succumbed to the search for power by Alexander the Great, and Israel was conquered by the Romans, who had buried their own republic in favor of imperial power.

Crucial elements of the Jewish and also of the Greek tradition were taken up by *Christianity*, which renewed the hope of a reversal of cultural degeneration in the face of the triumphant Roman Empire. I do not want to deny that the hope of early Christianity had a transcendental dimension, which cannot be expressed by talking about cultural regeneration. What matters in this context, however, is the fact that in its origins Christianity did not separate this dimension from the hope of a historical transformation toward a life without slavery and war. Who were the agents that were supposed to carry out this transformation? Salvation was still seen as the work of God, but now God was understood as inviting every human being to participate in that work.

The door to the Kingdom of Heaven was said to be wide open for the poor, but it was not altogether closed to the rich either. The human agents fostering cultural regeneration were by no means restricted to some pre–defined political community. The Jewish idea that all human beings are equal, because they are all made in the image of God, actually began to apply to all human beings. In particular, the goal of emancipation from slavery found new nourishment in the Gospel. It took nearly two thousand years before the society of nations began to treat slavery as unlawful, but the transformation did occur. Together with the emergence of democratic institutions, this is a second major process of cultural regeneration.[7]

The Jerusalem–based idea of human equality[8] worked its way toward the abolition of slavery through a long series of elaborations and transformations. The medieval mendicant orders were an important step in this process, and so were the peasant revolts, which in some countries marked the end of the Middle Ages. A third step, sometimes

---

[7] There are more slaves in today's world than there were in the world of Caesar's times for the simple reason that total human population has experienced substantial growth. The abolition of slavery is still an unfinished task, and it is directly linked to the task of abolishing the misery reigning in large parts of the so–called Third World. The reason why I talk about an actual process of cultural regeneration with regard to slavery is related to the fact that today slavery is an exception, does not provide the normal basis of economic life, and is considered immoral and unlawful by the society of nations.

[8] Putnam [225].

closely associated with these revolts, was the Reformation. The emphasis on the direct relation between every individual soul and the Lord favored a much more egalitarian spirit than the hierarchical edifice of faith developed by the Catholic Church. Finally, the Enlightenment generated a secularized version of the biblical idea of human equality. Human beings are equal, because each of them can and must think for himself or herself. We are equal, because we share the faculty of reason in a world full of open questions. Whether this faculty is a sign that we are made in the image of God is just one of the questions we can think about.

With the *Enlightenment*, the idea of human equality could be turned not only against political authority, but also against ecclesiastical authority. The abolition of serfdom by the French revolution was part of an explicit confrontation not only with absolute monarchy, but also with a Church which seemed to have all but forgotten its origins in the communities of free citizens and slaves established by St. Paul. The Enlightenment helped to separate this Church from the state, and thereby renewed the hope which lay at the origins of the former. The Enlightenment also helped to restore the view that not only the members of some predetermined political community, but all human beings are able to foster cultural regeneration.

With this development, human beings were largely expected to stand alone, without much hope of divine assistance. This was connected to the fact that the separation of church and state was achieved by establishing another link, this one between the state and an institution claiming privileged access to truth, namely modern science.

Both the Jewish and the Christian versions of the biblical tradition, as well as the democratic institutions and the philosophical thinking of Ancient Greece, were formed before the emergence of vocational life as a separate socio–cultural reality. Therefore, their anticipation of cultural regeneration bears more directly on private and public life than on possible transformations of today's world economy. The Reformation and the Enlightenment are different in this respect; in fact, our notion of vocational identity owes much to them. Still, the main ideas of the Reformation and of the Enlightenment were developed before Adam Smith described the invisible hand of the market. I will now turn to a conscious attempt to develop a process of cultural regeneration within the realm of the market economy, an attempt which has already begun to shape the history of humankind—the experience of the *labor movement*.

The labor movement arose in reaction to the suffering of wage earners, which the operation of the invisible hand of the market brought about at the time of industrialization. Throughout a long history of struggle, the labor movement succeeded in improving the lot of wage earners to a remarkable extent. A main instrument of this success was the organization of wage earners in trade unions, worker's cooperatives, and political parties. Pressure in the economic realm, in particular by means of strikes, combined with political action in the public sphere, enabled the movement to regulate labor contracts between employers and employees. Such regulation restricted unfair practices stemming from the unequal bargaining positions between the owners of business firms and the people needing employment to make a living. A crucial outcome of this struggle for regulation was the development of labor laws.

Given this background, it is quite understandable that the labor movement arrived at a new answer to the question of who would be the human agents of cultural regeneration. They were no longer identified as the members of a specific political community, as in the Jewish or Greek tradition, nor were all human beings seen as potential agents of cultural regeneration, as by early Christianity and later by the Enlightenment. Instead, the Christian emphasis on the poor as agents of salvation was taken up and transformed into a view of wage earners as the main agents of social progress.

The experience of the labor movement also made plausible a specific idea concerning the form such progress was to assume, namely the idea that social progress consists in the taming of economic forces by political means. This idea found its extreme expression in the Marxist project of a planned economy. The historical failure of this project makes it all too easy to ignore the tremendous intellectual challenge presented by the breakdown of Marxism. For over a century, this theory crystallized a critique of existing political and economic institutions and offered hope for the transformation of these institutions so as to eliminate much human suffering. The breakdown of this critique, and of the hope associated with it, prepares the ground for a dangerous dilemma. On the one hand, cynicism becomes a tempting perspective for those finding themselves in a reasonably comfortable position in a world in which excessive suffering is the fate of a large part of humankind, while the biosphere is threatened by anthropogenic environmental disruption. On the other hand, fundamentalist visions can ignite the imagination of those who do not find cynicism a viable alternative, either because their position is not comfortable enough, or because they find it morally and intellectually unacceptable.

In order to avoid this dilemma, it is important to at least roughly understand the reasons for the failure of Marxism, without vaguely claiming that Marxism is simply a fundamentally flawed ideology. For this purpose, it may be useful to consider the easily forgotten fact that there is a period in the history of Western Europe which presents many important parallels to the fate of socialism in Eastern Europe, namely the period of absolutism. The tensions which once forced the absolutist kingdoms of Europe to yield to an autonomous economic system bear remarkable similarities to the tensions forcing socialist regimes to similar steps.[9] In both cases, the attempt to keep economic development under the control of the state resulted in a totalitarian system of political domination until the operation of money forced political power to accept its new limits, which were drawn by the dynamics of the world economy.

In the context of cultural evolution, the experience of planned economies can be understood as one form of the transition from human ecological systems characterized by the dichotomy between private and public life toward systems including a third autonomous realm—the one of vocational life. In this transition, the state is forced to accept the autonomy of an emerging economic system. Absolutism and socialism, in the sense of planned economies, are two forms of this process. However, abandoning political planning of the economic process in favor of a market economy based on private property achieves the second step of cultural macro–evolution, while not contributing to a process of cultural regeneration. To be sure, such a process does gather momentum when democratic forms of political life begin to replace the monopolistic power of absolutist kings or of communist parties in control of the state, but this reduces common madness in the political realm, not yet in the economic realm.

The political possibilities brought about by the failure of planned economies are impressive. Not only can processes of cultural regeneration advance in the context of internal political institutions of various

---

[9] In this respect, there are interesting similarities between the fate of feudal aristocracy and the fate of the communist *"nomenclatura"*. In both cases, an elite in control of political power is forced to deal with the fact that its power cannot be maintained in the face of economic processes which it had not foreseen. The greater the willingness and the ability of the old elites to learn to cope with the new situation, the smaller the turmoil and the violence associated with the end of its regime.

nations, but there is also a definite opportunity for the development of a world–wide society of nations, which could realize far–reaching processes of disarmament. With regard to the possibility of cultural regeneration, the fate of peace movements in the 20th century deserves special attention. While on the eve of World War I such movements were completely unsuccessful, in the 60's they contributed to America's withdrawal from Vietnam. Since the development of war as an institutionalized practice, this was the first time a powerful nation was able to desist from seeking victory in a war which was highly questionable on moral grounds. Twenty years later, the demand for nuclear disarmament by international peace movements entered into the arena of political negotiations between the U.S. and Russia, which are no longer divided by the opposition between capitalism and communism.

The labor movement has always searched for processes of cultural regeneration not only in the political, but, at least to an equal extent, in the economic sphere. This search, however, was biased by attempts to achieve such regeneration by negating the autonomy of the world economy with regard to the political system. This holds true for Marxist theory, as well as for the more libertarian, if less influential, anarchist tradition. It also holds true for the more moderate views of Keynes, which after the great depression were embraced by the labor movement in nearly all industrialized countries.[10] Keynes did not preach revolution, but instead proposed to correct the operation of the invisible hand by macro–economic policy.

In the long boom period after World War II known as "the golden age of capitalism",[11] this approach seemed to work with amazing success. Economic growth at nearly full employment was realized in a growing number of countries, international trade expanded under a regime of fixed exchange–rates geared to the US–dollar, and business cycles never experienced a sharp downturn. Governments and national banks monitored the development of key economic variables and tried to keep them on a long–run growth path with the instruments of deficit–spending and variations in the rates of interest, in some cases supplemented by periodical adjustments of exchange rates. Trade unions took advantage of tight labor markets to obtain persistent increases in wage

---

[10] Keynes [155].

[11] Marglin and Schor [179]. This period is often studied under the heading of "Fordism", emphasizing the role which Henry Ford played in shaping some of its main characteristics. See Lüscher [172] for a contribution linking the themes of Fordism, refusal of labor, and personal identity.

incomes, and private households experienced unprecedented levels of consumption.

The heyday of Keynesian economic policy greatly reinforced the external character of the relation between the means and ends of economic activities. The paradigmatic case of such a relation was the mass-production of automobiles by the unskilled workers lined up along the assembly lines of car factories. Wage labor was considered to serve the purpose of consumption, and therefore the development of personal identity had no role to play in the context of vocational traditions. In purely economic terms, the cloven hoof of this strategy lay in the difficulty of controlling labor productivity. Detailed job descriptions, together with various schemes of efficiency wages, were used for this purpose, but they were a weak substitute for the commitment generated by lively vocational traditions.

This difficulty became manifest in the USA during the 60's, when problems of labor productivity began to figure as a main characteristic of the American economy—a role which they have maintained in the following decades. An acute expression of these problems were rising rates of absenteeism, as well as forms of passive and sometimes even active resistance against foremen and plant managers. While increases in labor productivity slowed down, increases in wage costs accelerated. This was due in part to industrial actions organized by trade unions, but also to actions such as wildcat strikes, which by-passed the traditional decision structures of trade unions. An important factor in the increase of wage costs was the growth of income taxes and social security contributions, a process which resulted from the general strategy of countering economic problems by political measures. The whole process may be described as a broad *refusal of labor*, a refusal to engage in activities characterized by external means–end relations.[12]

Entrepreneurs and managers first reacted to the combination of productivity problems and wage increases by price increases. As this was a very widespread phenomenon, competition did not prevent it. The result was accelerating inflation and a weakening dollar. These effects were amplified by the government's deficit–spending to finance the Vietnam war. In this context, it must be noted that the deficit–spending was still part of the Keynesian approach to economic policy,

---

[12] It is a remarkable fact that the same period saw a massive refusal of the labor of war (with regard to the Vietnam war) and a great enthusiasm for new forms of artistic creativity (with regard to rock music). Since the times of Aristotle, music and dance are often considered as paradigmatic examples of internal means–end relations.

making an important contribution to tight labor markets and thereby furthering wage increases and additional inflation. However, as inflation began to get out of control, the government was forced to end its full employment policy.

The oil shock of 1973, itself in part a reaction of OPEC to the devaluation of the dollar, provided a welcome opportunity for this purpose; governments did not need to assume responsibility for increasing unemployment, and could instead blame it on oil prices. Thus, the debate about limits to growth took a strange turn. Growth actually slowed down because of the social conflict generated by the external relation between means and ends of economic activities, but this slow–down was perceived by many as a foreboding of things to come as a consequence of finite resources. This obfuscated the relations between economic growth and environmental risks on the one hand, and between means and ends of economic activities on the other hand.

During the 60's, the refusal of labor spread from the USA to Western Europe, where it generated similar economic dynamics.[13] Even Japan was not exempt from this process, although for historical reasons[14] the refusal of labor was less pronounced than in Europe and North America.[15] In any case, after the first oil shock it was clear that something fundamental had been torn in the fabric of the world economy. Managers, entrepreneurs, trade unions, governments, economists, environmentalists, and many others began searching for ways to cope with the new situation, sometimes without bothering to analyze it in much detail.

In retrospect, the 70's and 80's present themselves as a period in which this search led to a wide variety of attempted solutions. The transfer of huge amounts of credit to third world countries, a practice leading to a persistent debt crisis, was one such attempt.[16] Another one was the policy of "Reaganomics", combining deregulation, especially of labor markets, with tax cuts, with high interest rates, and with deficit–spending financed by foreign capital attracted by those high interest

---

[13] Its economic implications are known as the "wage explosion" of the 60's and early 70's, documented in Armstrong, Glyn, and Harrison [6]; Bowles, Gordon and Weisskopf [35], Jaeger and Weber [146]; Nordhaus [200].

[14] Discussed by Morishima [196].

[15] It would be interesting to study the breakdown of communism in Eastern Europe in relation to the fact that the refusal of labor reached these countries, too.

[16] Interestingly, similar strategies can be documented for earlier periods of crisis in the world economy (Suter, Stamm and Pfister [270]).

rates.[17] A third attempt was the introduction of new technologies like industrial robots, and local as well as world–wide computer networks. The list could be extended almost indefinitely, especially if I were to include some less intensely pursued attempts. However, what matters here is the question of whether this search can contribute to a process of cultural regeneration which is adequate to cope with the problems of global environmental change.

Until now, I have discussed several processes of cultural regeneration, all of which seem to be incomplete. Would it not seem reasonable to try to accept the world as it is and to stop searching for the Kingdom of Heaven on earth, even in the disguised form of the age of reason? Maybe the world in which we live really is the best of all possible worlds, not in the sense of being perfect, but in the sense that a perfect world is not possible. However, the environmental crisis does not allow for such a convenient answer. Coping with the risks of global change will require far–reaching transformations of the human ecological systems in which humankind presently exists. The result may not be a perfect world, but it will be very different from the one we know—and there is much to be said for the attempt to make it a better one. Finding adequate answers to the problems of global change will mean going ahead with processes of cultural regeneration which our ancestors have started.

While neither cultural macro–evolution nor cultural micro–evolution can reasonably be described as progress from an inferior to a superior state of affairs, cultural regeneration does represent such *progress*. In the context of biological evolution, birds are not "better" than fish only because they arrived later in the evolutionary process, but even in the biological realm it makes good sense to say that a sick bird is worse off than a healthy one. The metaphor may become misleading when cultural regeneration is confused with biological healing, but it can help to avoid an unwarranted cult of progress. The healing of a sick organism only reverses its falling into sickness, it does not transform it into another kind of organism. Cultural regeneration is real progress, but it may only help humankind to reverse the loss of sustainable life–forms which has occurred in the course of cultural degeneration.

Nevertheless, the result will not be a return to archaic human ecological systems. The differentiation of human existence into a private,

---

[17] Deficit–spending took place on a huge scale, although its avoidance was a declared goal of the general political approach.

a political, and a vocational realm is the result of cultural macro-
evolution, not of cultural degeneration. The latter results in the common madness with which that differentiation is handled, not in the
differentiation as such. A process of cultural regeneration oriented toward solving environmental problems cannot be understood as restoring
archaic systems by dismantling political and vocational life. Instead,
the emancipation from common madness—"man's release from his self-
incurred tutelage"[18]—implies a transformation of human existence in
its private, political, and vocational dimensions.

More precisely, what is required is a *transformation of labor into human
agency* in these three realms. Consider private life first. Co–presence
is a necessary condition for the development of interpersonal accountability relations. Therefore, putting an end to the absence of men in
the realm of housework is a pre–requisite for the transformation of this
kind of labor into an experience of human flourishing. But co–presence
is only a necessary, not a sufficient condition. Sexuality, which provides the generalized end of action in the private realm, needs to be
re–integrated into interpersonal accountability relations. This is, first
of all, a very personal problem experienced in the context of individual existence. But at the same time it forms a crucial element in the
immense problem of worldwide population growth.[19] In purely numerical terms, humankind is plainly growing beyond any reasonable limits.
Changing this situation will require far reaching changes in the situation of women in developing countries. This will hardly be possible
without considerable economic growth. But it will also hardly be possible unless sexual motives will find an appropriate place in everyday
conversations. Such a re–integration of sexual motives in accountability relations seems also necessary to overcome the immense suffering
engendered by gender conflicts in highly industrialized countries. This
suffering ranges from the fate of single mothers and their children in
the slums of contemporary cities to the psychological distress caused by
the crisis of the family in more affluent parts of society. As I discussed
in chapter 3, the need of re–integrating sexual motives in accountability conversations runs into nearly insurmountable obstacles in a culture
which describes sexual relations along the lines of a misleading rhetoric
of love. Embedding sexual goals of action in relations of love becomes
very difficult, indeed, as long as the words needed to distinguish them

---

[18] Kant [152, p. 3].
[19] Another element of paramount importance are the desperate economic conditions
to which a large part of humankind is subjected.

unaffectedly are wanting. The rhetoric of love, at present, is taken care of primarily by artists and entertainers, and to a lesser but still highly influential degree by psychotherapists. Still, this rhetoric represents only the tip of the iceberg which religious traditions form in our secularized culture. Any serious change in the rhetoric of love involves, in the first place, religious traditions. However, in our world of innovation waves and future shocks, religious traditions often seem to share the immobility of fossils buried deep underground, and this fact suggests that cultural regeneration in this realm will be a long and difficult process.

An important arena for such change is provided by the everyday lives of a growing number of housewives. Preparing food, disposing of garbage, taking care of children's health, as well as other household tasks, have all become occasions for raising environmental awareness. The development of environmental awareness in the context of private lives endows housework with a new relevance as a topic of accounting conversations. Such conversations begin to re–establish the dignity of human agency for important aspects of housework. Given this background, it is at least possible to speculate about a future in which tasks like preparing food and taking care of a household will be viewed as essential contributions, not just to physical survival, but also to the very core of human culture.

If in private life the labor of housework could be transformed into human agency in the context of environmental awareness, what would an analogous transformation mean in the public sphere? Today, a crucial form of labor in public life is military service. The development of the practice of war was no doubt a major step in the development of common madness. A process of cultural regeneration which would put an end to common madness would have to establish a situation in which nations would not feel compelled to prepare for war in order to be able to live in relative peace. As the nuclear arms race has led to the accumulation of a stock of weaponry providing the capacity of global overkill, the need for a comprehensive disarmament process has become a major item on the agenda of world politics. Such a process could be viewed as the simple dismantling of armies, but a transformation of labor into human agency would imply something different: a transformation of military service into forms of meaningful community service.

An extremely important aspect of such a transformation concerns the exclusion of women from large portions of political life. Military service is a stronghold of male–dominated politics, as well as of the pursuit of power as an external goal of political activity. A community service which would treat power as an internal goal rooted in the interpersonal relations between citizens would also offer the possibility of public happiness being shared by men and women. A sensible community service could include activities of environmental protection like garbage collection or activities of social solidarity like taking care of the homeless. Such exercises of modesty could be effective contributions to public happiness, but obviously the contribution of highly developed personal skills is important as well. Public authorities have much to gain from citizens who participate in the elaboration of political decisions without renouncing vocational activities outside of political institutions.

A transformation of private and public lives along the lines sketched above would reverse the process of cultural degeneration as far as it was linked to the first step of cultural macro-evolution. Envisaging such a transformation is more than wishful thinking; important processes pointing in this direction are underway and can be documented. A major example is the attempts of women to reshape the conditions of their existence. Feminist debates about sex, love, housework, and politics are a part of this process, but the process itself is by no means limited to feminist circles. The participation of women in political and also in vocational life has been gradually increasing for several generations. More recently, growing numbers of women have actively begun to avoid patriarchal forms of family life. So far, the main outcome of this tendency seems to have been a reduction of population growth in industrialized countries together with a surge in the number of one–person households. While these phenomena can hardly be interpreted as a successful transformation of labor into activity, they surely represent very real challenges to age old patterns of cultural degeneration.

However, cultural degeneration was not limited to the first step of cultural macro–evolution, rather it was renewed in the context of the second step. While the Enlightenment made major contributions to cultural regeneration in the political and also the private realm, its achievements remain painfully incomplete with regard to the economic realm. By now, however, environmental problems are forcing us to reconsider precisely this problem. The task we are faced with is nothing less than overcoming the limits which restricted the project of the Enlightenment.

4.2 The Legacy of Mechanistic Thinking

The limits of the Enlightenment are highly relevant with regard to debates about the current environmental crisis. Many people, both specialists and lay–persons, seem to believe that the global environmental crisis basically presents an engineering problem which can be solved by relying in a mechanistic way on scientific computations. In this view, humankind and its global environment form one encompassing ecosystem, which has reached a highly complex ecological equilibrium characterized by a great number of biological populations and a large set of physical and chemical processes.[20] This global ecological equilibrium is stable only within critical thresholds of some of the variables involved, thresholds beyond which the system is presently being driven by human activities.

In this section, I will begin exploring this picture of the environmental crisis by discussing similarities between a basic model of population dynamics in biological ecology and a highly simplified "world–model" of the interactions between humankind and the biosphere. I will then compare both models to an elementary simulation model of a galaxy of stars, which move according to Newtonian laws of motion. I will use this comparison to show how the first two models rely on the use of mechanistic metaphors. This will lead me to consider the role of classical mechanics as an integrative research tradition. I shall conclude this section by criticizing the unwarranted generalization from classical mechanics to mechanistic thinking.

Consider first the models of *population dynamics* of the Lotka–Volterra type. In the simplest case, there is a population X of predatory animals and a prey population Y. The number of births in X increases with its own size, but also with the size of Y. I express this relation by multiplying the product of X and Y with the constant rate x_b. The number of deaths in X depends on the size of X, which is multiplied by the constant death rate x_d. Deaths in Y increase both with its own size and with the size of X. Again, I multiply the product of both populations by the constant rate y_d. Finally, births in Y increase

---

[20] A highly speculative, but fascinating version of this view has been proposed by Lovelock [167], who, in his Gaia–hypothesis, compares this global ecosystem to a living organism. This leads him to be quite optimistic about the system's ability to control physical variables like global temperature. Obviously, the same analogy may be used to stress the vulnerability of the system with regard to various dangers. A forerunner of the global ecosystem approach is Vernadsky [286], who explicitly considered humankind as "a large–scale geologic force".

with the size of Y, but only up to the carrying capacity N of the habitat. I therefore multiply Y by the birth rate y_b but also by the factor $1 - Y/N$, which becomes negative if population exceeds the carrying capacity. In both cases, population growth (x and y) equals the difference between births and deaths.

$$x = x_b \cdot X \cdot Y - x_d \cdot X$$
$$y = y_b \cdot Y \cdot (1 - Y/N) - y_d \cdot X \cdot Y$$

(4.1)

In discrete time, this yields a non–linear system of two difference (in continuous time: differential) equations, which may be used as a model of an ecosystem involving such a pair of populations. Depending on the parameters and initial conditions, the dynamics of the ecosystem may lead to its disappearance, to a steady state, to cyclical, or to chaotic changes. If an actual ecosystem of this type is found to display cyclical behavior or a steady state, it is important to look for critical changes in the parameters or variables which would lead to its breakdown.[21]

It is a remarkable fact that ecosystems of this type do not necessarily reach a state of equilibrium. Within the Lotka–Volterra framework, this may be shown in three ways. First, the processes leading to equilibrium take time and may never be completed because of the continuous emergence of new species. Second, the completion of endogenous processes converging toward equilibrium may be prevented because exogenous processes, such as climatic change, often modify the conditions defining carrying capacities. Third, even under fixed conditions and without the appearance of new species, the system may follow an unending chaotic trajectory. Carrying capacities will set upper limits on population sizes, but below those limits population sizes may vary forever in unforeseeable ways, just as the digits of a transcendental number like π vary between 0 and 9 without ever converging toward a cyclical pattern or a fixed number.

This argument holds true for cases where obvious physical boundaries can be indicated, as for the biosphere as a whole. In situations where boundaries are difficult to find, for example when just a part of a

---

[21] More sophisticated models can be built by considering the possibility that the carrying capacity for one population depends on resources which are shared with the other population. Evolutionary processes may be introduced by adding new populations resulting from random modifications of the genetic traits of existing populations. New genetic features may be thought of as modifications both of morphological properties and of behavioral traits of organisms.

meadow is considered, talk about ecosystems is far from trivial. Finding an ecological equilibrium in such situations is remarkable and rather unexpected. Whether a mathematical apparatus of the Lotka–Volterra kind can be applied in a meaningful way will depend on empirical conditions; however, even when its application is warranted, we are still a long way from having identified a state of ecological equilibrium. Still, this apparatus is quite useful, and we may attempt to proceed by asking whether it can be modified to represent the population dynamics of humankind in the context of global ecological problems.

Suppose a total human population M has a tendency to grow exponentially at a constant rate m_r in a global ecosystem whose carrying capacity for human beings is impaired by increasing pollution.[22] I measure pollution by some index P and define carrying capacity by a pollution threshold T beyond which additional population m becomes negative. Instead of equations (4.1) I now write:

$$m = m_r {\cdot} M {\cdot} (1 - P/T) \qquad (4.2)$$

There is only one population now, but we still get a second equation for the dynamics of pollution. I assume that pollution does not increase as long as total population stays below a threshold S, because human garbage and debris can be resorbed by natural cycles. In every year in which population stays above this threshold, additional pollution p is generated by a constant amount p_a of pollution per head:

$$p = p_a {\cdot} (M - S) \quad \text{for} \quad M > S$$
$$p = 0 \quad \text{for} \quad M \leq S \qquad (4.3)$$

In discrete time, this again yields a non–linear system of difference equations which may be used as a model of the global human ecosystem. In fact, this is the kind of *world–model* which following the Club of Rome's famous report[23] has shaped many discussions dealing with human ecology.[24] Within such a framework, it is easy to show that no path of exponential growth can be followed forever.[25] This is obviously relevant because presently both total human population and

---

[22] For a discussion of the following example, see Hund [136, p. 63ff].

[23] Meadows et al. [188].

[24] Clark and Cole [49] offer an evaluation of world models.

[25] Note that I am speaking of the growth of population and pollution, not of monetary magnitudes.

many forms of pollution are, in fact, growing along exponential lines. A more elaborate analysis could then be used to establish the conditions under which a system experiencing a phase of exponential growth can be stabilized as it approaches the environment's carrying capacity, and under which other conditions such a system will instead break down or enter a cyclical or chaotic trajectory.

The language of mathematics used in these models is often perceived as an indication of strictly deductive arguments as opposed to analogical thinking. The issue is not as simple as that. In both kinds of models which I have sketched above, population growth is considered in analogy to the laws of motion known from Newtonian physics. The use of classical mechanics as a metaphor for the study of all kinds of realities is a hallmark of what I will call mechanistic thinking.[26]

In order to understand the role of this analogy, one can use a simple simulation *model of a galaxy*.[27] The galaxy is composed of a set of stars indexed with $i = 1...n$. Each star has a physical mass m_i. At a given moment each star may be localized in space by a vector q_i; a second vector v_i identifies the velocity (as distance covered in one time unit) of each star at the same moment. Each ordered pair of stars i, j is characterized by a distance vector $d_{i,j}$ directed from q_i toward q_j. By dividing $d_{i,j}$ by its scalar length $d_{i,j}$ one obtains the normalized direction of the force of attraction $k_{i,j}$ operating on star i. Following Newton, the amount of this force is equal to the product of the two masses divided by the square of the distance separating the two stars. Accordingly, the attraction experienced by star i towards star j is described by the following equation:[28]

$$k_{i,j} = \frac{m_i \cdot m_j}{d_{i,j}^2} \cdot \frac{d_{i,j}}{d_{i,j}} \qquad (4.4)$$

For any star i, the sum for all $j \neq i$ yields the total force k_i operating on the star. Again following Newton, the acceleration b_i equals this force divided by the star's mass:

$$b_i = \frac{k_i}{m_i} \qquad (4.5)$$

---

[26] In my use of this concept, I draw on the work of authors like Dijksterhuis [59], Hund [137], Rust [235], Whitehead [293].

[27] The model has been formulated by Dewdney [57].

[28] The notation treats physical dimensions as implicit. The gravitation constant is set to one by choosing suitable measurement units.

In discrete time, the place q' of a star after a unit of time may be approximated by modifying its original place according to its velocity and acceleration:[29]

$$q'_i = q_i + v_i + b_i \qquad (4.6)$$

The smaller the time unit, the more accurate the prediction of the new place will be. Equations (4.4) – (4.6) describe the dynamics of our galaxy as long as no star collision occurs (further equations could be provided for this case). With such models, computer simulations may be performed until the limits of computing capacity are reached. The effect of a modification of initial conditions on later states of the system may be negligible if the initial modification is small enough. This need not be the case in this kind of models, but during the development of classical physics the focus was on situations where it was the case. These are the situations which lend themselves to the kind of astonishingly accurate forecasts which are the privilege of astronomy.

In physics as in other areas of study there exists a myriad of specialized research traditions. Each research tradition forms a human ecological system within the larger system of science. Clearly, such traditions may overlap and can also be embedded in each other. I do not, however, consider classical mechanics to be merely one more specialized field of research, but think of it in different terms, namely as an *integrative research tradition*. It integrates a wide variety of specialized areas of research concerned with physical phenomena by relating these phenomena to the operation of gravitation, which cannot be perceived by direct observation or by observation through instruments like microscopes.[30] We can observe a sunrise, the fall of a stone, or a moon of Jupiter, but identifying the operation of gravitation in all these phenomena is not a matter of additional observation; for this purpose it was necessary to establish an integrative research tradition, which was able to support the specialized study of these phenomena.

Newton's principles of mechanics helped to crystallize this integrative research tradition, which complements specialized research concerned, for example, with astronomy, with hydrodynamics, or with acoustics, and which enables researchers from very different fields to learn from each other and to contribute to a shared understanding of

---

[29] For an explicit treatment of physical dimensions, velocity and acceleration would need division by dimensional variables for time and squared time, respectively.

[30] In particular, the human organism has no sensory organ to perceive energy as such.

physical phenomena. An inquiry into the puzzle of human ecology[31] needs to consider integrative research traditions concerned with human beings.[32] It may therefore be helpful to examine the existence of such a tradition in the context of physics. In fact, classical mechanics was the first truly successful integrative research tradition ever established, and for a long time it remained the only one. This situation contributed to its extraordinary impact on the whole fabric of modern culture.

Classical mechanics deals with objects which at any given moment in time may be described in a satisfactory way by an array of real numbers, which correspond to possible results of empirical measurement. Change is described as motion through space. The so–called laws of motion specify how any configuration of initial conditions determines its subsequent development. This specification can be extended to cover the intervention of an external influence, for example when a human agent interferes in the internal functioning of a mechanical device. The influence of such an agent can be treated as part of the total configuration, a part which is then not further analyzed in mechanical terms.

For an inquiry into the puzzle of human ecology, it is useful to develop at least an elementary notion of the concept of equilibrium in the context of mechanical systems. If a child playing on a beach gently rolls a ball into a depression between two dunes the ball will come to rest at the bottom of the depression. To raise the ball above this level would require additional energy; equilibrium in this context means a state of minimal energy. From any place around the equilibrium point, the ball will tend to roll again into the minimal energy state: equilibrium is not only a situation which persists in the absence of external influences,

---

[31] In chapter 1, I characterized the puzzle of human ecology with the question: "How can the only species which has begun playing havoc with the biosphere learn to take care of it?"

[32] The famous concept of scientific paradigm proposed by Kuhn [159] is sometimes used to describe integrative research traditions, and so are similar concepts proposed by a large number of authors. I talk about integrative research traditions in order to distinguish them from specialized research traditions, on the one hand, and from comprehensive socio–cultural traditions, on the other hand. Kuhn uses the term paradigm not only for integrative research traditions like evolutionary biology or classical mechanics, but also for highly specialized research traditions (for example, in chemistry) and for the broad cultural tradition which in the Middle Ages offered an integrated account of Christian religion and Greek philosophy. Stegmüller [263] emphasizes the role of paradigmatic examples for the constitution of research traditions; Harré [118] discusses the ability of such traditions to identify entities such as magnetic fields, which lie beyond possible experience.

it is also a situation which tends to be restored after such influences. If the child makes a small depression on top of a dune and puts the ball there, it will again be in equilibrium. But this time the minimum energy state holds only within a very narrow range. The equilibrium is stable in its immediate local context, but it is unstable with regard to greater external impacts.

The last case illustrates a kind of situation which is quite often assumed to be characteristic of the biosphere as a whole. One also should not ignore the possibility of the child playing on a relatively flat beach, where the ball can easily be pushed around and where it will come to rest in one of the numerous small depressions making up the beach. Furthermore, there may be the danger that the child will get lost while playing with the ball, and there may be other problems as well, but in such cases the use of mechanistic metaphors will cease to be relevant.

In order to assess the significance of *mechanistic thinking* to human ecology, one must first acknowledge the fact that whereas in mechanical systems initial configurations may vary from case to case and may have to be measured ad hoc, this is not the case with the dynamic structure described by equations (4.4) through (4.6). The causal connections asserted by Newtonian mechanics are characterized by a quantitative structure which is not subject to ad hoc measurements, but is, rather, a basic feature of gravitation. It is precisely because an integrative research tradition integrates a whole series of specialized research traditions that the knowledge organized by the former does not depend on measurements which are specific to one of the latter. Instead, such knowledge depends on an overarching argument which integrates results of different specialized research traditions in order to identify underlying causal connections. When mechanistic thinking treats population dynamics and world models in analogy to physical motion, however, the causal connections underlying the dynamics of mechanical systems cease to apply.

Mechanistic thinking relies heavily on five beliefs, which are highly plausible in the context of classical mechanics. First, all relevant description takes the form of measuring and counting. Second, initial conditions may be arbitrary, but the patterns of change are not. Third, measurement data describing initial conditions, together with laws of motion, allow reliable forecasts of future conditions. Fourth, if initial conditions can be modified, future conditions may be controlled. Fifth, the behavior and development of the phenomena under study can and must be explained in terms of atomistic entities which interact with each other.

This list provides a partial description, not a strict definition. I consider mechanistic thinking to be a cultural phenomenon just like modern architecture, for example, not as an abstract discovery of a timeless human mind. At the moment I may merely illustrate it by recalling Lord Rutherford's ironic statement: "I was brought up to look at the atom as a nice hard fellow, red or grey in colour, according to taste." [33] Although this metaphor has a long lineage reaching back to ancient Greece, it has acquired paramount importance only with the development of classical mechanics as a highly successful integrative research tradition. It is in this context that the beliefs mentioned above were linked as part of a conceptual scheme which was to exercise great cultural impact.

While classical mechanics is an integrative research tradition organizing the work of scientists studying problems linked in one way or another to the effects of gravitation, mechanistic thinking is a way of framing arguments in all kinds of debates, both within and without the context of scientific inquiries. Strangely, mechanistic thinking very often seems to suggest that no integrative research tradition is needed for the study of phenomena which do not belong to the realm of mechanics. The fact that the so–called laws of motion in this realm express our knowledge of gravitation is forgotten, and the dynamics of systems where no comparable knowledge is at hand are self–confidently described on the grounds of ad hoc measurements or even simple guesses.

Mechanistic thinking was fruitful where it led to new applications of classical mechanics. This was the case in a large number of specialized research traditions, such as acoustics, hydrodynamics and statistical thermodynamics. Mechanistic thinking was also fruitful where it could be used to develop integrative research traditions other than Newtonian mechanics. This was the case in electrical engineering, where the study of electrical circuits can to a large extent be undertaken in analogy to mechanical systems (for example, networks of hydraulic pipes), but where, in fact, a very different integrative research tradition is applied. This tradition originated with Maxwell's equations for the interaction between electric and magnetic fields. These fields, which again cannot be perceived by either assisted or unassisted human senses, are used to explain a great variety of phenomena ranging from lightning to

---

[33] Quoted from Eve [75, p. 384].

magnetic effects, from solar light to radio transmission. The study of sound waves became a specialized research tradition embedded in the integrative research tradition of classical mechanics, while the study of electromagnetic waves was to become part of a very different integrative research tradition, but in both cases mechanistic thinking was instrumental to the study of the respective phenomena.

It is much less clear how fruitful mechanistic thinking is in instances where there is no integrative research tradition warranting a mechanistic description of the relevant phenomena. Consider first the case of population dynamics in biology. As we have already seen, population growth may be described in analogy to physical motion. The first belief of mechanistic thinking seems quite appropriate in the context of population studies, as both the size and the change of a population are easily expressed by natural numbers. The second belief seems much less warranted; the patterns of population growth seem to be highly contingent in a way that the laws of motion of classical mechanics are not. One could attempt to explain this away by claiming that no integrative research tradition appropriate to the study of populations of organisms has yet been found; however, I prefer to think that the research tradition of evolutionary biology, while being quite adequate for the study of living beings, does not specify quantitative laws of change which would be analogous to the laws of motion in classical mechanics. In other words, there seems to be no such thing as a set of laws of motion for biological evolution.

Still, in some respects, evolutionary biology fits in quite well with mechanistic thinking. For example, the fifth belief concerning atomism may be accommodated by treating genes as atomistic entities in a biological context (and possibly in a further step by attempting to explain their operation in chemical, and finally in physical terms). On the other hand, even in the case of purely quantitative descriptions of population dynamics, mechanistic beliefs concerning forecasting and control are vulnerable to objections from non–linear dynamics: it may be impossible to forecast and to control chaotic trajectories because the system can amplify imperceptible chance events to macroscopic dimensions.

The last point is based on the mathematical structure of the equations describing population dynamics. It is closely related to an insight concerning the physical structure of systems known from so–called non–linear thermodynamics. Consider again the second belief of mechanistic thinking mentioned above, namely the existence of causal laws independent of initial conditions. Suppose that the energy flows in some part of the biosphere could be described in detail and would be shown to follow regular patterns. This could well be possible for open systems far from thermodynamic equilibrium. But it would not mean that these patterns involve a fixed mechanism, which would remain unchanged if the initial conditions were modified. Quite the opposite: If the biosphere were to advance toward thermodynamic equilibrium, not only would the initial conditions for the dynamic patterns of the biosphere as one knows it be modified, but all dynamic patterns involving living organisms would disappear, because in a state of thermodynamic equilibrium no metabolic processes would be possible.

We need not search for a final assessment of the scope and limits of mechanistic metaphors in the context of biological ecology, but it may be useful to note that some serious limits are indeed likely to exist. In the context of human ecology, further doubts are appropriate. The second belief will hold even less for humans than for animals or plants, since the demographic growth of human populations seems to depend on complex circumstances, which can surely not be reduced to some sort of pseudo–Newtonian law of motion.

As soon as a phenomenon like global pollution is taken into consideration, even the first belief loses much of its plausibility. One may measure the amount of lead or carbon dioxide spread around the globe by humankind, but it is doubtful whether global pollution as a factor influencing demographic growth can be described adequately by any weighted index of physical measurements: it is conceivable that an adequate concept of pollution would have to incorporate cultural categories of what is considered to be dirty, dangerous, and so forth. There is little reason to assume that such categories would be amenable to quantitative treatment akin to the measurement operations of classical mechanics. The difficulties of forecasting and control may be formulated again on the grounds of non–linear dynamics, but now they are compounded by the impossibility of reducing the description of human affairs to measurement and calculation. Last but not least, the belief in atomism is highly questionable in the context of human societies.

Given these facts, the widely accepted notion that humankind is embedded in a highly complex global ecosystem, whose fragile equilibrium is threatened by human activity, loses much of its plausibility. I am, of course, far from claiming that there is no problem of global environmental disruption, but rather I am going to assert that the problem has a moral dimension, which is much less trivial than is commonly believed. In order to appreciate this, it may be helpful to consider the historical connection between the contemporary debate about environmental issues and the possibility of human self–destruction by means of nuclear warfare.

During the years immediately following the destruction of Hiroshima and Nagasaki, it had become a matter of common sense that starting a nuclear war would trigger a global catastrophe on an unprecedented scale. This belief has erected a moral barrier against the use of nuclear weapons, which, even now, has proved to be effective. Its effectiveness is, to a large extent, based on the fact that here we are dealing with a very clear–cut situation: Either humankind with all its joys and sorrows continues to exist or our world as we know it perishes. The line separating these two options is a thin one and can be crossed at any time by the performance of certain actions. It would be extremely difficult to guarantee that these actions will never be undertaken by anyone, and it seems very difficult to assess the moral legitimacy and the long run feasibility of a system of mutual threat of nuclear war designed to deter such a war. However, the moral issue involved in banning actions which would trigger a nuclear war is relatively trivial; indeed, it is on this triviality that the force of the ban relies.

In the meantime, the knowledge that the existence of humankind could be jeopardized by certain actions has become relevant with regard to ecological risks as well. This realization has given rise to the understandable attempt to identify the threshold of catastrophe. Finding a definite threshold would help to avoid the difficult moral problems which arise when no clear–cut limits exist, such as when we face a large field of possible actions involving ill–defined ecological risks with no definite limits. In this context, two points may be made about mechanistic thinking.

First, mechanistic thinking, in its cruder though quite influential version, is unable to cope with any moral problems at all. Such problems are considered to lie beyond the scope of scientific research and, therefore, of rational argument. Finding a well–defined threshold of catastrophe, which would allow us to treat ecological problems as morally trivial, would thus become imperative. Otherwise, no solution to ecological problems would be possible because of unending moral arguments about what should and should not be done.

Second, mechanistic thinking seems to indicate a way out of this impasse, because it lends prima facie plausibility to models which define the threshold of ecological catastrophe. Such models seem to be as reliable as the application of hard science in the development of modern technology. If the identification of the catastrophic threshold is not yet completely satisfactory, then what we need is more of the same, namely a hardening of the description based on better measurements, better experiments, better computations, better models of our environment—and not the study of a highly intractable subject such as the moral orders in which human beings live.

What is the relevance of mechanistic thinking to the problems of global environmental change? It was instrumental to the discovery of these problems and it may be a hindrance to their solution. An anecdote may help to explain this apparent paradox.[34] At a party, a woman tells her friend: "Do you see the man over there who is just pouring himself a glass of gin and tonic?" He nods, they approach the man and realize that it is not a man but a woman and that she is drinking vodka on the rocks. Clearly, the initial utterance was erroneous in several respects. Nevertheless, it was perfectly successful as an act of identifying a real entity which could then be described more accurately. Mechanistic thinking plays a comparable role with regard to today's environmental crisis.

Using a model with a similar structure to the one of equations (4.2) and (4.3), the Club of Rome and similar voices made claims to the general public that humankind was driving the process of demographic and economic growth beyond the earth's carrying capacity. The situation was widely perceived in mechanistic terms involving the idea of a global ecosystem whose equilibrium would be destroyed by growth paths generated by humankind. Computer simulations seemed to show that catastrophe was to be expected within the next few decades. The computations were based on highly questionable assumptions, whose plausibility was more due to the prima facie plausibility of mechanistic thinking in contemporary culture than to a sound study of the problems at hand. In general, much of the talk about ecosystems and their disruption by human beings is flawed by such assumptions. Yet the claim that humankind is actually running into major ecological problems has crystallized a growing consensus, both within the scientific community and among the general public as well.

With the benefit of hindsight, one may wonder whether the woman at the party should not have said: "Do you see that person pouring herself or himself a glass of liquid?" However, there is no guarantee that she would not then have discovered that the person was in fact a puppet. It is quite reasonable to start identifying a situation with the help of categories and descriptions which are readily available. If the identification is successful, it is not impaired by correcting what-

---

[34] The anecdote is discussed by Harré [118, p. 97].

ever errors occurred in the first place. With regard to environmental problems, mechanistic thinking helped to identify a real world situation of considerable interest. In the study of this situation, important shortcomings of mechanistic thinking must be overcome. In order to discuss the significance of such shortcomings, one needs at least a minimal understanding of the contrast between mechanistic thinking and the tradition which it helped to displace.

4.3 Tracing an Older Tradition

I will begin this section by assuming the point of view of self–confident mechanistic thinking, which was a crucial component of the Enlightenment. I will then consider the older tradition which was displaced by mechanistic thinking. This tradition can be described as a morphological cosmology, which once combined the Catholic religion with Greek philosophy. I want to argue that morphological cosmology was a stage in a comprehensive tradition of inquiry, which reaches back to the development of the Old Testament. The integrative research tradition of classical mechanics presented a major challenge to this tradition of inquiry.

To meet this challenge would have meant embedding the new research tradition in a renewed version of the more comprehensive tradition of inquiry. This did not happen, although the emergence of Protestantism pointed in such a direction. As a result, the integrative research tradition of classical mechanics developed in a kind of cultural vacuum. In this situation, mechanistic thinking became a surrogate for a comprehensive tradition of inquiry. Meanwhile, mechanistic thinking has come under attack both from within the scientific community and from various quarters in society at large. Maybe an evolutionary cosmology is in the making, which could help to embed scientific research traditions again in a more comprehensive tradition of inquiry.

How are the origins of mechanistic thinking seen from its own point of view? Galileo, so the story goes, claimed that the earth circles around the sun, while the church defended the older view, according to which the earth is at rest in the center of the universe. The older view was linked to Aristotelian physics and metaphysics and was defended by using the authority of the Bible. Aristotelian physics assumed that uniform linear motion required the continuous operation of a uniform force. Aristotelian metaphysics described a hierarchical universe governed by God, the unmoved mover. The church justified its own hierarchical structure, as well as the political hierarchy of the feudal system, by a combination of Christian theology and Greek philosophy. Sensory experience and the study of nature were downgraded by its doctrine, which blended the biblical contrast between flesh and spirit with the Platonic distinction between the world of appearances and the reign of ideas.

Galileo, following Copernicus, stated that the earth was not at rest, but in motion. According to Newton's concept of inertia, any moving body continues to move uniformly in the absence of external forces. The heroes of modern science, people like Galileo, Copernicus, and Newton, replaced Aristotelian physics with a different approach, which attempted to observe and describe facts independently of any worldly or spiritual authority or tradition. This involved much more than the mere correction of certain beliefs concerning facts of astronomy and physics. It marked the end of a comprehensive world view, which had shaped many centuries of occidental history. It also signalled the beginning of the *Enlightenment* and the abandonment of authoritarianism, superstition, and widespread misery in favor of democracy, scientific technology, and mass prosperity.

The optimistic tone of this story is challenged by rising environmental awareness. There are serious reasons for thinking that the very scientific progress so emphatically celebrated by the Enlightenment is leading humankind towards a tremendous ecological disaster. On the other hand, even the analysis of the so–called ecological crisis can hardly proceed without further scientific progress: satellites were necessary to discover the ozone hole. The Enlightenment seems to be characterized by a rather amazing, as well as dangerous, dialectic, as Horkheimer and Adorno argued during the second world war.[35] They focused on the German branch of the Enlightenment, whose most remarkable fruit is Kant's critique of pure reason. Meanwhile, another attempt to disperse the illusions generated by the Enlightenment has been undertaken by Foucault and other French authors, understandably preoccupied mainly by the French version of the Enlightenment, the "siècle des lumières".[36] In the next chapter, I will argue that the puzzle of human ecology requires a careful scrutiny of the fruits of the Enlightenment in Scotland, where it led to a major discovery, which for our discussion may be even

---

[35] Horkheimer and Adorno [130].
[36] Foucault [84].

more important than Newtonian mechanics: Adam Smith's theory of the invisible hand which coordinates the world economy.

The origins of mechanistic thinking are relevant for an assessment of the relevance of Smith's discovery to the environmental crisis of our times. I therefore need to discuss a number of topics whose relation to this crisis is not always easy to recognize. This will be all the more necessary as we cannot afford to simplify the moral dimensions of the environmental crisis along the lines of mechanistic thinking. We cannot avoid an explicit study of the ways in which classical mechanics generated a whole family of highly influential metaphors for the description of human life and of the world as a whole. Why did Newton's new physics contribute to a mechanistic thinking, which was then applied to the discussion of everything, ranging from light to chemistry, from living organisms to human affairs? In order to understand the cultural impact of mechanistic thinking, one must examine the history of the cosmology which it displaced.

There are two ways of recounting this history. I could begin with Greek philosophy and its origins in the Greek myths, and then proceed to the encounter of this tradition with Christianity. One difficulty with this approach is that the tradition of Greek philosophy was only faintly present in the Middle Ages when European monks started to read Aristotelian texts passed on to them by Moslem scholars. It is thus rather problematic to talk about one continuous tradition starting with Greek philosophy and leading to medieval scolasticism, and from there to modern philosophy. Greek philosophy actually leads to a cross–roads of traditions. There is the encounter with the Christian religion during the latter's formation, a later encounter with the world of Islam, then the contact between Christianity and Islam, in which the Greek heritage plays a major role, and finally, in more recent times, there is the formation of a specialized philosophical tradition, distinct from religion as well as from scientific research. The analysis of this network of traditions lies beyond the scope of my present inquiry.

The other possibility, of which a brief sketch will be given here, commences with the Bible. In a sense, this enhances the contrast with the Enlightenment, because thinkers like Voltaire felt much deeper respect for Greek philosophy than for Jerusalem–based religions. On the other hand, it should not be forgotten that the idea that all human beings are equal, which was so strenuously propagated by the Enlightenment, was unknown to the Greek philosophers, and actually stems from the Old Testament. As Putnam notes: "The idea of equality appears in the Jewish Bible as the idea that all human beings are created in the image of God."[37]

In a world where the earth seemed to be at the disposal of powerful kings, where slavery was as common as the right of the stronger, the Bible crystallized an alternative tradition defying such ways of life. It described its own origin as the work of divine revelation. While it espoused many of the brutalities then common, it also affirmed a notion of justice which denied the right of the stronger, both within the Jewish community and in relations with other people.

This tradition also entertained a peculiar awareness, which in modern day terms may be described by saying that there is something deeply wrong with the current state of the world, and that sooner or later this will have to be corrected. The history of the chosen people expressed a shared hope oriented toward a future in which the seemingly inescapable cycle of human atrocities would come to an end. This historical hope represented an unprecedented attitude towards the destiny of humankind, quite different from the many projects which people usually attempt to realize in their individual lives, and also quite different from the goals of conquest and glory which shaped large parts of human history.

So far, I have simply taken for granted that the existence of traditions is a fact of life, and I have begun to describe one of them. For my purposes here, the word "tradition" may be used as a synonym for "human ecological systems". Next, we need to distinguish different kinds of traditions. Earlier I talked about research traditions, both specialized and integrative. Clearly, such research traditions would be impossible without a wide range of other traditions, which enable the researchers to talk, to nourish themselves, and so on. The Jewish tradition actually includes the preservation of such things as a natural language and eating habits. Perhaps it would not have been able to survive without continuous contact with non–Jewish traditions, but it does offer a context, not just for specific activities like scientific research, but for whole human lives. In this sense, it is a comprehensive tradition which must be distinguished from partial traditions like those of scientific research.

Time and again, the biblical tradition was challenged both by the rise of internal problems and by encounters with other traditions. This is, of course, bound to be the fate of every tradition which persists for a sufficiently long time; the beliefs supported by the tradition will thus

---

[37] Putnam [225, p. 44].

rarely survive without modification. Such challenges may come to pass without any retrospective attempt ever undertaken to understand or justify the ensuing modifications. However, the growth of the biblical texts documents a process of inquiry involving a long series of just such attempts. With regard to this process, one may call the biblical tradition a *comprehensive tradition of inquiry*. This implies that it cultivated the skills of rational debate, especially in a legal context, and that it tried to identify, correct, and remember what it considered to be its own experiences of ignorance and error.[38]

A turning point in this process was reached with the writing of the New Testament, which opened the biblical tradition to all humankind. Thus, for example, the idea of human equality was intensified by the Gospel so as to undermine the legitimacy of slavery during the further course of history. The dramatic shift away from the history of the chosen people to the message of humankind's salvation led to a painful breach in the biblical heritage between the Jewish people, on the one hand, and the Catholic church, on the other—and further splits were yet to come.

It was with the Catholic version of the biblical tradition that the ideas defended by Galileo and the other pioneers of classical mechanics clashed, and it is therefore this version which we need to consider here. In this context, a crucial aspect of Catholicism is its relation to Greek philosophy. This latter tradition had already left its traces on the New Testament, where God was said to be the "word", the *"logos"* of the ancient Greeks. Few people would disagree that Greek philosophy is a tradition of inquiry. However, I would like to emphasize that this is not so much a property of some static philosophical framework as it is a dynamic aspect of a tradition, namely its ability to learn in an explicit way from its past shortcomings.

This aspect is particularly impressive in the transition from Plato to Aristotle (and a similar argument could be developed with regard to the transition from Socrates to Plato). Both Plato and Aristotle viewed a well-formed political community as closely related to individual rationality.[39] In their opinion, a rational individual will desire

---

[38] I do not distinguish between cognitive and moral errors here. This contrast is an important feature of mechanistic thinking, not of the older tradition with which I am now concerned. I would like to avoid a notion of rationality which simply assumes specific claims of mechanistic thinking. Rationality may be a matter of organizing factual knowledge, but it may also denote the search for wisdom.

[39] On this view, the political community is considered to be the highest form of social life. This involves the danger of confusing two issues discussed in chapters 2 and 3:

such a community, and without the background of at least a partially well–formed political community—such as the *polis*, the Greek city–state—no human individual can become a rational being. But what does "well–formed" mean in this context? The Greek tradition considered the whole world, the *"cosmos"*, to be well–formed in the sense that every natural being occupies the place which it deserves. A well–formed political community had to fit into the order of the cosmos. Although this idea has an obvious ecological relevance, Greek philosophy did not perceive ecological destruction (like the massive deforestation which led to soil erosion) to be a problem. What did constitute an issue was whether the citizens of a *polis* were assigned the status which they deserved, given their specific abilities and merits. One such ability of paramount importance was the capability to discuss problems in a rational manner. The structure of a *polis* had to be such that political decisions would be based on this ability: the institutions of the Persian empire were barbaric because they lacked the public debate taking place in a democratic assembly.

For Plato, a well–formed community was an ideal which could be described by philosophers without being attainable in the realm of practical politics. He tried to understand the tension between everyday reality—in which the murder of Socrates could take place—and the ideal of rational debate—to which the Athenian culture at least paid lip–service—in order to be able to take this ideal seriously. He thus distinguished between a reign of ideas and a reign of appearances. Our everyday life takes place in the dark cave of appearances, but philosophy offers a way to contemplate ideas in the light of reason. A powerful metaphor for this tension is offered by the relation between pure geometrical forms, such as a circle, and the imperfect approximation of such forms by material objects, such as a discus.

Aristotle re–defined the notion of a well–formed *polis* as a more dynamic entity. Plato had formulated his idea in a way which enabled him to criticize the actual state of affairs in Athenian politics, but he failed in his attempt to at least partially realize his ideal community in the Sicilian *polis* of Syracuse. Indeed, his way of distinguishing between ideas and appearances entails the inevitability of such failure—no stone can ever attain the perfect shape of the circle contemplated in geometry. Aristotle retained the critical potential of Plato's approach, but described a perfect political community as a *telos*, as a goal which

---

the relationship between persons and societies, and the emergence of politics in the course of cultural evolution.

can and should be reached by actual political practice. (Interestingly, this allows for the possibility that the ideal can only be hinted at, since it may be impossible to describe it in full as long as it has not yet been attained.) The relevant metaphor was no longer taken from mathematical forms, but rather from the way biological growth directs a plant towards its final shape.[40]

The tradition of inquiry embodied in Greek philosophy never developed any historical hope comparable to the one expressed by the biblical tradition, but both traditions had a remarkable critical potential. They were both able to deny the right of the stronger, because they could question a person's right to exercise specific forms of political power, and both argued that nobody was entitled to exercise absolute power. This is one reason why St. Paul could tell the Athenians that what was folly in their eyes, namely the wisdom of God, was actually the wisdom they were looking for, and that there was an awareness of God in their tradition, too. However, the encounter between the biblical and the Greek tradition occurred in a situation where the political dimensions of both traditions had become highly problematic. It had been a long time since the Greek *polis* had been destroyed by Aris-

---

[40] As philosophy has been said to consist of a series of footnotes to Plato, a footnote on the platonic flavor of logic (Wittgenstein [298, p. 89]) is in order here. For Plato, the pure forms of Geometry were paradigmatic examples of what "ideas" referred to. The "laws of thought" which were codified in Aristotle's logic can be seen in a similar way. They then appear as descriptions of perfect thought processes, of an ideal which the human mind cannot realize in our earthly existence. This view of one of Aristotle's greatest discoveries has a tremendous importance for the whole fabric of Western culture. In particular, contemporary notions of rationality as opposed to an irrational realm of emotions owe much to a picture of the human mind which emphasizes the possibilities of logical coherence discovered by Aristotle, but which ignores the step from Plato's ideas to Aristotle's notion of a *telos*. How, then, could logic be understood in a more Aristotelian way? A good start might be to consider how Aristotle treats logical coherence as a property, not just of sets of beliefs, but of sets of beliefs and actions. An example is the so–called practical syllogism, whose consequence is not a sentence, but the performance of an action. I may knock at a door as a consequence of two reasons: (1) I know that if that door is closed, I must knock before entering; (2) The door is closed and I want to enter. This pattern displays a coherence between beliefs and actions which in everyday life is the *telos* of continuing accounting conversations. Logic, then, can be seen as one way of hinting at this *telos*. Formal logic may help to check such coherence and, to some extent, even to attain it. However, coherence in this sense requires more than the absence of logical contradictions, it also means that different beliefs are connected by relations of entailment, overlap, analogy, etc., and that they help to shape a coherent life, or, in more modern terms, a personal identity. This is obviously related to the topics of accounting conversations and personal identity discussed in chapters 2 and 3.

totle's pupil Alexander the Great. The emerging Christian community
had no obvious political expression; both the Jewish and the Roman
authorities perceived it as a dangerous threat. Under these conditions,
political matters played a rather marginal role in the early synthesis
of the biblical and the Greek tradition. This may have corrected the
Greek habit of overrating politics, but it did not make it easier for the
church to come to terms with the reality of the state.

The destruction of the Jewish state by the Roman empire fostered
apocalyptic visions, which introduced the idea of revolution in occidental history.[41] The first Christians renewed the historical hope of
the Old Testament with their belief that Christ would soon return to
install the Kingdom of Heaven on earth. Furthermore, they probably
had little doubt that the Roman emperor would have to yield to this
kingdom. Since its inception, the Bible had defended political institutions formed to a greater or lesser degree within its tradition against
the danger of being overruled by the right of the stronger. Given the
destruction of the Jewish state and the hostility of Roman authorities toward the Christian community, an appeal was made to a law
which could overturn even a firmly established imperial order. It is
clear that the idea of human rights is often used in a similar spirit in
the contemporary world. Today, human ecology deals with a situation
where apocalyptic visions are proclaimed by many who do not perceive
themselves as belonging to the biblical tradition.

After a period of persecution, Christianity was accepted by the Roman empire. In this context, it encountered for the second time the
tradition of Greek philosophy. The process of inquiry stimulated by
this second confrontation was no longer documented in additions to
the Bible, but rather in separate texts like the ones written by St. Augustine. Here, I am less concerned with Augustine's theological contribution than with the fact that he helped to conceptualize the tension
between contemporary political institutions and the biblical tradition.
The latter involved a notion of justice which made it permissible to
criticize the former; but now it was conceivable for Christians to take
an active part in public life. This situation was analogous to the one
faced by Plato when he formulated his utopia while participating in the
admittedly imperfect *polis* of Athens. With the city of God in mind,
Christians could take part in the political institutions of their time in

---

[41] Under the impression of the Third Reich, Taubes [273] wrote a careful study of
the link between apocalypse and revolution. For the link between the idea of
revolution and the Jewish experience of Exodus, see Walzer [287].

a similar way as did the philosopher who participated in the public life of Athens while contemplating the realm of ideas.

St. Augustine also provided his tradition with an account of human agency involving an important innovation, which is highly relevant to human ecology. Following St. Paul, he developed a notion of human will, which was absent in Greek philosophy.[42] According to Greek philosophy, human beings act because they are moved by causes ranging from physical appetites to intellectual arguments. To which specific action these causes will lead depends, on the one hand, on external circumstances and, on the other hand, on the faculties which the person in question has been able to develop by suitable exercise and instruction. The idea of acts of will, which seems so self–evident today, played no role. This view has an important moral implication. If a human being knows what she or he should do in a given situation, then this knowledge will cause them to act accordingly, unless they are unable to do so. This lack of ability may depend on external circumstances, but may also be due to lack of training.

What would have been necessary to make Alexander the Great foster the institutions of the Greek *polis* instead of destroying them to suit the purposes of his empire? According to Aristotle, what he needed was an appropriate education which would have made him understand why it was a crime to destroy Greek democracy, along with exercises to direct his desire for power in accordance with his understanding. St. Augustine went farther than that. He took it for a fact of life that human beings are endowed with a will, which constitutes an autonomous cause of action. The human will is free to do very different things, even when they are known to be evil; nothing can force such a will to recoil from evil. What could help? According to St. Augustine, the experience of true love. There is no reason to suppose that Aristotle did not love his pupil Alexander, but while Aristotle developed an incredibly thoughtful account of the institutional setting of the Greek *polis*, he failed to recognize the threat his pupil posed to the city–state. St. Augustine probably would have been more realistic.

The biblical tradition involved ideals of equality and justice, which permitted a highly critical attitude toward the Roman authorities. When these authorities began to accept Christianity, the transformation of the Roman institutions according to those ideals failed to materialize. Gradually, the expectation of the Kingdom of Heaven was transferred from the historical future to another world. Combined with

---

[42] This point is elaborated by MacIntyre [173, p. 152ff]. See also section 2.1.

the realism with which Christianity was able to consider acts of human will, the Aristotelian understanding of an ideal as a *telos* could have proved helpful. Catholicism, however, had no access to the Aristotelian texts until the 13th century.

The encounter with Aristotelian philosophy took place in the Middle Ages through the mediation of Moslem scholars, who read and discussed Aristotle's texts long after Greek thinkers had ceased to occupy themselves with the tradition of philosophy. For the Catholic church, the newly discovered Aristotelian doctrines were hard to reconcile with the ideas which it had developed thanks to the contributions of St. Augustine and others. It was the great achievement of St. Thomas Aquinas to overcome this contradiction.

The Platonic heritage tends to neglect our bodily existence and our everyday activities for the sake of the contemplative life, the *vita contemplativa*, directed towards a higher, eternal reality, which the material world obfuscates.[43] Aquinas by no means refused contemplation. In a Christian context, he insisted on the Aristotelian notion of happiness as the contemplation of God. He chose to join one of the monastic orders, which in his time emerged as a reaction to the feudal power and wealth of the established church. From Aristotle, however, he derived a respect for the world of the senses, and therefore also for the life of action, the *vita activa*, which engages us in this world. This led him to defend the *vita mixta* of those who, inspired by contemplative experiences, intervened actively in the world of their time.

The idealization of a contemplative life by feudal elites clearly implied that others had to carry the burden of labor. While the Bible proclaimed that labor was the condition of humankind banned from paradise, a Neo–Platonic vision of contemplation contributed to the perpetuation of this condition, rather than offering salvation from it. Aquinas moved in another direction: The opposition of action and contemplation was to be transformed in ways which were unknown both to St. Augustine and to Aristotle. However, whereas Aquinas indicated the importance of such a transformation in the context of personal existence, he did not inquire very much into its relevance to social institutions. This is not to say that he was blind to questions of social justice. It is quite important to note that in his view, justice puts clear limits on property rights. He had little doubt that the poor are entitled to avoid starvation by using the stocks of their wealthy neighbors.

---

[43] For a comparison between the Platonic and the Aristotelian approach to contemplation, i.e., *theoria*, see Huber [135].

What Aquinas did not ask was how to transform the idea of human equality into a historical goal, how to set up social institutions which would be better suited than the feudal ones to the vision of the *vita mixta*.

An important reason for this shortcoming was the way Aquinas embedded the concept of a *telos* in a metaphysical scheme which combined Aristotelian natural philosophy with a literal reading of the Bible's account of the creation of the world. In Aquinas' view, every being—be it a natural species, like trees, or an individual being, like the tree in front of my window—has an essence, a nature, which is its idea as conceived by divine providence. This idea is the being's *telos*, which it strives to realize: The inconspicuous seed gradually grows until it becomes a majestic tree. If one takes the liberty to use the Platonic notion of a form, a *"morphe"*, in this transformed sense too, then one may say that medieval Catholicism elaborated a *morphological cosmology* inspired by Greek philosophy. This cosmology clearly was the major result of a comprehensive tradition of inquiry, and whatever its shortcomings, it surely preserved many of the best fruits of this inquiry.

However, morphological cosmology was not very helpful in inventing new institutions, because it had little to say about the links between human creativity and social reality. In a sense, this cosmology takes its point of departure from the situation of a man who builds a house according to a plan which he has made for it. This situation is considered to be analogical to the creation of the universe by God, and the idea of a house becomes part of God's plan. The *telos* of house–building, then, is to realize God's idea of a house. Because in God's plan every human being is assigned some place in human society, the good life involves finding one's place in society.

This account pays little attention to the fact that human activities like the building of a house differ, for example, from animal nest–making, since human activities presuppose social settings which define possible goals and standards of excellence for the given activities. Human creativity is embedded in a social context, which affords possible goals, and it can occasionally transform this context so that other goals become possible. Such a thought was hard to reconcile with the basic tenets of morphological cosmology. This is not to say that the medieval scholars were not creative, but their creativity did not reach far enough to design a historical project which would have restored the biblical sense of hope.

Morphological cosmology saw the invention of something new as the discovery of a pre–existing idea and considered the transformation of both natural beings and human artifacts as being governed by the *telos* set by such ideas. One may wonder whether such a cosmology is therefore committed to a basically intolerant approach towards the variety of ways of life developed by humankind. After all, if the *telos* of humankind is to realize a pre–existing idea, it is hard to see how different ways of life could coexist peacefully, unless they were explicitly integrated into the one right way of life defined for human beings.

To discuss this question in detail would require an analysis of the struggle between medieval Christianity and the expanding world of Islam—a struggle which left little opportunity to develop the virtue of tolerance. Important as such a discussion would be for its own sake, it would distract us from the task of assessing the relevance of mechanistic thinking to human ecology. What we do need for this purpose, and what I have attempted to sketch in the foregoing paragraphs, is a minimal description of the comprehensive tradition of inquiry which was able to merge Christian religion with Greek philosophy. It is this tradition which was challenged by the emergence of an integrative research tradition concerned with mechanical systems.

Galileo, Copernicus, Newton, and the other pioneers of classical mechanics were enthusiastic about the prospects of a scientific tradition which, in its conceptual elegance, resembled a jewel of Greek culture, the geometry elaborated by Pythagoras, Thales, Euclid, and others. Geometry, understood as a study of pure forms, fit well into the image of the world conceived by morphological cosmology. Things are more complicated in the case of physics. Morphological cosmology comprised valuable physical knowledge, contributed by Aristotle, Ptolemaeus, Archimedes, etc. This knowledge was often related to the movement of physical bodies through a viscous medium. Uniform linear motion then requires the operation of a constant moving force; heavy bodies sink while light ones rise. Such observations were used as metaphors to illustrate how every being tries to find its place in the world. The place of the earth, around which the sun and the stars circle, was in the center of the universe.

These observations and metaphors did not form a coherent body of knowledge referring to physical phenomena. Rather, knowledge about physics was scattered in different places in the comprehensive fabric of morphological cosmology, where it was instrumental in the generation of metaphors referring to metaphysical entities. Similar metaphors were generated by the observation of living beings growing into their final shape. From the perspective of morphological cosmology, the world is organized by a hierarchy of forms, which provide every being with its goal. The "good life" of human beings is directed by such forms much as is a plant blossoming in the sun, or a stone slowly sinking to the bottom of the sea. The fact that human actions are governed by socially shared standards of excellence, as well as by individual goals, is set in analogy with the way nature is moved by God, the unmoved mover.

It is therefore quite misleading to directly contrast the scientific research tradition of classical mechanics with "Aristotelian physics". What one must consider instead is the relationship between a comprehensive tradition of inquiry and a newly emerging integrative research tradition concerned with physical reality. In the context of the biblical tradition, there was no such thing as an integrative research tradition; what we would today call scientific knowledge consisted of scattered elements of a comprehensive tradition of inquiry. This was also true for the philosophical tradition which originated in the Greek *polis*.

Why, then, could classical mechanics not be integrated into the broader context of the biblical tradition of inquiry? As a matter of fact, it is not evident that this could not have happened; all we do know is that it did not happen. Clearly, classical mechanics represented a major challenge to morphological cosmology. A whole series of metaphors, which were used in this cosmology, collapsed. The idea of natural events governed by forms, which were to be realized in the future, was discarded. Instead, natural events were explained by referring to earlier events, whose consequences could be determined according to scientifically established laws. Moreover, the plausibility of a literal interpretation of the Bible was shaken, at least as far as astronomy was concerned. For Catholicism, there was no way of meeting this challenge without being transformed substantially. As I have already mentioned, such experiences of learning are inevitable for any tradition of inquiry; the biblical tradition had gone through a number of such episodes during its complex encounters with Greek philosophy.[44] This

---

[44] MacIntyre [174] has re-constructed the Aristotelian notion of a *telos* of human actions by considering how any such *telos* relies on the social embeddedness of human action. This allows for an Aristotelian approach to the moral dimensions of human action which is not hampered by the shortcomings of Aristotle's views on biology and physics. Could Catholicism have answered the challenge of modern science by elaborating such an approach? This depends, in part, on the question of whether an analogy between socially embedded human creativity and the creativity of the single God of the Bible could make sense. The doctrine of Trinity as a union of divine persons could have enabled medieval thinkers to develop such an analogy. I mention this possibility to emphasize that I do not at all claim that the breakdown of morphological cosmology was inevitable; I only

time the outcome was different: instead of being transformed, morphological cosmology became a rigid scheme, which lost contact with contemporary common sense.

What one needs to understand is not simply why classical mechanics presented a challenge to morphological cosmology, but also why the tradition of inquiry which had expressed this cosmology failed to integrate classical mechanics into its own much broader context. To answer this question, one must consider the additional fact that while the newly emerging integrative research tradition in physics did not challenge Catholicism on its own ground, the establishment of Protestant churches did. 1564, the year in which Galileo was born in Pisa, was also the year of Calvin's decease. By that time, Lutheran and Anglican churches had been firmly established. Why should the emergence of *Protestantism* be relevant in the context of human ecology? First of all, because it is part of the cultural crisis without which classical mechanics would hardly have inspired mechanistic thinking. Moreover, one should remember Weber's thesis that the "spirit of capitalism" relies on the Protestant ethic—and the spirit of capitalism is far from irrelevant to the dynamics of global environmental change.[45]

I have already mentioned this theme in chapter 3; here I should note that Thomas More, Henry VIII's antagonist, actually identified the crucial point of the crisis of Catholicism in his novel "about the optimal state of public affairs and the new island of utopia". Had Catholicism taken utopian thinking seriously enough to restore the historical hope which characterized its origins, the Protestant movement might well have contributed to advances in the Catholic church's process of inquiry instead of leading to its standstill. One may, however, also point out that Henry VIII did not renew that historical hope, either. Some of the Protestant movements on the European continent tried restoring the utopian spirit, but even these attempts did not really revitalize the historical hope in their time.

As a result, when morphological cosmology was challenged by classical mechanics, it was already ceasing to operate as a plausible expression of a comprehensive tradition of inquiry. The resistance of the Catholic church against the development of the new integrative research tradition was a sign of much deeper decay. Morphological cosmology had degenerated to a matter of endless philosophical disputes, and there seemed to be no longer any comprehensive tradition of inquiry

---

claim that this breakdown greatly contributed to the development of mechanistic thinking.

[45] Weber [289].

into which an integrative tradition of scientific research could have been embedded. The science of physics developed in a cultural vacuum, or, to put it in sociological terms, the new scientific institutions emerged into a highly anomic society.

Under these circumstances, one might say that in a sense the new integrative research tradition usurped the role of a much more comprehensive tradition of inquiry. The exciting discovery of mechanical systems was exaggerated into the belief that the whole world is made up of mechanical systems. This characterizes the relationship between classical mechanics and mechanistic thinking. In this situation, the study of systems which cannot be described adequately in mechanistic terms became a particularly difficult endeavor; and we have every reason to think that human ecological systems belong precisely in this category.

The atomism of mechanistic thinking was intimately related to the rise of individualism, which is so characteristic of modern history. There is a strong analogy between the explanation of natural events in terms of the movements of atomistic particles and the reduction of social reality to the activities of atomistic individuals.[46] It is quite obvious that such an individualism can be developed in a highly egalitarian spirit: no king or queen is entitled to ignore the will of his or her fellow citizens in the name of an independently existing authority. In the context of the Enlightenment, mechanistic thinking actually became the heir of the utopian ideal which the biblical tradition had made possible, but which it had subsequently neglected. Any critique of mechanistic thinking has to respect the effort of the Enlightenment to take seriously the historical task set by the ideal of human equality.

Discussing cultural regeneration in the context of today's environmental crisis makes little sense without taking into account the ambiguities of the Enlightenment: on the one hand, the atomistic view of nature, which fits in well with an individualistic view of society, on the other hand, the moral claims of equality and freedom, which can hardly be stated in a sensible way if moral orders are not allowed to form a legitimate subject of scientific research. Nobody expressed this tension more dramatically than Kant with his distinction between the world of experience, which is accessible to scientific knowledge, and the noumenal world of things in themselves. It is precisely because he tried to endure

---

[46] Freudenthal [88] offers a remarkable inquiry concerning the relationships between atomism and individualism.

this tension without resorting to inadequate solutions that he prepared the ground for a search leading well beyond mechanistic thinking.[47]

This search is inspired by the hope, shared by Kant, Lessing, and many others, that though there may be many churches, there is only one religion. Calling this not just a belief, but a hope, emphasizes the reality that until now mutual understanding between, say, Jews, Moslems and Christians has not been attained, as is evidenced by the on–going violence in the area surrounding Jerusalem. The history of the last few centuries has convincingly demonstrated that secularization does not hinder the perpetuation of warfare either. What Kant was advocating was not the convenient attitude of ignoring religious differences on the ground that religion makes no difference anyway. Rather, he tried to contribute to the historical growth of tolerance and mutual understanding which would enable humankind to put an end to warfare. Such mutual understanding would actually constitute a tradition of inquiry shared by all humankind—without having to eliminate the existence of the different churches or of the different languages. The development of such a tradition is precluded, however, as long as mechanistic thinking prevents us from appreciating the tradition of inquiry which once expressed morphological cosmology.[48] Combining that tradition with insights which science, philosophy, and religion have produced in different contexts still remains a fascinating challenge.

In the Germany of the 1930's, which was becoming an arena of unprecedented collective madness, Husserl searched for a way beyond mechanistic thinking in his discussion of the crisis of the European sciences.[49] Two decades earlier, in the trenches where the disintegration of the Austro–Hungarian empire was consummated, Wittgenstein prepared his first contribution to the same search, based on the feeling that even if all scientific questions could be answered, our real problems would still remain untouched.[50] Eventually, this led Wittgenstein to a forceful critique of mechanistic thinking, which involved a radical re–assessment of the philosophical heritage resulting from Plato's view of mathematical ideas.[51] While such philosophical arguments are discussed mainly in specialist circles, mechanistic thinking has come

---

[47] This view of Kant owes much to Putnam [225].
[48] Such an appreciation could be facilitated by a theology of a "sociable divinity" (Marti [181]; Buber [40]; and also Jonas [150]), which is currently discussed by feminist authors (Heyward [129]).
[49] Husserl [139].
[50] Wittgenstein [297, p. 73].
[51] See Shanker [253] and Bouveresse [34].

under attack from a strong current of public opinion as well. There are obvious signs of growing mistrust of technical solutions proposed by scientific experts, and this apprehension is nurtured by the repeated experience of the unexpected negative side effects brought about by technical innovations.

The strength which the criticism of mechanistic thinking has gained during the 20th century is also due to the fact that physicists themselves lost their confidence that sooner or later all natural phenomena could be explained in terms of classical mechanics.[52] The development of electrodynamics by Maxwell and others was a major step along this road.[53] Electrodynamics is an integrative research tradition as elegant and powerful as classical mechanics, and it is impossible to reduce the former to the latter. Besides the reality of material bodies, there is also a reality of electrical and magnetic fields, which follow their own laws. The attempt to find a common framework which could accommodate both mechanics and electrodynamics inspired not one but two integrative research traditions: relativity theory and quantum mechanics.

Physicists are still struggling to formulate a grand unified theory, which would afford them a unique integrative research tradition. Even if they should succeed, however, it would be difficult to revive mechanistic thinking. The history of science has led to the important and influential experience that integrative research traditions can coexist as well as be transformed and supplanted. This fact gains additional relevance when evolutionary biology is taken into consideration, as this integrative research tradition was consolidated quite independently of the upheavals taking place in theoretical physics.

In fact, the discovery of biological evolution seems to offer an alternative to mechanistic thinking. Attempts to develop an *evolutionary cosmology* depict the evolution of life as a major episode in the process of cosmic evolution. According to this view, the universe we live in has a limited age, which can be assessed more or less accurately. In the course of time, the universe separated into molecules, planets, and galaxies; on one such planet, life started evolving. This view of natural history is widely accepted as a common framework within which specific scientific studies can be endeavoured.

Evolutionary cosmology is not atomistic; the combination of elements into more comprehensive wholes simultaneously represents a differentiation of yet larger wholes into more varied parts. In such a

---

[52] For a recent assessment cf. Primas [224].

[53] The importance of this step is emphasized, for example, by Hund [138] and Whitehead [293].

context, the process of cosmic evolution is seen as a sequence of unique events, during which new realities emerge. The development of non–linear thermodynamics has been quite influential here, because it offers examples of macroscopic systems which come into existence thanks to the amplification of random events occurring on a microscopic scale. Recently, several authors have suggested that some version of evolutionary cosmology should become the world–view of the future.[54]

However, there is a serious danger in criticizing mechanistic thinking in the name of a new world–view, such as evolutionary cosmology, and then attempting to use this world–view as a master key, which would allow us to solve historical problems like the puzzle of human ecology straightaway. Such an approach ignores the need to take integrative research traditions seriously, and it regards as obsolete the search for a tradition of inquiry which would embed scientific research into a more comprehensive cultural context. As long as mutual understanding between human beings is so feeble as to allow wars, it is pretentious to claim implicitly or explicitly that further efforts to renew a comprehensive tradition of inquiry are obsolete.[55] And if we remember that mechanistic thinking was inspired by the development of classical mechanics, we have little reason to think that the development of a comprehensive tradition of inquiry could take place independently of the development of integrative research traditions.

4.4   Ecosystems and Moral Orders

The study of environmental problems often relies on a core concept which can be framed both in terms of mechanistic thinking and in terms of an evolutionary cosmology: the concept of an ecosystem. Obviously, this notion has a major role to play in biological ecology. However,

---

[54] Jantsch [148] offers a highly speculative view on these matters. Nicolis and Prigogine [199] proceed more cautiously in a similar direction.

[55] Evolutionary cosmology is probably the most interesting, though by no means the only, inducement for such pretension. General systems theory, which in its newer versions is often combined with an evolutionary world view, has claimed since its beginnings to provide an alternative to mechanistic thinking. Talking about self–organizing systems can indeed help to avoid some of the pitfalls of mechanistic thinking, but systems terminology still lends itself quite well to mechanistic arguments. With regard to human ecology, the theory of general systems—or any other theoretical construct—fails whenever it is supposed to render obsolete two crucial and interrelated tasks: the search for a tradition of inquiry offering a reasonable cultural context for scientific research, and the careful study of integrative research traditions referring to human ecological systems.

talking about ecosystems can become rather superficial when their development is not related to biological evolution. Therefore, in this section I will also consider evolutionary biology as an integrative research tradition. This will lead me to argue that the relation between the development of ecosystems and biological evolution is more complex and also more controversial than might be expected. In particular, it does not seem possible to decide whether human interference in biophysical processes is acceptable or not by relying simply on the results presented by the natural sciences. Instead, one has to engage in a careful study of moral orders as well. This is all the more appropriate as the existence of moral orders based on interdependent cultural rules marks a major difference between human ecological systems and purely biophysical ecosystems.

The study of *ecosystems* originated in plant ecology. The concept was proposed explicitly for the first time by Tansley in a paper on "The use and abuse of vegetational concepts and terms".[56] Meanwhile, the term "ecosystem" has found widespread use and abuse, too. It refers first of all to states such as found in a tundra where populations of different plant species coexist on a common ground in more or less stable ways. Such situations have specific names in many languages, "tundra" being one of them. Specialists of various disciplines—including botanists, foresters, geographers, and soil scientists—have studied these kinds of situations under different headings.[57]

An important reason for the acceptance of the idea of ecosystems was its affinity to the notion of ecological equilibrium. Several decades before Tansley introduced the term ecosystem into scientific debate, plant ecologists had begun to study how on certain soils plant populations succeed one another in an orderly fashion. Such a succession can eventually lead to situations where the various plant populations are more or less stable. This so–called climax is often conceptualized as a state of ecological equilibrium. Ecosystems may be characterized not only by their climax state, but also by the processes of succession which lead to the climax.

The notion of an ecosystem is used differently by different authors. Here I am interested in four attributes which are often ascribed to

---

[56] Tansley [272].

[57] As an illustration, consider the notion of "biochore" used by the Swiss soil scientist Pallmann [205]. This notion helped to organize a research tradition about which two decades later Major [175, p. 13] was to write: "Present Swiss plant ecology is a splendid example of the acceptance and use of the ecosystem idea."

ecosystems. First, such systems involve populations of organisms living in a shared environment. An example are the animals, plants, and microorganisms living in the Amazonian rain forest. An important connection between these populations is quite often established by the existence of food webs. Second, the shared environment is delimited by boundaries in physical space. For example, the boundaries of a rain forest are its edges, the canopy layer on its surface, and the ground on which it stands. Ecosystems are not isolated from the rest of the world, they are open systems. Their boundaries are crossed by flows of energy and matter, as well as by migrating organisms. If some portion of physical space works as a boundary, this is shown precisely by the fact that relevant flows cross it in systematic and not in purely random ways.

Third, ecosystems have equilibrium states in which whole sets of physical and biological variables—including proportions between the relevant populations, as well as geographical distributions and densities of these populations—are maintained either through cyclical patterns or as steady states. In the case of rain forests, such equilibria have been maintained for millions of years. Fourth, these equilibria are climax states toward which characteristic paths of ecosystem development converge. Rain forests were formed along such paths long before human beings came into existence. While there is a convergence toward equilibrium along these paths, there need not be any convergence towards equilibrium when states which do not lie on these paths occur: if human beings clear a major portion of a rain forest, processes of erosion can make a spontaneous regeneration of the forest totally impossible.

Once one accepts that ecosystems characterized with the above mentioned four features do exist, one may think of them in two very different ways. First, one could hold the existence of ecosystems to be a remarkable but rather exceptional fact, on a par with phenomena such as the aurora. Secondly, one could consider them to be a fundamental condition of all living beings, much as gravitation seems to be a basic feature of all matter. Of course the truth could also lie somewhere between these two extremes. However, Tansley thought that ecosystems were actually the basic units in which all life is organized.[58]

This thought was taken up by E. Odum, who generalized the notions of succession and climax in order to identify "The Strategy of Ecosys-

---

[58] The idea of "Ecosystem as the basic unit in ecology" was explicitly proposed in an influential note by Evans [74].

tem Development".[59] He suggested that biological reality is characterized by a set of interrelated processes of growth and of the combination
of biological populations under various environmental conditions. In
his view, these processes define a strategy under which, in a given
spatial setting, biomass accumulates through a succession of different
populations until a maximum is reached by some hierarchy of populations with a dominant species on top. Humankind's current ecological
problems could be solved if we stopped disrupting this strategy, which
has been developed by nature itself. One can, however, seriously doubt
whether the indicated strategy actually describes a general rule. Of
course, even if this were not the case, one could still ask whether the
life of organisms is embedded in some general pattern of ecosystem development, which we should learn to respect. However, developmental
models of ecosystems may be appropriate in some cases, while being
quite misleading in others.[60] Therefore, one should be well aware of
the fact that the notion of a general strategy of ecosystem development
represents a sweeping generalization from certain plant populations to
all kinds of life, including human existence.

This is not to deny that there is something which all living beings
have in common. Yet as far as we know, what living beings do share
is not the membership in ecosystems, nor is it some individual property which could be described as life. Rather, it is the participation
in the vast process of *biological evolution*. This process cannot be observed directly, but rather it is identified with the help of some standard examples of phenomena such as fossil records, which can hardly
be explained except as results of genetic variation and environmental
selection. The discovery and explanation of evolution are associated
with the work of Lamarck, Darwin, and other pioneers of modern biology. This work helped to crystallize an integrative research tradition
which complements specialized research concerned, for example, with
plant morphology or molecular genetics. Unlike integrative research
traditions in physics, the research tradition concerned with biological
evolution is not framed in mathematical language (although mathematics is used in many of its applications). Moreover, it is very weak
at forecasting. Nevertheless, thanks to its main achievement, it has
had a tremendous cultural impact. It has succeeded in connecting
scattered evidence about organisms which died long ago with findings

---

[59] E. Odum [201].
[60] See Drury and Nisbet [62] for a similar argument.

about contemporary living beings in such a way as to explain past steps of biological evolution.

Nobody pretends that evolutionary biology could explain everything about the process of biological evolution just because it is able to identify it. One must merely keep in mind that this process involves a specific interplay of variation with selection. This interplay has led time and again to astonishing correspondences between various environments and the organisms which inhabit them. Much talk about ecosystems is an attempt to emphasize such correspondences. If the word ecosystem is taken in such a loose sense, one may indeed say that being a member of an ecosystem is a common feature of all living beings. This term then denotes the fact that the process of biological evolution produces organisms which fit into specific, but often interlocked, environments.

Given this background, the current environmental crisis can be approached by asking whether humankind is destroying such correspondences in a multitude of situations. Presently, mass extinction of species is taking place on earth because humankind is destroying the environments into which the concerned species fit. Furthermore, human beings possess the ability to produce comprehensive synthetic environments for which biological evolution has made no provision. These developments are highly problematic, because they deprive humankind of the company of plants and animals which were part of our original habitats. We may already be caught in a trap which we have constructed ourselves. One would expect increasing emotional and behavioral disturbances from organisms finding themselves in an environment for which evolution has not prepared them. Are we not facing such disturbances both in everyday experience and in the frightening events of recent human history? These conjectures can at least help us in our study of human ecology, but they are by no means linked to the existence of ecosystems in a more specific sense. The process of biological evolution implies a general relevance of ecosystems only if we use the notion of an ecosystem to focus on the correspondences between an organism and its specific environment.

If, however, the concept of an "ecosystem" denotes situations where populations of different species share a common environment in a stable way, then we should not expect biological evolution to necessarily lead to the establishment of ecosystems. To see why this is so, it may be useful to recall some of the basic features of the process of biological evolution. This process involves organisms which have a limited life–span and which are capable of biological reproduction. The lifetime of different organisms varies depending on genetic factors and on environmental conditions. The number of offspring which an organism can have in a given period of time is influenced both by environmental conditions and by genetic factors. Environmental conditions may change suddenly, but in general the changes take greater intervals of time than the rhythm of biological generations. Occasionally, new genetic properties emerge. Environmental conditions will lead to the selection of those properties which present a reproductive advantage— either because they increase average lifetime or because they increase reproduction frequency.

Darwin described this process by using the example of animals which migrated from the South American continent to the Galàpagos islands, and which adapted themselves to the new environmental conditions by gradual change, stretching from generation to generation. Should this example be used as a paradigmatic instance of biological evolution, then the fact that these islands are relatively small territories with obvious physical boundaries must be bracketed. According to Darwin, evolution is supposed to take place on the Asian continent as well. If one looks at the geographical distribution of various populations of plants and animals, one usually finds that their boundaries do not coincide. In one region, plant A coexists with plant B, while in another region, with plant C. Under such conditions, talk about ecosystems can become quite misleading, and it may be better to focus on the way in which evolution leads to correspondences between each species and its specific environment. Where ecosystems cannot be identified in terms of geographical boundaries, one should not expect the steady states or recurrent cycles of the ecological equilibria associated with such systems. Rather, one may find unending shifts and changes in the size and distribution of the various populations. In fact, such situations may arise even on a small island with neat boundaries.

How, then, does the development of ecosystems fit into an evolutionary framework? To deal with this problem, Bateson assumed that organisms are not the only elements of biological evolution.[61] Rather, he proposed to substitute ecosystems for organisms as evolutionary units. An organism, after all, is part of the environment of another organism, so the evolution of different organisms may be interdependent. Instead of speaking of an evolution of species, Bateson therefore tends to emphasize what may be called the co–evolution of ecosystems. In support of this substitution for organisms as evolutionary units, one

---

[61] Bateson [16, p. 425–426].

may mention that not only organisms, but also genes seem to behave as elements of evolutionary processes. One may picture evolution as a multi–levelled process, with the evolution of genes occurring at a low level, the evolution of organisms at an intermediate level, and the evolution of species at a yet higher one.[62]

Given this view, all three layers of evolution exhibit the characteristic distinction between variation and selection. Environmental conditions cause the latter, while the former is a matter of genetic processes which are largely screened from environmental conditions. Without this separation, all kinds of processes could take place, but not biological evolution. Bateson's argument is important here precisely because it emphasizes that any attempt to treat ecosystems as the basic units of ecology runs into the difficulty that the development of ecosystems is by no means a necessary consequence of biological evolution.

This is not to say that the difficulty is insurmountable.[63] The point is that we face here unsettled questions of biology, which we will have to leave unresolved. This, however, requires some caution. Accordingly, I will consider ecosystems to be an important biological phenomenon, though not to be the organizing principle of the biophysical environment in which humankind has evolved.[64] The discovery that ecosystems exist, and that many of them are actually being destroyed by human activity, is crucial to the puzzle of human ecology; it is not, however, the key to its solution.

The Lake of Zurich is said to be an ecosystem, and so is the Amazonian rain forest. The latter is not expected to survive much longer; around the globe, the ecosystems of rain forests are threatened by human activities. There is, however, a great difference between saying that people clear a forest and asserting that humans destroy an ecosystem. The two phrases have different moral connotations. Interestingly, the concept of an ecosystem lends itself quite well to arousing moral feelings. Is this an unwarranted collusion between scientific analysis and ethical issues? I argue that this is not the case. If one wants to be able to tackle the puzzle of human ecology, one must accept the fact that now, towards the end of the twentieth century, the disappearance of forests has become a moral issue. Solving the puzzle will hardly

---

[62] The possibility of evolution as a multi–levelled process is discussed by Gould [103, p. 173ff].

[63] Bateson [16] elaborated a rather sophisticated argument to overcome the difficulty in question. Freese [85] proposes a different approach to the same problem.

[64] The same position is defended by Smith [259].

be possible without studying the rather obscure connections between ecosystems and *moral orders.*

The reason for the obscurity can best be explained by pointing to the fact that even when the familiar distinction between value judgements and descriptive propositions is sharply drawn, one is still allowed to combine the two types of judgements in such a way as to maintain the belief that humankind ought not to destroy natural ecosystems while it is actually doing so. Let us imagine a society in which sentences would be classified as falling unambiguously into either the descriptive or the normative category. Under such conditions, normative conclusions could obviously be drawn from normative premises, but not from sets of purely descriptive sentences. They could, however, also follow from a combination of descriptive and normative sentences. If, in such a combined argument, some of the descriptive premises were modified, different normative conclusions would follow in a perfectly coherent way.

Suppose the society in question widely espoused the normative belief that self–interest is a positive value, requiring every individual to attempt to preserve his or her individual existence and also requiring humankind to try to preserve its existence as a species. These beliefs would not only justify each individual's struggle for survival, but also the search by superpowers for compromises to avoid nuclear war. Still, the society in question could be destroying its natural environment in numerous ways without considering this to be a serious problem. If, however, researchers made purely descriptive claims stating that natural ecosystems exist, that they had been in equilibrium until humankind had started disrupting them, and that furthermore this latter process is threatening individual existences because it leads to new epidemics, famines, etc., and finally that the process is accelerating to such an extent as to threaten the very existence of humankind, then these claims would generate a serious moral problem.

The problem could be avoided by transforming the existing moral order in such a way that both individual and collective self–destruction would become perfectly acceptable. However, as long as such a transformation is not undertaken, the problem would evoke a different response: scientists would be asked to inform the public about the necessary conditions for the maintenance of the equilibrium of various natural ecosystems so that appropriate policy measures could be implemented to preserve or to restore these conditions. One could expect scientists to be quite pleased with this prospect, as it would increase their social prestige and improve their financial resources. On the whole, this development would presumably lead to the belief that the preservation of ecosystems is a morally good thing, while their disruption is morally bad. In such a framework, what would need to be studied in order to solve the puzzle of human ecology would not be the moral orders involved in human existence but the ecosystems making up humankind's environment. Such an approach is quite influential in contemporary societies. Without being modified in its normative core, a moral order emphasizing self–interest is sometimes applied to ecology by introducing the notion of an ecosystem.

If, in a society largely governed by self–interest, a moral problem arises because researchers claim that humankind is threatening itself by destroying natural ecosystems, then one must face the possibility that the researchers are exaggerating their case. Perhaps the existence of ecosystems is not such a fundamental feature of the biosphere that the destruction of even a great number of them would make the earth uninhabitable for human beings. Long before the appearance of humankind, large ecosystems, such as the forests which were transformed into coal, disappeared. If human beings destroy tropical forests, this may be deplorable for a number of important reasons, but it need not pose a threat to human existence. The same holds true with regard to the extinction of species. Dinosaurs disappeared for reasons which had nothing to do with human beings, and yet the biosphere continued to evolve. If now human beings are causing the extinction of other species, this need not deprive humankind of its habitat.

It all then comes to a question of degree. Which ecosystems can be damaged, and to what extent, without threatening human self–interest? How many species can we exterminate without endangering ourselves? Similar questions can be asked even at the purely physical level. How much carbon dioxide can humankind discharge into the atmosphere without incurring unacceptable risks of climatic change? Obviously, a possible answer involves arguing that more environmental research is required in order to assess these questions. Does it really make sense, however, to carry out such research without devoting a similar effort to the study of moral orders, without which we would not even have the notion of an unacceptable risk?

As the discussion of cultural rules in chapter 2 indicates, the existence of moral orders is a major feature of human ecological systems, i.e., ecosystems involving human beings and their biophysical environment. Surprisingly, perhaps, the difficulties which we encountered when examining the notion of an ecosystem in a biological context are less threatening with regard to human ecological systems. In a seminal study, Rappaport identified such systems by considering the boundaries drawn by the members of certain tribes.[65] The conclusions of his study were quite controversial, but his method remains perfectly sensible. Human beings are territorial animals and they have many effective ways of drawing boundaries. Nations, for example, consist of people with shared traditions and a territory with boundaries known to the inhabitants as well as to the neighbors. Boundaries can be fuzzy, they can shift, be contested, and misused, but they are a fact of life. This is true not only for nations, but also for households or for businesses, to mention only a few such cases. One should not doubt the existence of human ecological systems just because they can be disconnected in space and time—as may be seen from the example of a multinational company, which operates plants all over the world.

A garden, as such, is no human ecological system, but a city like Hong Kong is, as is a village with its fields, pastures, and woodlands.[66] The latter example refers to what is often called a cultural landscape, but nobody would use that label for the biosphere as a whole. However, one of the most important developments of the 20th century, and one intimately related to human ecology, is the fact that the biosphere has actually become a human ecological system. Its future fate depends crucially on the present behavior of humankind. There may have been a time when human ecological systems were embedded in natural ecosystems; today the opposite is the case: all existing natural ecosystems are increasingly embedded in the global human ecological system. This is a result of the dynamics of the global economy which has emerged with the second step of cultural evolution. Analyzing this dynamic in the context of cultural evolution is the task of the next chapter.

---

[65] Rappaport [229].
[66] Hong-Kong has been studied in a human–ecological framework by Boyden et al. [38], a remarkable study of a mountain village has been realized by Bachmann-Voegelin [11].

The great lights of commercial juris-
prudence, international confraternity,
and biological deviation, of all ages,
all civilizations, and all nationalities,
from Zoroaster down to Horace Gree-
ley, have (...) wrestled with this great
subject, and the greatest among them
have found it a worthy adversary, and
one that always comes up fresh and
smiling after every throw.

Mark Twain, Political Economy.

Chapter 5

Transforming the Economy[1]

Eco–eco problems, that is, problems situated at the interface between
economy and ecology, can be analyzed by trying to include ecological
phenomena into the highly elaborated theoretical apparatus provided
by the discipline of economics.[2] This is the strategy usually followed
by environmental economists.[3] Conversely, one can try to include economic phenomena in the framework of ecological analysis, especially in
conjunction with systems theory. This is the way of thinking which
has led to the well known debate about limits to growth. Both approaches have their merits and will no doubt stimulate much further
research. However, the challenge presented by today's eco–eco problems is so formidable that there is also a need for a line of research
which does not try to study these problems as special cases within an
already established theoretical scheme, but which takes them as the
starting point for the development of a new conceptual network.

This option, which corresponds well with the spirit of human ecology, provides the perspective which I will adopt in this chapter. I

---

[1] Chapters 5 and 6 rely in part on Jaeger [141].
[2] Folke and Kåberger [82] give a useful overview of eco–eco problems.
[3] For example Archibugi and Nijkamp [5].

will analyze eco–eco problems relying on Max Weber's method of ideal types.[4] Ideal types are often considered to be synonymous with scientific abstractions. They are then seen as including frictionless motion, ideal gases, as well as perfect competition. To Weber, however, ideal types meant a specific method appropriate for the moral sciences only. In a nutshell, with this concept he tried to organize the search for historical possibilities which are morally relevant for some human community. An ideal type relates historical facts and moral norms in such a way as to enable the researcher to understand major causal links in human history. In this sense, researchers interested in ancient Greece may try to elaborate an ideal type of democracy as well as one of tyranny.

In this chapter, the focus on the current environmental crisis will lead me to discuss ideal types of quantitative growth, qualitative growth, and a steady–state economy. A section of the chapter will be devoted to each of these types. I will prepare this discussion in the first section by describing some of the cultural rules which shape the operation of business firms and the dynamics of market processes.

5.1   A Fresh Look at Eco–Eco Problems

This section prepares the ground for the analysis of various ideal types of economic dynamics. The operations of business firms are subject to rules of accounting which draw a distinction between what does matter for the firm's performance and what does not. Important aspects of environmental problems may well fall into the second category. In the framework defined by those rules, managers and entrepreneurs develop projects for their firms. In these decision processes, they rely on a shared knowledge of normal product specifications, including normal prices.

Normal prices are crucial elements in the network of rules which constitutes the world economy. They indicate price levels at which supply and demand can be expected to match. When capacity limits prevent such matching at normal prices, it is brought about by rising or falling market prices. The difference between market and normal price, then, gives an incentive to the corresponding producers for investing or

---

[4] See Weber [290], Weber [291], and Burger [43]. Recently, the methodology of ideal types has been advocated by Morishima [194] for the purposes of integrating sociological and economic analysis, a task which is no doubt essential for an understanding of the current environmental crisis (Price [223]).

disinvesting until demand can again be satisfied at normal prices. Markets are informational systems: the difference between market prices and normal prices signals short run scarcity due to capacity limits and enables the system to adjust these limits to changing conditions. If public authorities try to modify the working of markets—for example, for the purposes of environmental policy—it is important to preserve this precious institutional arrangement.

For the analysis of eco–eco problems, one needs a minimal notation for the description of interlocked human activities taking place in a physical setting. This notation should, as far as possible, be compatible with the conceptual schemes used by economists and ecologists dealing with such problems. A notation fulfilling this requirement can be based on the concept of social structures elaborated in chapter 2. This concept draws attention to the spatial trajectories which human beings and human artifacts follow in the course of time. In many cases, this can be done by means of two–dimensional diagrams, with vertical lines indicating that an entity keeps its place, and diagonal lines indicating spatial movements. Horizontal lines are impossible, because movement takes time.

In chapter 2, the focus was on social structures in general. Now, the concepts introduced there need to be specified so as to apply to business firms. Figure 5.1 gives a simple example. A firm is situated in buildings equipped with machinery, its site remains unchanged during the period under consideration. People enter the plant in the morning and leave it in the evening. Moreover, energy, materials, and information are fed into the plant on a regular basis. These inputs are continuously transformed into the plant's stock of semi–finished products and then into its final output, which includes products as well as waste products.

A highly significant aspect of patterns like the one displayed in figure 5.1 is the fact that they are usually reproduced again and again, thus providing pathways for routinized action. If this is the case, they form a social structure in the sense elaborated in chapter 2. I will designate social structures obtained in business firms as *socio–economic structures*. Such structures are not static entities, but relatively stable features of highly dynamic processes, which can reproduce themselves in a recursive fashion. Economic life involves plenty of socio–economic structures as defined above. In particular, any technique for the production of industrial products like cars, computers, etc., usually implies a whole set of such structures. It should be noted that in socio–economic structures material objects play a crucial role. This holds true not

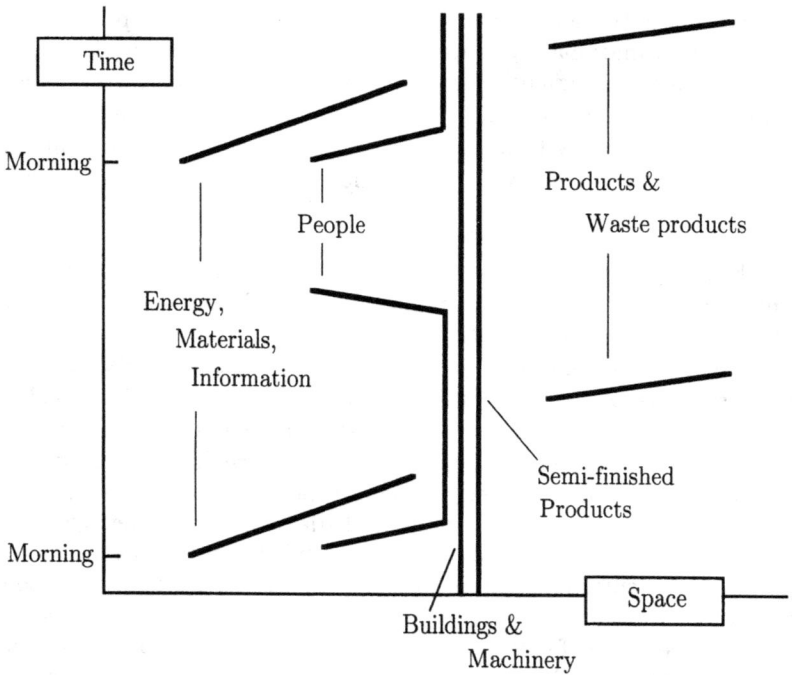

Figure 5.1: A business firm.

only in farms and manufacturing plants but also in firms providing various kinds of services. Obviously, socio–economic structures also include immaterial goods like consulting or entertainment, which can be represented as information items.

Contemporary economic institutions draw a crucial distinction between two different components of human ecological systems.[5] By their reliance on rules of business accounting, these institutions make visible all those events which directly affect the profitability of business firms. This is the case with events which modify the monetary value of a firm's assets and liabilities, including modifying the firm's stock of semi–finished goods by producing new ones. From the point of view of the economic system, other aspects of human ecological systems, in particular their embeddedness in a biophysical environment which is not reckoned as part of the firm's assets, are hidden.

---

[5] This point has been emphasized by Luhmann [168].

The difference between economically *visible and hidden aspects* of human ecological systems can be expressed with a simple algebraic notation if one considers a socio–economic structure during a fixed time span. Given the recursiveness of social structures, one can choose this time span so that the situation at its beginning is equal to the one obtained at its end. In the case of figure 5.1, this can be done by considering the period from one morning to the next. For the chosen time span, one can list all the inputs of the structure as a vector d and the outputs as a vector b. The structure can then be represented by a mapping from the input vector into the output vector.

The economically visible part of the structure is then a submapping, which maps the economically visible inputs d_v into the economically visible outputs b_v. The economically visible outputs for a given period consist of all the goods and services which business firms have sold during that period, plus the goods which they own at its end. These goods and services include capital equipment which is not yet written off. I will treat the input of human labor separately and designate it with a vector for human activities, a_v. Each element of this vector indicates the amount of time which people with the same kind of vocational skills have contributed to the process under consideration.

Such a mapping can be defined not only for single socio–economic structures, but also for sets of such structures, including the world economy as a whole. If the (row) vectors for the different structures are written one below the other, one gets an input and an output matrix, D_v and B_v, together with a human activity matrix, A_v. However, in an aggregated system like the world economy, single structures can be combined in very different proportions and older structures can be replaced by newer ones. The three matrices are time dependent, and, therefore, I mark them with a time index t:

$$D_{v,t}, A_{v,t} \rightarrow B_{v,t} \qquad (5.1)$$

The sums over the columns of the three matrices form an input vector, $d_{v,t}$, a human activity vector, $a_{v,t}$, and an output vector, $b_{v,t}$. An important advantage of this notation is its affinity with the notation of input–output analysis, which is well established in economics.[6]

Clearly, for many purposes it is essential to consider the economically invisible outputs, too. In order to analyze the interface between economy and ecology, it is extremely important to be aware of the dis-

---

[6] In the latter framework, the ecological relevance of the distinction between visible and hidden processes has been analyzed by Perrings [215].

tinction between what is economically visible and what is not. This
distinction does not depend on how some statistical office estimates
GNP and similar measures of economic performance. It depends on the
rules of accounting applied by business firms in their operations.

For the subsequent discussion, I next need to consider briefly a simple accounting relation which necessarily applies to the world economy
as a whole. If one multiplies the output vector for a given time span
with the average prices ruling in this time span, p_t, one obtains the
value of total output. If one multiplies the input vector (which includes
fixed capital) with the same prices one obtains total input costs. In the
actual world economy, output value exceeds input costs. The difference feeds total gross wages plus total gross profits.[7] If one divides
total profits by the value of total capital K_t, one obtains the rate of
profit, r_t. Total wages are the product of the human activity vector,
a_t, with the vector of wage rates for different kinds of labor, w_t. One
can then write:

$$b_{v,t} \cdot p_t = d_{v,t} \cdot p_t + a_{v,t} \cdot w_t + K_t \cdot r_t \tag{5.2}$$

Rates of profit are crucial for the analysis of eco–eco problems because
they serve as a guideline for management decisions in a market economy. In such an economy, the decision about which socio–economic
structures are reproduced and which ones are displaced by new ones is
made at the level of individual firms, in particular in the form of decisions about gross and net investment. The multitude of management
decisions results in the dynamic process in which the input and output
matrices are modified over the course of time. This modification can
be described by a decision matrix, M_t, which maps the block matrix
consisting of the input and output matrices of one period in a similar,
but usually different block matrix for the next period:[8]

$$[D_{v,t+1}; B_{v,t+1}] = [D_{v,t}; B_{v,t}] \cdot M_t \tag{5.3}$$

---

[7] Alternatively, one could consider net wages, net profits, plus taxes.

[8] In principle, the dynamics of decision matrices through time could be recon-
structed ex post by observing the input and output matrices of various periods
and solving equation (5.3) for M $_t$. However, forecasting the interdependent outcome of future management decisions is hardly a sensible exercise, except for
narrowly limited time horizons of maybe two or three years. But even if decision
matrices cannot be specified in detail, it may still be possible to indicate certain
general properties of such matrices. Two such properties are the tendency to
increase labor productivity by means of technical progress and the tendency to
shift production towards more sophisticated goods as incomes increase.

Equation (5.3) describes the dynamics of the economic system. It should be noted that the rank of $D_{v,t}$ and $B_{v,t}$ can change as new products are invented and old ones are displaced.

The decision matrix is the aggregate outcome of a multitude of management decisions. Many of the decision processes involved consist of the development of entrepreneurial projects. Such projects usually involve specific combinations of goods. Clearly, the relevant quantities are only roughly defined, but it would be preferable to get approximately the right amounts rather than getting too much or too little. In other words, entrepreneurial *projects generate preference orderings*. A crucial question in this chapter will be to ask how the projects carried out within socio–economic structures interfere with the economically hidden part of human ecological systems.

In general, having one unit too much of something will still be preferable to having one unit too little. Moreover, in some cases a lack of one product may be compensated by additional quantities of another product. However, the original project can be modified only within certain limits, beyond which it will simply fail. For the case of a project involving just two goods, the preferences entailed by the project can be represented by a preference surface in two–dimensional space. The possibility to generalize to n–dimensional space is obvious. The two–dimensional case is represented in figure 5.2, where the darker areas are preferred to the lighter ones.

No manager could define sensible investment projects without considerable knowledge about the relevant technologies and markets. In particular, she or he needs to have fairly accurate ideas of what are the normal properties of various goods, including what are the normal prices of these goods.[9] Moreover, investment projects usually are defined in terms of some financial budget. Normal prices of various goods then define the possible combinations which can be paid for out of the given budget.

In the case of two goods, such combinations can be represented by a budget line, as in figure 5.3a. The corresponding project is represented by figure 5.3b. If possible, one will buy combinations lying along some optimum range of the budget line. If, for some reason, this turns out to be impossible, the preference surface entailed by the project defines alternative courses of action. Such a situation is represented by figure 5.3c. The market price for one of the goods has risen, and,

---

[9] This idea lies at the core of Hayek's influential critique of socialism (Hayek [126, 124]).

Good B

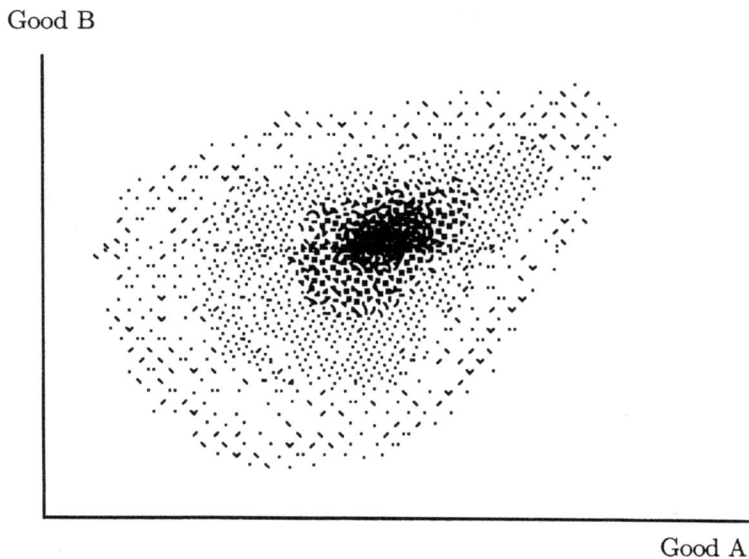

Good A

Figure 5.2: Preference surface for a project with two goods.

therefore, the actual budget line shifts away from the original one. The
consequence is a standard result of micro–economics: the good whose
price has risen is partially substituted by the good whose price has
remained unchanged. As with other projects, however, the difficulties
of realization can become so great as to make the project unrealistic
altogether.

An analysis of preferences in terms of projects has the advantage
of showing an important asymmetry between price increases and price
reductions. If prices rise (or if incomes fall), it becomes impossible
to realize the project in the form which was originally considered to
be optimal. As long as the project is not dropped altogether, it will
be necessary to reduce some expenses in order to overcome the difficulty. If prices fall (or if incomes rise), the feasibility of the project is
not impaired. Additional money is available, and new projects can be
planned. As planning a project requires time, however, there will be

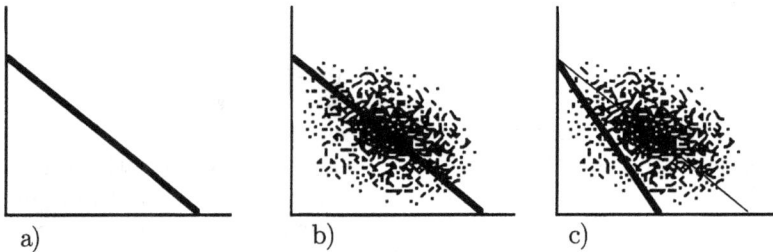

Figure 5.3: A project to spend money on two goods; a) Budget; b) Original Project; c) Modified Project.

good reasons to save at least part of the additional money for a certain period of time.[10]

In order to carry out an entrepreneurial project, a firm will usually demand certain goods. Demand is more than desire. Wishing to buy a computer while having no money to do so would not constitute economic demand. Having the same wish and the money required, it would still be strange to talk about demand unless one put an advertisement in the paper or chose some other way of actually looking for a computer. What about collecting information in a computer shop out of curiosity, though without excluding the possibility of actually purchasing a computer? Things become clearer if one thinks in legal terms. Somebody may propose a contract so as to be committed to the contract if another person accepts the proposal. Such a proposal is a speech act, an action which is performed by using certain words in the appropriate cultural setting.[11] A classical example is the ceremony of baptism, where words are used not to describe a given fact, but first of all to achieve it. Speech acts of supply and demand constitute a large set of possible contracts, some of which are actually realized.

Such speech acts can be addressed not only to specific individuals, but also to sets of potential partners. The commitment to engage in potential contracts may become somewhat weaker, but it still lies at the core of various actions signalling supply and demand. This is the case, for example, with newspaper advertisements or with the display of

---

[10] Besides the projects which they are actually pursuing, managers like other people usually entertain large sets of more or less clearly defined possible projects. These may become increasingly relevant if prices fall or incomes increase.

[11] Cf. Austin [7].

commodities bearing a price tag in a department store. If a computer is expected to cost $1,000, then people can say in a straightforward manner how many computers they are prepared to buy and sell. If every transaction had to be prepared by considering all possible prices between zero and infinity, no world economy would exist. There is an important analogy between prices and product specifications here. The network of economic transactions would break down if before every single transaction, the fully detailed specifications of the item to be traded had to be provided. Just as the operation of the world economy relies on the existence of normal products, it also relies on the existence of normal prices. *Normal prices* are cultural rules which together with other rules referring to product specification help to constitute a market.

As long as the total quantity of normal products demanded at normal prices does not differ from the total quantity offered at the same prices, transactions will take place at normal prices and the rules establishing them will be consolidated. What happens if excess demand arises? Contracts will no longer be settled at normal prices. Typically, some buyers will begin demanding the commodity in question at a price above its normal price, and sellers will be happy to settle contracts at this new level. Adam Smith already described such situations[12] by saying that market prices could rise above natural prices if there was a deficiency of "the quantity which is actually brought to market" in comparison with "the demand of those who are willing to pay the natural price of the commodity".[13] In the case of negative excess demand, the reverse happens, and market prices fall below normal prices.

Even people fond of Smith's metaphor of the invisible hand often ignore that his use of this metaphor referred to the differences in economic behavior generated by *differences between market prices and normal prices*. It is by no means easy to understand the role which these differences play in the dynamics of business life, but without such an understanding, an inquiry into today's environmental crisis would not get very far.

---

[12] On this point see the discussion in Schefold [243].
[13] Smith [258, p. 73]. I prefer the concept of normal prices elaborated by Marshall [180, p. 289f.] to Smith's older term of natural prices. For a recent restatement of the classical doctrine of natural prices, see Pasinetti [213]. For a discussion of some important weaknesses and strengths of Marshall's analysis of markets, see Becattini [17].

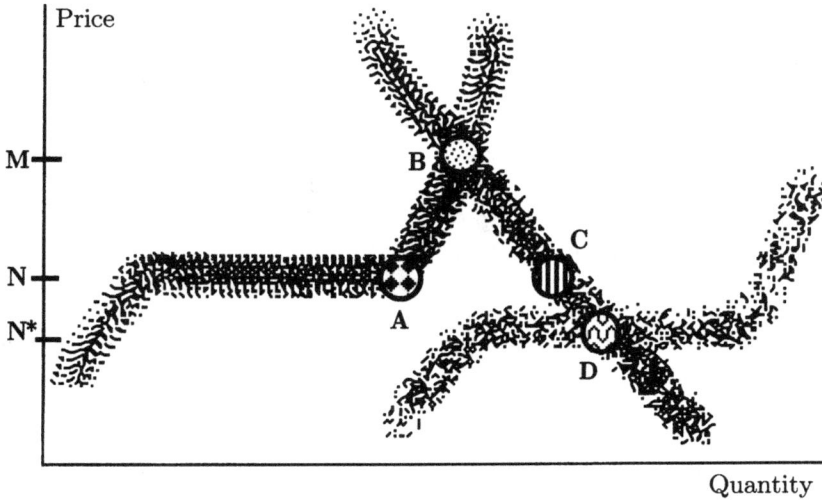

Figure 5.4: Normal price and market price.

The reduction of excess demand by the interplay of normal and market prices can be analyzed by using the graph in figure 5.4.[14] N is the level of normal prices. At this level, firms usually have some latitude in the quantities they can supply. This is due in part to inventories, and in part to the flexibility of production systems which allow the accomodation of fluctuations in demand. Possible supply quantities at normal prices are indicated by the horizontal beam to the left of point A. I avoid using a pure line because normal prices are rough estimates, not precise figures. Prices always vary with the specific circumstances of the different transactions, including variations in product specification.

Point A represents the upper limit of the quantities which can be supplied at normal prices. As long as demand lies within the range of flexibility represented by the horizontal beam, no particular problem arises. If demand at normal prices moves to the right of A, excess demand is created. Its size is indicated by the distance between A and C. To produce the quantity demanded at C, capacity must be expanded, which requires time. In the short run, it is difficult to augment supply beyond A, and this will be attempted only if market prices rise steeply.

---

[14] Scott [250, p. 57] uses a similar graphic technique for studying networks of firms.

This is indicated by the upwardly directed beam starting at A. The whole step–curve which runs through A and B is the supply curve corresponding to normal prices N. The end of the beam which falls to the left hand side indicates the willingness of suppliers to sell below normal prices if demand falls below their range of flexibility. It should be clear that this supply curve cannot be used to explain normal prices. Quite the opposite, the existence of normal prices is needed to explain this curve. What it can help to understand is the deviation of market prices from normal prices under conditions of excess demand.

The downward sloping curve connecting B and C is the demand curve. The adjustment effect described in figure 5.3 can help to understand why demand for a good falls if its price rises. However, this kind of analysis applies only as long as most other prices remain stable. Otherwise, incomes as well as purchase possibilities could vary in most surprising ways, and there would be no such thing as a demand curve connecting the demand for varying quantities of a single good with its market price. The existence of demand curves can be taken for granted only as long as a pattern of normal prices can be considered as given.

If excess demand corresponds with the distance between A and C, actual trade occurs at point B, which indicates both demand and supply at market prices M. The quantity demanded is lowered from C to B as the price rises from N to M: firms and households have to modify some of their projects for investment and consumption, as they get less for the same expenditure.

Smith argued that, if market prices rise above natural prices, more resources will be devoted to the production of the commodity, and the quantity brought to the market "will soon be sufficient to supply the effectual demand".[15] As a result, the supply curve shifts to the right, as indicated by the lighter step–curve in figure 5.4. As soon as capacity is sufficiently increased, excess demand disappears, and market prices again approach normal prices. However, as Smith already knew, the expansion of capacity is linked to all sorts of socio-technical innovations. In particular, labor often becomes more productive as the extent of the market increases. In figure 5.4, this effect is represented by the distance

---

[15] Smith [258, p. 75].

between the old level of normal prices N and the new level N^*.[16] As a result, excess demand will be eliminated at point D, not C.

As this happens with all commodities, relative prices need not vary a great deal. It is a remarkable fact that over the course of time nominal wages are much less stable than the relative prices of many goods and services.[17] The stability of relative prices is all the more remarkable as the precise specifications of goods and services are continuously being modified in the process of technological innovation.

The difference between normal price and market price is a signal of short run *scarcity*. However, the scarcity expressed by this difference is not a matter of human wants facing limited natural resources. Rather, the difference between market price and normal price signals a situation where historically given capacity limits hinder the satisfaction of a demand which would become effective at normal prices. Clearly, this signal is of great significance when investment decisions to modify existing capacity limits are made, but it has nothing to do with scarcity due to limited natural resources. This is a different matter, which requires a closer scrutiny of normal prices in the context of economic growth.

5.2 The Juggernaut of Quantitative Growth

In the present section, the dynamics of the world economy which has led to the contemporary environmental crisis is described with the ideal type of quantitative growth. This pattern of economic dynamics is characterized by a positive rate of economic growth associated with positive rates of physical growth. Rates of physical growth refer to quantitatively measurable environmental impacts of the production and consumption of various goods and services. Economic growth as such is a consequence of cultural rules which stabilize positive rates of profit and of interest. Under these conditions, money becomes an external goal of action pursued by billions of people in an institutional setting

---

[16] Recently, authors like Romer [232] and Schwartz [248] have emphasized how in an innovative economy production costs tend to fall when the extent of the market increases. One may then draw a curve falling from A to D and consider it as a long run supply curve with increasing returns to scale.

[17] As Schwartz [249, p. 43] notes, in America, during the 4 business cycles from 1919 to 1938, the average factory pay in years of boom lay 40% above the average pay in years of recession. The quantity of manufactured goods varied by similar factors. On the other hand, relative (wholesale) prices varied by only 10% or less.

which systematically disregards the environmental impacts of economic growth.

With regard to eco–eco problems, one of the most important properties of the decision matrices which have characterized the world economy so far is the fact that they have led to positive economic growth. More precisely, under conditions of positive profits usually a positive fraction of these profits is used for net investment and thus leads to economic growth. Therefore, the positive profits which have prevailed in the history of the world economy have consistently led to economic growth: the rate of growth of net output valued at constant prices, $g_{e,t}$, is usually positive:[18]

$$g_{e,t} = \frac{(\boldsymbol{b}_{v,t+1} - \boldsymbol{d}_{v,t+1}) \cdot \boldsymbol{p}_t}{(\boldsymbol{b}_{v,t} - \boldsymbol{d}_{v,t}) \cdot \boldsymbol{p}_t} - 1 \qquad (5.4)$$

This rate as such does not yet tell much about the ecological implications of economic growth. In order to analyze these implications, one must, to some degree, be able to describe the relation between the economically visible part of human ecological systems and their hidden part. For this purpose, one needs some measure of environmental impact for the various components of net economic output. In the case of problems like the anthropogenic greenhouse effect, for example, such measures can be estimated in the form of greenhouse gas emission coefficients, which indicate how much greenhouse gas is generated by the production and consumption of one unit of various goods. If and only if a vector $\boldsymbol{i}_t$ of such impact factors can be at least roughly estimated, an environmentally meaningful rate of physical growth, $g_{p,t}$, can be defined for the economic system:

$$g_{p,t} = \frac{(\boldsymbol{b}_{v,t+1} - \boldsymbol{d}_{v,t+1}) \cdot \boldsymbol{i}_t}{(\boldsymbol{b}_{v,t} - \boldsymbol{d}_{v,t}) \cdot \boldsymbol{i}_t} - 1 \qquad (5.5)$$

In the case of the greenhouse problem, it is known that there is a positive impact vector of greenhouse gas emission coefficients, even if its components can be estimated only very roughly. It is important to

---

[18] In order to obtain vectors of the same number of components for different periods, I consider a vector space with a separate dimension for all kinds of goods and services produced at least in one of the two periods. The output vectors then contain zero components for the goods and services not produced in the period to which they refer. The components of the price vector indicate prices prevailing in period t, except for the goods and services which are produced only in period t+1.

notice that the impact coefficient associated with a gallon of gasoline does not only indicate the carbon dioxide emitted when the gasoline is actually burned down. The impact coefficient includes the greenhouse gas emissions associated with the refinery where the gasoline was produced and with the transportation of the gasoline to the point of sale. One must also include the emissions associated with the processes of building the refinery, the gas station, etc.

In the actual world economy, fossil fuels are basic goods in the sense that they are used at least indirectly for the production of every good and service. Therefore, the greenhouse impact vector is strictly positive, because even goods which do not contain a single molecule of carbon cannot be produced without using fossil fuels. For decades, the average physical growth rate associated with this vector according to equation (5.5) has been strictly positive. More generally, *quantitative growth* means economic growth based on physical growth of economic goods.

To say that quantitative growth is not sustainable basically means that there is a limit G which the world economy's environmental impact should not exceed for a given period.[19] Actually that limit may decrease as the biosphere's resilience is impaired by the impact of economic growth, but, for my present purposes, it is sufficient to consider G as an upper boundary for all time–dependent limits which may be additionally specified. It is, then, obvious that, if the average rate of physical growth defined by a specific impact vector is positive without converging to zero, there always is a period t^* after which environmental impacts exceed the limit G by an increasing margin. Sustainability with regard to such a limit, however, would be defined as the state of affairs described by formula (5.6):

$$(b_{v,t} - d_{v,t}) \cdot i_t \leq G \qquad \text{for all} \quad t \qquad (5.6)$$

In the case of the greenhouse problem, the claim that a quantitative limit of sustainability exists relies on properties of the climate system. However, this does not mean that such a limit could not be crossed. The

---

[19] This notion of lacking sustainability can be used for different environmental problems for which a sensible impact vector can be defined. This is the case with the problem of the ozone hole and with many problems of waste products. However, there are other enironmental problems, for example with regard to biodiversity, for which an impact vector can hardly be defined in a meaningful way. I therefore use formula (5.6) to define the notion of sustainability in the context of the greenhouse problem only, and leave open the question of how this notion should be understood in other contexts.

claim is that the limit should not be crossed for economic, political and moral reasons, although it is actually possible to do so. This implies that many courses of action are ecologically sound if and only if they are not performed at an excessive scale. The burning of fuelwood produces carbon dioxide, which can contribute to the growth of new trees. In principle, this is a perfectly acceptable state of affairs. Yet there is a growing awareness of the dangers involved in unlimited anthropogenic production of carbon dioxide. It is not known where the critical limits precisely are, as they depend on intricate features of the highly complex climate system, but there can be little doubt that such limits can be crossed only with grave consequences.

The triadic human ecological system which has emerged in Europe at the end of the Middle Ages has developed a pattern of quantitative growth which leads it to cross local and global thresholds of sustainability. A crucial factor leading to this pattern is the prevalence of positive *rates of profit*. The rates of profit of different firms can be described by a probability distribution like the one in figure 5.5.[20] In a given period of time, there will usually be some firms making a deficit, and therefore obtaining negative rates of profit. A major feature of the world economy as we know it is that it tends to generate positive rates of profit. This is indicated in two properties of their probability distribution. The distribution is skewed, and its expected value r^* is greater than zero. It is often said that capitalism is based on the search for profit, and it is not difficult to find impressive illustrations for this thesis. It is, however, important to distinguish between the role of profit as a goal of entrepreneurial action, and the role of profitability as a criterion for investment decisions. An entrepreneur may be driven by a vision of some technological and social possibility, and this vision may lead him or her to design appropriate investment projects. When deciding whether to realize a specific project, an essential criterion will be the comparison of the project's expected profitability with a normal rate of profit, i.e., a rate of profit which is considered normal in the business in question. If the entrepreneur consistently fails to meet this criterion, she or he will be driven out of business. The profitability criterion can work with very different levels of the normal rate of profit, including a zero level. In this case, the criterion is identical to the avoidance of losses.

---

[20] When constructing such a probability distribution out of empirical data, it is reasonable to weigh the rates of profit of different firms with the size of the respective capitals.

probabilities

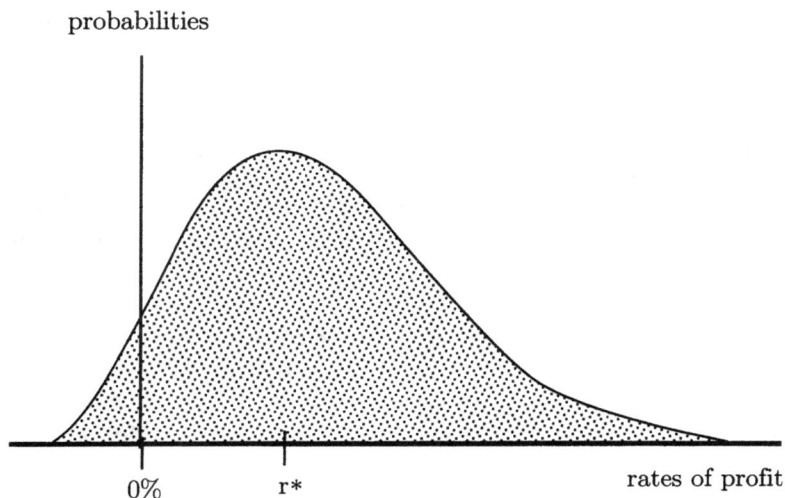

Figure 5.5: Probability distribution of rates of profit.

How then are rates of profit determined? The distinction between normal rates and market rates is crucial here. *Market rates of profit* come about as the result of daily operations by single firms on various markets. Consider the example of an investment project. Over some period of time, such a project generates a series of costs and a series of revenues. Three factors are especially important for the shape of these two series. First, technology: the introduction of a new computer system may be expected to yield a higher rate of profit as it increases output dramatically. Second, organization: the transformation of an internal department into an external supplier may be expected to yield a higher rate of profit as it reduces costs and improves quality. Third, marketing: if a firm is able to establish something like a working relationship with its customers, it will be able to sell what it produces and to produce what can best be sold. Obviously, these three factors interact in many important ways. Together, they make up nothing less than the process of socio–technical change. For the single firm, then, socio–technical change is a major determinant of rates of profit.

It is not the only one. A firm can try to keep input prices, especially wages, low while trying to keep output prices high. Competition with other firms will set limits to such strategies, but there often is considerable latitude for successful efforts in this direction. Moreover, rates of profit can depend critically on the scale of production. I have already noticed Adam Smith's statement that the productivity of labor often increases dramatically if the scale of production can be expanded. On the other hand, there are thresholds of organizational size which are difficult to cross. For a small firm of 5 people, it is usually quite easy to grow to 7 people. Somewhere around a dozen employees lies an important threshold which in most cases requires the introduction of new organizational hierarchies. Other thresholds, often strongly dependent on technology, exist for larger sizes. In many cases, additional investment can be expected to lead to higher rates of profit up to a critical limit, beyond which the inverse effect becomes probable.

While this kind of reasoning may be perfectly satisfactory for somebody interested in the fate of a specific firm, it is of remarkably little help for somebody interested in rates of profit for the economic system as a whole. The reason is straightforward. When a firm makes a decision about an investment project, it presupposes a pattern of normal prices. These prices, however, already imply rates of profit for the economy as a whole.[21] Moreover, in the evaluation of possible investment projects, these are usually compared with what is considered to be a normal rate of profit for the business in question. The economy as a recursive system reproduces normal rates of profit together with normal prices. Their origins coincide with the origins of the world economy. Meanwhile, what matters is not how rates of profit were determined in the first place, but how they are modified in the interrelated processes of socio–technical change and economic growth.

From the point of view of firms, *normal rates of profit* represent a crucial property of their economic environment. In many cases, normal rates of profit can be specified for given industries in given economic regions. Firms often try to achieve a rate of profit which is at least as high as the normal one. Much effort is devoted to the problem of identifying strategies which enable firms to achieve such goals. However, this kind of analysis does not explain the normal rate of profit. For this purpose, one needs to change the unit of analysis and consider the economic system as a whole.

For the system as a whole the rate of profit r_t during an accounting period t can be defined as total profits divided by the value of the capital goods advanced at the beginning of the period.[22] If in formula (5.2)

---

[21] See Harcourt [116] for an account of a remarkable controversy concerning these matters.

[22] Rates of profit can be defined in several ways, and in some cases it is quite reasonable to consider several definitions in parallel. Important differences arise,

the value of capital, K_t, is expressed as the product of the vector $\boldsymbol{k}_{v,t}$ of capital goods multiplied by the price vector,[23] the rate of profit can be expressed by formula (5.7):

$$r_t = \frac{\boldsymbol{b}_{v,t} \cdot \boldsymbol{p}_t - \boldsymbol{d}_{v,t} \cdot \boldsymbol{p}_t - \boldsymbol{a}_{v,t} \cdot \boldsymbol{w}_t}{\boldsymbol{k}_{v,t} \cdot \boldsymbol{p}_t} \qquad (5.7)$$

The accounting structure on which the economic system relies puts a heavy penalty on continued losses: they lead firms into bankruptcy and are therefore incompatible with the reproduction of the economy as a whole. Continued profits, on the other hand, present no problem, but rather quite the opposite. Socio–technical change will therefore be obviously biased toward increasing profits, at least in the short run. No firm wants to introduce a new technology or a new form of organization which would lead to lower rates of profit, while all firms will be glad to introduce any innovation leading to higher rates of profit. There can be no doubt that since the origins of the world economy this mechanism has been continuously fostering forms of socio–technical change which tend to increase r_t. The most important pattern was identified already by Adam Smith, namely the fact that $\boldsymbol{b}_{v,t}$ and $\boldsymbol{d}_{v,t}$ grow significantly faster than $\boldsymbol{a}_t$.[24] An important question, then, is whether the tendency to increase r_t in the short run is offset by some counter–tendency in the longer run.

This counter–tendency is the rise in wage costs $\boldsymbol{w}_t$. For several generations, the processes of socio–technical change and economic growth have gone hand in hand with the long run tendency to increase wage incomes per hour. Moreover, social security contributions as well as income taxes also contribute substantially to rising wage costs. These are indisputable facts. The question is whether the long run rise in wage costs is linked to short run increases in rates of profit in such a way as to reproduce these rates more or less at their prevailing level. There are three such links. First, a perception of persistently rising rates of profit often leads to demands for higher gross wages. It is very difficult to run a business without a minimal consent of the wage earners, and this consent may be jeopardized if rates of profit are allowed

---

for example, if there is a stock market and one is interested in dividing profits by the value of the firm's total stock. These differences can be quite important for an analysis of single firms. For a discussion of the long run dynamics of rates of profit in the economy as a whole, equation (5.7) gives a satisfactory basis.

[23] $k_{v,t}$ is smaller than $d_{v,t}$ because some inputs don't need to be financed in advance.

[24] Whether this increase in the productivity of labor is due mainly to the causes described by Smith is another matter, which I do not want to consider here.

to rise systematically. After all, if the economy can work with stable rates of profit, why should productivity gains be used to increase those rates? There are very influential notions of *fairness* which justify the claims of wage earners to participate in the enjoyment of productivity gains.[25] These claims are presented both directly with regard to net wage incomes and indirectly as political pressure toward improved social security and the like.

Clearly, claims leading to higher wage costs can be resisted if there are enough unemployed people willing and able to work for lower wages. But the second link between increasing rates of profit and rising wage costs results from the fact that increasing rates of profit encourage investment and thus accelerate economic growth. This tends to produce shortages on the labor market, which obviously lend force to the demands of wage earners for increased income. Such shortages can appear even under conditions of substantial unemployment, because the unemployed often lack the qualifications required by the fastest growing sectors of the economy.

It is quite plausible that at the time of the origin of the world economy this problem was less severe than it is today. Moreover, in the 18th century the idea of more or less constant incomes seemed quite natural to most people. Finally, increases in overall rates of profit were hard to perceive. The beginnings of the world economy, therefore, could have been more favorable to rising rates of profit than is the present. This could help explain how positive rates of profit became established in the first place. Once they had become normal, the two mechanisms keeping them in check started to operate.

The third link reverses the causal order. In many cases, it is not wages which adjust to a rise in the rates of profit due to socio–technical change, but the other way around. Rising wages can force entrepreneurs to look for socio–technical changes which enable them to maintain existing levels of rates of profit. These levels do not need to be uniform. Contrary to a picture conveyed by many theoretical models, rates of profit differ widely among industries as well as among nations. The interesting fact is that these various levels are not experiencing a persistent increase due to socio–technical change. It is this fact which can be understood in terms of the three mechanisms just expounded.

The last of these mechanisms actually leads to the reverse question: Are there any checks to avoid a persistent decline in rates of profit? This question is especially, but not exclusively, relevant for the analysis

---

[25] Elster [70] offers a careful account of the role of social norms in wage bargaining.

of wage bargaining. Again, normal rates of profit come into play. If managers and entrepreneurs have strong ideas about what should be their normal rate of profit, they will not consider a situation of declining profits as offering prospects for good business, and as a result, their *state of confidence* will be worsened. This can lead to a drastic reduction of investment decisions. Reduced investment decisions lead to an excess supply of various goods, market prices fall below normal prices, and excess capacity and unemployment rise.[26] As a result of all this, rates of profit fall even more than managers and entrepreneurs expected. Their state of confidence surely will not be restored by this development. The economic system enters into a major crisis.

Experience shows that this is not the end of the story. An intense search for new business opportunities begins. Socio–technical change leads to new products and processes. Such innovation can reduce the labor input needed to produce a given output. The economic crisis, especially increasing unemployment, dampens the increase in wage costs. Public expenditure for armaments and other purposes can help to reduce excess capacity. Taken together, these developments can restore normal rates of profit and thus economic growth.[27]

The crisis will come to an end if the state of confidence of the relevant investors is restored. Until now this usually meant that rates of profit returned to more or less the levels which were considered normal in the times preceding the crisis. This is a mechanism which can keep in check a decline of the rates of profit as far as the economy as a whole is concerned. On the other hand, I have already discussed how an increase in such rates is kept in check, too. Both socio–technical change and economic growth tend to leave rates of profit for the economy as a whole more or less stable.

I do not want to argue that normal rates of profit are immutable. However, the importance of norms of fairness in wage bargaining and of the state of confidence in investment decisions mean that, once some level of the rate of profit is accepted as normal, there are strong mechanisms to keep market rates fluctuating around that level. As the world economy since its very beginnings is characterized by positive levels

---

[26] Inflationary expectations are built into normal prices once inflation itself is considered to be unavoidable. Market prices then fall below normal prices as soon as they increase by less than the rate of inflation which management considers to be normal.

[27] These were the general features of the way in which the world economy overcame the great depression of the 30's. As I will discuss in more detail in chapter 6, the present situation of the world economy indicates that there are also other possibilities of overcoming a situation of persistent economic crisis.

of normal rates of profit, global economic growth is one of the salient features of the triadic human ecological system which has increasingly shaped the global environment.

A crucial element which has to be added to the above analysis is the role of *interest rates*. They should not be confused with rates of profit. One may perhaps imagine that in some idealized state of economic equilibrium interest rates and rates of profit would have the same size, but even then there would not be a single ratio with two different names, but a quantitative correspondence between two different variables. One way to emphasize the difference between the two ratios is to relate them to speech acts of supply and demand. Rates of interest are a part of contracts referring to credits. There are speech acts of demanding and offering credits at various rates of interest. If an agreement is reached, a rate of interest is agreed upon by the parties involved in the contract. Rates of profit are not fixed by contract, they are the result of an accounting procedure applied to economic activities. Rates of profit are not regulated by speech acts of supply and demand for capital, they are the result of performing the whole complex set of operations needed to realize an economic activity.

Obviously, rates of interest and rates of profit are interdependent. If a rate of interest of 5% can be obtained by lending a sum of money on the credit market, few people will invest in an economic activity from which they could not expect a rate of profit of more than 5%. Rates of interest set a lower limit to rates of profit.[28] With a given pattern of normal prices, one can imagine entrepreneurs and managers ordering their investment projects according to the expected rates of profit. The projects with an expected rate of profit reasonably higher than the rate of interest for credits of similar duration will be executed. The higher the rate of interest, the smaller the number of projects which will be realized. Rates of interest then exert some influence on rates of profit and on investment activity as well.

If entrepreneurs expect rates of profit around 15%, they may be willing to seek large amounts of credit as long as the relevant rate of interest is only 5%. Excess demand for credit may ensue and rates of interest will rise until supply and demand for credit are matched again. If, on the other hand, entrepreneurs expect rates of profit to drop to 2% or 1%, while rates of interest still lie around 5%, then demand for credit will be lowered. Moreover, entrepreneurs and other investors

---

[28] In order to be equally attractive, rates of profit usually must exceed rates of interest, as the former are uncertain while the latter can be fixed by contract.

will increase the supply of credit with money which they no longer want to use for industrial investment. Therefore, rates of profit exert some influence both on demand and supply for credit.

The demand curve for credit, as represented in figure 5.6, has a peculiar property: it extends into the realm of negative rates of interest. In the case of an industrial product, it is not clear what a negative price could mean. If I want to get rid of my car and I pay $100 to somebody who is willing to take it, I am not selling the car for a negative price. Whether the car will be recycled, shredded, etc., I am buying a service of waste disposal for a positive price of $100. In the case of credit, things are different. A credit couples the right to spend a certain amount of money now with the duty to pay back a comparable amount of money later. In principle, there is no reason why the second amount should always be greater than the first one.[29] If I get a credit of one billion dollars, I have the commitment to pay it back after a certain amount of time. Taking a credit makes sense mainly if I want to spend the money now, while confidently expecting to earn a similar amount of money later on. Even with negative rates of interest, such an expectation could be unwarranted. Therefore, demand for credit can be limited to a finite quantity both at positive and at negative rates of interest, as shown in figure 5.6.

Negative rates of interest can arise if the rate of inflation is higher than the nominal rate of interest. For centuries, rates of interest have become negative only under exceptional conditions.[30] The reason is represented in figure 5.6 by the peculiar shape of the supply curve. Under normal conditions, this curve has a lower bound i^*, below which no credit is offered. In an uncertain world, holding cash has the crucial advantage of providing liquidity. Few people and even fewer institutions are willing to give up this advantage unless it be either for the acquisition of some good or, in the case of credit, for a tangible rate of interest. Therefore, i^* is said to express the liquidity preference of the public. Empirically, it lies in the order of magnitude of a few percent.[31] However, it should be emphasized that the behavior of the

---

[29] Suppose that between the beginning and the end of a credit with an interest rate of 10% the price of trucks goes down by 20%. The money rate of interest in terms of trucks is 38%, because the money paid back can buy 38% more trucks than the money lent at the beginning. Now suppose that during the same period of time the price of houses goes up by 20%. The money rate of interest in terms of houses is then -8%.

[30] Nominal rates of interest have been negative in Switzerland at times when large inflows of foreign funds threatened the financial stability of this small country.

[31] This was emphasized by Gesell [97].

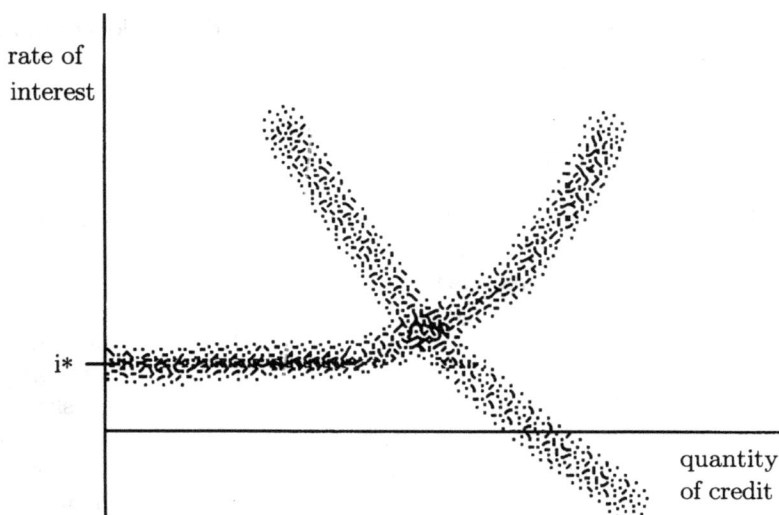

Figure 5.6: Supply and demand for credit.

so–called public here is determined to a considerable extent by the rates of interest which national banks require for their credits.

The cultural rules governing the supply of credit as well as the rules maintaining normal rates of profit at positive levels establish the core mechanism of economic growth: the accumulation of capital along a path of compound interest.[32] Persistently positive rates of profit and interest make economic growth look like the overall goal of the global economy. As I discussed in chapter 2, goals and projects are pursued by persons. To say that a human ecological system like the world economy is a goal–directed system is a highly metaphorical, and possibly misleading, way of talking. The goals pursued in and maybe by the world economy need closer scrutiny.

Is the game of tennis a goal–directed system? First of all it is goal-defining: the players are assigned certain goals like trying to get the tennis–ball over the net and trying to win the game. By inducing many people to pursue these goals, the game of tennis can contribute to the

---

[32] The first comprehensive analysis of the accumulation of capital is to be found in the work of Marx [182]. Scholars shouldn't ignore this achievement because of the limits of Marx' theoretical approach. For a promising attempt to learn from Marx in view of a better understanding of environmental problems see Dickens [58].

overall fitness of these people. This latter effect may be regarded as a goal of tennis by public health authorities, tennis clubs, etc.

The world economy is also a goal–defining system. In particular, it assigns the goal of making money literally to billions of people. Human beings carry out projects, and in so doing they set for themselves an amazing variety of goals which they pursue in their activities. The emergence of the world economy meant that a shared goal was established which human beings could try to reach all over the world. The world economy is a moral order because it treats the pursuit of money by all humankind as an honorable and desirable activity. Nobody expressed this more convincingly than Adam Smith, moral philosopher and founding father of economics.

For the majority of the people, the only realistic way of making money is to earn a wage. The activity performed is the means, money is the end. A worker observes a control panel, an employee fills in a form, both are earning their money. Earning money allows for a deep dissociation between means and ends. This is a possibility and often a reality, but it is not always the case. I have argued in chapter 2 that human agency in general implies an internal relation between means and ends. It is impossible to learn what food is without learning what eating is, and the converse is also true. To say that somebody is dancing typically refers both to bodily movements and to harmony with a rhythm. There are also human activities where the relation between means and ends becomes an external one. Charlie Chaplin's "Modern Times" presents a paradigmatic series of such situations. As discussed in section 2.4, I use the term "labor" for activities where an *external relation between means and ends* is established.[33] Making money is in no way the only end which can be dissociated from its means in such a way, but clearly it is an example of major importance, especially with regard to environmental problems.

Obviously, money can be a means as well as an end. Earned money will usually become a means to purchase consumption goods. This actually aggravates the dissociation between means and ends which is so widespread in situations of wage labor. Moreover, as I have already mentioned with regard to figure 5.3, money does not simply provide the means to realize given projects. Rather, there are many cases where people carry out projects to spend money. If making money becomes an external goal of economic activities, unlimited economic

---

[33] MacIntyre [174] discusses human practices in the context of internal means–end relations.

growth becomes a self–evident joint project of the people participating in the world economy.

Actually, economic growth is a basic feature of the recursive process in which the world economy has reproduced itself since its beginnings at the end of the Middle Ages. The input of capital goods systematically exceeds the amount needed for replacement, and this process of capital accumulation leads to a continuous increase in productive capacity. As long as positive rates of profit prevail, they provide both the means and the incentive for net investment and thus for economic growth. Moreover, a positive rate of profit is a stronghold of money as an external goal for economic activities. The desire to make money for its own sake finds strong institutional support in a situation in which any sum of money can be increased by investing it.[34] This links the persistence of positive rates of profit and interest to the external relation between means and ends of economic activities.[35]

5.3   Mechanisms of Qualitative Growth

Quantitative growth generates increasing environmental impacts. The possibility of avoiding such impacts by avoiding further economic growth deserves careful discussion, and I will look at it in section 5.4. On the other hand, it is important to investigate the possibilities of

---

[34] Marx was profoundly upset by the historical impact of this desire and by the indifference associated with it for the actual misery of the working population. However, money can become an external goal not only for entrepreneurs and managers, but for employees and workers as well. This role of money as an external goal is not an unavoidable social structure; it is an important fact of contemporary life, no more, no less. Here again, the study of human ecology requires prudence, not fast conclusions.

[35] Here we touch on the limits of economic theory as we know it. This theory is unable to offer a realistic account of the difficulties involved in an external means–end relation. Quite the opposite, economic theory actually assumes such a relation as its starting point. Following Robbins [231], neoclassical economists do this very explicitly. Despite the significant differences between, say, classical, neoclassical, and Keynesian economists, they actually share the view of labor as an activity which is related to its goals externally. This approach greatly contributes to the unity of economics as a scientific discipline. Moreover, it has the great advantage of combining simplicity with remarkable explanatory power— an advantage which helped to establish economics as the discipline which more than any other shapes the conceptual framework of actual decision processes in the contemporary world. Nevertheless, the problems of human ecology require the ability to venture beyond the limits involved in such an approach to economic reality.

decoupling economic from physical growth. This is the task of this section. Such a decoupling can happen if impact vectors can be reduced. An important example is the introduction of abatement activities in those cases where an environmental impact can be reversed with suitable technologies. The service provided by these activities then adds a new element to the economically visible output.

On the input side, the discussion of economically invisible inputs leads to an analysis of the rent mechanism. This mechanism makes limited inputs economically visible and fosters processes of qualitative growth by decoupling economic growth from further use of the resources in question. Rents indicate the existence of limited inputs, and thereby convey an important scarcity signal to economic agents. The analysis of these signals will be extended to exhaustible resources and then to the case of environmental thresholds. Such thresholds occur when gifts of nature should not be used beyond certain limits, because otherwise irreversible environmental degradation would occur. Public authorities can enforce these thresholds with the instrument of limited permits, for example for the production of commercial energy. These permits then generate a specific kind of rent. Energy permits can be shown to be—at least in the longer run—preferable to energy taxes. They can also be shown to be compatible with democratically established standards of fairness.

To consider the case of *reversible environmental effects*, imagine a firm producing, together with marketable goods, some toxic waste. The goods form the economically visible part of its output. However, there is also an economically invisible part, namely toxic waste. There is no trade with this waste, and if one wants to include it in the firm's accounting framework, one must assign it a fictitious zero price. Precisely for this reason it would not make sense to include the information about toxic waste in the firm's regular accounting framework.

Still, the waste is harmful by any reasonable standard. It involves what economists call an external effect.[36] To measure the effect one could point to the volume or the weight of the waste in question. Assigning a pecuniary value, however, may prove to be totally mistaken. Usually, it makes little sense to measure problems in monetary units,

---

[36] The notion of external effects was introduced in economic debates by Marshall. Pigou [219], Coase [50], Meade [186] and, with more empirical grounding, Kapp [153] provide the cornerstones of the large structure of arguments which has been built around this concept. See Mishan [193] for its history and Siebert [256] for a textbook approach with regard to environmental economics.

though an external effect is basically a problem generated by some economic activity. One may be faced with a serious moral problem because some toxic waste fosters malformation in human babies. This would no doubt represent a worrying external effect, but it would certainly be insane to think that the damage created could be expressed in a satisfactory way as a sum of money.

This does not exclude the possibility that external effects—including many cases of environmental disruption—may be avoided by resorting to a strategy which involves well defined sums of money as its essential instrument. An important case of this kind is given where an environmental impact can be reversed with the help of suitable technology. Even if some toxic waste leads to damage which cannot be assessed in monetary units, a technology for decomposing the waste products into harmless components may be developed, and such a technology would involve well defined costs. It would then become feasible to forbid any economic activity which would release toxic waste into the environment, even if the given product was deemed to be indispensable. As a result, the use of abatement technology could become a service offered on the marketplace by specialized firms.

This procedure may be described as the internalization of an external effect. It does not assign a price to the toxic waste nor to any natural resources affected by this waste, but an additional price is introduced: the price for the new service of decomposing the toxic by–products of the firm's main activity. This is the case of reversible environmental effects. Economic activities produce a potentially harmful effect on the environment, but technologies which reverse this effect are available. In such situations the maxim "polluter pays" has a clear meaning and can easily be satisfied by enforcing the use of such technologies.

Interestingly, there are two ways of realizing this solution. One approach would rely on a market for the new service, the other one would levy an emission tax in order to finance waste processing facilities operated by public authorities. The working of the invisible hand of the market, described in section 5.1, yields a strong argument in favor of the market solution, but as I will show below, there may be other reasons which could make the second alternative more attractive. Public authorities, however, play a crucial role in the market solution as well: By simply prohibiting pollution effects, public authorities can create a market for the use of abatement technologies provided by business firms.

In the notation introduced in section 5.1, this process can be described by considering an economic system yielding an output consisting of an economically visible part and an invisible part:

$$D_{v,t}, A_{v,t} \rightarrow B_{v,t}, B_{i,t} \tag{5.8}$$

The system can then be modified so as to eliminate the economically invisible output by increasing both the visible input and the visible output by a new economically visible good, the abatement service:

$$\widetilde{D}_{v,t}, \widetilde{A}_{v,t} \rightarrow \widetilde{B}_{v,t} \tag{5.9}$$

The input matrix $\widetilde{D}_{v,t}$ is equal to the matrix $D_{v,t}$ enlarged by an additional row and column representing the provision and use of the abatement service. The same is true for the output matrices.[37] Two consequences follow. First, demand for an additional product has been created, and this provides opportunities for further economic growth. Second, in order to produce the same net product without generating waste products, total production must increase to provide abatement services; this generates opportunities for new jobs.[38]

However, the costs for the abatement service can generate inflationary pressure and conflict about the distribution of income. In order to discuss this effect I introduce the concept of a standardized rate of profit. Take the vector of goods which were bought with an average wage unit in the last period.[39] Call this vector x_{t-1} and insert its monetary value in place of the elements of w_t in formula (5.7).[40] The resulting magnitude ζ_t indicates the rate of profit which would be obtained in period t if wage incomes were such as to allow wage earners to go on with their previous per capita consumption patterns:

$$\zeta_t = \frac{(b_{v,t} \cdot p_t - d_{v,t} \cdot p_t - a_{v,t} \cdot (x_{t-1} \cdot p_t) \cdot e)}{k_t \cdot p_t} \tag{5.10}$$

Standardized rates of profit are a good approximation of potential growth rates at a given level of consumption. Here, I am introducing them in order to make the familiar argument that, in the future, environmental conditions will make it increasingly costly to increase or even to maintain a given standard of living. The use of abatement technologies increases the costs of other products, therefore constant real

---

[37] The labor matrix is enlarged by an additional row, but not necessarily by an additional column.

[38] As was emphasized by Leontief [162].

[39] This includes both direct consumption by wage earning households as well as the goods bought from social security pensions.

[40] The vector e = $(1, 1, 1, \ldots, 1)$ is used to obtain a scalar product.

wages would imply increasing nominal wages and a falling standardized rate of profit. Under these circumstances, the introduction of an abatement technology requires the ability to handle possible conflicts about the question of who should carry the additional costs. One possible approach would be to try to speed up technological change so as to offset the economic costs of abatement technology. Moreover, these costs are associated with clear benefits as the toxic waste is eliminated. As these benefits may be considered a public good, financing abatement services by the state can help to avoid conflicts about income distribution. This presupposes that goverment revenue is not increased but reallocated from other purposes to the task of reversing environmental impacts of quantitative growth.

Reversing environmental impacts with the use of abatement technologies lowers impact vectors and so dissociates economic from physical growth. Under these conditions, in the face of reversible environmental effects economic growth can continue and may even be fostered by the additional demand for abatement services. This offers a prospect of qualitative growth, at least for some time. In the long run, however, falling standardized rates of profit may restrict not only potential but also actual economic growth. I will discuss some related questions in section 5.4.

The argument that environmental conditions may make it increasingly costly to further increase a given standard of living is relevant not only for reversible environmental effects but also for *limited natural resources*. The classical example is the existence of a specific kind of land which is available only in a limited amount. For the production of a given good b_i, this kind of land, which I denote as L, offers an exceptionally profitable opportunity—be it because of its geological properties, climatic conditions, traffic access or other reasons. If the total quantity of L is insufficient to produce the amount of b_i in demand at its normal price, the market price of b_i will rise until supply and demand are matched by simultaneously stretching production to the limits and reducing demand by rising market prices. This process is represented in figures 5.4 and 5.7 by the price movement from N to M.

What information is conveyed by this transition? The difference between the market price at B and the normal price at A signals a capacity limit. In the case of fixed capital, such limits can be overcome by additional investment. Now we are faced with a limit which cannot be overcome in this manner. Additional investment plans may be in-

Price

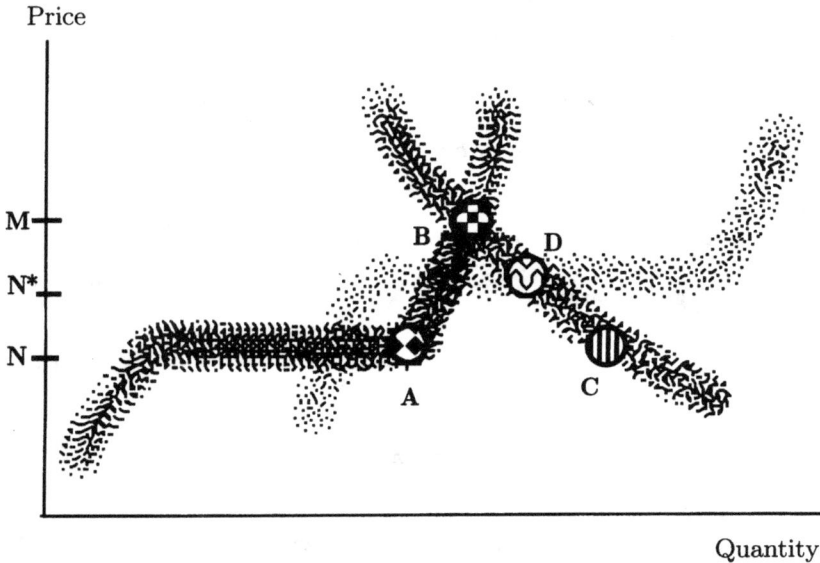

Quantity

Figure 5.7: Normal price and market price with increasing rent.

duced by the rise of market prices, but given the limited amount of L these plans will be impossible to realize until a way is found to satisfy the excess demand for b_i without using L.

Under this constraint, however, production of b_i may require considerably higher costs. Therefore, production will be persistently expanded only if the normal price for b_i rises above its previous level. The resulting movement of prices is represented in figure 5.7 by the transition from B to D. I deliberately speak here of a movement. We are facing a recursive system, in which normal prices at any given moment in time depend on demand patterns which in turn depend on normal prices at earlier stages. What information is imparted by the rise of normal prices from N to N^*? This is one of the most important questions about the functioning of a system of interdependent markets, and it is especially relevant for an inquiry into the relationship between economy and environment. I will approach it by considering a pattern of normal prices π and normal wages ω given during some period of economic activity.[41] For the same period, quantities of various kinds of human labor as well as inputs and outputs of various goods are given. One then can define normalized profits, Φ, as the profits which are obtained if all inputs and outputs are valued at normal prices:[42]

$$\Phi = b \cdot \pi - d \cdot \pi - a \cdot \omega \qquad (5.11)$$

From this we get:

$$a \cdot \omega = b \cdot \pi - d \cdot \pi - \Phi \qquad (5.12)$$

By defining the parameter:[43]

$$\gamma = (1 + \frac{\Phi}{d \cdot \pi}) \qquad (5.13)$$

we obtain:

$$a \cdot \omega = b \cdot \pi - \gamma \cdot d \cdot \pi \qquad (5.14)$$

and hence:

$$a \cdot \omega = (b - \gamma \cdot d) \cdot \pi \qquad (5.15)$$

This can be written:

$$a \cdot \omega = (b_1 - \gamma \cdot d_1) \cdot \pi_1 + \cdots + (b_n - \gamma \cdot d_n) \cdot \pi_n \qquad (5.16)$$

$(b_i - d_i)$ is the net output of the i–th good. I will call $(b_i - \gamma \cdot d_i)$ the growth–inducing output of the same good. This is the fraction of net output which remains if net investment maintains a growth rate of $1 - \gamma$ for the economy as a whole.[44] Equation (5.16) then states that total labor costs are equal to the sum of growth–inducing outputs valued at normal prices.

   If we differentiate total labor costs with respect to the growth–inducing output of an arbitrary good, we obtain a remarkable result:

---

[41] I use the symbols p and w for average prices and wages in a given period. Whether they are equal to normal prices and wages depends on the behavior of market prices in the period under consideration.

[42] The subscripts "v,t" are omitted for brevity.

[43] γ is defined to be equal to a given number in the study of a given price pattern, not as a function of variable prices and profits.

[44] It is possible to consider different growth rates for each good by using the device of sub–systems designed by Sraffa [261] and letting different subsystems grow at different growth rates. While the use of different rates yields important insights about the role of heterogeneous rates of profit, it would become too technical in this context.

$$\frac{\partial(a \cdot \omega)}{\partial(b_i - \gamma \cdot d_i)} = \pi_i \qquad (5.17)$$

The normal price of a good indicates the increase in total labor costs which would be needed if the economy were to expand the growth–inducing output of the good in question by one unit. I will denote this increase as the good's marginal labor cost.[45]

If the normal price of a car is \$20,000 and the normal hourly wage is \$20, the production of an additional car will require the economic system as a whole to employ an additional 1,000 hours of work. From the point of view of the worker, this means that she or he has to work 1,000 hours to buy a car; this is what the classical economists called the labor commanded by a product. In this terminology, equation (5.17) implies that the labor commanded by a good corresponds to the good's marginal labor cost. This is the focus of what Morishima aptly calls the marginal labor theory of value.[46]

The rise of normal prices from N to N^* in figure 5.7 indicates that the limitation of the natural resource L leads to an increase in the good's marginal labor cost. This increase is due to the fact that the process using the limited natural resource L had to be supplemented by a less profitable process operating without using L, because the amount of L available would be insufficient to satisfy demand at normal prices. Those producers which are able to use L will then make a rent equal to the difference between N and N^* for every unit of production. This is the phenomenon of a differential rent. As this rent is due to the use of a specific limited input, say the land L, it can define a normal price p_α of land use d_α. More precisely, p_α is the price for the right to use one unit of L during one period. If this right is not owned by the producer, she or he may be able to buy it from its original owner by exchanging it for the rent which can be obtained on the land in question.

The right to use natural resources is very often economically invis-ible, as the use of these resources is organized by cultural rules which are much older than triadic human ecological systems. When, how-ever, the right to use a natural resource during a given period yields

---

[45] In this terminology, marginal labor costs depend on growth–inducing outputs. If γ varies, marginal labor costs change.

[46] Morishima [195]. This approach to the economic theory of value blends core ele-ments of classical political economy with basic insights of neoclassical economists. By considering normal prices as rules developing in evolutionary processes, eco-nomic theory can then be developed as part of a more comprehensive theory of cultural evolution.

an economic rent, this right becomes an economically visible input of the economic process. The situation is similar to the one considered in (5.8) and (5.9), but now the invisible item under consideration is not an output, but rather an input.

$$D_i, D_v, A_v \rightarrow B_v \qquad (5.18)$$

$$\tilde{D}_v, \tilde{A}_v \rightarrow \tilde{B}_v \qquad (5.19)$$

The system (5.18) can be modified so as to render economically visible the previously invisible input. The total visible input is enlarged by a new economically visible good, the right to use a natural resource. At the same time, the process which used the invisible input is split into two processes, one which relies on the economically visible usufructuary right, and one which produces the same kind of output at a higher cost, but without needing this right.

As a consequence, in some cases a visible input is positive while the corresponding output is zero. Therefore, the denominator in figure (5.17) will turn negative. In order to yield a positive price, the nominator must be negative, too. This is the case because if a greater quantity of the resource considered were available, total labor costs could be lowered by expanding the less costly process and reducing the more costly one. The normal price of usufructuary rights for a limited natural resource indicates the reduction in total labor costs which would become possible if these rights could be expanded by an additional unit of the resource.

So far, I have considered only the price of the right to use a limited resource like land, not the price of the resource itself. The former price refers to usufructuary rights, which include the duty to preserve the resource itself in good state. The latter refers to ownership rights, which are temporally unlimited and which may even include the right to destroy the resource.[47] If a limited resource L can be confidently expected to yield a rent ϱ for an unlimited amount of time, ownership of this resource means owning a source of permanent income. In a world where credits bear interest such a source can be compared to a credit whose interest would be equal to ϱ. The price of the resource

---

[47] The development of the theoretical notion of property rights is discussed by Furubotn and Pejovich [92]. Land may be bought and sold independently of its use as an input for economic activity, and such trade may interfere with the processes of price formation described above. This, however, is not essential for my present topic, the possibility of qualitative growth.

will then be equal to the magnitude of this credit, and therefore to ϱ discounted at the prevailing rate of interest, i:

$$p_L = \frac{\varrho}{i} \qquad (5.20)$$

If a limited, but economically invisible natural resource is used up to its limit, the resource can become economically visible by generating a differential rent. Economic growth will then go on without increasing the use of the resource any further. Using the resource is an environmental impact, and the mechanism of differential rent lowers the corresponding impact vector: economic and physical growth are decoupled.

The emergence of a differential rent tends to lower the standardized rate of profit. The reason is that, in the production process using the limited resource, at constant real wages the rent must be detracted from profits. The higher costs in the process which avoids using the limited resource imply that the economic system displays diminishing returns, at least for a while. Economic growth is not necessarily slowed down by this process, as real wages can be lowered and/or labor productivity increased by socio–technical change. In any case, the mechanism of differential rent decouples economic growth from further use of the limited input for which the rent is paid. Therefore, not only reversible environmental effects, but also limited natural resources, can be integrated in a process of qualitative growth. Clearly, one may wonder whether this can happen indefinitely. I will come back to this question in section 6.2, but first it is useful to extend the analysis to the case of exhaustible resources.

The topic of *exhaustible natural resources* is sometimes treated, under the heading of intertemporal allocation of resources, as a special case of the problem of resource allocation. The market economy is then presented as a general problem solver for allocation problems, which in the case of exhaustible resources seeks a path of optimal depletion. The reader may become a bit skeptical if she realizes that this approach to exhaustible resources also entails a theory of optimal extinction, which can easily be applied to natural species from panda bears to blue whales.[48] This skepticism should help one to proceed with small, careful steps.[49]

Suppose there is an established way of producing some product Q at price p_q. An exhaustible resource is discovered which would

---

[48] I owe this sarcastic expression to Page [204].
[49] My procedure is similar to, but not identical with, the one used by Parinello [206].

make it possible to produce the same product at a lower price p'_q. This price includes various costs as well as profits at a normal rate. However, the amount of the resource available each year does not suffice to satisfy total demand for the product. Therefore the old and the new process are deployed in parallel. Under these conditions, the use of the resource yields a differential rent. The resource is found in a mine M. As a starting premise, I assume that the mining technology allows the extraction of a quantity R of the resource per year and that the mine contains the quantity $2R$. Design the amount of the resource needed to produce one unit of Q as s. By setting the rent per unit of the resource equal to D, we then get the following simple accounting equation, which represents the price of the product as the sum of the lower price p'_q and differential rent $s \cdot D$ per unit of output:

$$p'_q + s \cdot D = p_q \qquad (5.21)$$

The resource's price is nothing but the rent per unit of the resource, D. What is the price of the mine? The mine can be expected to yield an annual income of $R \cdot D$ for 2 years. Somebody who wants to sell the mine could therefore argue that the mine's value is equal to $2 \cdot R \cdot D$. In a world where positive rates of interest prevail, it would be hard to find a buyer at this price. Future income streams would be discounted at a positive rate of interest in order to compute their present value. The price of the mine therefore would be lower than $2 \cdot R \cdot D$. More generally, at positive rates of interest, the price of an exhaustible resource *in situ* is always smaller than the sum of the rents which can be obtained from the resource.

To determine its precise value, I will work backwards from the moment at which the resource is exhausted. After depletion, the mine's value will obviously be equal to zero. At the beginning of the depletion period, it will be equal to the discounted value of the rent which is expected for the end of this period. At a rate of interest i of 10%, it takes a capital of \$909 to grow to \$1,000 in a year's time. If with the same rate of interest a mine is expected to yield \$1,000 at the end of the depletion period, its value at the beginning of this period, $p_{m,k}$, will be \$909. In general terms:

$$p_{m,k} = \frac{R \cdot D}{(1+i)} \qquad (5.22)$$

From (5.21), this is equivalent to (5.23):

$$p_{m,k} = \frac{(p_q - p'_q)}{(1+i)} \cdot \frac{R}{s} \qquad (5.23)$$

which implies:

$$p_q' + p_{m,k} \cdot (1+i) \cdot \frac{s}{R} = p_q \tag{5.24}$$

This formula represents the value of a unit output of the depletion period as the sum of the lower price and differential rent per unit of product. Rent, however, is now represented as interest on the value of the mine.

For the previous periods, a similar formula applies, with the difference that the value of the partially depleted mine will appear on the output side as well, again discounted by one plus the rate of interest:

$$p_{m,k-1} = \frac{R \cdot D}{1+i} + \frac{p_{m,k}}{1+i} \tag{5.25}$$

With the help of 5.21, this can be rearranged as:

$$p_{m,k-1} = \frac{p_q - p_q'}{1+i} \cdot \frac{R}{s} + \frac{p_{m,k}}{1+i} \tag{5.26}$$

yielding the accounting equation:

$$p_q' + p_{m,k-1} \cdot (1+i) \cdot \frac{s}{R} = p_q + p_{m,k} \cdot \frac{s}{R} \tag{5.27}$$

For our two period case, formula 5.25 and 5.22 yields:

$$p_{m,k-1} = \frac{R \cdot D}{1+i} + \frac{R \cdot D}{(1+i)^2} \tag{5.28}$$

The value of two units of the resource *in situ* is smaller than two times the rent per extracted unit. The greater the rate of interest, the greater the difference. Applying formula (5.28) to a total rent of $2000 and a rate of interest of 10%, the initial price of the mine amounts to $1735. The difference of $ 265 is a clear incentive to accelerate the depletion process, and the higher the rate of interest, the greater the incentive to accelerate depletion.[50]

A major example of an exhaustible resource is oil. Known reserves may be roughly ordered by the different costs of production. Oil from the Middle East has low production costs, oil from the North Sea has high production costs. As reserves of different kinds are tapped simultaneously, large differential rents arise. In the course of time, the world economy uses increasingly more oil, and therefore reserves with

---

[50] This is a main point of the famous paper by Hotelling [133].

increasing extraction costs are tapped. Because of the greater difficulties which must be overcome in oil production, it takes an increasing amount of labor to produce an additional unit of oil. This tendency can always be countered by technological innovations or by the discovery of new reserves, but if the expansion of production continues, normal prices are bound to increase in the long run. Increasing normal prices, which lead to new differential rents, can stimulate technological innovations which help to reduce the use of oil. However, in a growing economy increasing normal prices make additional reserves available, they do not stop the extraction of available reserves.

The mechanism of differential rent for limited natural resources is no guarantee for an ecologically sound management of exhaustible resources. This is not always a serious problem. A small oil well in the desert may be exhausted fairly rapidly without creating major ecological problems; and after the well's depletion many other wells may be available. Obviously, serious problems of economic adjustment would arise if global oil reserves were to be completely depleted, but this would be a gradual process stretching over at least several decades. Although the discounting of future rents described above does provide an incentive for accelerating depletion, technological, financial, and political factors put an upper ceiling on depletion rates, as the policy of OPEC over the last two decades illustrates. Moreover, in the long run normal prices for oil will rise because production will shift towards increasingly costly sources. The corresponding price increases will then induce major socio–technical changes, which could make the transition from today's heavily oil–dependent economic structure towards a different structure less difficult than it seems to be now. Still, oil plays such an important role in today's world economy that such a transition would no doubt be an extremely difficult process. Severe breakdowns of the general standard of living as well as frightening military conflicts cannot be excluded at all.

In addition to the problems of final depletion, the development of urban air pollution and the risks of global climatic change show that oil use can create severe environmental problems long before oil reserves are exhausted. Similar problems arise with other exhaustible resources. Under such conditions, additional mechanisms are warranted to decouple economic from physical growth. One such mechanism, which deserves careful study, is the use of tradeable permits which maintain economical activities below critical *environmental thresholds*.

As a case in point, suppose that production and imports of commercial energy would be controlled by energy permits. Under such a scheme, producing coal from a coal mine, producing electricity from hydroelectric power, as well as importing oil from abroad would require energy permits.[51] Using solar energy to produce electricity for one's household does not constitute commercial energy, nor does the use of solar energy to grow corn. Using the same solar energy to produce crops which are sold as energy sources from biomass burning, however, is a way of producing commercial energy.

Firms engaged in the production of commercial energy would need to deliver a corresponding amount of energy permits to an independent government agency. A limited amount of permits would be sold every year by the same agency. These sales would take the form of several auctions per year, with the agency selling the annual amount of permits in such a way as to avoid sudden jumps in the price of permits. The permits would be freely tradeable, but their validity would expire after a fixed time span. The government agency would be free to buy back permits at market prices. Furthermore, I assume that the government revenue obtained from energy permits would be used to lower existing taxes and social security contributions so as to reduce wage costs.

Energy permits can be considered as emission permits for entropy. However, there is no need to measure the entropy actually emitted. Economic activities producing and importing commercial energy are easy to check; enforcing permits for this kind of activity would not require a big administrative apparatus. Such an apparatus would, however, be needed if the instrument of limited permits should target a whole series of specific emissions. This is a strong argument for focusing limited permits on a core parameter of whole human ecological systems, and not on a large series of emissions. By controlling the input of commercial energy many environmental impacts can be controlled, too. Important examples are noise production, traffic congestion and frequency of traffic accidents, many kinds of air, water, and soil pollution, and the overall production of technomass.

What amount of commercial energy is made available under such a permits scheme is a matter of political decision. As I discussed in chapter 4, there is no clear–cut border separating actions leading to environmental catastrophe from environmentally acceptable actions. Drawing such a border is always a moral decision. Scientific arguments about

---

[51] Some issues relating to effects of energy permits on international competition will be discussed in chapter 6.

the properties of ecosystems and the like are vital for such decisions, but they don't eliminate the necessity of a moral choice.

Suppose that such a choice has been made. Imagine that a political decision is made to reduce the use of commercial energy by 25% by issuing energy permits according to the rules specified above. To envisage the possible consequences of such a measure it is useful to consider a numerical example of an imaginary economic system. Such an example is presented in table (5.29). The table can be read as an equation stating that the value of output is equal to the sum of the remaining items. Most inputs (including depreciaton of fixed capital) are lumped together in a catch–all category; labor costs are differentiated into direct (i.e., net) wage costs and indirect wage costs (i.e., taxes and social security).

products	$100\beta \cdot 30\$/\beta$
various inputs	$80\alpha \cdot 10\$/\alpha$
commercial energy	$60\psi \cdot 5\$/\psi$
direct wage costs	$40\lambda \cdot 20\$/\lambda$
indirect wage costs	$40\lambda \cdot 20\$/\lambda$
profits	$300\$$

$$(5.29)$$

According to scheme (5.29), the system uses 60 units of commercial energy. From now on, however, it must operate with only 45 units. This enforces the introduction of a new, energy saving technology. The new technology, however, will not supplant the existing technology all at once. Rather, old and new technologies will coexist, with the new one expanding until the system as a whole can operate with the commercial energy available under the permits regime. Table (5.30) describes such a situation. The total output produced is the same as in (5.29), but now the system is split into two processes, one operating with the old technology, one with the new technology. A good example would be the use of buildings with excellent insulation based on new technology side by side with buildings with poorer insulation based on older technology.

	old technology	new technology
products	$50\beta \cdot 30\$/\beta$	$50\beta \cdot 30\$/\beta$
various inputs	$40\alpha \cdot 10\$/\alpha$	$40\alpha \cdot 10\$/\alpha$
commercial energy	$30\psi \cdot 15\$/\psi$	$15\psi \cdot 15\$/\psi$
direct wage costs	$20\lambda \cdot 20\$/\lambda$	$29\lambda \cdot 20\$/\lambda$
indirect wage costs	$20\lambda \cdot 5\$/\lambda$	$29\lambda \cdot 5\$/\lambda$
profits	150$	150$

(5.30)

The new technology uses less energy but more labor per unit of output. If the amount of energy permits available should be reduced even further, the new technology would expand in relation to the old one. The combination of the two technologies enables the total system to minimize the total labor required to yield a given output under given energy constraints.[52] If the old technologies were discarded altogether, total energy use would be further reduced while total labor costs would increase.

In the transition from table (5.29) to (5.30), the price of commercial energy follows the process of rising normal prices described in figure 5.7. As a result, the normal price for commercial energy rises from $5 to $15. At average wage costs of $25 per hour, an energy price of $5 implies that in order to produce an additional unit of commercial energy as net output, the economic system as a whole would require an additional 12 minutes of labor. The higher price of $15, then, implies that 36 minutes would be needed for the same purpose. But how can the net output of energy be augmented if energy permits limit total energy production? By reducing energy use in the production of other goods and services. In the example under consideration, this effect can be achieved by reducing the use of the old technology and increasing the use of the new one. This shift leads to the need for the additional 36 minutes.

What about the price of the permits themselves? The price of energy permits is a price of limited non–produced inputs, and may, therefore, be described as a rent. As in the case of differential rent, a cost difference between two technologies is neutralized by assigning

---

[52] In a system with positive rates of profit, what matters are growth inducing outputs.

a price to a limited non–produced input. In this case, the limited
input is used by both technologies, although with different intensity.
Accordingly, the price of the permits can be labelled as an *intensive
rent*.[53] As energy permits enter the system as an input without being
produced as an economic output, their price corresponds to a negative
marginal labor cost. It indicates how much labor could be saved in the
economic system as a whole if an additional unit of energy were made
available by additional permits.

In which sense does an intensive rent for energy permits internalize
an external effect? Environmental problems engendered by rising use
of commercial energy constitute external effects. They are caused by
economic activities but don't appear in the accounting schemes of these
activities. The introduction of energy permits would internalize the
problem in the sense that these permits would appear in economic
accounting schemes. However, what contributes to the solution of the
problem is not simply the price of the permits, but their limitation.
The price of the permits is the signal which enables the economy to
cope with the limitation by developing adequate forms of technological
change. Shifts in demand as a consequence of price movements are
not the crucial component of this process, although they will no doubt
occur. The crucial component is the stimulation of technological change
by limiting the use of a vital natural resource, namely the free energy
which the economic system receives as a gift from nature. I will come
back to the form of this change in chapter 6.

Once the permits have found a price through the operation of market processes, there is no need to assign a price to the amenity of landscapes, the integrity of the climate system, and other features of the
environment which were threatened by unlimited energy use. Energy
permits can internalize external effects without assigning a monetary
value to these effects or to the environmental systems protected by the
introduction of such permits. What becomes economically visible is the
environmental threshold set by the institution of energy permits, not
the series of external effects which are controlled by this threshold.

Intensive rents can arise not only with energy permits and similar
instruments, but also with a limited supply of natural resources like
land or oil.[54] If different kinds of such a resource exist, an intensive
rent for the most costly kind may then be combined with differential
rents for the less costly ones. In all these situations, an input is used

---

[53] The possibility of intensive rents was first described by Sraffa [261].

[54] In the case of raw materials, intensive rent can take the form of royalties for their
extraction.

which does not involve costs of production, because it is a gift of nature. In a sense, the use of such inputs is a trivial attribute of any human activity, because human beings are the result of an evolutionary process which has placed them into a pre–existing world. What is less trivial is the fact that some of the gifts which we receive from nature may involve environmental thresholds. In this case, it would be efficient to develop a mix of two technological processes to produce a single set of goods. In the absence of environmental thresholds, only the less costly of the two technologies would be used. Where such a threshold is established, the second technology will be required, too, because it allows the expansion of production without crossing the threshold.

If production increases, use of the technology with lower resource intensity will expand, so as to keep the system within the threshold. If demand continues to grow, simply shifting the quantitative relation between the use of two technologies will not do indefinitely. Sooner or later, a new technology with still lower resource intensity will have to be developed. The new technology can then supersede the more resource intensive of the two previous technologies. This will happen as soon as the intensive rent rises to a level which makes the new pair of technologies competitive. In the case of energy permits, this process would induce a sequence of technological advances leading to higher energy efficiency.

The mechanism of intensive rent offers the possibility of coping with environmental thresholds by establishing a pattern of qualitative growth. Economic growth occurs without increasing the use of a critical resource, in our case commercial energy. As in the case of differential rent, standardized rates of profit may fall with rising intensive rent. With instruments like energy permits sold by the goverment, however, there is an interesting possibilty to compensate the rent for these permits by lowering indirect wage costs. Moreover, technical change may help to maintain standardized rates of profit. I will come back to the interaction between technical change and environmental thresholds in chapter 6.

Next, however, it is important to focus on the difference between the introduction of energy permits and an *energy tax*. They differ in the way in which they handle the relation between prices and quantities. In the case of the tax, public authorities define a monetary magnitude, while the market finds a related physical quantity. With limited permits, public authorities define a quantity, while the market finds a corresponding price. There can be little doubt that in the case of envi-

ronmental thresholds the latter division of labor is more appropriate to
the respective institutional properties of markets and governments.

In a growing economy, a level of taxation which today leads people
to forgo the purchase of energy intensive products will loose its bite
a few years later. Therefore, it will be quite difficult to establish a
tax which keeps energy consumption persistently below a well defined
threshold. Moreover, it may well be that for two specific levels of an
energy tax two optimal technologies can be found, but that no technology is optimal for intermediate levels of the tax. As it is impossible
to know such connections in advance, a gradually growing tax may often lead to suboptimal results. Finally, in a rapidly changing economy
the time lags involved in economic adjustment processes can make it
impossible to find out which level of an energy tax would be needed
at a specific moment in time to reach a given target for energy use.
As a result, the political decision about energy use cannot be framed
in terms of a moral choice about an environmental threshold, but only
in terms of defining more or less arbitrary levels of taxation. Political
processes may then easily lead to results which do not make much sense
in environmental terms.

By contrast, limited permits would set a cost effective and clearly
perceived ceiling on the production of commercial energy. Firms would
have an immediate and persisting incentive to find paths of technological change which would keep overall energy use below that ceiling. Households could still choose for which purposes they wish to use
the limited commercial energy available in the economy in which they
live.

This is not to say that limited permits are always preferable to taxes.
I have already mentioned that in the case of reversible environmental
effects taxes can make sense if they cover the cost of a service which
reverses the relevant environmental effect. Moreover, in the political
process it may turn out to be possible to introduce an energy tax quite
rapidly while it would take a long time to establish energy permits. It
may then be appropriate to introduce an energy tax, which at a later
stage might be turned into a scheme of energy permits.

The implementation of energy permits raises important issues of *fairness*. Energy permits create new property rights: they entitle their
owners, and only them, to produce a certain amount of commercial energy. This is sometimes considered to be immoral because it is thought
to establish a "right to pollute". However, producing commercial energy engenders pollution only if relevant environmental thresholds are

crossed. Energy permits are an instrument for enforcing such thresholds. They fail to establish an acceptable situation if the threshold is set too high. This is not a consequence of using energy permits, but of not being strict enough in their use. Which level is appropriate, however, is a matter of public debate and political decision.

Other issues of fairness are raised by the initial distribution of the new property rights. The analysis along the lines of table (5.30) can be used to show that important effects of limited emission permits are quite independent of their initial distribution.[55] I have assumed that the permits are initially owned by the government. They would operate in the same way if they were owned by a private person, or by another institution. If the permits are initally owned by the government, but the government must use the receipts from their sale to lower taxes, then in an important sense the original ownership lies with the citizens of the nation in question. These citizen can allocate the receipts in a way which corresponds to their notions of fairness. In particular, receipts from selling energy permits may be used to specifically reduce taxes for disadvantaged groups, without in any way impairing the environmental functioning of the permits. This would apply even if the receipts were used to allocate a negative income tax to such groups, in order to compensate for raising energy prices. Clearly, energy permits cannot solve preexisting conflicts about the distribution of income and wealth, but they can be implemented in ways which correspond to democratically established notions of fairness.

Who should be required to buy energy permits? One approach would focus on private households. This is motivated by the idea that private households will change their consumption patterns if they are forced to spend additional money on energy permits. There is, however, a flaw in this argument: in a democracy, people will hardly accept a scheme which puts on their shoulders the burden of a technological development for which they were never responsible. This misstep can be avoided by an analysis in terms of intensive rents, because this analysis is not based on shifts in consumer demand, but on a mechanism ruling the production process. Excess demand for a limited input induces technological change, which increases efficiency in using that input. Later, consumption patterns will change because technological change affords new consumption possibilities. People started using gasoline after cars were invented, not the other way around. Humankind will

---

[55] This is reminiscent of the claim by Coase [50] that in some cases the effect of introducing property rights for the internalization of external effects is independent of the initial distribution of property titles.

save gasoline to the degree to which the technological infrastructure of
the world economy will make this an attractive possibility.

Therefore, it makes much more sense to require the producers and
importers of commercial energy to buy the permits, while other firms
and their clients simply have to pay a price which takes into account
the cost of the permits. This kind of arrangement could help the firms
which actually produce the relevant technological infrastructure to develop innovations directed toward increasingly efficient energy use. As
a result, consumption patterns of private households would shift toward
the newly developed goods and services. Along these lines, limited energy permits could help to establish an economic transformation from
quantitative towards qualitative growth.

5.4   A Steady–State Economy?

In section 5.2, I have discussed the close links between positive rates
of economic growth and positive rates of interest and profit. In this
section, I will discuss the ideal type of an economy in which these three
ratios all fluctuate around a zero level. This leads to the interesting
situation of infinite prices for rent–yielding assets. The intuitive idea
that the value of some ecosystems should be set beyond anything money
can buy applies quite literally to a steady–state economy. Lowering
rates of interest to zero, however, requires important modifications of
today's monetary institutions. Some kind of liquidity fee is needed for
this purpose, and one possibility to realize such a fee is given by the
prospect of a de–nationalization of money.

A steady–state economy presupposes a process of cultural regeneration in which money loses its present status as an external goal of
economic activities. In such a process, wage labor is transformed into
vocational activity, which is experienced primarily as an opportunity
for self–fulfilment. This can hardly be realized without new kinds of
vocational associations, which may emerge out of today's trade unions.
In particular, in a triadic human ecological system the polarity of private and public property rights needs to be supplemented by vocational
property rights. For this purpose, vocational associations can run pension funds which own business firms. In this way, individual biographies
can be linked to vocational traditions not only at a cultural level, but
also at a structural level. Money can cease to be an external goal which
transforms human activity into labor, and a sustainable world economy
becomes at least a long–run perspective.

It is often said that environmental problems are due to situations where environmental goods have no positive price.[56] In this context, it is usually assumed, without much reflection, that a good can only be either free or have a finite positive price. There are, however, environmental goods such as the ozone layer which, in a way, ought to have a positive *infinite price*. No sum of money, however large it may be, should be permitted to purchase the right to destroy the ozone layer. There may be good reasons for holding similar positions when dealing with certain tropical forests, the Antarctic, endangered species like the whales, or other beings of great ecological value.

There is no need to define a positive notion of ecological value here. It is sufficient to make the negative claim that not everything that human beings consider valuable can be made equivalent to a finite sum of money. There are things which money cannot buy, and there are beings which money should not be able to buy. In both cases, one may ask what economic arrangements would assign an infinite price to these beings. In many cases, there is a straightforward answer: A normal rate of interest of zero would assign an infinite price to any source of permanent income.

The possibility of zero rates of interest and profits affects the relation between stocks and flows in a remarkable way. Consider a piece of land which can be expected to yield a constant rent over an indefinite amount of time in the future. The rent is a flow, while the land is a stock. As indicated by equation (5.20), the rate of interest makes it possible to transform flows into stocks: The value of the stock is equal to the value of the flow divided by the rate of interest.

From equation (5.20) it follows that a decrease in the normal rate of interest leads to an increase in the stock's price. If, for example, rates of interest fall, the price of land tends to rise. At a rate of interest of 20%, a piece of land yielding a permanent rent of $1,000 is equivalent to a capital of $5,000; at a rate of interest of 5%, the same piece of land yielding the same rent is equivalent to a capital of $20,000. What happens at a zero rate of interest? The price of a stock which yields a permanent income becomes infinite. Trade in such stock will cease, because at a zero rate of interest no finite payment can be equivalent to a source of permanent income.

This is a remarkable result. Consider the example of a landscape whose beauty lies beyond anything money can buy. Tradeable permits to use this landscape in ways which preserve its beauty could be sold

---

[56] A highly influential paper along these lines is Hardin [117].

to the public just like other limited permits. Such rights are usufructuary, and they are, therefore, limited in time. They do not confer
possession of the landscape. The economic value of the landscape as
such is equal to the rent from the permits discounted by the normal
rate of interest. Only if this rate is zero will the landscape's economic
value be infinite.

A zero rate of interest establishes a profound distinction between
stocks and flows, a distinction which is lost at positive rates of interest.
With regard to ecological systems, positive rates of interest imply a
confusion between usufructuary rights and rights of possession. A world
economy with a normal rate of interest fluctuating around zero would
offer a setting where firms would be entitled to use landscapes, rare
species, etc., while being obliged to preserve them. Clearly, a serious
analysis of today's environmental crisis cannot omit a discussion of
these possibilities.

Perhaps at some future date limited inputs from the environment will
force a decline in standardized rates of profit which no amount of socio–
technological change will help to avoid. For a while, actual rates of
profit may then stay unchanged if wage increases are slowed down or
even reversed. If the decline of standardized rates of profit were to
continue, actual rates would have to fall as well. Economic growth
would probably slow down, and eventually stop in a situation of zero
rates of profit. This need not be an unpleasant situation. It could
be a *steady state* in which people would enjoy more economic wealth
than ever before and in which they would focus their projects on other
goals than further increasing their wealth.[57] Economic activities would
then make sense to the extent to which they were characterized not
by the opportunity to earn more money, but by an internal relation
between means and ends. The labor performed in the economic realm
would have been transformed into vocational activity. The point of
this activity would lie in the opportunities for self–fulfilment—on a par
with activities in the realms of private and public life.

If the world economy did reach a steady–state, socio–technical
change would go on, but economic growth would not. The probability
distributions of rates of profit and of rates of interest would both be
symmetrical with an expected value of zero. Profitability would still be
a crucial rule governing investment decisions, although it would refer

---

[57] Daly [56] has collected strong arguments for a steady–state economy, mainly
from an environmental point of view. In a seminal paper on the theory of saving,
Ramsey [228] even described the steady state as a state of bliss.

to a zero normal rate of profit. Firms would continue to compete for business opportunities and try hard to avoid losses which could throw them out of business altogether. As a result, markets would go on displaying the effects of the invisible hand.

Positive rates of profit provide a strong incentive for a kind of socio–technical change which leads to increased production. In a steady–state economy, this incentive would be ineffective. Socio–technical change would be directed primarily towards improving product quality and inventing new products. However, a steady–state economy could still engender flows of energy and technomass which are much too high from an environmental point of view. Therefore, the instrument of energy permits discussed in section 5.3 would have to be an integral component of the institutional setting of a steady–state economy. This instrument would then also help to channel socio–technical change in environmentally sensible ways.

Clearly, the transition to a steady–state economy would require that lower, and eventually zero, rates of profit be progressively considered as normal. Otherwise, breakdowns of confidence would inevitably lead to situations of economic crisis. A possible trigger of such crisis is the existence of a lower bound i^* for rates of interest.[58] If rates of profit were to decline below i^*, major economic crises would be inevitable unless the liquidity preference of the public could be lowered so that rates of interest could fall below i^*.

Liquidity preference could be persistently lowered by introducing time–marked money.[59] An elegant way of carrying this out is made available by the progressive substitution of traditional cash money by electronic instruments of payment like "smart" credit cards with a built in microchip. Every inflow of money could have a date, and after a year the money in question could lose its validity. It could then be exchanged for new money for a fee equal to i^*, say 3%. Another way of achieving the same end would be the introduction of a liquidity fee, which would make it unattractive to hold cash by reducing the value of hoarded money at some specified rate per day. More sophisticated approaches could involve random decay and other technicalities, but the main point is simple. If the validity of money had a time–limit, the public's liquidity preference could be lowered so as to make zero rates of interest possible.

---

[58] The existence of a lower bound for rates of interest at which credit is supplied was discussed in section 5.2.

[59] A possibility envisaged among others by Fisher [79], Gesell [97], Keynes [155]. A recent contribution in the same direction is Suhr and Godschalk [269].

A liquidity fee could be construed as a tax collected by national banks or another government agency, but this is not the only possibility. An important alternative is offered by recent proposals of a *de–nationalization of money*.[60] In chapter 3, I have discussed sex, power, and money as three generalized ends of action corresponding to the realms of private, public, and vocational life, respectively. Given this perspective, the fact that in today's world economy the operation of money is still rather closely linked to political power through the privileged role of national banks is something of an anomaly. De–nationalizing money could be a sensible way of freeing the currency system from problematic political interferences.

At least since Keynes' proposal of a single world currency the practice of national monetary policy has been questioned time and again by invoking the idea of a world–wide monetary authority—and the construction of the International Monetary Fund is seen by many as a step in that direction. Establishing a single global monetary authority is usually seen as a task for national governments engaged in the formation of supra–national bodies, maybe even of a world government. Such a perspective contributes little to a better differentiation between politics and economics, between power and money. However, a different development is at least conceivable, if Milton Friedmans suggestion that society should get rid of monetary authorities altogether is taken up in a more creative way than with so–called monetarist economic policy.[61]

Nation states could gradually transfer their right to define and create currency to suitable economic actors, for example to an appropriately defined category of banks. In turn, these actors would accept specific duties in order to guarantee sensible monetary institutions.[62] Instead of strengthening a central monetary authority like the international monetary fund, such a process would foster pluralistic competition between different actors trying to supply the world economy with liquidity in a reliable way. Suppliers of financial services could then be entitled to define currencies of their own choice, while being denied

---

[60] Such a proposal was formulated by Hayek [125]. See also Gerding and Starbatty [96], as well as Greenfield and Yeager [107].

[61] Friedman [90].

[62] For example, a bank's right to issue its own currency could be conditional on a maximum rate of inflation for the currency in question. Moreover, very strict liability rules would obviously be warranted for the case of bankruptcy. National banks could be maintained as actors in competitive currency markets. However, they would lose their present monopolistic position and would also have to finance their operations by charging a liquidity fee.

the possibility of financing themselves by charging interest on credit. Banks with the right to issue currency could not finance themselves from interest payments on the credit which they supply to others. Instead, they would need to charge the users of their currency a liquidity fee as the price for supplying a reliable currency. This fee would not be a tax, but simply the normal price for a specific economic service.

To convey the basic idea, it may be useful to imagine a bank which is entitled to issue its own currency, which may be called the Phoenix. The bank could give credit in Phoenix units at will, but it would not be allowed to charge interest on such credits. The bank would, however, be entitled to charge all users of Phoenix currency with a uniform liquidity fee. This fee would be equally charged to the bank's creditors and its debitors as long as they used the bank's currency. At the time of its introduction, the bank would define the purchasing power of the Phoenix by offering to exchange it at given rates against other currencies.[63] These rates could then be redefined in the course of time. If the Phoenix should be subject to inflation, the bank would face the danger that its clients would sooner or later stop using the Phoenix altogether. It could counteract this tendency by increasing its liquidity fee. This could restrict the amount of the Phoenix units available and raise its exchange rate with other currencies, thereby reducing the inflationary pressure on the Phoenix. Clearly, much research is needed to study the interrelated dynamics of rates of interest and rates of profit which can lead to a steady–state economy. This is, however, a research task of considerable importance for any long–term solution of the global environmental crisis.

A reduction of normal rates of profit and interest to zero would draw a sharp line between usufructuary and property rights with regard to rent–generating resources. What would be a sensible arrangement for property rights with regard to such resources? Maybe there is something to be learned from the Bible here. According to the Old Testament, the land belongs to God, and households can have usufructuary rights to it. A household or, in the context of the contemporary economy, a firm, could thus be entitled to use a rent–yielding natural resource for a limited time. This entitlement would entail the duty to preserve the resource for future use and to give it back upon the ex-

---

[63] Incidentally, this emphasizes that the purchasing power of money must be studied as the outcome of a historical process, not as the result of synchronic variables like quantities of money and quantities of various products existing at a single moment in time.

piration of the contract regulating the entitlement. The other partner
of such contracts would be a political community empowered with the
property rights to the natural resource in question. This community
would be entitled to make decisions concerning possible modifications
of rent–yielding resources, for example with regard to mining.

The old idea of public ownership of land, an idea vigorously defended even by L.Walras, one of the founding fathers of modern economics, would offer the obvious solution to the problem of *property
rights for the sources of rent*.[64] Such items would be subject to public
property rights, with public authorities selling freely tradeable usufructuary rights at periodic auctions. It would then appear natural that
rent–generating resources cannot be passed from parents to children
any more than the power of a judge or a prime minister could be inherited.

But does experience not show that public ownership of important
economic resources leads to inefficiency, mismanagement, and serfdom?
These are serious matters, and confusion lurks in the most unexpected
places. The first source of confusion lies between untradeable resources
with an infinite price and tradeable capital goods with a finite price.
I am here concerned exclusively with the former, and there is nothing
in my argument pointing in the direction of public ownership of, say,
machinery or whole economic firms. A second confusion involves the
distinction between *res publica* and *res nullius*.[65] An important cause
of environmental problems lies in situations where natural resources
are treated as free goods, and sometimes this is said to follow from
public property rights to such resources. In fact, a free good in most
cases is what the Romans called *res nullius*, an item without specified
property rights. Public property fits in less with a zero price than with
an infinite one. It implies explicit rules of conduct with regard to the
item in question, and such rules suit non–tradeable items especially
well.

It is useful to compare the problem of property rights to natural
resources with the problem of property rights to human beings. It took
a long historical process to establish that property rights to human
beings are immoral and illegal. While there is no nation which would
not subscribe to this view, slaves are still traded in several parts of the

---

[64] As Jaffé [147] rightly emphasizes, Walras' land–nationalization scheme was firmly
rooted in his view of a structural conflict between private owners of the sources
of rent and the rest of society.

[65] To avoid this confusion is a major concern of Perrings [215]. See also Berkes et
al. [23].

world. It will still take a great deal of further effort to reach a situation
in which the price of a human being will actually become infinite. This
effort could be linked to a different, but related task: establishing an
infinite price for rent–yielding natural resources. In both cases, variants
of usufructuary rights are important. An employer can use the abilities
of an employee for a limited time, and he is not allowed to do harm to
the employee during this time. There is a remarkable analogy between
wage labor as opposed to slavery, and the entitlement to use a natural
resource while preserving it, as opposed to the entitlement to destroy
a natural resource for one's particular purposes. In the case of human
beings, the people employed are entitled to a wage for their work. In the
case of natural resources, a rent arises, but it does not make sense to pay
it to the resource. Instead, both rent payments for usufructuary rights
to use land, to deplete mines, and to produce commercial energy could
become a main, maybe the sole, form of *government income.*[66]

If different kinds of property rights are carefully distinguished, the
idea of public ownership of rent–generating resources is actually compatible with private property of land. Imagine a landlord who is entitled to enjoy his or her land for private purposes as much as she or
he wishes. In order to put that land to an use which can yield a rent,
however, the landlord is required to buy tradeable permits for the use
in question. Under competitive conditions, the price of the permits
will be equal to the rent which they permit to obtain. If the permits
are originally sold by the government, public property rights provide
the possibility to collect a rent, while private property rights provide
access to the land. Under such circumstances, land could have a finite
price even at a zero rate of interest. The price of land would reflect the
preferences and projects of people selling and buying land. It would
be independent, however, of the rents which government would collect
from landlords via tradeable permits.

So far, I have discussed property rights within the polarity of private
and public life. This polarity, however, has ceased to be exhaustive
after the emergence of markets in which vocational organizations interact with each other, as well as with private households and public
authorities. The distinction between private and public property rights
was developed in a systematic fashion in the context of the Roman Empire and was elaborated and transformed by feudal kingdoms, which
combined basic traits of the Roman tradition with institutional forms

---

[66] It is worth remembering that the idea that taxes could be focused on rent was
dear already to Ricardo.

of various "barbarian" tribes. This distinction was quite appropriate for dual human ecological systems. With the emergence of the new realm of vocational life, the situation changed dramatically. There are strong arguments against attempts to bring business firms under the exclusive influence of public property rights. But is it really sensible to gear the world economy to the hereditary practices of families by defending private property rights over business firms?

Marx thought that private property rights to business organizations are incompatible with a socially responsible development of these organizations in the long run. He argued that public property would be more adequate. Although this idea seems to have been definitely discredited by the experience of planned economies, there can be little doubt that in the mixed economies of the present times public property of some assets is a welcome complement to private enterprise. Examples of such assets are certain transportation facilities as well as organizations like elementary schools and administrative authorities.

If the attempt to check irresponsible use of private property rights by their transformation into rights of public property has been successful only in restricted forms, the straightforward idea of a redistribution of private property rights with the goal of "people's capitalism" has gained new appeal. Before the development of stock holding there was a highly visible distinction between households living from wages and households living from profits or rent, although the distinction was blurred by the existence of small entrepreneurs like artisans, dentists etc. However, with the institution of stock holding even the existence of giant enterprises does not require the concentration of private property in a few hands. In fact, there is much to be said in favor of a broad distribution of the wealth of nations among their citizens.

The socialist critique of private property rights to capital can be re-stated so as to attack not the private character, but the unequal distribution of such property rights. However, while steps toward people's capitalism may actually strengthen the democratic character of public life, it is hard to see how they could check the problem of irresponsible behavior in the economic realm. Could the latter problem really be solved simply by entitling a multitude of stock holders to appoint the managers of big firms? In public life, a similar process takes place in the form of elections. However, the "one man, one vote" rule is a necessary, but not at all sufficient condition for democratic government. Still required is the existence of institutions like a free press, institutions which nurture a lively public opinion. If this second condition is found wanting, elections degenerate into a dangerous mix of demagogy and chance events. Such a situation is still better than tyranny, but all too often it has prepared the grounds for dictatorship. What is the counterpart of public opinion in economic life? When it comes to moral questions, businessmen have little more to rely on than public debates, on the one hand, and their private religious and ethical beliefs on the other hand.

In his classical analysis of the division of labor, Durkheim argued that in order to overcome the anomie of industrial capitalism, vocational associations had to play a pivotal role.[67] This would mean that vocational ethics would provide the counterpart to public opinion in the economic realm.[68] What would be the counterpart to democratic government? Durkheim thought of an institutional arrangement where vocational associations would set the overall production goals for the economy. As an illustration, one may imagine an artisan economy, where people cooperate in a multitude of workshops following well established vocational traditions. These traditions would be sustained by vocational associations similar to the guilds formed by craftsmen of the past. For the purposes of this analysis, it is important to distinguish between vocational organizations like firms, which coordinate people of different and complementary occupations in their everyday work, and vocational associations such as guilds or maybe some transformed kind of trade unions, in which people of similar occupations try to solve common problems.

In a steady-state economy, where wage labor would have been transformed into vocational activity, such associations could be kinds of trustees of vocational knowledge and competence. Could they reasonably be expected to set macro-economic production goals? This looks quite feasible in the context of a small settlement of people. Yet already at the scale of a nation, like Durkheim's France, the picture becomes absurd, even if one supposes that vocational associations were strongly supported by the state. Moreover, vocational systems engender activities which easily transcend national contexts in a world-wide network of cooperation. If the production of every good or service was to be based on central decisions by vocational associations, a tremendously complex normative field would be needed. This normative field would have to specify a similar amount of information as the one that would be needed to run a world-wide planned economy. The truly

---

[67] Durkheim [66].
[68] I have discussed the phenomenon of vocational ethics in chapter 3. The revived interest in the relations between economics and ethics (Sen [251]; Rich [230]) could find an important focus in this phenomenon.

critical point concerns innovations. Many innovations would require world–wide modifications of a multitude of normative fields. The time required to work out these modifications would quite obviously exceed the rate of change due to shifting external circumstances and to human creativity.

Durkheim, who took over the problem of the division of labor from Adam Smith, could have avoided this problem by relying on the invisible hand discovered by Smith. If excess demand leads to an increase of market prices above normal prices, and if this difference stimulates additional production, while excess supply works the other way around, then adaptations to innovation may turn out to be quite simple as long as this price mechanism works at a speed more or less in line with the rate of change of innovation. Market dynamics make the self–reproduction of a changing economy possible.

Both the Marxist design of a planned economy and Durkheim's intuition of an economy controlled by vocational associations share a fundamental mistrust of monetary institutions. This mistrust probably confuses the real danger of monetary institutions lacking an adequate system of checks and balances with an imaginary danger associated with the existence of money as such. Monetary institutions introduce a casino character into the modern economy, as Keynes remarked. To some degree, this kind of roulette may be essential to maintaining the necessary flexibility of the world economy, and if it can offer acceptable opportunities for play and adventure, all the better. The danger of the present form of "casino capitalism"[69] consists of being led to a situation where the survival of humankind and the fate of the biosphere are at the mercy of monetary institutions unchecked by suitable forms of social responsibility. A world economy characterized by flourishing vocational ethics, by rates of interest and rates of profit both fluctuating around zero, by public property of rent–yielding assets and freely tradeable usufructuary rights for such assets could provide the necessary institutional checks and balances. It would be able to solve the environmental problems of global change by embedding the generalized end of action represented by money in reliable networks of interpersonal responsibility.

This could be achieved by developing *vocational property rights*, which would supplement private and public ones. In a historical context, this possibility may become important, for example, with regard to the role of trade unions in the current transformation of socialist

---

[69] Strange [268].

economies into market economies. It is also relevant with regard to the "pension fund socialism"[70] of contemporary Western societies and to the future role of trade–unions in market oriented economies.

In the contemporary world, pension funds are among the greatest investors and often play a crucial role in the ownership of large corporations. Durkheim rightly stressed that a major role of vocational associations such as guilds was to offer their members a network of social security, on which the members' life–plans could rely to a considerable extent. On the other hand, in countries with elaborate systems of vocational education like Germany and Switzerland, certain vocational associations play a major role in the organization of the educational system. Given this background, it seems worthwhile to investigate the possibility of a new kind of vocational association, which would have strong institutional ties to the life–course of their members, with regard both to education and to pension funds.

How could vocational property rights evolve? I will not try to answer this question here. Rather, I want to insist that this question deserves a long–term effort both in terms of research and of institutional innovation. One line of research could clearly be devoted to the various traditions of workers' cooperatives and similar forms, including workers' councils which have arisen in situations of social turmoil. These traditions stem from forms of public life and public property developed by medieval communities, which adopted rules of public property originating outside the Roman Empire. In the attempt to apply such forms to vocational organizations, steps have been taken which hint in the direction of vocational property. Unfortunately, experiences such as the one made in the former Yugoslavia strongly suggest that the problem of group egotism cannot be solved by the tradition of workers' cooperatives alone.

This is why the possibility of rooting vocational property rights in vocational associations, which are distinct from business firms, is so important. As an illustration, imagine a society where several dozen occupational fields are defined in terms of education patterns, occupational activities, and vocational associations. These associations run large pension funds, which in turn are the main owners of stock.[71] Firms would be owned in various proportions by these associations.

---

[70] Drucker [60].

[71] The pension payments of any given year would be financed mainly by the contributions of the association's members in the same year. The stock owned by the association would work as a buffer to absorb differences between these two magnitudes.

Obviously, an association of occupations related to chemical activities would tend to own large parts of chemical firms and would attempt to influence the management of these firms according to the association's priorities. The same association would also try to own significant amounts of shares of other firms which are relevant to the working lives of its members. Clearly, it would be sensible for such an association to try to own shares of other firms which seem to have a bright economic future, and maybe also of firms which have a strategic importance for the overall development of the economy. This kind of situation could be of increasing relevance in the transformation of public property rights as they have been established in planned economies. Its importance could also increase in the mixed economies of the OECD area, which are presently characterized by a combination of private and public property rights.

It may well be that the future importance of trade unions, both in socialist and in mixed economies, will critically depend on the unions' ability to re–define their role so as to fit into the framework of such a scheme. This would require far reaching transformations, because vocational associations could no longer be limited to wage earners. Instead, as organizations they would have to support life–styles which are quite distant from the proletarian patterns of the past. It would no longer be admissible to consider as irrelevant biographies such as the following. A girl learns a certain vocational activity and starts earning her living as an employee; she stops working for a while in order to have time for her children; later she starts a small business of her own, which grows to considerable size; the firm goes public and vocational organizations become its owners; the woman in question retires from business, but from time to time works as a part time employee. In the future, vocational associations should provide help in the shaping of such success stories, as well as in the case of more or less dramatic impairments of vocational life.

The historical dynamics of the labor movement can contribute to the realization of a steady–state economy by its tendency to transform present economic institutions. However, a basic difficulty with traditional strategies of the labor movement lies in their attempt to control the economy from the outside. Interestingly, a similar attempt is often observed with regard to environmental problems. Even the mainstream of environmental economics suggests that the real responsibility for ecological disruption does not lie with economic agents, but rather with governments, which neglect the task of internalizing external effects, be it by taxes, emission certificates, or other instruments. More radical environmentalists tend to talk more aggressively about business firms, but again, the remedies they propose usually emphasize political controls.

My analysis suggests a different perspective. A steady–state economy would be a deeply transformed economy, but not an economy subjugated to political controls. This point can be well illustrated with the example of factor markets.[72] Consider first the case of rent–generating resources like land. I have argued that in the long run a sustainable world economy should be characterized by rates of profit and rates of interest both fluctuating around zero. I have also discussed how a process leading to zero rates of interest would transform markets for rent–generating resources into markets for usufructuary rights, while rent would become a main form of government revenue, possibly replacing present forms of taxation. Obviously, this would lead to very different dynamics of land use, mainly because usufructuary rights require maintenance efforts which can be avoided under a regime of temporally unlimited possession. Land use would still be regulated by market processes, and there would be no need to subsume the corresponding markets under political control. Factor markets could be modified so as to yield a *sustainable world economy*, without trying to subordinate the economic process to the mechanisms of political power.

A similar argument is applicable to capital markets with rates of interest fluctuating around zero. Obviously, such a situation would lead to very different dynamics of capital markets, mainly because the desire of money for its own sake would cease. Capital markets would not disappear, though, nor would they yield their autonomy to governments. People would still want to save money for future consumption, and firms would still want to save in order to invest in the future. Conversely, other firms would look for credit to finance current investment, and private households would demand consumer credit. Variations in demand and supply for credit would induce fluctuations in interest rates and liquidity fees. Still, a zero level of normal rates of interest would be the outcome of large-scale historical processes. These processes will never come about unless the very possibility of economic agents transforming the operation of the economy is contemplated.

With regard to labor markets, the analysis of chapter 3 suggests that in the economic realm the transformation of labor into activity

---

[72] The following argument recalls Polanyi's [221] analysis of "the great transformation" from markets subordinated to political processes towards an autonomous economic reality, but without sharing Polanyi's nostalgia for the former situation.

implies a growing emphasis on vocational identities. Given such a perspective, markets for broadly specified vocational services would become even more common than they already are. Again, labor markets would not disappear, nor would they become objects of political control. Instead, a process of cultural regeneration would transform labor markets by transforming the cultural definition of the goods traded on these markets.[73] Different vocational traditions define different services, to each of which corresponds a separate labor market. On the other hand, markets for an undifferentiated labor–force would have, at best, a secondary role to play in a sustainable world economy.

---

[73] For a more detailed discussion, see Jaeger [143].

Yes, Mr.Twain, as I was saying in the beginning (said Mr. McWilliams), the rules for preserving people against lightning are so excellent and innumerable that the most incomprehensible thing in the world to me is how anybody ever manages to get struck.

Mark Twain, *The McWilliamses and the Lightning.*

Chapter 6

Managing the Environmental Crisis

In the introduction, I have discussed some of the problems which make it so difficult for humankind to behave responsibly in the face of global environmental change. They can be represented by the model of a prisoner's dilemma without iterations. I have pointed out that in order to find viable solutions, familiar notions of human agents as rationally pursuing given interests must be questioned. In chapter 2, I have proposed a more comprehensive view of human agents as accountable beings. In chapter 3, I have expanded this approach into a theory of cultural evolution. This theory can be used to study not only patterns of interpersonal accountability, but also the historical processes in which such patterns have given way to widespread irresponsibility with global consequences. In chapter 4, countervailing tendencies have been discussed, and the difficulty which these tendencies meet in the economic realm have been emphasized. In chapter 5, I have analyzed the possibility that the contemporary world economy would undergo a transformation which would enable humankind to behave responsibly in an era of global change.

In the course of such a transformation, humankind would reach a responsible economy, an economy which would restore the dignity of

247

human beings as moral agents, while preserving the wealth and efficiency provided by competitive markets.[1] A major reason to look for such a transformation is given by the worrying reality of unemployment in highly industrialized countries. The influential idea that markets automatically find socially desirable equilibria is hard to reconcile with persistent unemployment. Therefore, a brief analysis of multiple equilibria on labor markets shall prepare the ground for this concluding chapter.

Consider an economy in which money wages are fixed once per year in a central bargaining process between workers and capitalists. Once wages are fixed, workers determine in a complex informal process how carefully and effectively they will perform their tasks and how far they will try to improve their personal skills. Assessing whether the wage deal is fair or not plays a major role in this process. As a result, high or low productivity may result, and wage costs per unit of product will vary accordingly. In turn, managers react to the workers' behavior. If wage costs rise throughout the economy, they reduce real wages by raising product prices. Moreover, if managers feel that wage costs are increasing too fast, they may generate unemployment by slowing down investment. And after a year, the whole process starts over again.

Whatever each actor does, the outcome is always co–determined by the actions of the other actor.[2] This kind of situations can be represented as a repeated non–zero–sum game with two actors. According to the "folk theorem" of game theory, any conceivable distribution of the total payoffs can be an equilibrium as long as the workers are not driven into starvation and the capitalists are not driven into bankrupcy.[3] This result makes it difficult to believe that unemployment will be easy to avoid. In game theory, an equilibrium is a situation in which no actor can improve the outcome of a given combination of strategies by unilateral action. In this sense, a large set of stable situations on the labor market are characterized by persistent unemployment.

The difficulty is not due to the presence of only two players. If a competitive labor market is represented by curves of demand and

---

[1] This perspective fits well with recent efforts to develop a better understanding of economic reality by devoting more explicit attention to its socio–cultural dimensions. Kreps [157] gives a brilliant introduction to this task from a micro–economic perspective; Abbott [1], Etzioni [73], Granovetter [105] and Swedberg [271] provide important sociological contributions.

[2] Elster [70] analyses scandinavian wage bargaining along such lines.

[3] The folk theorem owes its name to the fact that it creeped into the literature as an obvious result about repeated games, without being accredited to a single author.

Labor

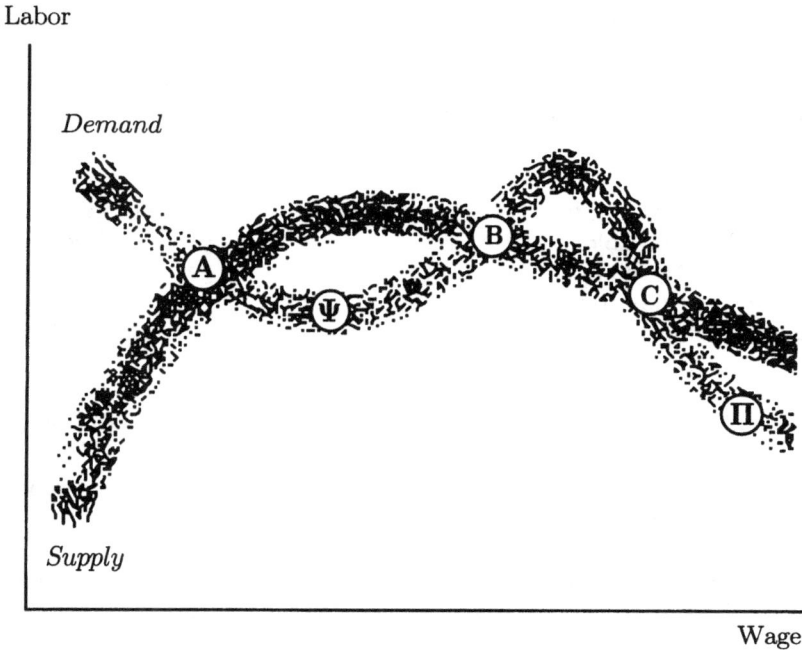

Figure 6.1: The unemployment trap.

supply, these need not show a unique point of intersection, but may as well share a whole set of common points, as illustrated by figure 6.1.[4] This may be due to the fact that demand for labor need not fall with rising wages, because wage increases may create additional demand, and because rising wage costs may lead to rising prices for various products, including labor saving machinery. It may as well be due to the fact that the supply of labor need not increase with rising wages, because wage increases enable people to work less in order to get a better education, to take care of their children, and to enjoy life.

Presently, labor markets in OECD countries are trapped in a situation like the one of point Ψ. On the one hand, managers and entrepreneurs identify the goal of full employment with point A, where

---

[4] Such curves must be handled with care, as they suggest a static framework, which easily disguises important dynamic processes. They are, nevertheless, useful tools for the study of labor markets. The relevance of multiple equilibria for economic analysis is discussed by Kreps [157] and, in a polemical vein, by Kirman [156].

labor supply would be reduced because of lower wages. On the other hand, wage–earners and their organizations want to move towards point B or C, where full employment is reached because higher wages lead to higher effective demand and lower labor supply.[5] If the economy moves in that direction, however, monetary authorities will block that process by rising interest rates, because they fear uncontrollable inflation.

This policy is grounded in the experience of the late 60s and early 70s, when the golden age of the post–war era came to an end in a situation like the one of point C. Full employment gave a strong bargaining position to wage earners. At the same time, the role of money as an external goal of economic activities was so pervasive that fighting for higher wages seemed the obvious thing to do. A complex series of events led to a sudden increase in unemployment, which can be represented by a movement from C to Π. Meanwhile, the share of wages in the total product has been reduced again, especially in the U.S. As a result, the economy has moved, as it were, from Π to Ψ and is now trapped in a situation of persistent unemployment.

As the unemployed often lack the opportunity to learn essential skills required by a rapidly evolving economy, this situation is reinforced through a deepening divide between insiders and outsiders on the labor market. Without major programs of vocational training, the outsiders have very limited chances of reentering into vocational life. Unless the economy moves towards full employment, however, such training programs make little sense.

Reaching a responsible economy is no easy solution to this problem, but it might well offer the only realistic strategy to overcome the plague of persistent unemployment. The point of this strategy would be to decouple full employment from the danger of uncontrollable inflation by offering an attractive alternative to inflationary wage increases. (As a matter of fact, it is this danger which leads monetary authorities to avoid situations of full emplyoment.) This alternative, which managers and entrepreneurs could and should offer to wage–earners, is an increasingly meaningful vocational life.[6]

In the contemporary world, this requires the fulfillment of three conditions. First, the world economy must, step by step, stop producing means of environmental, military, and also cultural destruction. Second, the tremendous gap between economically advanced countries and so–called developing countries must gradually disappear. Third, these

---

[5] Point B may be highly unstable, so point C would be preferable.
[6] Jaeger and Weber [146].

macro–processes must go along with micro–processes through which vocational life can, step by step, become an experience of personal self–fulfilment.

In the next two sections, the prospect of reaching a responsible economy will be explored on the global and regional level. Then, the instrument of energy bounds will be proposed as an essential policy means on the national level. Finally, I will discuss the importance of situations of multiple control for realistic attempts to cope with global change.

6.1 Global Change and Sustainable Development

In chapter 5, the rate of economic growth was defined as the ratio between today's and yesterday's economically visible net output, both valued at constant prices.[7] Then physical growth was defined by multiplying physical output vectors not with a price vector but with a vector of impact coefficients. Without such coefficients the notion of physical growth would make little sense. Next, I used the same impact vector to define the notion of sustainability in terms of a given limit for acceptable impacts per period. In chapter 4, I argued that such a limit does not depend simply on properties of ecosystems, but that it involves moral choices with regard to our environment. Now it is time to introduce the notion of development in the context of the present analysis. For this purpose, it is useful to distinguish between an advanced and a developing part of the world economy, with labor productivity being much larger in the former than in the latter. Then one can define development as the process diminishing this difference by means of faster economic growth in developing countries than in advanced ones. Economic growth is thus a necessary, but not a sufficient condition for development.

Until recently, a division of the global economy into a first, highly industrialized world, a second world comprising the centrally–planned economies, and a third world lacking a high degree of industrialization seemed plausible. Meanwhile, the collapse of the USSR and the Eastern European economies marks the end of the "second world". Clearly, these nations hope to become part of the first world, thus striving for

---

[7] For the definitions mentioned in this paragraph see formulas (5.4–5.6) in chapter 5.

the same goals as the group of third world countries. So there are good reasons to reduce the former division of the globe in three worlds to a simple bipartition between advanced and developing countries. Several countries in South–East Asia have successfully crossed the line between developing and advanced countries, yet for the majority of countries on the developing side a transition seems to be rather a mirage than a sizeable opportunity.

Successful *development* means that developing economies grow faster than advanced ones and that, in the same process, their labor productivity is dramatically improved. Such improvements cannot be achieved without profound social and cultural changes, in the course of which the advanced economies have to share with the developing ones their technical knowledge, their vocational skills, and probably even their concept of personal identity, which they have evolved for generations. Or, to put it in terms of cultural macro–evolution, which I introduced in chapter 3, successful development basically implies the transition from dual human ecological systems towards a triadic system.[8]

Archaic human ecological systems have nearly disappeared today. Whether it is desirable that people living in these contexts should reproduce the first step of cultural macro–evolution and begin sharing the culture of political systems is open to debate. Yet it is hard to imagine how such a development could be avoided. As to dual human ecological systems, however, the situation is different. Although they are deeply influenced by the world economy, they persist without developing integral vocational cultures; and they still comprise the majority of humankind. A number of them are characterized by vain efforts to control their economies by merely political means. Again, one may wonder whether it would not be sensible to preserve older life–forms, for which the realm of an autonomous economic life would be at best marginal—the recent rise of Islamic fundamentalism involves major efforts in such a direction. But up to now, economic dynamics as well as the wishes of most people have contributed to a massive tendency toward a slow, but seemingly inevitable, integration of all nations into the web of the world economy. Monetary institutions have permeated the lives of most people in the world in ways that may well be irreversible. It is probably simply too late to avoid the second step of macro–evolution.

---

[8] Analyzing the problems of developing countries in terms of cultural macro–evolution is especially relevant in order to understand the role of politics and so–called state–classes (Elsenhans [69]) in these countries.

If this is true, development means to complement processes that are already under way by establishing the institutions required to support a viable vocational culture. This implies a huge cultural transfer in which highly complex systems of rules and beliefs are made accessible to developing economies. An important vehicle for this purpose is the export of capital goods from advanced to developing economies. For investors of advanced countries, the prospect of higher economic growth in developing countries would no doubt provide a strong incentive in favor of this kind of capital flow. Capital accumulation in developing economies, then, would not only depend on domestic net investments, but also on foreign investments from advanced economies.

For the purpose of successful development, however, an inflow of foreign capital is useful only to the extent that it helps to organize an inflow of capital goods which become vehicles of "international learning".[9] This proviso is crucial because the difficulties of developing economies are not simply caused by a lack of capital, but rather by a situation of low and only slowly increasing labor productivity. There are complex social and cultural reasons for that situation, which can be explained as the outcome of an exposure to a triadic human ecological system without sharing its cultural resources. One may speculate whether it would not be desirable to achieve a state of peaceful coexistence between the triadic system and its predecessors. Most people living today, though, badly need and strongly desire increases in economic well–being, which imply a successful transition to the triadic system.

As actual development requires both economic growth and capital accumulation to proceed faster in developing economies than in advanced ones, it is very likely that environmental impacts caused by developing countries will increase. It would be nice if development could happen according to the ideal type of qualitative growth, but this hardly seems a realistic perspective. Instead, one must acknowledge that the task of achieving successful development at a global scale makes the problems of global environmental change even more difficult.

If development should fail, the lives of billions of humans already marked by misery would offer no prospect of hope. In particular, the persistence of very low standards of living would make it extremely difficult to slow down the rates of population growth. If, however, development in the sense of replicating the second step of cultural macro-

---

[9] This point has been carefully elaborated by Pasinetti [213].

evolution should actually succeed, a rising number of nations could experience the mixed blessing of economic growth combined with tremendous environmental disruption. In order to avoid such a perspective, development needs to be combined with a comprehensive process of cultural regeneration. Without this combination, sustainable development will be impossible.

Consider the example of anthropogenic emissions of carbon dioxide, which are likely to cause climatic change.[10] Although carbon dioxide emissions caused by advanced countries have been more or less constant since 1973, emissions are still increasing in the rest of the world. This is quite understandable, considering the fact that emissions per capita are at least ten times smaller in China and Brazil than in the US.[11] In 1991, humankind produced annual carbon emissions at a level of nearly 1 metric ton per capita with a total population approaching 6 billion people. The average level for developing countries lies well below this mark, while the US level is about 5 tons per capita. It is perfectly clear that developing countries will strive to emulate the standard of living of the richest countries on Planet Earth and that this is a highly legitimate effort. And there seems to be a very simple answer to the problems of global environmental change, which will arise inevitably if the contemporary ways of life of the richest countries spread over the whole planet. Namely, these countries should develop sustainable ways of life, which can actually be generalized to the whole planet.

In Japan, annual carbon emissions per capita amount to less than half the US level, i.e., to 2 metric tons. If the richest countries of the world undertake a substantial effort to reduce their carbon emissions, they will have a fair chance of attaining the level of 1 metric ton per capita, which is the present world average. Setting this level as a goal for the whole world would slow down the increase in world emissions to the speed of world population growth. This would still increase carbon emissions in the coming decades by some factor ranging between two and four, but not by the factor somewhere between ten and twenty which would result from a generalization of present US levels. Instead of continuing to expand along their previous path of quantitative growth, advanced countries can change course. They actually can achieve eco-

---

[10] The figures about carbon emissions are from UNEP and The Beijer Institute [284] and from Flavin [81]. Other greenhouse gases could be discussed in a similar manner with regard to the ideal types of qualitative growth and sustainable development.

[11] Emissions have also dramatically increased in the former USSR, where they are already higher than in Germany.

nomic growth with constant global impacts at a considerably reduced level.

Unfortunately, the ideal type of qualitative growth does not fit the situation of developing countries. These countries, where the majority of the world population is living, urgently need a physical increase of their capital equipment. Thus, the ideal type of qualitative growth is immediately ruled out as a viable path for them. Moreover, they need to achieve growth rates well above the average rate for the world economy as a whole. Both goals will no doubt entail an increase in environmental impacts caused by developing countries. Thus, their potential ways of development will hardly be compatible with the condition of qualitative growth. Successful development will require at least some physical growth. Obviously, a development trying to emulate present emission levels of advanced countries could hardly be considered sustainable. Even if developing countries should, from the outset, aim at those reduced impact levels which advanced countries will hopefully achieve within several decades, this would still imply an increase of environmental impacts above current levels. If, therefore, development is to be sustainable, the positive rate of physical growth in developing economies must be offset by negative rates of physical growth in advanced economies.

At least for a limited time–span, this seems compatible with positive economic growth in advanced countries. However, a moment will come when advanced economies may still be able to achieve economic growth while keeping environmental impacts stable, but will no longer be able to reach any further reductions of impacts. Therefore, a process of sustainable development requires developing economies to have caught up with the advanced ones by this time, so that physical growth will no longer be necessary for either part of the world economy.

Sustainable development must fulfill two conditions: the physical growth in developing countries must be compensated by a reduction of environmental impacts in advanced countries; and it has to be successfully completed before the potential for such reductions is exhausted. If one understands development as attaining the levels of labor productivity which prevail in advanced countries, then sustainable development is not a process of infinite duration. Rather, it means advancing from today's state of affairs to a specific social goal in accordance with specific ecological conditions.

In principle, the transition from human ecological systems characterized by the duality of private and public life into a triadic system which also comprises the third realm of vocational life might well go along with a comprehensive cultural regeneration. As already mentioned, this combination constitutes a process of sustainable development. This process would differ significantly from the transition which occurred in Europe at the end of the Middle Ages: it would realize an opportunity which was missed at that time. The possibility of this prospect will, however, deeply depend on processes of cultural regeneration taking place in advanced countries.

Qualitative growth in advanced countries is essential to support the process of sustainable development in the rest of the world. Such a support will consist, on the one hand, in reducing environmental impacts caused by advanced countries, so that a moderate increase from developing countries can be tolerated; on the other hand, it will consist in providing foreign investment so as to foster international learning in developing countries. Sustainable development is compatible with the basic processes of cultural evolution. Yet considering the actual way these processes have evolved so far, sustainable development faces difficulties of frightening dimensions.

One such difficulty lies in dealing with the entropy margin of the biosphere. In the industrialized countries, energy use per capita has already risen to a level which is most likely to cause severe environmental disruption. If completing the second step of cultural macro–evolution should entail an extension of this level of energy use to the entire world population, the problems of global change would be amplified by a huge factor. And world population will doubtlessly increase much further before a decline and, finally, stability of energy use is reached.

Can humankind as a whole truly participate in the worldwide triadic human ecological system while total energy use actually declines? Technically, there is no reason to rule out this possibility. It even presents a fascinating challenge for industry and governments as well as for private households. Developing countries will, however, hardly be able to meet this challenge unless the developed ones drastically reduce their total energy use. This means that sustainable development implies a fundamental shift towards a new kind of socio–technical change, a shift which will stress the mutual interdependence between advanced and developing countries. As an inevitable consequence, sustainable development cannot be achieved by applying known solutions to well defined technological problems. The only way of approaching it is a comprehensive innovation process, in which new solutions to ill defined technological and social problems are found.

6.2 Innovation Processes and Regional Milieus

Both the ideal types of qualitative growth and sustainable development require a *decoupling of economic from physical growth.* Consider again the example of carbon dioxide emissions in order to better understand this decoupling process. In the period from 1950 to 1973, those emissions increased steadily at an annual rate of about 4% in advanced countries. For reasons discussed in the preceding section, emissions continue to grow in developing countries. It is a remarkable fact, however, that after 1973 emissions caused by advanced countries have not increased for at least two decades. An important reason for this new situation is the fact that average rates of economic growth in advanced countries are substantially lower since 1973 than they were in the post–war period. A second reason is the structural change towards an increasing share of services in total output. Service provision requires fossil fuels too, but less than the production of manufactured goods.[12]

Finally, the various measures by which OPEC limited oil production since 1973 are a third reason. As a result of production limitations, oil became more costly; and this had two important consequences. First, there are substitution effects. If fuel prices rise, private households may reduce fossil fuel consumption, for example by reducing car trips in the evening and amusing themselves with video–tapes instead. Analogous shifts will happen with business firms. Pure substitution effects do not expand the range of known technologies, they are just a different choice among the technologies available for the satisfaction of given preferences. More important than pure substitution effects are the innovation processes induced by the oil price shocks of '73 and '89, and subsequent political measures to increase energy efficiency. In part, these innovation processes might also have happened independently of such dramatic events. The precise links between changes in normal prices and technological innovations are very difficult to assess.[13] Whether they are price–induced or not, however, technological innovations have fostered a remarkable decoupling of economic growth and fossil fuel use in the past decades.[14]

---

[12] The importance of structural change for qualitative growth is discussed by Simonis [257].

[13] See Neuburger [198] for a skeptical view about such links with regard to oil prices.

[14] As a matter of fact, economic growth has been decoupled to a considerable extent from energy use in general (Kümmel [160]). Among the first to draw attention to this possibility were Mazur and Rosa [184].

Relevant innovations include changes in automobile technology leading to increased energy efficiency of cars, changes in manufacturing technology leading to decreased energy requirements for heat generation in industrial production processes, and changes in construction technology which lower the energy used for the heating of buildings. But relevant innovations also include cases where lower use of energy per unit of production is an unintended effect. Above all, this happens in service industries—for example, in software development or in psychotherapy—where quite often the economic value of a product can be increased from period to period while the flows of energy and materials involved remain more or less unchanged.

In such cases, the new products rely on fossil fuels no less, but also no more, than the old ones. Waste production as well as input flows of energy and materials are more or less constant, while the increase in product quality is due to improved information inputs. Impact coefficients can then be constant, and in terms of the corresponding impact vector no physical growth occurs:

$$(\boldsymbol{b}_{v,t+1} - \boldsymbol{d}_{v,t+1}) \cdot \boldsymbol{i}_t = (\boldsymbol{b}_{v,t} - \boldsymbol{d}_{v,t}) \cdot \boldsymbol{i}_t \qquad (6.1)$$

In the absence of physical growth, product innovation can be successful only if it leads to higher quality for the new products. On the other hand, if this is the case, these products may well be more expensive than the older ones. Under such conditions economic growth can be generated with constant or even decreasing environmental impacts:

$$(\boldsymbol{b}_{v,t+1} - \boldsymbol{d}_{v,t+1}) \cdot \boldsymbol{p}_t > (\boldsymbol{b}_{v,t} - \boldsymbol{d}_{v,t}) \cdot \boldsymbol{p}_t \qquad (6.2)$$

Clearly, if there were only one output good, a similar situation could not arise. If formula (6.1) holds for a single output good with a positive environmental impact coefficient, it follows immediately that physical output does not change from one period to the next; and therefore formula (6.2) cannot be true. This case has served as an argument in many discussions about ecological limits to economic growth.[15] In reality, the world economy produces a myriad of different goods and services, and product innovation is continuously modifying the composition of this multidimensional output.

The conditions under which positive economic growth can go on without generating positive physical growth can be formulated by considering the difference between the net output in period t and the pre-

---

[15] van den Bergh and Nijkamp [22] provide a recent example.

vious period. It can be analyzed by means of two semipositive vectors
of goods and services, $b_{g,t}$ and $b_{z,t}$:

$$(b_{v,t+1} - d_{v,t+1}) - (b_{v,t} - d_{v,t}) = b_{g,t} - b_{z,t} \qquad (6.3)$$

$b_{g,t}$ represents the difference between net outputs for those items for
which this difference is positive; for all the other items, the elements
of $b_{g,t}$ are zero. Conversely, $b_{z,t}$ represents the size of the difference
between net outputs for those items for which it is negative. It then
follows that (6.1) and (6.2) will hold if:

$$b_{g,t} \cdot p_t > b_{z,t} \cdot p_t \quad \text{and}$$
$$\qquad\qquad\qquad\qquad\qquad\qquad (6.4)$$
$$b_{g,t} \cdot i_t = b_{z,t} \cdot i_t$$

The remarkable fact about this condition is that the impact coefficients
do not need to diminish in the course of time for qualitative growth to
be achieved. It is sufficient that technical innovations lead to improved
product quality with non–increasing impact coefficients. This process
may be described as an ideal type of qualitative growth realized by
product innovation.

According to this analysis, a highly innovative world economy could
continue to grow indefinitely without increasing carbon dioxide emissions, even if fossil fuels were not replaced by other energy sources.
The basic mechanism of this kind of qualitative growth would be the
introduction of new goods of better quality than older ones, but with
similar impact coefficients per physical unit. If the higher quality of
new goods results in higher prices per physical unit the effect would be
a lowering of impacts per monetary unit of output while impacts were
kept constant per physical unit. Qualitative growth requires a different
kind of technological progress than the one which was dominant in the
golden age of economic growth after World War II. Fortunately, this
new kind of technological progress is already operating quite successfully in economically advanced countries.[16]

These considerations refer to a non–increasing impact vector. Such
a situation would, admittedly, lead to actually increasing global environmental impacts because of physical growth in developing countries.
Real impact decreases are needed to offset those increases. Fortunately,
they seem achievable in many areas. Yet, the basic mechanism of qualitative growth consists in improving product quality while keeping environmental impacts constant.

---

[16] Block [29] offers a sociological discussion of relevant trends.

An adequate answer to the present environmental crisis clearly requires major technological advances. These advances cannot be based on a few technological breakthroughs, though. The crucial prerequisite is a continuous process of product innovation. Such a process could take advantage of the development of *innovative regional milieus*, a development which in the last few years has been documented under different headings in a rapidly growing body of literature.[17]

The emergence of innovative regional milieus is a major outcome of the refusal of labor which I discussed in section 4.1. In the late 60's and early 70's, sluggish productivity growth combined with dramatically rising wage costs undermined the state of confidence of managers and entrepreneurs in advanced countries, especially as governments and national banks abandoned the goals of full employment and of steady growth in order to try to restore monetary stability. Business firms became more reluctant to invest than they had been in the post World War II period, and their investment decisions became more erratic. As a result, the world economy became more volatile, and single markets became less foreseeable and more fragmented. This trend was further accentuated by the breakdown of the regime of fixed exchange rates. Under the new conditions, flexibility became the first requirement of economic success.

Plenty of experiences seem to indicate that single firms can be much more flexible when they operate in regional networks. In central Italy and southern Germany, in New England and in Japanese provinces, such networks have evolved to the point where they have gained a competitive edge on world markets. A process of self–organization has started in regions distributed over nearly all industrialized countries.[18] This form of regional development was fostered by a remarkable process of spatial decentralization, which was observed in all industrialized countries during the 70's.[19] The result is not at all a reduction of spatial inequalities in favor of a homogeneous spatial structure, but rather the emergence of patterns of multiple hierarchies, in which a given region can be peripheral in some respects while being central in others.[20] Multiple hierarchies are also an important characteristic of the new, flexible

---

[17] See Sabel [236] for an overview. The concept of innovative milieus is elaborated, for example, in Aydalot [9]. Relations with environmental awareness are explored in Jaeger [142].

[18] Among the first authors to document this reversal of Tayloristic strategies for the organization of industrial labor were Piore and Sabel [220] and Kern and Schumann [154].

[19] See, for example, Berry [24], Ernste and Jaeger [72], Frey and Speare [89].

[20] This theme is further explored in Jaeger and Dürrenberger [144].

organizations which make up regional networks of firms. Temporally limited project groups, which are formed to solve new problems and which often cut across established bureaucratic hierarchies, represent a noteworthy example.

The emergence of regional innovative milieus is an important opportunity for both advanced and developing countries. It could be used in the coming decades for orienting global economic growth toward building an economically sound and ecologically viable infrastructure for the developing countries. Therefore, pilot regions in industrialized countries could engage successfully in the necessary processes of trial and error and pass their experiences over to other regions. That role would offer them new export possibilities for goods and services which make their newly developed know–how available. In so far, it would be a sound economic perspective. Without such examples from advanced countries, developing countries will hardly consider sustainable development a promising strategy.

A crucial difference between sustainable development and the older development strategies lies in the fact that the latter forced developing countries to engage in a desperate catch up race, while the former offers the prospect of a new goal, which is not yet realized both in the developing and in the developed countries. Cultural regeneration is a task for humankind as a whole, and in some respects the poor may have less difficulty in attaining it than the rich. Pilot regions for sustainable development may emerge in advanced economies as well as in developing ones. The latter possibility can be fostered by efforts to strengthen vocational traditions in developing countries, thereby completing the second step of cultural macro–evolution.

In advanced and in developing economies, strengthening regional vocational cultures intensifies interpersonal accountability relations and emphasizes the competence and know–how of the people engaged in vocational activities. Innovative regional milieus can contribute to a process of cultural regeneration by embedding vocational activities in the comprehensive web of social life. Even though they live in a global economy, most people carry on their private lives at a local scale. Therefore, an integration of private, political and vocational life is hardly conceivable without relying to a considerable extent on regional social networks.

In the introduction, I mentioned the threefold differentiation of contemporary cities as a major research finding of human ecology. Contemporary urban regions can be shown to be shaped by the interact-

ing dynamics of economic, private and public life.[21] Clearly, modern
urban planning has systematically fostered a large–scale separation between private and vocational life while sacrificing most spaces of urban
public life to car traffic.[22] This territorial structure is a remarkable
expression of a degenerated triadic human ecological system. The in-
novativeness of regional networks offers a potential to counteract this
degeneration.

The remedy, however, has little to do with a simple contrast between
a nostalgia for the life–world of primordial institutions and the awesome
reality of large–scale organizations.[23] Innovative regional milieus are
important precisely because they recombine the global reality of today's
economy with the local reality of private lives. This recombination
could be a necessary condition for the innovation processes required to
decouple economic from physical growth. To be sufficient, however, it
has to be complemented by explicit political action aiming at the same
effect.

6.3   The Energy Challenge

Political action is necessary, among other reasons, because a world economy characterized by positive rates of profit and growth has a built–in
tendency to engage in rising environmental risks. To understand why,
let us look at figure 6.2, representing two investment projects. They
can be interpreted as plants which are built in the first year and used
in the following years. Both projects last five years. In the first year,
project A requires a net investment equal to the area covered by black

---

[21] In these regions, the dynamics of public life are closely related to racial and ethnic
identities.

[22] Dürrenberger et al. [67].

[23] This contrast has inspired a long series of brilliant writers. Habermas [110] builds
a complex theory of communicative action around it and tries to define conditions
for a "peaceful coexistence" of primordial institutions and large–scale organizations. Perrow [216] argues that it may be necessary and possible to scrap most if
not all such organizations. Coleman [51] interprets the same contrast the other
way around and proposes to construct the conditions for a life without primordial
institutions. Each one of these analyses deserves careful consideration. Nevertheless, they all share a somewhat naive view of primordial institutions. Feminist
critiques of kinship structures in contemporary societies suggest that primordial
institutions and the world of large–scale organizations may have more in common
than the mentioned authors seem to believe. An effective process of cultural regeneration will need to transform the realm of private life as well as the world of
politics and economics.

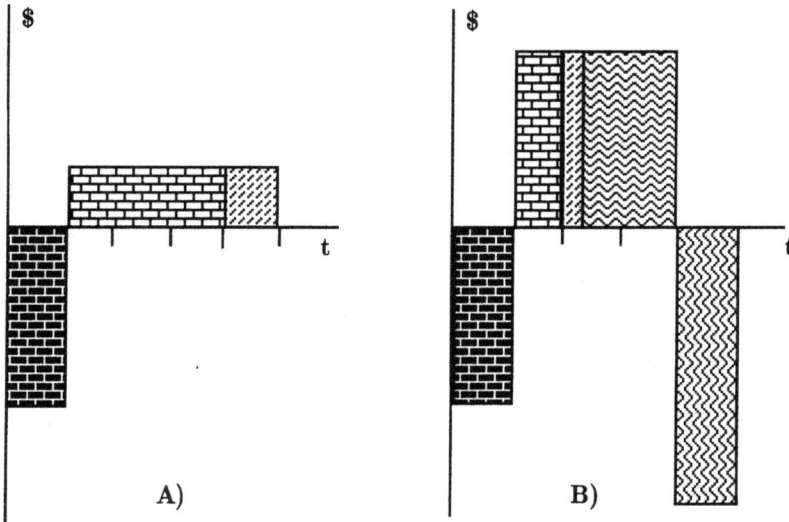

Figure 6.2: Pay–off periods and delayed costs.

bricks, say 1.2 mio dollars.[24] In the following four years, the project yields a net income of \$ 1.6 mio, i.e., \$ 0.4 mio per year.[25] The initial investment costs are recovered one year before the project ends: the first four years are the pay–off period of the project. The net income of these years is represented by the area covered by white bricks, which is different in shape, but equal in surface to the black bricks area. The net income of the fifth year, symbolized by the hatched area, is equal to the total profits accruing to the project, which amount to \$ 0.4 mio.

Project *B* begins with the same investment, again represented by an area covered by black bricks. The project yields the same amount of profits, again represented by a hatched area. However, project *B* differs significantly from the first project: its annual net income is much higher, and additional costs arise at the end of the project. They

---

[24] Comparing dollars over various periods raises the problem of inflation. As we are interested in rates of return, we should use the same standard of value which is used by firms when they assess such rates for themselves. A usual procedure is to use monetary units with constant purchasing power, for example, dollars deflated by the current rate of inflation. This makes sense as long as the goods actually purchased in the various periods are at least roughly comparable from one period to the next.

[25] Gross income would include the costs of running the factory in the current year. Without loss of generality, I ignore these costs in this example.

could arise, for example, from having to deal with toxic waste resulting
from the operation of the plant. I assume that these costs amount to
$ 2.0 mio, represented by the vertically undulated area. This money
does not have to be advanced, because it is earned as net income during
the third and fourth year, represented by the horizontally undulated
area.

Because in project B the annual net income of the second year is
much higher than in project A, the pay–off period for project B is only
two years, that is, half the pay–off period of project A. In a world where
positive rates of profit prevail, this is a decisive argument to prefer
project B. A dollar today is better than a dollar tomorrow, because
in the meantime it can be augmented. Therefore, it pays to postpone
costs toward the end of a project. The higher the rate of profit, the
greater the gains to be obtained from cost delaying. The existence
of positive rates of profit implies a practice of *discounting the future*.
This practice corresponds to basic features of economic growth: in a
growing economy, future costs matter less than present ones because in
the future more economic resources will be available.

Two important criticisms may be raised against this practice.[26]
First, business enterprises do not use the actual growth rate of the
world economy to assess their investment plans, but rather a discount
rate which is considerably higher. The discount rate depends in part
on average rates of profit, which are usually more than twice as high
as growth rates. Second, it is conceivable that economic growth will
not go on indefinitely. At some stage, further growth may become un-
feasible, undesirable, or both. But if economic growth should come
to an end, the whole fabric of postponed costs could suddenly become
an unbearable burden. Important as these objections may be, there
is an even more serious argument based on the indeterminacy of the
future. Future events which depend on human decisions are uncertain
by definition, and only some aspects of them can be known in advance.
If this is described as a problem of bounded rationality, it is important to understand that the idea of an unbounded rationality would be
conceptually incoherent.

Figure 6.2 compares two investment projects whose outcome seems
to be well known in advance. The figures may be interpreted as expected values of probability distributions, but in reality even probability distributions for future costs and incomes are known only in a

---

[26] Early critics were Ramsey [228] and Pigou [219]. For recent critiques related to
   environmental problems, see Perrings [215] and Broome [39].

restricted domain. In real life, there are rules of thumb which help to draw a boundary between what can be considered a reasonable expectation and what lies in a future too distant to be taken into consideration. Nobody could live without such rules of thumb. The difficulty in justifying the practice of discounting the future lies precisely in the inevitability of such rules. Today's world economy is characterized by the interdependent features of positive rates of profit and of economic growth, which lead to a systematic preference for postponing the responsibility for environmental risks. This preference is combined with the human tendency to ignore remote possibilities; the necessity of taking into account risks of increasing size is thus postponed beyond the time–horizon of economic actors.

No doubt, there are huge *environmental risks* ahead, and the practice of discounting the future amplifies these risks while at the same time postponing them to a future which is distant enough to be all but ignored by economic agents. Discounting the future creates serious problems, which are not reflected in the accounting framework on which the world economy relies. In other words, we are facing intertemporal external effects. How could they be internalized?

Internalizing the intertemporal external effects involved in the practice of discounting the future would require the normal rate of profit to drop to zero. This corresponds to the steady state economy discussed in section 5.4. We must, however, face the fact that in the actual world economy positive rates of profit persist. As long as economic growth will be deemed necessary—especially in order to raise the standard of living in developing countries—this situation will hardly change. As a result, increasing controversies and conflicts about environmental risks are to be expected.

The ozone hole, the greenhouse effect, desertification, and so forth are all highly dynamic phenomena. Crossing environmental thresholds today may lead to serious, but often unpredictable consequences tomorrow. Such thresholds can be "internalized" into market processes by establishing limited inputs like emission permits. In section 4.4, I have emphasized, however, that such thresholds do not constitute a clear–cut borderline separating acceptable from unacceptable actions. Environmental thresholds are no substitute for moral choices. Quite the opposite, politically implemented moral choices will often be necessary for the social definition of environmental thresholds. Therefore, defining environmental thresholds is a matter of difficult political negotiations.

Such choices have already been made with many pollution standards. There is, however, a serious problem of overregulation here.[27] As the dynamics of the world economy entail growing environmental risks, the attempt to regulate them on a case by case basis leads to an expanding network of regulations, which will become increasingly difficult to implement and which may seriously impair economic efficiency. Every threshold and its connected risks must be identified, new property rights and their allocation must be negotiated, and the economy must adjust to the new limited inputs. The attempt to substitute the working of the invisible hand by direct political regulation of technologies and production processes would make things even worse. Obviously, it would be an attractive alternative if an overall environmental threshold could be defined which would enable the economic system to avoid at least a large class of environmental risks.

Such a threshold can be set by limiting the input of commercial energy available for economic use. I will call this the instrument of *energy bounds*.[28] Limiting the amount of available commercial energy would strongly reduce many problems of pollution. The emissions produced by traffic and heating systems, by heavy industry and agriculture, and by many other sources are strongly linked to energy use. And so is the reduction of biodiversity: biodiversity is often threatened by the destruction of suitable habitats, which, in turn, is made easy by the availability of cheap energy. Moreover, major environmental risks like the one of global warming are closely coupled to energy use, too. Even epidemiological risks for human beings and for other organisms are fostered by high mobility fuelled by seemingly unlimited energy inputs.

It would be absurd to suggest that the contemporary environmental crisis is simply due to cheap energy supplies, and that substantially increasing energy prices would be a sufficient measure to overcome this crisis. Energy bounds would be clearly insufficient to deal with the ozone hole; this problem requires banning the use of certain chemical compounds. Limiting the energy supply may well be a necessary measure to overcome the environmental crisis, yet it will hardly be sufficient. Nevertheless, energy bounds deserve special attention for

---

[27] More precisely, the problem is one of anomic regulation, in which the web formed by environmental regulations and other rules implies contradictory requirements.

[28] For a brief proposal to implement energy bounds see Imboden, Jaeger, and Müller–Herold [140]. A related instrument is the dynamic energy tax proposed by Mauch, Iten, von Weizsäcker, and Jesinghaus [183]. For a discussion of energy policy with regard to the problem of discounting future risks, see Lind [164].

two reasons. First, they can help to counteract in an effective manner the tendency to let environmental risks grow through a practice of discounting the future. Second, they can foster qualitative growth by triggering an ongoing innovation process of the kind described in section 6.2.[29]

Introducing energy bounds in order to support a transition from quantitative to qualitative growth means modifying the *interface between politics and economics*. This is no easy task. The modern economic system is a worldwide reality while the political system is structured by boundaries between nations; hence some of the difficulties to subordinate the economic system to political goals. Since its beginnings, the research tradition of economics has emphasized the importance of acknowledging the relative autonomy of the economy with regard to politics. This autonomy is due to a large extent to the crucial feedback mechanism on which the economic system is based: the production of capital goods which are then used as input of the economic system itself.

Figure 6.3 represents this feedback, together with various interfaces between the economic system, understood as the universe of business firms, and other systems. The economy is a recursive system, in the sense that in each accounting period firms use as input capital goods which were part of the output of the system in the preceding period. As a great portion of capital goods lasts for more than one accounting period, a considerable inertia of the world economy is inevitable.[30] For this reason, there is always a remarkable historical continuity in the process of socio–technical change. Besides the very fact of ongoing change, this continuity is nearly the only predictable feature of socio–technical change as distinguished from economic growth. Time and again, new products and new production processes emerge in an unpredictable manner. The world economy experiences a gradual process of socio–technical change, which can go on indefinitely without repeating itself.

The ability of the economic system to reproduce itself is, among other things, due to the existence of normal prices, the pattern of which

---

[29] Romm and Lovins [233] provide an impressive overview over relevant innovations.

[30] Only very rough estimates can be made for the relation between capital stock and gross product. Such estimates for today's world economy are about 4:1. About 1/5 of the gross product is used for gross investment. As these figures have remained quite stable over the last decades, the average lifetime of capital stock should be about $4 \cdot 5 = 20$ years.

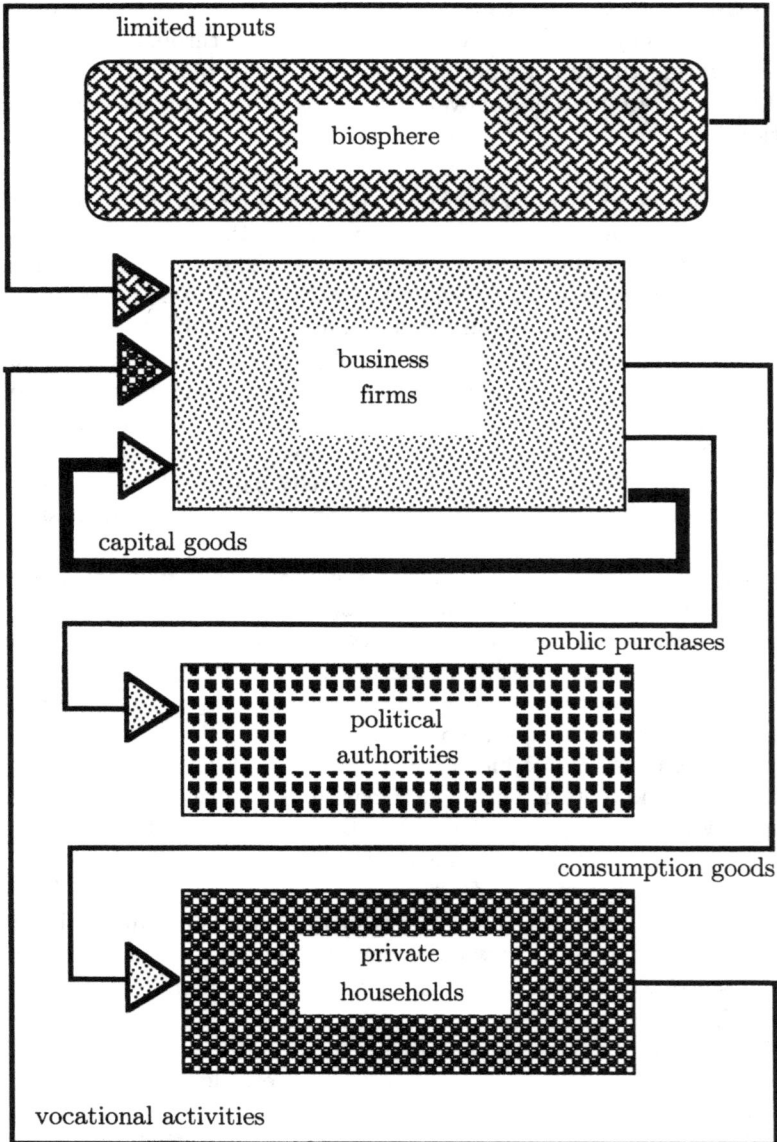

Figure 6.3: Interfaces of the world economy.

can be called the general equilibrium of an interdependent system of markets. But it should not be forgotten that in the world economy the interplay between market prices and normal prices never comes to a rest. If this is to be called an equilibrium, then it is a rather busy one. Supplementing the metaphysical metaphor of an invisible hand with the physical metaphor of an equilibrium can help to describe economic phenomena. But the equilibrium metaphor becomes severely misleading when it is used to suggest that the internal dynamics of the economy is controlled by the consumption patterns of private households. If the economy is regarded as following an equilibrium path shaped by consumer preferences, the reality of economic dynamics is missed. It is more realistic to assume autonomous economic dynamics as modulated by changes in the environment of the economy, which includes private households and public authorities, as well as the biosphere as a whole.

Political authorities are advised by the research tradition of economics to accept the relative autonomy of the economy and to be satisfied with limited possibilities to modulate its internal dynamics. For this purpose, several instruments are available. They include all kinds of legal prescriptions and interdictions, and in particular the possibility to levy taxes. From the point of view of the economic system, however, taxes are completely arbitrary, as they are fixed outside the market process.

Now consider the interface between the economy and the biophysical environment. Biological evolution has embedded humankind, like any other species, in the biosphere. Therefore, human activities presuppose a myriad of life–sustaining processes taking place on earth. In particular, free inputs from the environment as well as free outputs into the environment are presupposed by any economic activity. By definition, free inputs and free outputs do not appear in the book–keeping framework of the economy. This framework structures value flows which can be paid for in monetary units. Nature, however, accepts no monetary payments, nor does it pay back in cash.

As discussed in section 4.3, interactions between the biosphere and the economic system can sometimes become visible within the framework of monetary book–keeping. The owners of land can earn a rent which appears in the book–keeping of any business taking place on that land. Environmental thresholds can be represented by limited inputs like emission permits. The corresponding payments are made not to the environment as such, but to the owners of the respective property rights.

The interface between economy and private households is characterized by two kinds of transactions: the economy receives vocational activities as inputs and provides consumption goods as outputs. The relations with the biosphere and with political authorities, however, are one–sided. From the biosphere, the economy gets limited inputs, but it cannot sell goods to it. To political authorities, it can sell all kinds of goods, but the public goods provided by these authorities are not supplied through market processes.

Implementing energy bounds offers a remarkable opportunity to reduce the arbitrariness of taxation schemes. If political authorities get a revenue by regularly selling a limited amount of energy permits through an auction system, the price of these permits will be defined by market processes, much as the rent for land.[31] As discussed in section 5.3, the corresponding revenue could be used to lower traditional forms of taxation. This is important for several reasons. It helps to avoid inflationary pressures from rising energy prices as well as reductions in investment due to the same reason.[32] It offers a possibility to reduce income taxes in a differentiated way in order to meet politically accepted standards of fairness with respect to different income categories. Moreover, the instrument of energy bounds avoids a crucial difficulty connected with taxes on pollutants: the contradiction between the government's interest in high revenues and the environmental goal of reducing the level of pollution. Commercial energy as such is not a pollutant, and there is no need to try to reduce its use to zero. In a growing economy, energy bounds can help to reduce environmental risks and at the same time let government revenue grow with the economy as a whole.

6.4 Human Agency and Cultural Regeneration

Energy bounds are a precious possibility to contribute to the solution of environmental problems. They can help to reshape the interface be-

---

[31] As I already mentioned in section 5.4, political authorities could also require that certain forms of land use presuppose the regular acquisition of corresponding permits. For example, the total amount of office space on a given territory could be limited by political decision. A limited number of tradeable permits for office space would be sold regularly by public authorities through an auction system. The rent for office space would accrue to public authorities without the need of an economically arbitrary taxation scheme. As a result, the price of land would be defined by those uses for which no permit would be necessary.

[32] Pearce [214] discusses macro–economic implications of carbon taxes in ways which can be generalized to the case of energy bounds.

tween politics and economics, avoiding delusive attempts to establish political control over the economic process as a whole, while contributing to a more rational system of raising government revenue.

Any such rearrangement, however, must come to terms with the relation between national polities and the global economy. One is easily tempted to dream of a world government being able to overcome this problem. But attempts to control the world economy with political means are futile and dangerous. Futile because they are bound to fail, dangerous because they nourish a concentration of power which undermines democratic institutions. If political measures are to contribute to a solution of the current environmental crisis, they have to be enacted by a society of nations, not by a world government. This, however, implies multiple control and cooperative problem solving. The relation of environmental problems to conflicting interests, already discussed in the introduction, has to be taken into account in the conclusion, too.

The dream of a *world government* is a venerable one. It is linked to the first Enlightenment's hope for a world without war. Kant was inspired to think about such a world by the motto "eternal peace" on a dutch inn, combined with the painting of a graveyard. He insisted that a world without war is a historical possibility, even if he accepted the bitter fact that he had no chance to witness its realization. He saw a world government as the logical form for the attainment of this goal, but he considered the establishement of a federative scheme of united nations as a more realistic second–best solution. The new Enlightenment, which will be needed to tackle the environmental crisis, shares with the first the historical project of eliminating the practice of war. It differs in the insight that only a society of nations, and no world government, can realize this project.

The difference is due to the demise of mechanistic thinking. The idea that a world government would be needed to solve global problems stems from the mechanistic idea that an agent can be rational in a solipsistic mode. If, however, rationality presupposes relations of accountability between several actors, the idea of an enlightened world government loses much of its plausibility. As I have argued in chapter 2, a person can develop only in a world in which she is not the only person. It is highly doubtful that a peaceful government could emerge in a world in which it was the only government. Obviously, in such a situation there could be no war with another government, but there could be tyranny as well as civil war to the same extent that war and tyranny can exist among a multitude of nations.

To prevent organized violence by public authority, it is of little use to look for a unique global authority. It is much more promising to foster a society of nations structured by strong accountability relations. Such relations must hold not only between various governments, but also between government and citizens within each nation. Otherwise it is hard to see why governments should display responsible behavior in their international relations. If, however, governments are held accountable by their citizens, there is no reason why nations should not learn to stick to peaceful means when dealing with each other. Clearly a society of such nations can try to persuade other nations to follow similar rules.[33]

There is an important analogy between the problem of world peace and the problem of global environmental change. In both cases, one may imagine that a solution is impossible without an enlightened world government. In both cases, a process of rule evolution in a society of nations is more realistic. But while the problem of war and peace is basically a political one, things are different with the environmental crisis. Here the main difficulty lies beyond the realm of politics, in the dynamics of the world economy.

In a sense, this simplifies things for national governments. No nation can expect to avoid the problems of global environmental change if it implements a scheme of energy bounds without most other nations taking a similar step. Given the very real conflicts of interests in the international arena, however, the chances of reaching a global agreement on energy bounds are very small, indeed. Introducing energy bounds, then, is a realistic strategy only if it promises substantial rewards independently from its effect on global environmental change. Fortunately, such *rewards* can be identified. First, energy bounds help to reduce local environmental problems. Limiting energy use limits many sources of pollution as well as many kinds of technological risks. Second, a shift of current systems of taxation towards energy bounds helps to direct technical change towards solutions which save energy rather than human labor. Given the persistent problems of unemployment in advanced as well as in developing economies, such a reorientation of technical change may become one of the most important goals

---

[33] As long as some governments keep using organized violence both to oppress their own citizens and to deal with other governments, even a society of democratic nations may have strong reasons to engage in a military conflict. Nevertheless, it would be a dangerous illusion to believe that nations could be forced to support democratic institutions and peaceful policies. Such support may be fostered, it cannot be commanded.

of future economic policy. Third, the possibility to gain first–mover advantages in new technological fields is a specific incentive to introduce energy bounds without waiting for competing nations to take the same step. Finally, introducing energy bounds helps to reestablish a sense of ecological responsibility in an economic system which is all too often perceived as a machine of cynical money–making. An ecologically sound economy would be able to treat money not as an external, but as an internal goal; and one should not underestimate the importance of such a transformation both in terms of personal well–being and of political legitimacy. These rewards may be of different importance for different nations, but it is quite plausible that at least some nations have good reasons for introducing energy bounds without waiting for worldwide international agreements.

A discussion of specific scenarios for the interaction between world economy and environmentally sound policies at a national level lies beyond the scope of this work. Such a discussion would have to include the realities of private life, especially with regard to the tremendous problems of population growth and migratory movements. It would have to pay careful attention to the interface between the economy and the private and the political realm. Economic activities often impair non–commercial goods, like the silence of a landscape, by attaining commercial ones, like the opening–up of a region for tourism. This relation between commercial and non–commercial goods deserves close scrutiny. Obviously many other problems of great theoretical and practical importance would require consideration. I leave their analysis to other, more detailed studies.

What should be emphasized here is the general point that no single actor, neither individual nor collective, can bring about a solution of that crisis. The environmental crisis is the result of a myriad of human actions enmeshed in complex patterns of cultural evolution. Only if a huge process of cultural degeneration can be reversed into a fairly rapid process of cultural regeneration, is there a chance of overcoming the environmental crisis. Cultural regeneration lies beyond the control of human agency, although it cannot take place without the active participation of many people in very different social positions.

It is quite obvious that the problems of global change require innovation processes of staggering proportions, both in the technological and in the institutional dimension. It would be naive to expect that such innovation could be managed by some central authority on a planetary scale. International organizations have an essential contribution to make to a process of cultural regeneration leading to a sustainable world economy, but they cannot control such a process—no single institution, let alone individual, will be able to do that. This is obviously to be welcomed by anybody committed to the ideals of democracy and of human equality. Moreover, the differentiation of the realm of vocational life from the political realm also implies that effective cultural regeneration will not be primarily the work of political authorities. This is the reason why national economies cannot be expected to be the building blocks of a sustainable world economy. If, on the other hand, a transformation of wage labor into vocational activity can be observed at the regional level, then this offers a remarkable starting point for sustainable development.

After all, who seems better equipped to meet the challenges of global change than innovative regional milieus? Their approach to world markets has already proved their ability to cope with new challenges on a global scale. The very fact of their limited size allows them to engage in processes of trial and error which would be irresponsible and often impossible on a larger scale. So it seems sensible to rely on innovative regional milieus for a decoupling of economic from physical growth.

Implementing energy bounds at a national scale can be a highly effective measure to stimulate such a decoupling and to foster a transition from quantitative growth to qualitative growth and sustainable development. Once again it should be emphasized, however, that the environmental crisis can be solved only if a very large number of actors deliberately engage in situations of *multiple control*, in which no single actor can act independently of the others.

It may be helpful to enumerate some of the most important actors, starting in the economic realm. Business firms will play a crucial role. Structures of communication and cooperation between such firms will be indispensable. If the orientation of economic activities toward external goals is to be modified by strengthening internal goals such as self–fulfilment in the context of vocational traditions, business firms cannot be the only actors in the economic realm, though. Another kind of economic organizations is needed, namely vocational associations. Trade unions are the obvious candidates for this role, but other possibilities may become important should trade unions continue to define their constituencies as wage–earners rather than transforming these constituencies by sustaining personal identities rooted in vocational traditions. Apart from business firms and vocational associations, scientific institutions also play a major role in a possible solution of the environmental crisis by their shaping socio–technical change.

As to the political realm, again a large number of actors will be indispensable for effective cultural regeneration—nations, international organizations, political parties, local authorities, non–governmental organizations. Finally, it would be a major error to neglect social actors rooted in the private realm. Churches are of paramount importance in this field; single families also have influential roles to play, especially in the context of regional milieus. Last but not least, individual persons will necessarily have their autonomous say in any process of cultural regeneration.

The point of this list is to make clear that a practical solution to the current environmental crisis can be found only as a result of joint action, not as a strategy implemented by a single actor. Saying this, I do by no means intend to discredit any attempts of designing and elaborating strategies for specific actors, quite the opposite. Yet I want to stress that the acknowledgment of situations of multiple control and mutual interdependence, of interaction and of dialogue is a *conditio sine qua non* for any viable strategy. Moreover, although reaching a responsible economy is a task for humankind as a whole, no single actor can develop a viable strategy for coping with this problem without a careful consideration of his or her specific situation. Therefore, I now conclude by inviting the reader with her or his particular experiences, abilities and competences to join this effort.

Bibliography

[1] ABBOTT, A., *The System of Professions* (Chicago University Press, Chicago, 1988).

[2] ADORNO, T.W., FRENKEL–BRUNSWIK, E., LEVINSON, D.J., SANFORD, R.N., *The Authoritarian Personality* (Harper & Row, New York, 1950).

[3] AKERLOF, G.A., YELLEN, J.L. (EDS.), *Efficiency Wage Models of the Labor Market* (Cambridge University Press, Cambridge, 1986).

[4] ANDERSON, P., *Passages from Antiquity to Feudalism* (Humanity Press, London, 1974).

[5] ARCHIBUGI, F., NIJKAMP, P., *Economy and Ecology: Towards Sustainable Development* (Kluwer, Dordrecht, 1989).

[6] ARMSTRONG, P., GLYN, A., HARRISON, J., *Capitalism since World War II* (Fontana, London, 1984).

[7] AUSTIN, J.L., *How to do things with words* (Oxford University Press, Oxford, 1962).

[8] AXELROD, R.E., *The Evolution of Cooperation* (Basic Books, New York, 1984).

[9] AYDALOT, P. (ED.), *Milieux innovateurs en Europe* (Gremi, Paris, 1986).

[10] BACCINI, P., BRUNNER, P.H., *The Metabolism of the Anthroposphere* (Springer, Heidelberg, 1991).

[11] BACHMANN–VOEGELIN, F., *Blatten im Lötschental. Die traditionelle Kulturlandschaft einer Berggemeinde* (Haupt, Bern, 1984).

[12] BAKER, G.P., HACKER, P.M.S., *Language, Sense & Nonsense* (Basil Blackwell, Oxford, 1984).

[13] BARGATZKY, T., *Einführung in die Kulturökologie. Umwelt, Kultur und Gesellschaft* (Reimer, Berlin, 1986).

[14] BARNES, B., *The Nature of Power* (University of Illinois Press, Urbana Ill., 1988).

[15] BARROWS, H.H., Geography as Human Ecology, *Annals of the Association of American Geographers*, **13**, 1–14 (1923).

[16] BATESON, G., *Steps to an Ecology of Mind* (Granada Publishing, London, 1978).

[17] BECATTINI, G., L'interpretazione sraffiana di Marshall, *Economia e politica industriale*, **12**, 5–23 (1985).

[18] BENEDICK, R.E. (ED.), *Ozone Diplomacy: New Directions in Safeguarding the Planet* (Harvard University Press, Boston, 1991).

[19] BENJAMIN, J., *The Bonds of Love: Psychoanalysis, Feminism, and the Problem of Knowledge* (Pantheon, New York, 1988).

[20] BENJAMIN, W., The Work of Art in the Age of Mechanistic Reproduction, in: *Illuminations*, Benjamin, W., 219–253 (Fontana, Glasgow, [1936] 1973).

[21] BENOIST, J.-M., *L'identité. Séminaire interdisciplinaire dirigé par Claude Lévi-Strauss* (Grasset, Paris, 1977).

[22] BERGH, J.C.J.M. VAN DEN, NIJKAMP, P., Aggregate dynamic economic-ecological models for sustainable development, *Environment and Planning A*, **23**, 1409–1428 (1991).

[23] BERKES, F., FEENY, D., McCAY, B.J., ACHESON, J.M., The Benefits of the Commons, *Nature*, **340**, 91–93 (1989).

[24] BERRY, B.J.L. (ED.), *Urbanisation and Counterurbanisation* (Sage, Beverly Hills, 1976).

[25] BERRY, B.J.L., KASARDA, J.D., *Contemporary Urban Ecology* (Macmillan, New York, 1977).

[26] BHASKAR, R., *Reclaiming Reality* (Verso, London, 1989).

[27] BHASKAR, R., *The Possibility of Naturalism* (Harvester, Brighton, 1979).

[28] BHASKAR, R., *A Realist Theory of Science* (Harvester, Brighton, 1978).

[29] BLOCK, F., *Postindustrial Possibilities. A Critique of Economic Discourse* (University of California Press, Berkeley, 1990).

[30] BORDEN, R.J., in Collaboration with JACOBS, J. and YOUNG, G.L. (EDS.), *Human Ecology. A Gathering of Perspectives* (Society for Human Ecology, College Park, Md., 1988).

[31] BOSERUP, E., *The Conditions of Agricultural Growth* (Aldine, Chicago, 1965).

[32] BOURDIEU, P., *The Logic of Practice* (Stanford University Press, Stanford, 1990).

[33] BOURDIEU, P., *Outline of a Theory of Practice* (Cambridge University Press, Cambridge, 1977).

[34] BOUVERESSE, J., *La force de la règle* (Minuit, Paris, 1987).

[35] BOWLES, S., GORDON, D.M., WEISSKOPF, T.E., *Beyond the Waste Land* (Anchor Books, New York, 1984).

[36] BOYD, R., RICHERSON, P., *Culture and the Evolutionary Process* (University of Chicago Press, Chicago, 1989).

[37] BOYDEN, S., *Western Civilization in Biological Perspective. Patterns in Biohistory* (Clarendon Press, Oxford, 1987).

[38] BOYDEN, S., MILAR, S., NEWCOMBE, K., O'NEILL, B., *The ecology of a city and its people. The case of Hong Kong* (Australian National University Press, Canberra, Australia, 1981).

[39] BROOME, J., *Counting the Cost of Global Warming* (The White Horse Press, Cambridge, 1992).

[40] BUBER, M., *I and Thou* (Macmillan, London, 1978).

[41] BUCHMANN, M., *The Script of Life in Modern Society: Entry into Adulthood in a Changing World* (University of Chicago Press, Chicago, 1989).

[42] BUDYKO, M.I., *The Evolution of the Biosphere* (Reidel, Dordrecht, 1986).

[43] BURGER, T., *Max Webers Theory of Concept Formation. History, Laws and Ideal Types* (Duke University Press, Durham NC, 1987).

[44] BURNS, T.R., DIETZ, T., Cultural Evolution: Social Rule Systems, Selection and Human Agency, *International Sociology*, **7**, 259–283 (1992).

[45] BUTTEL, F.H., New Directions in Environmental Sociology, *Annual Review of Sociology*, **13**, 465–88 (1987).

[46] CARLSTEIN, T., *Time Resources, Society and Ecology*, Vol. I, Preindustrial Societies (George Allen & Unwin, London, 1982).

[47] CATTON, W.R.JR., DUNLAP, R.E, A New Ecological Paradigm for Post–Exuberant Sociology, *American Behavioral Scientist*, **24**, 15–47 (1980).

[48] CATTON, W.R.JR.,DUNLAP, R.E., Environmental Sociology: A New Paradigm, *The American Sociologist*, **13**, 41–49 (1978).

[49] CLARK, J., COLE, S., *Global Simulation Models. A Comparative Study* (John Wiley & Sons, London,1975).

[50] COASE, R.H., The Problem of Social Cost, *Journal of Law and Economics*, **3**, 1–44 (1960).

[51] COLEMAN, J.S., The Rational Reconstruction of Society, *American Sociological Review*, **58**, 1–15 (1993).

[52] COSTANZA, R., What is Ecological Economics, *Ecological Economics*, **1**, 1–7 (1989).

[53] COTGROVE, S., *Catastrophe or Cornucopia: The Environment, Politics and the Future* (John Wiley, New York, 1982).

[54] COULTER, J., *The Social Construction of Mind* (Macmillan, London, 1979).

[55] DAHRENDORF, R., Wenn der Arbeitsgesellschaft die Arbeit ausgeht, in: *Krise der Arbeitsgesellschaft?, Verhandlungen des 21. Deutschen Soziologentages in Bamberg 1982*, edited by Matthes, J. (Campus, Frankfurt, 1983).

[56] DALY, H.E., *Toward a Steady State Economy* (Freeman, San Francisco, 1973).

[57] DEWDNEY, A.K., How Close Encounters with Star Clusters Are Achieved with a Computer Telescope, *Scientific American*, **254**, 12–16 (1986).

[58] DICKENS, P., *Society and Nature. Towards a Green Social Theory* (Temple University Press, Philadelphia, 1992).

[59] DIJKSTERHUIS, E.J., *The Mechanization of the World Picture: Pythagoras to Newton* (Princeton University Press, Princeton NJ, 1986).

[60] DRUCKER, P., *The Unseen Revolution. How Pension Fund Socialism Came to America* (Harper & Row, New York, 1976).

[61] DRUCKER, P., *The End of Economic Man* (Harper Colophon Books, New York, [1939] 1969).

[62] DRURY, W.H., NISBET, I.C.T., Interrelations between Developmental Models in Geomorphology, Plant Ecology and Animal Ecology, *General Systems*, **16**, 57–68 (1971).

[63] DUNLAP, R.E., CATTON, W.R.JR., Environmental Sociology, *Annual Review of Sociology*, **5**, 243–273 (1979).

[64] DUNLAP, R.E., MERTIG, A.G., *American Environmentalism. The U.S. Environmental Movement, 1970–1990* (Taylor & Francis, Philadelphia, 1992).

[65] DUNLAP, R.E., VAN LIERE, K.D., The 'New Environmental Paradigm': A Proposed Measuring Instrument and Preliminary Results, *Journal of Environmental Education*, **9**, 10–19 (1978).

[66] DURKHEIM, E., Préface de la seconde édition. Quelques remarques sur les groupements professionnels, in: *De la division du travail social*, edited by Durkheim, E. (Presses universitaires de France, Paris, [1902] 1967).

[67] DÜRRENBERGER, G., ERNSTE, H., FURGER, F., JAEGER, C., STEINER, D., TRUFFER, B., *Das Dilemma der modernen Stadt* (Springer, Berlin, 1992).

[68] DÜRRENBERGER, G., *Menschliche Territorien. Geographische Aspekte der biologischen und kulturellen Evolution* (Geographisches Institut ETH, Zürich, 1989).

[69] ELSENHANS, H., *Development and Underdevelopment: The History, Economics and Politics of North–South Relations* (Sage, Newsbury Park CA, 1991).

[70] ELSTER, J., Wage Bargaining and Social Norms, *Acta Sociologica*, **32**, 113–136 (1989).

[71] EMERY, F.E., TRIST, E.L., *Towards a Social Ecology* (Plenum Press, London, 1972).

[72] ERNSTE, H., JAEGER, C., Neuere Tendenzen schweizerischer Migrationsströme. Teil 1: Eine Literaturübersicht zum Phänomen der Entstädterung, *Geographica Helvetica*, **41**, 111–116 (1986).

[73] ETZIONI, A., *The Moral Dimension. Towards a New Economics* (The Free Press, New York, 1988).

[74] EVANS, F.C., Ecosystem as the Basic Unit in Ecology, *Science*, **123**, 1127–1128 (1956).

[75] EVE, A.S., *Rutherford. Being the Life and Letters of the Rt Hon. Lord Rutherford, O.M.* (Cambridge University Press, Cambridge, 1939).

[76] FEYERABEND, P., *Erkenntnis für freie Menschen*, Veränderte Ausgabe (Suhrkamp, Frankfurt, 1980).

[77] FIRESTONE, S., *The Dialectic of Sex* (W. Morrow and Company, New York, 1970).

[78] FISCHER, H.R., *Sprache und Lebensform: Wittgenstein über Freud und die Geisteskrankheit* (Athenäum, Frankfurt am Main, 1987).

[79] FISHER, I., *Mastering the Crisis. With Additional Chapters on Stamp Scrip* (Allen & Unwin, London, 1934).

[80] FLANNERY, K.V., The Cultural Evolution of Civilizations, *Annual Review of Ecology and Systematics*, **3**, 399–426 (1972).

[81] FLAVIN, C., *Slowing Global Warming: A Worldwide Strategy. Worldwatch Paper 91* (Worldwatch Institute, Washington DC, 1989).

[82] FOLKE, C., KÅBERGER, T., *Linking the Natural Environment and the Economy: Essays from the Eco–Eco Group* (Kluwer, Dordrecht, 1991).

[83] FOUCAULT, M., *Madness and Civilization: A History of Insanity in the Age of Reason* (Random, New York, 1988).

[84] FOUCAULT, M., *Order of Things: An Archaeology of the Human Sciences* (Random, New York, 1973).

[85] FREESE, L., Evolution and Sociogenesis, Part 1: Ecological Origins, Part 2: Social Continuities, in: *Advances in Group Processes*, edited by Lawler, E.J., Markovsky, B., Vol. 5 (AI Press Inc., Greenwich CT, 1988).

[86] FREUD, S., *Totem and Taboo* (Norton, New York, [1912] 1990).

[87] FREUD, S., *Beyond the Pleasure Principle* (Norton, New York, [1920] 1990).

[88] FREUDENTHAL, G., *Atom und Individuum im Zeitalter Newtons. Zur Genese der mechanistischen Natur– und Sozialphilosophie* (Suhrkamp, Frankfurt, 1982).

[89] FREY, W.H., SPEARE, A., *Regional and Metropolitan Growth and Decline in the United States* (Russell Sage Foundation, New York, 1988).

[90] FRIEDMAN, M., *Capitalism and Freedom* (University of Chicago Press, Chicago, 1962).

[91] FRIEDRICHS, J., *Stadtanalyse. Soziale und räumliche Organisation der Gesellschaft* (Rowohlt, Hamburg, 1977).

[92] FURUBOTN, E.B., PEJOVICH, S., Property Rights and Economic Theory: A Survey of Recent Literature, *Journal of Economic Literature*, **10**, 1137–1162 (1972).

[93] GAZZANIGA, M.S. (ED.), *Handbook of Cognitive Neuroscience* (Plenum Press, New York, 1984).

[94] GEERTZ, C., *The Interpretation of Cultures* (Basic Books, New York, 1973).

[95] GEORGESCU–ROEGEN, N., *The Entropy Law and the Economic Process* (Harvard University Press, Cambridge Mass., 1971).

[96] GERDING, R., STARBATTY, J., *Zur Entnationalisierung des Geldes. Eine Zwischenbilanz* (J.B.C. Mohr, Tübingen, 1980).

[97] GESELL, S., *The Natural Economic Order* (Portr., London, [1916] 1958).

[98] GIBSON, J.J., *The Ecological Approach to Visual Perception* (Houghton Mifflin, Boston, 1979).

[99] GIDDENS, A., *The Constitution of Society. Outline of the Theory of Structuration* (University of California Press, Berkeley, 1984).

[100] GIDDENS, A., *Central Problems in Social Theory. Action, Structure and Contradiction in Social Analysis* (Macmillan, London, 1979).

[101] GOODMAN, N., *Ways of World–Making* (Harvester, Hassocks, 1978).

[102] GORE, A., *Earth in the Balance: Forging a New Common Purpose* (Earthscan, London, 1991).

[103] GOULD, S.J., *Hen's Teeth and Horse's Toes. Further Reflections in Natural History* (Penguin, Harmondsworth, 1984).

[104] GOULDNER, A., *For Sociology. Renewal and Critique in Sociology Today* (Allen Lane, London, 1973).

[105] GRANOVETTER, M., Economic Institutions as Social Constructions: A Framework for Analysis, *Acta Sociologica*, **35**, 3–11 (1992).

[106] GRANOVETTER, M., Small Is Bountyful: Labor Markets and Establishment Size, *American Sociological Review*, **49**, 323–34 (1984).

[107] GREENFIELD, R.L., YEAGER, L.B., A Laissez–Faire Approach to Monetary Stability, *Journal of Money, Credit and Banking*, **15**, 302–315 (1983).

[108] GROEBEL, J., HINDE, R.A. (EDS.), *Cooperation and Prosocial Behaviour* (Cambridge University Press, Cambridge, 1991).

[109] GROH, D., Mobilität als Strategie und Ressource—Das Beispiel von Jäger–Sammlern und Hirtennomaden, *GAIA*, **1**, 144–152 (1992).

[110] HABERMAS, J., *The Theory of Communicative Action*, 2 Vols. (Beacon Press, Boston, 1989).

[111] HABERMAS, J., *Toward a Rational Society: Student Protest, Science and Politics* (Beacon Press, Boston, 1970).

[112] HÄGERSTRAND, T., What about People in Regional Science, *Papers of the Regional Science Association*, **24**, 7–21 (1970).

[113] HALL, E.T., *The Hidden Dimension. Man's Use of Space in Public and Private* (The Bodley Head, London, 1969).

[114] HALLER, M., HOFFMANN–NOWOTTNY, H.-J., ZAPF, W. (EDS.), *Kultur und Gesellschaft* (Campus, Frankfurt, 1989).

[115] HANNAN, M.T., FREEMAN, J., *Organizational Ecology* (Harvard University Press, Cambridge Mass.,1989).

[116] HARCOURT, G.C., *Some Cambridge Controversies in the Theory of Capital* (Cambridge University Press, Cambridge, 1972).

[117] HARDIN, G., The Tragedy of the Commons, *Science*, **162**, 1243–1248 (1968).

[118] HARRÉ, R., *Varieties of Realism. A Rationale for the Natural Sciences* (Basil Blackwell, Oxford, 1986).

[119] HARRÉ, R., *Personal Being* (Basil Blackwell, Oxford, 1983).

[120] HARRÉ, R., *Social Being* (Basil Blackwell, Oxford, 1979).

[121] HAWLEY, A.H., *Human Ecology: A Theoretical Essay* (University of Chicago Press, Chicago, 1986).

[122] HAWLEY, A.H., Human Ecology: Persistence and Change, in: *The State of Sociology. Problems and Prospects*, edited by Short, F.Jr. (Sage, Beverly Hills, 1981).

[123] HAWLEY, A.H., *Human Ecology: A Theory of Community Structure* (Ronald, New York, 1950).

[124] HAYEK, F.A.v., *The Fatal Conceit: The Errors of Socialism* (Routledge, London, 1988).

[125] HAYEK, F.A.v., *The Denationalization of Money* (Institute of Economic Affairs, London, 1976).

[126] HAYEK, F.A.v., *Collectivist Economic Planning. Critical Studies on the Possibility of Socialism* (Routledge, London, 1938).

[127] HECKHAUSEN, H., *Motivation und Handeln* (Springer, Berlin, 1989).

[128] HEINTZ, P., *Einführung in die soziologische Theorie*, zweite, erweiterte Auflage (Ferdinand Enke, Stuttgart, 1968).

[129] HEYWARD, C., *The Redemption of God. A Theology of Mutual Relation* (University Press of America, Washington D.C., 1982).

[130] HORKHEIMER, M., ADORNO, T.W., *Dialectic of Enlightenment* (Continuum, New York, [1947] 1975).

[131] HORKHEIMER, M. (ED.), *Studien über Autorität und Familie. Schriften des Instituts für Sozialforschung, Vol. V.* (Alcan, Paris, 1936).

[132] HÖSLE, V., *Philosophie der ökologischen Krise, Moskauer Vorträge* (Beck, München, 1991).

[133] HOTELLING, H., The Economics of Exhaustible Resources, *Journal of Political Economy*, **39**, 137–175 (1931).

[134] HOUGHTON, J.T., JENKINS, G.J., EPHRAUMS, J.J. (EDS.), *Climatic Change: The IPCC Scientific Assessment* (Cambridge University Press, Cambridge, 1990).

[135] HUBER, G., Bios theoretikos und bios praktikos bei Aristoteles und Platon, in: *Arbeit Musse Meditation. Betrachtungen zur vita activa und vita contemplativa*, edited by Vickers, B. (vdf, Zürich, 1985).

[136] HUND, F., *Grundbegriffe der Physik. Teil 1* (Bibliographisches Institut, Mannheim, 1979).

[137] HUND, F., *Geschichte der physikalischen Begriffe. Teil 1: Die Entstehung des mechanischen Naturbildes* (Bibliographisches Institut, Mannheim, 1978).

[138] HUND, F., *Geschichte der physikalischen Begriffe. Teil 2: Die Wege zum heutigen Naturbild* (Bibliographisches Institut, Mannheim, 1978).

[139] HUSSERL, E., *The Crisis of European Sciences and Transcendental Phenomenology: An Introduction to Phenomenological Philosophy* (Northwestern University Press, Evanston JL, 1970).

[140] IMBODEN, D., JAEGER, C., MÜLLER–HEROLD,U., Projekt Energieschranke, *Gaia*, 1, 128 (1992).

[141] JAEGER, C., Sustainable Regional Development: A Path for the Greenhouse Marathon, *Advances in Human Ecology*, 2, 129–156 (1993).

[142] JAEGER, C., Innovative Milieus and Environmental Awareness, *Sociologia Internationalis*, 28, 205–216 (1990).

[143] JAEGER, C., Die kulturelle Einbettung des europäischen Marktes, in: *Kultur und Gesellschaft*, edited by Haller, M., Hoffmann–Nowottny, H.–J., Zapf, W. (Campus, Frankfurt, 1989).

[144] JAEGER, C., DÜRRENBERGER, G., Services and Counterurbanization: the case of central Europe, in: *Services and Metropolitan Development*, edited by Daniels, P.W., (Routledge, London, 1991).

[145] JAEGER, C., BIERI, L., DÜRRENBERGER, G., Berufsethik und Humanisierung der Arbeit, *Schweizerische Zeitschrift für Soziologie*, 13, 47–62 (1987).

[146] JAEGER, C., WEBER, A., Lohndynamik und Arbeitslosigkeit, *Kyklos*, 41, 3, 479–506 (1988).

[147] JAFFÉ, W., Walras' Economics as Others See It, *Journal of Economic Literature*, 18, 2, 528–549 (1980).

[148] JANTSCH, E., *The Self-Organizing Universe* (Pergamon, Oxford, 1980).

[149] JENSEN, U.J., HARRÉ, R. (EDS.), *The Philosophy of Evolution* (St. Martin's Press, New York, 1981).

[150] JONAS, H., *Der Gottesbegriff nach Auschwitz. Eine jüdische Stimme* (Suhrkamp, Frankfurt, 1987).

[151] JUNG, C.G., The Relation Between the Ego and the Unconscious, in: *The Collected Works of C. G. Jung, No. 7: Two Essays on Analytical Psychology*, edited by Adler, G. et al. (Princeton University Press, Princeton,[1928] 1966).

[152] KANT, I., What is Enlightenment, in: *On History*, edited by Kant, I. (Library of Liberal Arts, Indianapolis NY, [1784] 1957).

[153] KAPP, K.W., *The Social Costs of Private Enterprise* (Harvard University Press, Cambridge Mass., 1950).

[154] KERN, H., SCHUMANN, M., *Das Ende der Arbeitsteilung? Rationalisierung in der industriellen Produktion* (Beck, München, 1984).

[155] KEYNES, J.M., *The General Theory of Employment, Interest and Money* (Macmillan, London, [1936] 1970).

[156] KIRMAN, A., The Intrinsic Limits of Modern Economic Theory: The Emperor has no Clothes, *The Economic Journal*, **99**, 126–139 (1989).

[157] KREPS, D.M., *A Course in Microeconomic Theory* (Harvester Wheatsheaf, New York, 1990).

[158] KREILCAMP–CUDMORE, A., *Language as Wittgenstein's Way of Life* (Boston University Press, Boston, 1973).

[159] KUHN, T., *The Structure of Scientific Revolutions* (University of Chicago Press, Chicago, 1962).

[160] KÜMMEL, R., *Energie als Produktionsfaktor und Entropie als Verschmutzungsindikator in der Marktökonomischen Modellierung* (manuscript, 1989).

[161] LEHMANN, D., KOUKKOU, M., Psychophysiologie des Traums, in: *Der Traum in Psychoanalyse und analytischer Psychotherapie*, edited by Erdmann, M. (Springer, Berlin, 1983).

[162] LEONTIEF, W., Environmental Repercussions and the Economic Structure: an Input–Output Approach, in: Leontief, W., *Essays in Economics*, Vol. II, 78–98 (Basil Blackwell, Oxford, 1977).

[163] LEWIN, K., *Field Theory in Social Science: Selected Theoretical Papers* (Harper & Row, New York, 1951).

[164] LIND, R.C. ET. AL., *Discounting for Time and Risk in Energy Policy* (Resources for the Future, Washington, D.C., 1982).

[165] LOCKE, J., *Two Treatises on Government* (Cambridge University Press, Cambridge, [1689/90] 1960).

[166] LOUBSER, J.J., BAUM, R.C., EFFRAT, A., LIDZ, V.M., *Explorations in General Theory in Social Science. Essays in Honor of Talcott Parsons*, Vol. II (The Free Press, New York, 1976).

[167] LOVELOCK, J.E., *Gaia. A New Look at Life on Earth* (Oxford University Press, Oxford, 1979).

[168] LUHMANN, N., *Ecological Communication* (University of Chicago Press, Chicago, 1989).

[169] LUHMANN, N., *Soziale Systeme. Grundriss einer allgemeinen Theorie* (Suhrkamp, Frankfurt, 1984).

[170] LUHMANN, N., *Macht* (Enke, Stuttgart, 1975).

[171] LUHMANN, N., Zur Theorie symbolisch generalisierter Kommunikationsmedien, *Zeitschrift für Soziologie*, **3**, 236–255 (1974).

[172] LÜSCHER, R.M., *Henry und die Krümelmonster* (Konkurs-buchverlag, Tübingen, 1989).

[173] MACINTYRE, A., *Whose Justice? Which Rationality?* (Duckworth, London, 1988).

[174] MACINTYRE, A., *After Virtue* (Duckworth, London, 1987).

[175] MAJOR, J., Historical Development of the Ecosystem Concept, in: *The Ecosystem Concept in Natural Resource Management*, edited by Van Dyne, G.M. (Academic Press, New York, 1969).

[176] MALCOLM, N., *Ludwig Wittgenstein: a Memoir* (Oxford University Press, Oxford, 1984).

[177] MALMBERG, T., *Human Territoriality* (Mouton, The Hague, 1980).

[178] MANN, M., *The Sources of Social Power* (Cambridge University Press, Cambridge, 1986).

[179] MARGLIN, S.A., SCHOR, J.B. (EDS.), *The Golden Age of Capitalism. Reinterpreting the Postwar Experience* (Oxford University Press, Oxford, 1990).

[180] MARSHALL, A., *Principles of Economics. An Introductory Volume* (Macmillan, London, [1890] 1982).

[181] MARTI, K., *Die gesellige Gottheit. Ein Diskurs* (Radius, Stuttgart, 1989).

[182] MARX, K., *Capital,* (Buccaneer Books, Cutchoque NY, [1885] 1988).

[183] MAUCH, S., ITEN, R., WEIZSÄCKER, E.U. VON, JESINGHAUS, J., *Ökologische Steuerreform. Europäische Ebene und Fallbeispiel Schweiz* (Rüegger, Chur/Zürich, 1992).

[184] MAZUR, A., ROSA, E, Energy and Life–Style; Massive energy consumption may not be necessary to maintain current living standards in America, *Science*, **186**, 607–610 (1974).

[185] MCKINLAY, R.D., LITTLE, R., *Global Problems and World Order* (Frances Pinter, London, 1986).

[186] MEADE, J.E., *The Theory of Economic Externalities: The Control of Environmental Pollution and Similar Social Costs* (Sijthoff, Leiden, 1973).

[187] MEADOWS, D.H., MEADOWS, D.L., RANDERS, J., *Beyond the Limits* (Earthscan, London, 1992).

[188] MEADOWS, D.H., MEADOWS, D.L., RANDERS, J., BEHRENS, W.W., *The Limits to Growth* (Universe Books, New York, 1972).

[189] MEYER–ABICH, K.M., *Wege zum Frieden mit der Natur. Prak-tische Naturphilosophie für die Umweltpolitik* (Hanser, München, 1984).

[190] MICHAELS, C., CARELLO, C., *Direct Perception* (Prentice–Hall, Englewood Cliffs, 1981).

[191] MICKLIN, M., CHOLDIN, H.M. (EDS.), *Sociological Human Ecology: Contemporary Issues and Applications* (Westview Press, London, 1984).

[192] MILBRATH, L.W., *Envisioning a Sustainable Society. Learning our Way Out* (State University of New York Press, Albany NY, 1989).

[193] MISHAN, E.J., Literature on Externalities, *Journal of Economic Literature*, **14**, 1–29 (1971).

[194] MORISHIMA, M., Ideology and Economic Activity, *Current Sociology*, **38**, 51–77 (1990).

[195] MORISHIMA, M., *Ricardo's Economics. A General Equilibrium Theory of Distribution and Growth* (Cambridge University Press, Cambridge, 1989).

[196] MORISHIMA, M., *Why Has Japan 'Succeeded'? Western Technology and the Japanese Ethos* (Cambridge University Press, Cambridge, 1982).

[197] MÜLLER, H.M., *Evolution, Kognition und Sprache. Die Evolution des Menschen und die biologischen Grundlagen der Sprachfähigkeit* (Paul Parey, München, 1987).

[198] NEUBURGER, H., Energy use in an era of rapidly changing oil price - how OPEC did not save the world from the greenhouse effect, *Environment and Planning A*, **24**, 1039–1050 (1992).

[199] NICOLIS, G., PRIGOGINE, I., *Self-Organization in Nonequilibrium Systems* (John Wiley & Sons, New York, 1977).

[200] NORDHAUS, W., The Worldwide Wage Explosion, *Brookings Papers on Economic Activity*, **2**, 431–465 (1972).

[201] ODUM, E., The Strategy of Ecosystem Development, *Science*, **164**, 262–270 (1969).

[202] ODUM, H.T., An Energy Circuit Language for Ecological and Social Systems: Its Physical Basis, in: *Systems Analysis and Simulation in Ecology*, edited by Patten, B.C., Vol. II (Academic Press, New York, 1972).

[203] ORRÙ, M., *Anomie. History and Meanings* (Allen & Unwin, Boston, 1987).

[204] PAGE, T., *Conservation and Economic Efficiency. An Approach to Materials Policy* (Johns Hopkins University Press, Baltimore, 1977).

[205] PALLMANN, H., *Bodenkunde und Pflanzensoziologie*, Kultur– und Staatswissenschaftliche Schriften, Heft 60 (Polygraphischer Verlag, Zürich, 1948).

[206] PARINELLO, S., Exhaustible Natural Resources and the Classical Method of Long Period Equilibrium, in: *Distribution, Effective Demand and International Economic Relations*, edited by Kregel, J.A. (Macmillan, London, 1983).

[207] PARK, R.E., The Urban Community as a Spatial Pattern and a Moral Order, in: *Urban Social Segregation*, edited by Peach, C. (Longman, London, [1925] 1975).

[208] PARK, R.E., *On Social Control and Collective Behavior* (The University of Chicago Press, Chicago, 1967).

[209] PARSONS, T., *Social Systems and the Evolution of Action Theory* (The Free Press, New York, 1977).

[210] PARSONS, T., On the Concept of Political Power, in: Parsons, T., *Sociological Theory and Modern Society* (The Free Press, New York, 1967).

[211] PARSONS, T., SHILS, E.A. (EDS.), *Towards a General Theory of Action. Theoretical Foundations for the Social Sciences* (Harper & Row, New York, 1951).

[212] PARSONS, T., SMELSER, N., *Economy and Society* (The Free Press, New York, 1956).

[213] PASINETTI, L.L., *Structural Change and Economic Growth. A Theoretical Essay on the Dynamics of the Wealth of Nations* (Cambridge University Press, Cambridge, 1988).

[214] PEARCE, D.W., The role of carbon taxes in adjusting to global warming, *Economic Journal*, **101**, 938–948 (1991).

[215] PERRINGS, C., *Economy and Environment* (Cambridge University Press, Cambridge, 1987).

[216] PERROW, C., A Society of Organizations, *Theory and Society*, **20**, 725–762 (1991).

[217] PERROW, C., *Normal Accidents. Living with High–Risk Technologies* (Basic Books, New York, 1984).

[218] PICHT, G., Ist Humanökologie möglich?, in: *Humanökologie und Frieden*, edited by Eisenbarth, C. (Klett, Stuttgart, 1979).

[219] PIGOU, A.C., *The Economics of Welfare* (MacMillan, London, 1920).

[220] PIORE, M.J., SABEL, C.F., *The Second Industrial Divide. Possibilities for Prosperity* (Basic Books, New York, 1984).

[221] POLANYI, K., *The Great Transformation. The Political and Economic Origins of Our Time* (Rinehart & Co, New York, 1944).

[222] POPPER, K.R., Natural Selection and Emergence of Mind, *Dialectica*, **32**, 339–355 (1978).

[223] PRICE, M., Humankind in the Biosphere: The Evolution of International Interdisciplinary Research, *Global Environmental Change*, **1**, 3–13 (1990).

[224] PRIMAS, H., Umdenken in der Naturwissenschaft, *GAIA*, **1**, 5–15 (1992).

[225] PUTNAM, H., *The Many Faces of Realism* (Open Court, La Salle Ill., 1987).

[226] PUTNAM, H., *Reason, Truth, and History* (Cambridge University Press, Cambridge, 1981).

[227] QUINE, W.V., *Set Theory and its Logic* (Harvard University Press, Cambridge MA, 1971).

[228] RAMSEY, F.P., A Mathematical Theory of Saving, *The Economic Journal*, **38**, 543–559 (1928).

[229] RAPPAPORT, R., *Pigs for the Ancestors* (Yale University Press, New Haven, 1967).

[230] RICH, A., *Wirtschaftsethik*, 2 Vols. (Mohn, Gütersloh, 1984/1990).

[231] ROBBINS, L., *An Essay on the Nature and Significance of Economic Science* (Macmillan, London, 1937).

[232] ROMER, P.M., Are Nonconvexities Important for Understanding Growth?, *American Economic Review*, **80**, 97–103 (1990).

[233] ROMM, J.J., LOVINS, A.B., Fueling a competetive Economy, *Foreign Affairs*, **72**, 46–62 (1992).

[234] ROUGEMONT, D. DE, *Love in the Western World* (Schocken, New York, 1990).

[235] RUST, A., *Die organismische Kosmologie von Alfred N. Whitehead* (Athenäum, Frankfurt, 1987).

[236] SABEL, C., Flexible Specialisation and the Re–emergence of Regional Economies, in: *Reversing Industrial Decline? Industrial Structure and Policy in Britain and Her Competitors*, edited by Hirst, P., Zeitlin, J. (Berg, Oxford, 1989).

[237] SABINI, J., SILVER, M., *The Moralities of Everyday Life* (Oxford University Press, Oxford, 1982).

[238] SACK, R.D., *Human Territoriality* (Cambridge University Press, Cambridge, 1986).

[239] SAHLINS, M., *Stone Age Economics* (Tavistock Publications, London, 1974).

[240] SANDERSON, S.K., *Social Evolutionism. A Critical History* (Basil Blackwell, Oxford, 1990).

[241] SARTRE, J.-P., *The Family Idiot: Gustave Flaubert 1821–1857*, 3 Vols. (Chicago University Press, Chicago, 1981/1987/1989).

[242] SAUSSURE, F. DE, *Course in General Linguistics* (Fontana, London, [1916] 1974).

[243] SCHEFOLD, B., *Ökonomische Klassik im Umbruch* (Suhrkamp, Frankfurt, 1986).

[244] SCHIEVE, W.C., ALLEN, P.M. (EDS.), *Self-Organization and Dissipative Structures: Applications in the Physical and Social Sciences* (University of Texas Press, Austin, 1982).

[245] SCHMIDHEINY, S. WITH THE BUSINESS COUNCIL FOR SUSTAINABLE DEVELOPMENT, *Changing Course* (The MIT Press, Boston, 1992).

[246] SCHNAIBERG, A., *The Environment* (Oxford University Press, Oxford, 1980).

[247] SCHNEIDER, W., Die postindustrielle Zeit; die neue Aufklärung, in: *Wissenschaft in Sorge um die Umwelt*, edited by ETH Zürich, Forum für Umweltfragen (Birkhäuser, Basel, 1990).

[248] SCHWARTZ, J.T., America's Economic–Technological Agenda for the 1990s, *Daedalus (Journal of the American Academy of Arts and Sciences)*, winter (1992).

[249] SCHWARTZ, J.T., *Lectures on the Mathematical Method in Analytical Economics* (Gordon and Breach, New York, 1963).

[250] SCOTT, A.J., *Metropolis* (University of California Press, Berkeley, 1988).

[251] SEN, A., *On Ethics and Economics* (Basil Blackwell, Oxford, 1987).

[252] SEN, A., Goals, Commitment and Identity, *Journal of Law, Economics and Organization*, **1**, 341–355 (1985).

[253] SHANKER, S.G., *Wittgenstein and the Turning-Point in the Philosophy of Mathematics* (Croom Helm, London, 1987).

[254] SHOTTER, J., *Social Accountability and Selfhood* (Blackwell, Oxford, 1984).

[255] SHOTTER, J., GERGEN, K.J. (EDS.), *Texts of Identity* (Sage, London, 1989).

[256] SIEBERT, H., *Economics of the Environment. Theory and Policy* (Springer, Berlin, 1987).

[257] SIMONIS, U.E., Ecological modernization of industrial society: three strategic elements, *International Social Science Journal*, **41**, 347–361 (1989).

[258] SMITH, A., *An Inquiry into the Nature and Causes of the Wealth of Nations* (Clarendon Press, Oxford, [1776] 1976).

[259] SMITH, E.A., Anthropology, Evolutionary Ecology, and the Explanatory Limitations of the Ecosystem Concept, in: *The Ecosystem Concept in Anthropology*, edited by Moran, E.F. (Westview Press, Denver, 1984).

[260] SPERRY, R., *Science and Moral Priority. Merging Mind, Brain, and Human Values* (Columbia University Press, New York, 1983).

[261] SRAFFA, P., *Production of Commodities by Means of Commodities. Pelude to a Critique of Economic Theory* (Cambridge University Press, Cambridge, 1960).

[262] STEFAN, V., *Häutungen: autobiographische Aufzeichnungen, Gedichte, Träume, Analysen* (Frauenoffensive, München, 1975).

[263] STEGMÜLLER, W. *The Structuralist View of Theories. A Possible Analogue of the Bourbaki Programme in Physical Science* (Springer, Berlin, 1979).

[264] STEINER, D., WISNER, B., *Humanoekologie und Geographie*, Human Ecology and Geography, Zürcher Geographische Schriften, Nr.28 (Geographisches Institut ETH, Zürich, 1986).

[265] STEWARD, J.H., *Theory of Culture Change* (University of Illinois Press, Urbana Ill., 1955).

[266] STIERLIN, H., *Individuation und Familie* (Suhrkamp, Frankfurt, 1989).

[267] STOESSEL, M., *Aura. Das vergessene Menschliche. Zu Sprache und Erfahrung bei Walter Benjamin* (Hanser, München, 1983).

[268] STRANGE, S., *Casino Capitalism* (Basil Blackwell, Oxford, 1986).

[269] SUHR, D., GODSCHALK, H., *Optimale Liquidität—eine liquiditätstheoretische Analyse und ein kredittheoretisches Wettbewerbskonzept* (Fritz Knapp Verlag, Frankfurt, 1986).

[270] SUTER, C., STAMM, H., PFISTER, U., External Public Debt of the Periphery: A Recurrent Problem of World Society, in: *World Society Yearbook*, edited by Bornschier, V., Lengyel, P., Vol. 1 (Stiftung Weltgesellschaft, Zürich, 1989).

[271] SWEDBERG, R., Economic Sociology, *Current Sociology*, **35** (1987).

[272] TANSLEY, A.G., The Use and Abuse of Vegetational Concepts and Terms, *Ecology*, **16**, 284–307 (1935).

[273] TAUBES, J., *Abendländische Eschatologie* (Francke, Bern, 1947).

[274] TAYLOR, F.W., *Scientific Management* (Harper and Brothers, New York, [1911] 1947).

[275] THE WORLD COMMISSION ON ENVIRONMENT AND DEVELOPMENT, *Our Common Future* (Oxford University Press, Oxford, 1987).

[276] THEWELEIT, K., *Male Fantasies*, 2 Vols. (University of Minnesota Press, Minneapolis, 1987/1989).

[277] THRIFT, N., On the Determination of Social Action in Space and Time, *Society and Space*, **1**, 23–57 (1983).

[278] TIMMS, D., *The Urban Mosaic. Towards a Theory of Residential Differentiation* (Cambridge University Press, Cambridge, 1971).

[279] TODD, E., *The Explanation of Ideology: Family Structure and Social System* (Basil Blackwell, Cambridge MA, 1988).

[280] TÖRNQVIST, G., Contact Systems and Regional Development, *Lund Studies in Geography*, **B**, 35 (1970).

[281] TOURAINE, A., *The Self–Production of Society* (University of Chicago Press, Chicago, 1977).

[282] TRIST, E., *The Evolution of Socio–Technical Systems. A conceptual Framework and an Action Research Program* (Ontario Quality of Working Life Centre, Toronto, 1981).

[283] TRONTI, M., *Operai e capitale* (Einaudi, Turin, 1971).

[284] UNEP AND THE BEIJER INSTITUTE, *The Full Range of Responses to Anticipated Climatic Change* (UNEP, Geneva, 1989).

[285] VARELA, F., *Principles of Biological Autonomy* (Elsevier, New York, 1979).

[286] VERNADSKY, V.I., The Biosphere and the Noosphere, *American Scientist*, **33**, 1–12 (1945).

[287] WALZER, M., *Exodus and Revolution* (Basic Books, New York, 1985).

[288] WATERS, F., *Book of the Hopi* (Penguin, Harmondsworth, 1978).

[289] WEBER, M., *The Protestant Ethic and the Spirit of Capitalism* (Peter Smith, Magnolia MA, [1920] 1984).

[290] WEBER, M., Roschers und Knies und die logischen Probleme der historischen Nationalökonomie, in: Weber, M., *Gesammelte Aufsätze zur Wissenschaftslehre* (J.C.B. Mohr, Tübingen, [1903–1906] 1951).

[291] WEBER, M., Die Objektivität sozialwissenschaftlicher und sozialpolitischer Erkenntnis, in: Weber ,M., *Gesammelte*

Aufsätze zur Wissenschaftslehre (J.C.B. Mohr, Tübingen, [1904] 1951).

[292] WELLMAN, B., BERKOWITZ, S.D. (EDS.), *Social Structures: A Network Approach* (Cambridge University Press, Cambridge, 1988).

[293] WHITEHEAD, A.N., *Process and Reality* (The Free Press, New York, [1929] 1978).

[294] WHORF, B.L., *Language, Thought, and Reality* (Massachusetts Institute of Technology, Cambridge Mass., 1956).

[295] WINSON, J., *Brain and Psyche: The Biology of the Unconscious* (Anchor Press/Doubleday, Garden City NY, 1985).

[296] WITTGENSTEIN, L., *Remarks on Frazer's Golden Bough* (The Brynmill Press, Doncaster, 1979).

[297] WITTGENSTEIN, L., *Tractatus logico–philosophicus* (Routledge & Kegan Paul, London, [1921] 1961).

[298] WITTGENSTEIN, L., *Philosophical Investigations* (Basil Blackwell, Oxford, [1953] 1958).

[299] YOUNG, G.L., Human Ecology as an Interdisciplinary Concept: A Critical Inquiry, in: *Advances in Ecological Research*, edited by Macfayden, A., **8**, 1–105 (Academic Press, New York, 1974).

[300] YOUNG, G.L. (ED.), *Origins of Human Ecology* (Hutchinson Ross, Stroudsburg Penn., 1983).

Subject Index

accountability, *see* accounting conversations; relations, of accountability

accounting conversations, *see also* relations, of accountability, 14, 25–26, 29, 32, 34, 35, 41, 48, 49, 66, 69, 70, 89, 92, 111, 119, 120, 122, 144, 145

agency, 5–7, 19, 25–28, 38, 40, 41, 50, 59, 69–71, 74, 91, 93, 95, 97, 102, 108, 110, 122, 128, 131, 134, 136, 138, 144, 145, 152, 167, 211, 247, 248, 271

anarchy, 112, 140

anomie, 20, 55, 67, 70, 74, 112, 124, 131, 173, 241

atomism, 38, 52, 56
   of classical mechanics, 9, 154
   of mechanistic thinking, 132, 154–156, 173

beliefs, 20, 21, 23–28, 37, 45, 51, 59, 92, 162, 173, 183, 253
   nonsensical, 54–55, 59–60, 63, 65–69, 131

biographies, 20, 38, 44–47, 53, 57, 112, 117–118

biological evolution, *see* evolution, biological

biological motives, *see also* sexual motives, 19, 21, 27, 32, 44, 86–87, 89, 90

biophysical environment, *see* environment, biophysical

boundaries, 40, 43, 44, 68, 70, 77–78, 96–98, 109, 115, 119, 148, 178, 181, 267

Chicago School, 8–12

Christianity, 132, 133, 136–137, 161, 166–168, 170

civilization
   emergence of, *see* emergence, of civilization

climatic change, 2, 101, 148, 184, 200, 201, 224, 254–255

common madness, *see* madness, common

consciousness, *see also* unconscious
   discursive, 21, 26, 28, 41, 97

practical, 21, 26, 28, 41, 87, 97, 118
conversation of humankind, 115, 119
cosmology
   evolutionary, 15, 132, 159, 175–176
   morphological, 132, 159, 169–172, 174
cultural
   degeneration, *see* degeneration, cultural
   evolution, *see* evolution, cultural
   macro–evolution, *see* evolution, cultural: macro–evolution
   micro–evolution, *see* evolution, cultural: micro–evolution
   regeneration, *see* regeneration, cultural
cultural reality, 40, 41
culture, 20, 29, 41–44, 92, 94, 103, 111, 122

degeneration
   cultural, 74, 75, 95, 111–113, 123, 126, 131, 134, 143, 144, 146, 262, 273
   of human agency, 74, 95, 108, 109
   of relations of accountability, 95
democracy, 17, 102, 106, 107, 131, 133, 135, 231, 240, 271, 274
developing countries, 5–6, 16, 126–127, 144, 250–256, 261

development, *see also* sustainable development, 251–255
double–bind hypothesis, 60–62, 64–67

ecological crisis, *see* environmental crisis
ecological paradigm, 13, 15
economic
   life, 124, 136, 189, 234, 240–241, 245, 252, 274
   system, 110, 190, 193, 200, 226, 267, 269, 273
economics, 15, 16, 81, 123, 187, 191, 211, 238, 241, 244, 269
economy, 115–116, 125, 127, 185, 232, 267
   global, *see* world economy
   market, 111, 137, 139, 189, 192, 196, 214, 217, 221
   planned, 138, 139
   steady–state, 16, 188, 232–246, 265
ecosystem, 133, 147–149, 156, 158, 176–185
emergence
   of archaic systems, 89, 92, 98
   of civilization, 54–56, 62, 114
   of democratic institutions, 135
   of dual systems, 94, 99, 101, 113
   of economic systems, 139

of political power, 105, 107

of political systems, 94, 100, 102, 108–109, 111, 122, 125

of the world economy, 113, 126, 211

of triadic systems, 118

of vocational systems, 117–119, 122, 125, 137

emergent causality, 21, 23, 29

energy

bounds, 251, 266–267, 270–274

flow of, 73, 84, 128, 155, 178, 235, 256, 258

permits, 213, 224–232, 235, 270

tax, 213, 229–230

Enlightenment, 15, 74, 131–134, 137, 146–147, 159–161, 173, 271

new, 132–133, 271–272

entropy, 225

flow of, 84–85

margin, 73, 84–85, 127, 128, 256

production of, 85, 89, 128, 129

environment

biophysical, 2, 3, 11, 12, 14, 21, 74–77, 80, 81, 89, 94, 147, 178, 180–182, 190, 269

specific, 77–81

environmental

awareness, 145, 160

crisis, 1–7, 20, 54, 62, 71, 76, 111, 131, 132, 134, 143, 147, 158, 160,

161, 180, 196, 199, 260, 272–275

disruption, 55, 62, 67, 71, 73–75, 127, 128, 133, 156, 214, 254

effects, *see* reversible environmental effects

impact, 3, 74, 89, 113, 199–201, 212–214, 216, 221, 225, 251, 253, 255, 256, 258

risks, *see* risks, environmental

threshold, *see* threshold, environmental

evil, 14, 71, 112, 167

evolution

biological, 19, 20, 22, 23, 27, 63, 75, 86, 89, 90, 94, 98, 132, 133, 143, 155, 175, 177, 179–182, 269

cultural, 4, 14, 19, 21, 42, 73, 82, 93, 94, 99, 104, 106, 111, 126, 139, 185, 247, 256, 273

degeneration, *see* degeneration, cultural

macro–evolution, 73–75, 100, 101, 105, 112, 120, 122, 123, 125, 126, 139, 143, 144, 252

micro–evolution, 73, 93, 94, 98, 100, 101, 116, 118, 125, 143

regeneration, *see* regeneration, cultural

external effects, 111, 213–214, 228, 244

external relations, *see* relations, external

flow
    of energy, *see* energy, flow of
    of entropy, *see* entropy, flow of
    of material, *see* technomass
fossil fuels, 2, 75, 83–84, 128, 129, 201, 257–259
Frankfurt School, 55, 58, 59, 112

game theory, 2, 6, 248
gender, *see also* relations, of gender; sexuality, 87, 88, 91, 97, 98, 100, 118
generalized end of action, 74, 109, 110, 112–113, 123, 144
global change, 143, 158, 172, 247–251, 253, 254, 256, 272–274
goal of action, 42, 74, 109, 110, 144, 202
    external, 16, 74, 111, 112, 123, 124, 131, 134, 135, 146, 199, 212, 232, 250, 273, 274
    internal, 135, 146, 273
Greeks, 117, 133, 135–137, 161, 163–167, 169
greenhouse effect, 2, 3, 84, 129, 200–202, 265
growth
    economic, 5, 16, 111, 140, 144, 158, 199–201, 204, 205, 207, 208, 210, 212, 213, 215, 216, 221, 224, 229, 234, 251, 253–255, 257, 258
    of population, *see* population growth
    physical, 149, 199, 213, 216, 221, 224, 251, 255, 258
    qualitative, 188, 213, 216, 221, 229, 232, 253, 255, 256, 259
    quantitative, 188, 199, 201–202, 212

habits, 19–21, 26–28, 32, 44, 86–87, 98
hidden beings, 77, 80
human agency, *see* agency, 14, 69–70
human ecological system, 14–15, 73, 76, 77, 80, 81, 86, 89, 92, 94, 95, 98, 100, 104, 107, 115, 117, 139, 151, 162, 173, 177, 184–185, 190, 191, 225
    archaic, 15, 74, 87–89, 91, 92, 94, 98, 100, 103, 104, 107, 110, 113, 115, 125, 143, 144, 252
    dual, 74, 99, 110, 114, 120, 125
    political, 15, 100, 102–104, 106, 110, 117, 119, 125, 140
    private, 102, 103, 119
    triadic, 15, 74, 118, 119, 125, 202, 208, 232, 252, 253, 255, 262

vocational, 15, 74, 115–122, 124, 125, 134
human ecology, 8–13, 75, 149, 153, 156, 166, 167, 170, 180, 185, 187
  puzzle of, 4, 7, 13–17, 110, 152, 160, 176, 182, 184

ideal type, 188, 199, 232, 253, 255
identity
  gender, 53, 87, 91, 97, 103
  national, *see* identity, political
  personal, 7, 14–15, 20, 44–45, 50–54, 68–70, 91, 92, 97, 98, 104, 108–109, 120, 121, 126, 141, 252, 274
  political, 104, 105, 108
  vocational, 120, 126, 137, 246
impact, *see* environmental, impact
individualism, 11, 20, 48, 173
infinite price, *see* price, infinite
innovation, *see also* socio-technical change, 198, 199, 205, 207, 224, 232, 242, 243, 256–262, 267, 273
innovative regional milieu, 260–262, 274, 275
instructions, 29–32, 48, 53
interaction distances, 99, 119
interests, 110–111

conflicting, 5–6, 111, 271, 272
internal relations, *see* relations, internal
investment, 116, 192, 193, 198–200, 202–204, 206–209, 212, 216, 218, 234, 245, 248, 253, 260, 262–264, 267
invisible hand, 137, 138, 140, 161, 196, 214, 235, 242, 266, 269

Judaism, 133–137, 162

kinship, *see also* relations, of kinship, 53, 91, 100

labor, 16, 70, 74, 108–112, 114, 115, 123–124, 126, 127, 131, 134, 144–146, 168, 191, 198, 211, 224, 227, 232, 234, 241–242, 245–246
  costs, *see also* wage, costs, 218–220, 227
  marginal, 219, 228
  market, 140, 142, 206, 245–246, 248–250
  movement, 112, 127, 134, 137–138, 140, 244
  refusal of, 108, 134, 141, 142, 260
  wage, *see* wage labor
language game, 30, 36, 38, 41, 42, 64, 92, 95, 105, 106
life form, 41, 42, 63, 64, 86, 95, 97

love, 17, 53–54, 120, 144–146, 167

madness
  common, 13, 14, 20, 28, 54–55, 59, 62–63, 67, 68, 70–71, 74, 95, 97, 107, 108, 111, 112, 129, 131, 133, 139, 144, 145, 174
  individual, 28, 53–55, 60–67
market economy, *see* economy, market
Marxist theory, 55, 57–59, 112, 125, 138–140, 240, 242
mechanics
  classical, 132, 147, 150–154, 156, 159, 161, 163, 170–173
mechanistic thinking, 9, 15, 24, 111, 132–133, 147–161, 170, 172–176, 271
milieu, *see* innovative regional milieu
modernization, 125
monetary institutions, 126
money, 15, 16, 74, 110, 123–124, 139, 199, 211–212, 232, 233, 235–237, 242, 245, 250, 273
  de–nationalization of, 232, 236–237
moral order, 8–9, 42, 45, 133, 158, 173, 177, 184, 211

motives, *see* biological motives, sexual motives, 28

nation, 100, 104–105, 107, 109, 115, 118–119, 126, 145, 185, 236, 273
nations
  society of, 17, 104, 105, 107, 115, 136, 140, 271, 272
natural resources, *see* resources, natural
neolithic revolution, 74
network
  social, *see* social relations, network of
normal price, *see* price, normal
normative field, 20, 29, 43–45, 59, 65, 67, 70, 78–79, 89–91, 101, 106, 113, 121, 124, 127, 241–242
  archaic, 90–93, 101
  political, 103, 107, 120, 123
  private, 120, 123
  vocational, 117, 120, 123

patriarchy, 94–95, 98, 108, 112, 114, 135
permits, *see also* energy permits, 213, 224, 233, 234, 239, 270
  emission, 16, 265, 269
personal identity, *see* identity, personal
persons, 14, 19, 21–23, 26, 28, 29, 32, 38–40, 44, 50–

54, 68, 75, 77, 87, 102–103, 107, 118, 210

political
life, *see also* public, life, 94, 95, 102, 107, 109, 139, 144–146, 261, 273–275
system, *see* human ecological system, political
population growth, 17, 101, 113, 128, 144, 146, 149, 150, 156, 253, 254, 273
power, 74, 105–107, 109–112, 123, 131, 133–135, 139, 146, 165, 167, 236, 271
preferences, 193–194, 209, 235, 265, 269
price, 194–196, 214, 220–222, 227–228, 233
infinite, 16, 232–233, 238, 239
market, 188–189, 193, 196–199, 207, 216–217
normal, 188–189, 193, 196–199, 204, 207, 208, 216–220, 224, 227, 267
prisoner's dilemma, 6–7, 247
private
life, 15, 17, 37, 57, 59, 74, 94, 95, 99–103, 108, 118, 119, 121, 123, 139, 144–146, 231, 234, 239, 261, 262, 273, 275

system, *see* human ecological system, private
projects, 20, 21, 24–28, 39, 40, 44, 48–49, 92, 110, 188, 193–195, 198, 202, 208, 210, 211
property rights, 220, 230–232, 234, 237–240, 242–244
Protestantism, *see* Reformation
psychoanalysis, 44, 45, 47, 55, 57–59
psychology, 45, 46
public
happiness, 110, 112, 146
life, *see also* political, life, 15, 37, 57, 74, 94, 95, 99–102, 108, 109, 118, 119, 121, 123, 139, 145, 146, 166, 167, 234, 239, 240, 262
system, *see* human ecological system, political
puzzle of human ecology, *see* human ecology, puzzle of

rate
of economic growth, 199, 200, 215, 232, 251, 265
of growth, 262
of interest, 16, 140, 142, 143, 199, 208–210, 212, 221–223, 232–235, 237, 242, 245

of physical growth, 199–201, 255

of profit, 16, 192, 199, 202–210, 212, 215–216, 221, 229, 232–235, 237, 242, 245, 262, 264, 265

rationality, *see also* tradition, 120, 122, 163–165, 264, 271

    scientific, *see also* science, 63

reasons, 20, 21, 23–28, 44

reciprocity, *see also* rules, of reciprocity, 74, 88, 91, 92

reductionism, 29–30

    psychological, 57, 58

    sociological, 57, 58

reference, 33–35, 37, 50

Reformation, 74, 117, 120, 132, 137, 159, 172

refusal of labor, *see* labor, refusal of

regeneration

    cultural, 75, 131, 133–140, 143–146, 173, 232, 254, 256, 261, 273–275

regional development, *see* innovative regional milieu

relations

    between means and ends, 16, 52, 54, 69–70, 109, 123, 131, 141, 142, 211–212, 234

    between stocks and flows, 233–234

external, 16, 20, 52, 68–70, 123, 141, 142, 211, 212

internal, 14, 20, 45, 52, 54, 68–70, 109, 118, 211, 234

of accountability, *see also* accounting conversations, 5, 14, 19, 20, 29, 33, 34, 45, 50, 54, 66, 67, 69, 70, 95, 97, 103, 106, 108–114, 126, 127, 135, 144, 242, 250, 261, 271–273

of gender, *see also* gender, 53, 89, 91, 95

of kinship, 87–88, 91, 95, 104

of reciprocity, 114

sexual, 17, 57, 98, 144

social, *see* social, relations

relationship

    human beings—environment, 69, 81, 88, 113–115

    human beings—nature, 1–4, 113–115

Renaissance, 74, 117, 118, 120

rent, 16, 213, 219–224, 232, 233, 237–239, 270

    differential, 219, 221–224, 228–229

    intensive, 227–229, 231

representation, 29, 30, 35–37, 39, 42, 107

    mental, 34, 35, 37, 49

resources

exhaustible natural, 213, 221–224

limited natural, 199, 216–221, 224

natural, 216–224, 237–239

responsibility, *see* accounting conversations; relations, of accountability

reversible environmental effects, 213–216, 230

risks, 184, 272

environmental, 3, 5, 142, 157, 262, 265–267, 270

rules, 20, 29–37, 40, 41, 43, 48–50, 67, 70, 77, 80, 87, 88, 91, 92, 94, 98, 100, 103, 106–107, 109, 111, 114, 121, 133, 177, 188–196, 199, 210, 219, 238, 243, 253, 272

emergence of new, 48–49

of accounting, 188, 190, 192, 205, 208, 213, 228

of endogamy, 56, 88, 104

of exogamy, 56, 88

of kinship, 74, 90, 91, 104

of reciprocity, 74, 88, 91, 114

transformation of, 49

science, *see also* tradition, 17, 121–123, 131, 133,

137, 151, 159, 160, 171, 173, 175–177

role of, 3, 15, 132, 183–184, 274

sex, 74, 112, 123, 146

sexual motives, *see also* biological motives, 17, 44, 47, 87, 91, 112, 135, 144

sexuality, *see also* gender; relations, of gender, 45–48, 144

slavery, 62, 67, 109, 112, 114, 125, 134–136, 162, 238–239

social

network, *see* social relations, network of

reality, 9, 19, 23, 29, 38, 40, 42, 44, 74, 77–80, 93, 95, 96, 105, 125, 137, 173

relations, 7, 22–23, 75, 92, 125

network of, 19–21, 23, 40, 87, 88, 101, 104, 119, 261

rules, *see* rules, social

structure, 20, 29, 38–44, 77, 92, 103, 189, 191

theory, 79–80

socialization, 91–92, 103, 120–121

socio–economic structure, 189–193

socio–technical change, *see also* innovation, 203–207, 221, 224, 228, 229, 234–235, 256, 267, 272, 274 speech act, 14, 23, 40, 106, 195, 208

steady–state
economy, *see* economy, steady–state

sustainability, *see also* sustainable development, 16, 75, 201–202, 245, 251, 274

sustainable development, *see also* sustainability, 2, 5, 254–256, 261, 274

taxation, *see also* energy, tax, 214, 229–230; 269, 270, 272

technomass, 73, 82–84, 86, 113–115, 127–129, 225, 235

territoriality, 98–100, 104, 118, 119

threshold
environmental, 85, 202, 213, 224, 228–231, 265–266, 269

trade unions, *see also* labor movement; vocational associations, 111, 138, 140, 141, 232, 241, 242, 244, 274

tradition
of inquiry, comprehensive, 132, 159, 163, 169–174, 176
philosophical, 133, 163–170
religious, 133–137, 145, 161–163, 165–170
research tradition, 8–13, 15, 79

integrative research tradition, 132, 147, 151–155, 159, 162, 170–173, 175–177, 179
specialized research tradition, 151–155, 162

unconscious, 27–28, 45, 46, 87, 97

unemployment, 207, 248–250, 272

urban ecology, 10–11

usufructuary rights, 134, 220, 234, 237–240, 242, 245

values, 42, 63

vocational
activity, 146, 232, 234, 241, 244, 261, 270, 274
associations, 232, 241–244, 274
ethics, 120–121, 124, 126, 127, 241, 242
life, 15, 117, 119, 121, 123, 139, 144, 146, 240, 244, 250, 251, 261, 262, 274
organizations, 239
system, *see* human ecological system, vocational

wage, 123–124, 192, 211, 216, 221, 248–250
costs, 74, 141, 205–207, 225, 229, 248, 260
labor, 74, 124, 125, 141, 211, 232, 239, 241, 274

war, 55–57, 62, 63, 67, 107, 109–112, 114, 127,

136, 140, 145, 157,
174, 176, 271

will, 24–25, 167–168

world economy, 17, 74, 84, 115,
116, 126–129, 139,
140, 142, 161, 188,
191, 192, 196, 199–
202, 204, 206, 207,
210–212, 224, 234,
236, 242, 250, 252,
255, 258–260, 262,
265, 269, 271, 272

Name Index

Abbott, 248
Adorno, 55, 59, 160
Akerlof, 124
Alexander the Great, 136, 166, 167
Allen, 85
Anderson, 109
Archibugi, 187
Archimedes, 170
Aristotle, 101, 102, 163, 165–168, 170, 171
Armstrong, 142
Austin, 195
Axelrod, 7
Aydalot, 260

Baccini, 82
Bachmann–Voegelin, 185
Baker, 32, 34, 64
Bargatzky, 12
Barnes, 105
Barrows, 10
Bateson, 12, 53, 54, 60, 62, 64, 181, 182
Becattini, 196
Benedick, 7
Benjamin, J., 46
Benjamin, W., 68
Benoist, 53
Berkes, 238
Berkowitz, 40
Berry, 10, 260
Bhaskar, 21, 24, 26, 38, 41

Bieri, 120
Block, 259
Borden, 12
Boserup, 101
Bourdieu, 26
Bouveresse, 174
Bowles, 142
Boyd, 94
Boyden, 12, 82, 185
Broome, 264
Brunner, 82
Buber, 23, 96, 174
Buchmann, 45
Budyko, 88
Burger, 188
Burns, 94
Buttel, 13

Calvin, 117, 172
Carello, 30
Carlstein, 89
Catton, 12, 13
Choldin, 11
Clark, 149
Coase, 213, 231
Cole, 149
Copernicus, 160, 170
Costanza, 3
Cotgrove, 13
Coulter, 53, 60

Dahrendorf, 70
Daly, 234

Darwin, 128, 179, 181
Dewdney, 150
Dickens, 210
Dietz, 94
Dijksterhuis, 150
Dostoevsky, 96
Drucker, 57, 243
Drury, 179
Dürrenberger, 27, 89, 98, 99, 120, 260, 262
Dunlap, 6, 12, 13
Durkheim, 124, 241–243

Elsenhans, 126, 252
Elster, 206
Emery, 11
Ephraums, 2
Ernste, 260
Etzioni, 248
Euclid, 170
Evans, 178
Eve, 154

Feyerabend, 64, 122
Firestone, 46
Fischer, 65
Fisher, 235
Flannery, 101
Flavin, 254
Folke, 187
Ford, 140
Foucault, 60, 96, 160
Freeman, 11
Freese, 182
Freud, 44, 45, 55–57, 59, 65, 105
Freudenthal, 173
Frey, 260
Friedman, 236
Friedrichs, 11
Furubotn, 220

Galileo, 159, 160, 163, 170, 172
Garibaldi, 41
Gazzaniga, 22
Geertz, 48
Georgescu–Roegen, 85
Gerding, 236
Gergen, 50
Gesell, 209, 235
Gibson, 80
Giddens, 26, 28, 38, 40, 42, 92, 123
Glyn, 142
Godschalk, 235
Goethe, 120
Goodman, 81
Gordon, 142
Gore, 2
Gould, 22, 182
Gouldner, 91
Granovetter, 119, 248
Greenfield, 236
Groebel, 56
Groh, 98

Habermas, 59, 96, 110, 112, 135, 262
Hacker, 32, 34, 64
Hägerstrand, 39
Hall, 99, 119
Haller, 42
Hannan, 11
Harcourt, 204
Hardin, 233
Harré, 38, 50, 91, 94, 96, 152, 158
Harrison, 142
Hawley, 11, 13
Hayek, 193, 236
Heckhausen, 50, 70
Heintz, 43

Henry VIII, 172
Heyward, 174
Hinde, 56
Hobbes, 56
Hösle, 4
Hoffmann–Nowottny, 42
Homer, 46, 76, 109
Horkheimer, 55, 59, 160
Hotelling, 223
Houghton, 2
Huber, 168
Hund, 149, 150, 175
Husserl, 174

Imboden, 266
Iten, 266

Jaeger, 120, 142, 187, 246, 250, 260, 266
Jaffé, 238
Jantsch, 176
Jenkins, 2
Jensen, 94
Jesinghaus, 266
Jonas, 174
Joyce, 43
Jung, 46

Kåberger, 187
Kant, 144, 160, 173, 174
Kapp, 213
Kern, 260
Keynes, 140, 235, 236, 242
Kirman, 249
Koukkou, 47
Kraus, 38, 96
Kreilcamp–Cudmore, 64
Kreps, 248, 249
Kümmel, 257
Kuhn, 116, 152

Lamarck, 179

Lampedusa, 41
Lehmann, 47
Leontief, 215
Lessing, 174
Lévi–Strauss, 53
Lewin, 43, 80
Lind, 266
Little, 107
Locke, 56
Loubser, 110
Lovelock, 147
Lovins, 267
Lüscher, 140
Luhmann, 38, 43, 110, 123, 190
Luther, 117

Machiavelli, 110
MacIntyre, 167, 171, 211
Major, 177
Malcolm, 41
Malmberg, 98
Mann, 105
Marglin, 140
Marshall, 196
Marti, 174
Marx, 57, 59, 105, 112, 125, 127, 210, 212, 240
Mauch, 266
Maxwell, 175
Mazur, 257
McKinlay, 107
Meade, 213
Meadows, D.H., 2, 149
Meadows, D.L., 2, 149
Mertig, 6
Meyer–Abich, 4
Michaels, 30
Micklin, 11
Milbrath, 13
Mishan, 213

More, 172
Morishima, 134, 142, 188, 219
Müller, 90, 92
Müller–Herold, 266

Neuburger, 257
Newton, 150, 151, 160, 161, 170
Nicolis, 176
Nijkamp, 187, 258
Nisbet, 179
Nordhaus, 142

Odum, E., 179
Odum, H.T., 105
Orrù, 67

Page, 221
Pallmann, 177
Parinello, 221
Park, 8, 9
Parsons, 38, 59, 110, 123
Pasinetti, 196, 253
Pearce, 270
Pejovich, 220
Perrings, 13, 82, 191, 238, 264
Perrow, 78, 262
Petrarca, 96
Pfister, 142
Piaget, 59
Picht, 11
Pigou, 213, 264
Piore, 260
Plato, 64, 101, 163–166, 174
Polanyi, 245
Popper, 21
Price, 188
Prigogine, 176

Primas, 175
Ptolemaeus, 170
Putnam, 36, 136, 162, 174
Pythagoras, 170

Quine, 64

Ramsey, 234, 264
Randers, 2
Rappáport, 185
Rembrandt, 59
Ricardo, 239
Rich, 241
Richerson, 94
Robbins, 212
Romer, 199
Romm, 267
Rosa, 257
Rougemont, 48, 96
Russell, 61
Rust, 150
Rutherford, 154

Sabel, 260
Sack, 98
Sahlins, 112
Sanderson, 94
Sartre, 51
Saussure, 35
Schefold, 196
Schieve, 85
Schmidheiny, 2
Schnaiberg, 13
Schneider, 133
Schor, 140
Schumann, 260
Schwartz, 199
Scott, 197
Sen, 7, 241
Shakespeare, 47
Shanker, 64, 66, 174

Shils, 38, 123
Shotter, 24, 30, 50, 53
Siebert, 213
Simmel, 39
Simonis, 257
Smelsers, 110
Smith, A., 137, 161, 196, 198,
   204, 205, 211, 242
Smith, E.A., 182
Socrates, 101, 163, 164
Speare, 260
Sperry, 21, 22
Sraffa, 41, 218, 228
St. Augustine, 24, 166–168
St. Paul, 137, 165, 167
St. Thomas, 168, 169
Stamm, 142
Starbatty, 236
Stefan, 48
Stegmüller, 152
Steiner, 10
Steward, 12
Stierlin, 62
Stoessel, 68
Strange, 242
Suhr, 235
Suter, 142
Swedberg, 248

Tansley, 177, 178
Taubes, 134, 166
Taylor, 124
Thales, 170
Theweleit, 57
Thrift, 80
Todd, 58
Törnqvist, 40
Touraine, 123
Trist, 78
Tronti, 70, 108

van den Bergh, 258
van Liere, 13
Varela, 96
Vernadsky, 147
Voltaire, 161
von Weizsäcker, 266

Walras, 238
Walzer, 134, 166
Waters, 97
Weber, A., 142, 250
Weber, M., 59, 117, 120, 121,
   125, 172, 188
Weisskopf, 142
Wellman, 40
Whitehead,   52,   61,   150,
   175
Whorf, 97
Winson, 28, 47
Wisner, 10
Wittgenstein, 29, 31, 32, 36–38,
   41, 45, 52, 59, 63, 64,
   66, 68, 90, 92, 95, 96,
   165, 174

Yeager, 236
Yellen, 124
Young, 12

Zapf, 42

For Product Safety Concerns and Information please contact our EU
representative GPSR@taylorandfrancis.com
Taylor & Francis Verlag GmbH, Kaufingerstraße 24, 80331 München, Germany

www.ingramcontent.com/pod-product-compliance
Lightning Source LLC
Chambersburg PA
CBHW070558270326
41926CB00013B/2352

* 9 7 8 1 0 4 1 1 4 7 0 2 2 *